# Introduction to Programming in Java

First Edition

J. N. Patterson Hume

Christine Stephenson

Holt Software Associates Inc.
Toronto, Canada

D1257427

Publisher:
HOLT SOFTWARE ASSOCIATES INC.
203 College St., Suite 305
Toronto, Ontario, Canada  M5T 1P9
(416) 978-6476   1-800-361-8324
http://www.holtsoft.com/java

ISBN 0-921598-39-4

First Edition

Printed in Canada by the University of Toronto Press

# Table of Contents

# Preface

This textbook, *Introduction to Programming in Java*, is intended to be used in a first computer science course in Java. It emphasizes the basic concepts of programming and the object-oriented programming paradigm. The programming language used in this book is Java..

*Introduction to Programming in Java* focuses on computing concepts with the ultimate goal of facilitating the broadest possible coverage of the core computer science curriculum. In an effort to provide material for courses covering the World Wide Web we have included an introductory chapter on creating web pages using HTML.

To begin, Java standalone application programs are used exclusively. Applets are covered in considerable detail in later chapters. Some of the more advanced notions of concurrency, exception handling, and graphical user interfaces have been omitted or are discussed in an abbreviated way.

This textbook package includes a CD containing the **Ready to Program with Java**™**Technology** software. **Ready** is a complete integrated development environment for Java that provides all the power of Java without the complexities that confuse learners.

(Additional references should be consulted if a complete syntax of Java or the Java class libraries is required.)

## Overview

This book covers the material in standard curricula for first courses in computer science. As well, it emphasizes the object-oriented paradigm.

The list of chapter titles outlines the arrangement of materials.
1. Computing Essentials
2. The Ready to Program with Java™ Technology Environment
3. Programming
4. Programming in Java

**Chapter 1** provides an overview of the history of modern computing, including hardware, software, programming languages, and number systems. By highlighting a number of key technological developments, it attempts to place Computer Engineering today in its scientific and social context. It also explores some of the current issues in computing such as employment, privacy, and access to information.

**Chapter 2** describes how to use the **Ready to Program with Java™ Technology** environment. The way to create standalone Java program classes and Java applets is outlined. The chapter also covers how syntax errors are reported and how they are corrected.

**Chapter 3** introduces some of the key ideas in computer science. As well as providing a description of programming, programming style, and the software development process it introduces the difference between the two major programming paradigms: the procedure-oriented paradigm and the object-oriented paradigm which is the paradigm of the Java programming language. Abstraction is introduced as a way of making programs easier to create and to understand.

Chapter 4 introduces a number of the basic elements of the Java syntax, particularly the idea of a class and a method. These are illustrated by graphic examples using the *Console* class. The details of all these concepts are explored in later chapters. Instructions are provided for the creation and running of Java standalone applications.

Chapter 5 presents the EBNF metalanguage for formally describing the syntax of a programming language. The primitive data types of the Java language are defined along with the way to declare variables of these types. Expressions for each type are also defined and the assignment statement presented. The chapter explains how values of the different types are output and formatted using the *Console* class. The role of comments in providing internal documentation to a program is also discussed.

Chapter 6 discusses how data can be input to a program. Ways in which a list of data items can be input by counted or conditional loops are shown. Input from the standard input, the keyboard, and input from a file are discussed. Ways to generate data, using random numbers, for purposes of testing programs are presented. The statistical analysis of numerical data is also described.

Chapter 7 deals with program structure. Algorithms can be programmed using three basic forms of control structure: linear sequence, repetition, and selection. The Java syntax for each of these is defined. The use of diagrams such as flow charts to supplement the program itself is discussed and shown to be unnecessary for a structured program which is properly paragraphed, and internally documented. Tracing execution of a program before trying to run it on a computer is encouraged

Chapter 8 introduces the string data structure which is implemented using the *String* class. Strings in Java are objects instantiated from the *String* class. Methods of the class are shown. The *StringBuffer* class is introduced as useful when the contents of a string are to be changed. The *StringTokenizer* class which permits the breaking of a string into tokens is illustrated.

Chapter 9 provides details about methods – components of a object that can be used by other objects to operate on the data of the original object. As with subprograms of earlier programming languages, methods fall into two principal classes: procedure-type methods that perform some action and function-type methods that yield a value. The differences in the way these two types of methods are defined and invoked is detailed. The relation between formal and actual parameters is explained. The scope of identifiers in a program is outlined. The signature, header, and specifications of a method are defined. Methods that call themselves (recursive methods) – and iterative methods that accomplish the same result – are dealt with. A case study illustrating the design of programs broken down into methods is provided.

**Chapter 10** shows how an object can encapsulate data and the methods that operate on the data, and illustrates how other objects that use that object are prevented from interfering with the encapsulated data. The class is the template from which an object is instantiated. A constructor method of the class is used to create a new instance of the class – the object. Examples are given of using and creating a class. Inheritance is introduced as a means by which new classes are created through modifications of a base class. By using the Java library of classes, multiple objects of the class can be created or new classes produced.

**Chapter 11** introduces Java applets. Applets are invoked by using a browser, such as *Netscape Navigator*™, and can be accessed through the *World Wide Web*. It is this feature of Java that is at the root of much of its popularity, as well as its being an object-oriented programming language. Graphical User Interfaces (GUIs) are introduced. This chapter covers many of the classes in Java's *Abstract Windowing Toolkit* (awt). A case study which examines the design decisions involved in the development of a GUI applet is provided.

**Chapter 12** explores the creation of web pages using HTML (Hypertext Markup Language). The use of HTML to format information, create tables, place pictures, and display lists is discussed in some detail. The chapter also discusses the details controlling the presentation of an applet: its size, location on the screen, and so on.

**Chapter 13** introduces the structured data type called an array. Individual elements of an array share the same name and data type but are distinguished from each other by having an index. An individual element of an array can be passed by value to a method whereas an entire array is passed, as any object is, by reference. When the method alters its array parameter the actual array is altered. The efficiencies of searching an array by a linear search and a sorted array by a binary search are compared.

**Chapter 14** concentrates on the higher concepts of object-oriented programming. These include abstract classes, class hierarchies, genericity, and Java interfaces. Object-oriented analysis is emphasized. The chapter also deals with the realities of programming in Java such as resource constraints and trade-offs between resource usage and program flexibility.

**Chapter 15** describes implementing records as objects and the reading from and writing to binary files. In Java, there is no standard way to store an object's fields in a record. As a result, it must be programmed The ways records can be input from or output to a file are shown, as is the storage of records in a binary form so that random access to individual records is possible. A simple linear search of an array of records is introduced as an example of using records.

**Chapter 16** presents algorithms for sorting lists of data stored in arrays. A comparison of the sort using the various algorithms is explored. The chapter also explains how methods depending on recursion, are more efficient than simple exchange algorithms.

**Chapter 17** gives details of self-referential classes and how they can be used to instantiate nodes to link objects together in simple linked lists. A *List* class is created and then modified to produce an *OrderedList* class by inheritance.

**Chapter 18** introduces many of the more advanced features of the graphical interface capabilities of Java's *Abstract Windowing Toolkit* (awt) by guiding students through the construction of a movie ticket seller applet and a simple paint applet. A case study which illustrates the use of menus in the design of a GUI application is provided.

**Appendix A** is a case study focusing on the creation of a library automation system with an emphasis on object-oriented design. It covers the development of the design specifications, the determination of the classes and class hierarchies to be used, and the Java program development.

# Conventions

This book uses a number of naming conventions for identifiers. These are not part of the Java language but are used to make programs understandable.

- All identifiers that are multiple words use an upper case letter to begin all words after the first
- Class names have the first letter capitalized.
- Variable and method names have identifiers beginning with a lower case letter.
- Constants have identifiers all in upper case.

# Flexibility

*Introduction to Programming in Java* has been organized to provide an introduction to the fundamental concepts of computer science. The object-oriented paradigm of the Java programming language is used to illustrate basic principles.

Differing course demands and student populations may require instructors to omit certain chapters or parts of chapters, or to insert additional material to cover some concepts in greater detail. For example, instructors wishing to address the historical information in Chapter 1 after students have more hands-on programming may choose to begin with a later chapter.

# The Java Programming Language

Java is a programming language that was developed at Sun Microsystems. Java standalone application programs provide all the features of other general purpose languages such as Pascal or C. Java applets add the flexibility of sharing programs via the World Wide Web and Internet. Java is an object-oriented programming language and has been provided with an extensive library of classes that can be used in creating programs. This library is being rapidly extended by its many users.

The language is portable; it can be used on any computer platform that has a Java interpreter. This means that software developers can confidently program in Java and know that their software will run on any such computer. As well, individuals can also share applets via the Web. Attempts are made to make the use of shared programs safe. For security, for example, no applet may read from or write to a file on the system on which it is being executed.

Java syntax is based on the C syntax but many of the difficult and error prone parts of C and C++, such as pointers, operator overloading, and multiple inheritance have been eliminated. In this book we have eliminated still more of the "tricks" that some C programmers delight in. Our approach is based on the fundamental principle of structured programming, namely keeping programs easy to understand.

Java with its class libraries has many additional features which are not part of C or C++. It provides for strings, graphics, concurrency, and exception handling, as well as a large number of data structures. Java also provides graphical user interface classes.

All of these features contribute to Java's attractiveness as both a commercial software tool and a means of addressing the core computer science concepts.

# Comments

Your comments, corrections, and suggestions are very welcome. Please feel free to contact us at:

Distribution Manager
Holt Software Associates Inc.
203 College Street, Suite 305
Toronto, Ontario, Canada M5T 1P9
E-mail: books@hsa.on.ca
USA or Canada phone: 1-800-361-8324
World Wide Web: http://www.holtsoft.com

# Acknowledgments

This book would not have been produced without the enthusiasm and help of Tom West who was invaluable in ironing out the technical details of Java, testing the programs, assembling the appendices, and providing the Library Automation Case Study in Appendix A.

Inge Weber entered much of the copy from handwritten drafts, Harriet Hume created the index, and Catharine Trenchard did our final page check. The book cover was designed by Brenda Kosky.

It was our good fortune again to work with such a cooperative and competent team.

J. N. Patterson Hume
Christine Stephenson

# Chapter 1

# Computing Essentials

# 1.1   Introduction

Computers are now part of our everyday lives. We do our banking by computer. When we buy something at the grocery store, the clerk runs the bar code over an optical scanner which then inputs the price from a computer database. We also use computers for recreation, for example, we play games that use simulation and computer animation.

Despite the fact that most of us use computers every day, many people still do not know exactly what is inside the computer, what its various parts do, and how they all work together.

This chapter begins with a brief history of computers and then describes the parts of the computer and how they function. Although this chapter discusses the history of computing and the person most-commonly associated with each new development, it is important to remember that what appears to be a great leap forward is often the result of many tiny steps, both forward and backward, taken not by one, but by many people. Like most scientific endeavors, advances in computing are usually the result of work by many people over long periods of time.

# 1.2   A Brief History of Computer Hardware

The history of computing goes back to the earliest days of recorded civilization and humankind's desire to find ways to calculate more accurately and reason more systematically. The Greeks, for example, helped to systematize reasoning and developed axiomatic mathematics and formal logic. The Babylonians and Egyptians contributed enormously to computational science by developing multiplication tables, tables for squares and roots, exponential tables, and the formula for quadratic equations.

In the late sixteenth and early seventeenth centuries a number of major discoveries contributed to our ability to perform complex mathematical operations. These included the development of Algebra (using letters for unknowns), logarithms, the slide rule, and analytic geometry.

The development of mechanical machines to assist with calculations began in 1623 when Wilhelm Schickard designed and built what is believed to be the first digital calculator. This machine did addition and subtraction mechanically and partially automated multiplication and division. About twenty years later Blaise Pascal developed a gear-based machine that was capable of performing addition and subtraction. Gottfried Wilhelm Leibniz (who invented calculus along with Sir Issac Newton) invented a device called the **Leibniz Wheel** that did addition, subtraction, multiplication, and division automatically.

The nineteenth century saw major advances in computation. Charles Babbage (who was a founding member of the Royal Astronomical Society in Britain) developed the concepts for two steam powered machines, which he called the **Difference Engine** and the **Analytic Engine**. The **Difference Engine** could perform mathematical computations to eight decimal places.

Although it was never actually built (and would have been the size of a railway locomotive if it had been) the **Analytic Engine** was truly an ancestor of the modern computer. It was to be a machine capable of performing mathematical operations from instructions on a series of punched cards. It had a memory unit, a sequential control, and many other features of a modern computer.

In 1854 Swedish printer Pehr George Scheutz succeeded in building a **Difference Engine** for calculating mathematical tables. Scheutz's machine consisted of a memory (which he called a "store") and a central processor (which he called a "mill"). It operated by a series of punched cards that contained a series of operations and data. His design was based on the **Jacquard loom** which used punched cards to encode weaving patterns.

What might be considered the first computer company was established in 1896 by Herman Hollerith. Hollerith was a mechanical engineer who was helping to tabulate the census of the population of the United States. In 1890 he invented a new punched card technology which proved much faster than traditional manual methods of tabulating the results and this allowed the *United States Census Bureau* to gather more information by asking more questions. Hollerith's company, the *Tabulating Machines Company*, later became *International Business Machines*, better known now as *IBM*.

In 1937 a British mathematician named Alan M. Turing made a significant contribution to computing with the development of an abstract machine called the **Turing** machine. During World War II, Turing was involved in top secret work for the British military and was responsible for breaking the German code, thus providing the allied forces with important information about Germany's war plans.

In the late 1930s and early 1940s *Bell Telephone Laboratories* began building more powerful machines for scientific calculations. In 1944, Howard T. Aiken, an electromechanical engineer, collaborated with a number of *IBM* engineers to design and build the **Mark I** computer. This machine could handle negative and positive numbers, carry out long calculations in their natural sequence, use a variety of mathematical functions, and was fully automatic. Rather than punched cards, the instructions for the **Mark I** were punched on a paper tape.

In 1945 John W. Mauchly and J. Presper Eckert Jr. designed and built the first large-scale electronic digital computer from 18,000 vacuum tubes and 1500 relays. This machine was called the **ENIAC** (electronic numerical integrator and calculator). **ENIAC** was a thousand times faster than the earlier electromechanical machines. It weighed 30 tons and took up 1500 square feet of floor space.

John von Neumann, who also worked on the **ENIAC** project, played a major role in the development of a machine that would improve on **ENIAC** in a number of ways. The new machine, called **EDVAC** (electronic discrete variable and calculator), was capable of storing a program in memory and breaking computations down into a sequence of steps that could be performed one at a time. **EDVAC** used **binary notation** to store and manipulate numbers whereas earlier machines used decimal arithmetic. (See section 1.4 for a more complete explanation of binary.)

In 1951 Mauchly and Eckert developed the **UNIVAC I** (universal automatic computer) for the *Remington-Rand Corporation*. **UNIVAC I** was considered by many to be the first commercially viable electronic digital computer.

In 1952 the University of Toronto purchased a computer from *Ferranti Electric* and called it **FERUT** (Ferranti University of Toronto). This machine, which replaced the University's original calculating punch equipment, used a punched paper tape system based on the teletype machine. It was actually a copy of the **Mark I** developed at the University of Manchester by Alan M. Turing. It is important to note the large number of women who programmed for **FERUT**. These included Audrey Bates, Charlotte Frose, Jean McDonald, Jean Tucker, and Beatrice Worsley.

In 1953 *IBM* entered the commercial market with the **IBM 701**. This was followed a year later by the **IBM 650**, which was a decimal machine designed as a logical upgrade to punched-card machines.

The next major breakthrough in computer hardware came in the late 1950s and early 1960s during which the expensive and often unreliable **vacuum tubes** were replaced with **transistors**. The transistor allowed for the design of computers that were more reliable and more powerful.

Between 1965 and 1970 the introduction of **integrated circuits**, each of which contained many transistors, made the previous generation of computers virtually obsolete. The wires connecting the transistors were printed as copper on a sheet of insulating material. The transistors were plugged into the insulating sheet, making contact with the wires as required. In modern computers, the integrated circuit is achieved by a process of printing metal onto a tiny chip made of silicon which acts as an insulator. Adding certain other elements to the silicon creates a transistor. Multiple transistors are be combined to create circuits.

Between 1970 and 1980 the move to **large-scale integration** (LSI) and **very large-scale integration** (VLSI) continued this miniaturization trend. High-speed **semi-conductor** technology has also led to significant improvements in memory storage.

The late 1970s saw the development of personal computers, the first computers small enough and affordable enough for the average person to buy. The development of the **Altair 8800**, the **Apple II**, and the **IBM PC** marked the first steps in what has now become a world-wide mega-industry.

In the 1980s **reduced instruction-set computers** (RISC), parallel computers, neural networks, and optical storage were introduced.

| Generation | Year | Hardware Development |
|:---:|:---:|:---|
| 1 | 1951-58 | vacuum tubes<br>card or paper tape input/output<br>magnetic drum memory |
| 2 | 1959-64 | integrated circuits (printed)<br>magnetic tape I/O<br>magnetic core memory |
| 3 | 1965-70 | integrated circuits (photographic)<br>minicomputers<br>magnetic disk I/O |
| 4 | 1970-80 | LSI<br>VLSI<br>virtual storage<br>microcomputers |
| 5 | 1980+ | RISC<br>parallel computers<br>optical storage<br>laser disk |

# 1.3 A Brief History of Programming

The person believed to be the very first computer programmer was Ada, Countess of Lovelace, the daughter of the English romantic poet Lord Byron. As a woman in the early 1800s, Ada Byron was largely self-taught in mathematics. This was both remarkable and necessary since at that time women were not allowed to even enter a library, let alone attend university. During her studies, Ada Byron corresponded with many of the important English mathematicians of her day and eventually came to work with Charles Babbage. While Babbage concentrated on designing the computer hardware, Ada Byron became the first person to develop a set of instructions, which came to be called a **computer program**, for Babbage's **Analytic Engine**.

As computer hardware evolved from those early prototypes or models to today's fast and powerful machines, the ways in which information and instructions were prepared for the computer also radically changed. Over time the emphasis shifted from making the instructions simple enough for the computer to understand to making them close enough to the spoken language for everyone else to understand.

Computers such as ENIAC and EDVAC stored information, both numbers and program instructions, as groups of binary digits; 0 and 1. Each instruction was often made up of two parts, a group of bits (binary digits) representing the **operation** to be performed, and a group representing the **operand**, that is, the machine **address** of data to be operated on. A program consisted of a series of such instructions written in this **machine code**.

The problem with machine language is that it required programmers to write very long series of numbered instructions and to remember the binary codes for the different commands in the machine's instruction set. They also had to keep track of the storage locations (addresses) of the data and the instructions. As a result, a single program often took months to write and was commonly full of hard-to-find errors.

A major improvement in programming languages began in the 1950s with the development of symbolic machine languages, called **assembly languages**. Assembly languages allowed the programmer to write instructions using letter symbols rather than binary operation codes. The **assembler** then translated these simple written instructions into machine language. A program written in assembly language is called a **source program**. After the source program has been converted into machine code by an assembler, it is called an **object program**.

Assembly languages have a number of advantages when compared to machine language. They are:

• easier and faster to write,

• easier to **debug** (to find and correct errors), and

• easier to change at a later date.

But assembly languages also have a major drawback. Because the communication is taking place at one step up from the machine, an assembly language is designed for a specific make and model of computer processor. This means a program written to run on one computer will not work on another. Assembly languages are therefore said to be **machine oriented**.

**Symbolic addressing** was another interesting programming language development. Symbolic addressing involves the use of symbols to represent the assignment of storage addresses to data. Programmers could thus create symbolic names to represent items of data, and these names could be used throughout a program. Programmers no longer had to assign actual machine addresses to symbolic data items. The processor automatically assigned storage locations when the program ran.

The development of **high-level languages** was the next important step in computing. Like a program written in assembly language, a program written in a high-level language still needed to be translated into machine code. High-level languages included their own translation software to perform this task. The translating program is called a **compiler**. Compilers often generated many machine instructions for each source code statement. Today, however, many personal computers use an **interpreter**, rather than a compiler. A compiler translates the source program into object code and then executes it; the interpreter converts each source program statement into machine language every time the statement is executed. It does not save the object code.

High-level languages provide a number of benefits. They:

- free programmers from concerns about low-level machine details such as memory addressing and machine dependency,
- can be run on different makes of computers,
- are easier to use than assembly languages, and
- are easier for programmers to learn.

Here is an example of a simple instruction which shows the high-level language, assembly language and binary versions.

```
High Level Language (Turing)

a := 5

put a                          .
```

```
8086 Assembly language program

mov  word ptr _a,0005H   [_a=824H]        c7 06 24 08 05 00

push _a                                    ff 36 24 08

call  printf_            [printf=421CH]    e8 1c 42

add  p,0004H                               83 c4 04
```

```
Binary program

11000111 00000110 00100100 00001000 00000101 00000000 11111111 00110110

00100100 00001000 11101000 00011100 01000010 10000011 11000100 00000100
```

Until the late 1950s computers were still being used primarily for mathematical and scientific calculation. Computers used binary arithmetic and it was not until machines were developed to use decimal arithmetic that they were practical for business calculations. In 1958, J. N. Patterson Hume and C.C. Gotlieb from the University of Toronto published the first book on using the computer for business, called *High-Speed Data Processing* (McGraw Hill, 1958). Hume and Gotlieb are credited with publishing many of the computer terms still used today, including: compiler, data processing, and keyboard. In many ways Hume and Gotlieb pioneered today's wide-spread use of computers in business.

The major problem with programming in the early days was that it was time-consuming and difficult work, and programs often did not work. The growing recognition of the potential use of computers in many fields led to the evolution of modern programming languages that allowed for programs that were easier to develop, use, and modify over time.

In 1954 John Backus began leading an *IBM*-sponsored committee to develop a new scientific-mathematical programming language. In 1957 this committee introduced a new high-level language called **FORTRAN** (Formula Translator) for the **IBM 704** computer. FORTRAN gained wide acceptance, especially among scientists and statisticians because of its usefulness for expressing mathematical equations and over the years many versions of FORTRAN have been developed.

As more businesses began to appreciate the potential for computers, new languages were developed to meet their particular needs. In 1961, Grace Murray Hopper helped to invent **COBOL** (Common Business-Oriented Language). COBOL was designed to process business data and for many years it was used heavily by the insurance and banking industries among others. The language **ALGOL** was also developed by an international committee for scientific use.

At the same time John McCarthy at the Massachusetts Institute of Technology developed **LISP** was designed to support research in the field of **artificial intelligence** (AI).

**BASIC** (Beginners All-purpose Symbolic Instruction Code) was developed by John Kemeny and Thomas Kurtz beginning in 1964 at Dartmouth College. Kemeny and Kurtz wanted to develop a language that undergraduate students could easily learn and use on a time-shared basis on a large computer. Although the original BASIC had a well-defined syntax (the grammar rules of a programming language), over the years many different non-compatible versions have been developed, so that today, there are many "dialects" of BASIC.

**LOGO** was developed in the 1960s by Seymour Papert at the Massachusetts Institute of Technology. Papert's goal was to help young children explore a mathematical environment by using an on-screen "turtle" to draw figures and create simple animations.

In 1970, **Pascal** (named after the seventeenth-century French mathematician Blaise Pascal) was developed by Niklaus Wirth at the *Federal Institute of Technology* in Switzerland. One of the major benefits of Pascal over BASIC, was that it was designed to support the concepts of **structured programming**. In the case of earlier languages such as BASIC, a program's structure could be quite complex and trying to follow the

## 1.4   What is a Computer?

Now that we have looked at how computers have evolved, it makes sense to look more closely at what exactly is meant by the term computer. A computer is a machine that takes in information, transforms it, and outputs it in a different form. Information used by the computer is called **data**. Data can take many forms. It can be text, numbers, graphics, and even sounds. More specifically, information put into the computer is called **input**. Information that comes out of a computer is called **output**.

While computers themselves can be very complex, there is a very simple model that represents how all computers work. There must be something to take in information, something to process it, something to store it, and something to output the result. Here is a simple model of a computer.

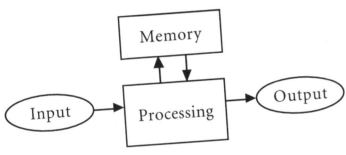

Figure 1.1

The part of the computer performing the input function receives information in the form of data or programs. Common examples of **input devices** include keyboards, disk drives, scanners, and the mouse.

One of the things that can be very confusing is that, while many kinds of devices (microwave ovens, bathroom scales, toasters, even singing birthday cards) use computer technology such as computer chips and memory, they are not really general purpose computers because they can only be used to perform the task for which they have been built. They cannot be programmed to perform a variety of tasks. Computers, however, are defined by their ability to process information in a variety of ways.

sequence of execution (how a program runs) was like trying to untangle a plate of spaghetti.

At the heart of structured programming is the idea that within a program there are groups of statements that are used to control the flow of information. These groups, often referred to as **control constructs**, are:

- **linear sequence**: where statements are executed one after the other in the order in which they are written,

- **repetition**: where a group of statements is to be executed repeatedly, and

- **selection**: where one group of statements is selected for execution from a number of alternatives.

Within a structured program, these control constructs are organized so that the program can be read from top to bottom. Each structure allows only one entrance and one exit. Indenting the instructions in a program printout helps someone looking at a program to understand its logic more easily.

The term structured programming now relates not just to program control logic, but to how programs are designed and developed. Today when people speak of structured programming, they are often referring to a systematic way of analyzing computer problems and designing solutions called **top-down programming**. In top-down programming, a problem is broken down into a series of smaller problems, each of which is then solved. Once the smaller problems are solved, the solutions are combined to solve the larger problem.

In the early 1970s Dennis Ritchie and Brian Kernighan of *Bell Labs* developed a programming language they called **C**. This language allowed for easy access to the hardware and was very efficient. C was designed to program large systems and so it became a favorite programming language of systems programmers. It was used to produce the **UNIX** operating system.

In 1975 the United States Department of Defense began a series of studies intended to support the development of a new programming language to be used by computer vendors and military programmers. The language, called **Ada** (after Ada Byron), was released by *CII-*

*Honeywell-Bull* in 1979 and was used extensively by the United States military.

| Year | Person | Developed |
|------|--------|-----------|
| 1800s | Ada Byron | first computer programs |
| 1954 | John Backus | FORTRAN |
| 1960s | Grace Murray Hopper | COBOL |
| | John Kemeny | BASIC |
| | Thomas Kurtz | |
| | Seymour Papert | LOGO |
| 1970s | Niklaus Wirth | Pascal |
| | Dennis Ritchie | Ada |
| 1980s | Brian Kernighan Dennis Ritchie | C |
| | Ric Holt James Cordy | Turing |
| 1990s | Bjarne Stroustrup | C++ |
| | James Gosling | Java |

**Turing** (named after Alan M. Turing) was developed by Ric Holt and James Cordy at the University of Toronto in 1984. Like Pascal before it, Turing was designed to suit personal computers, where the instructions are typed in directly. Turing was more powerful than Pascal and was designed to have a mathematically specified syntax (preventing the development of numerous incompatible versions) and that its syntax was much easier to understand.

## 1.3.1  A New Way of Organizing Large Programs

As computer programs and the tasks they perform have larger and more complex, programmers, scientists, and academ worked to find new ways of thinking about, developing, and mai these programs over time. The term **programming paradigm** the set of ideas which forms the basis of a particular programming.

The move from the unstructured to structured progra paradigm (see previous section) was a significant improvement programs were written and developed. By following the rules asso with structured programming, programmers made the logic of programs easier to follow. This meant that it was easier to locate a errors and to make changes to those programs as needed.

But the reality is that even structured programs are often consuming to write, hard to understand, and inflexible in that the designed for a specific task.

**Object-oriented** programming is a way of designing and wri programs based on the concept that a program can be created collection of **objects** which work together. Each of these objects is a se data and methods that operate on this set of data. The details of how data is stored and how the methods work are hidden from the user.

An object is created from a class from which many such objects be created. One class can **inherit** (or borrow) features from another cla Classes which perform specific tasks can also be reused in oth programs, thus speeding up program development. Current objec oriented programming languages include C++ (developed by Bjarn Stroustrup), **Java** (developed by James Gosling), and **Object Oriente Turing** (developed by Ric Holt).

## 1.4.1   The Central Processing Unit

The internal part of the computer that processes information is called the **Central Processing Unit** or **CPU**. The CPU does the work and determines the order in which operations are performed. There are three main sections of the CPU:

- the **primary storage** section,
- the **arithmetic-logic** section, and
- the **control** section.

The primary storage section or **main memory** is used four ways:

- the **input storage area** collects data that has been fed in until it is ready to be processed,
- the **program storage** area holds the processing instructions,
- the **working storage space** holds the data being processed and the intermediate results of that processing, and
- the **output storage area** holds the final results of the processing operations until they can be released.

The arithmetic-logic section is where all calculations are performed and decisions are made; in other words, where the data held in the storage areas is processed. Data moves from primary storage to the arithmetic logic unit and back again to storage repeatedly until processing is completed. Once the processing is completed, the final results are sent to the output storage section and from there to an **output device** such as the **computer screen** (also called a monitor) or the **printer.**

The control section maintains the order of the entire system by directing the data to the appropriate places. It is the traffic cop of the CPU. When processing begins, the control section retrieves the first instruction from the program storage area. The control section then interprets the instruction and signals the other sections to begin their tasks. Program instructions are selected and carried out in sequence unless an instruction is encountered to tell it to jump to another instruction or until the processing is completed.

## 1.4.2   Memory

Over the years the ways in which computers store information have changed remarkably. Initially information was stored using vacuum tubes. Vacuum tubes, which resemble light bulbs, are glass cylinders containing several filaments. A later generation of computers stored information using **magnetic core memory**, which consisted of donut shaped rings that were magnetized in one direction or another. Today, main memory is usually on **silicon** chips (see Section 1.5.2) and the time required to access information in main memory (**access time**) is measured in nanoseconds (billionths of a second) instead of the microseconds (millionths of a second) magnetic core memory required.

Main memory is broken down into two main types, **RAM** (Random Access Memory) and **ROM** (Read Only Memory). RAM stores programs, data, or information from input and output devices. This stored information can be manipulated by computer programs or input from or output to devices such as printers and scanners. RAM memory is lost when the computer is shut off. Saving RAM memory in secondary storage is essential if this information is required later. Creating a **back-up** (saving a second copy of the same information) is a good programming practice.

| Memory | Conversion |
|---|---|
| 1 bit | either 1 or 0 |
| 1 nybble | 4 bits |
| 1 byte | 8 bits or 2 nybbles |
| 1 kilobyte | 1000 bytes (approx.) |
| 1 megabyte | 1000 kilobytes |
| 1 gigabyte | 1000 megabytes |
| 1 terabyte | 1000 gigabytes |

ROM on the other hand stores information that the system needs in order to function. The contents of this memory are recorded at the time the computer is manufactured and are not lost when the computer is shut off, if there is an interruption in power, or if an application stops working properly (referred to as "crashing").

In early personal computers, the overall amount of memory was very limited. For example, when the **Commodore Pets** were introduced the total RAM was 8K and many people could not imagine needing any more memory than this. Today, however, personal computers contain far more RAM and sizes are now measured in gigabytes (millions of kilobytes).

Information that needs to be stored for future use can be kept in **secondary storage devices** such as floppy disks, hard drives, and Zip™ drives.

### 1.4.3    Output Devices

Once data is input and processed it often needs to be output in various forms. When the computer is used for numerical computation, for example, the numbers are input, then processed, and the result is output. Output devices can include monitors (the computer screen), printers, and synthesizers. Over time the technology underlying computer monitors has changed dramatically, and these changes have often been driven by the need for higher resolution especially for computer graphics and smaller, more portable computers. Different types of display technologies include CRTs (cathode ray tubes), LCDs (liquid crystal), and gas plasma displays.

# 1.5   Number Systems: Decimal and Binary

At its most basic, a computer is a machine that processes information, but before you can understand more explicitly how it does that, you have to know something about how that information is expressed at the machine level. As mentioned earlier in this chapter, machine language is based on the binary number system rather than the decimal number system. We will now look more closely at both of these systems and how they differ.

When human beings count, they use a number system which is based upon combinations of ten different digits. These are:

0  1  2  3  4  5  6  7  8  9

All numbers are combinations of these symbols. This number system is called the **decimal number system** or **base 10** since it is based on a set of ten digits. At the machine level, however, computers use only combinations of two different digits to represent all information that can be stored. These are:

0  1

This two-digit system is called the **binary number system**. It is also called **base 2**. When people need to communicate with computers at their most fundamental (machine) level, they need to be able to convert between binary and decimal representation.

An important aspect of each number system is that it has **place value**. The base 10 number (the decimal number) 987 has 7 in the units column, 8 in the tens column, and 9 in the hundreds column. Moving from the right column to the left, each column is multiplied by 10.

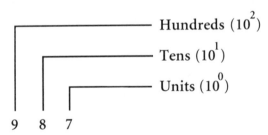

Figure 1.2

Therefore the base 10 number 987 equals

$$9 \times 10^2 + 8 \times 10^1 + 7 \times 10^0$$

In mathematics $10^0$ equals 1. The figures in superscript (smaller raised figures) represent the number of times the base number is multiplied by itself.

The binary number system also has place value. The binary number (base 2) 1101 has the right-most 1 in the units column, the 0 to its left is in the twos column, the 1 in the 2 squared (or fours column), and the left-most 1 in the 2 cubed column (eights column). Each column is multiplied by 2, moving from the right to the left.

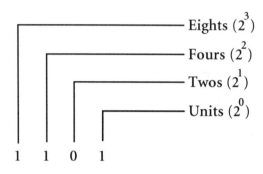

Eights ($2^3$)
Fours ($2^2$)
Twos ($2^1$)
Units ($2^0$)

1   1   0   1

Figure 1.3

For example, the binary number 1101 equals

$$1 \times 2^3 + 1 \times 2^2 + 0 \times 2^1 + 1 \times 2^0 \text{ or } 8 + 4 + 0 + 1 = 13$$

therefore

$$1101_2 = 13_{10}$$

In mathematics $2^0$ equals 1. The figures in **subscript** (smaller lowered figures) represent the number system being used.

All base 10 numbers have an equivalent binary number. Understanding the decimal and binary number systems is essential in order to understand how computers work.

Here is a chart showing the decimal and binary version of the first sixteen natural numbers in both systems.

| Decimal or Base 10 | Binary or Base 2 | Decimal or Base 10 | Binary or Base 2 |
|:---:|:---:|:---:|:---:|
| 0 | 0 | 8 | 1000 |
| 1 | 1 | 9 | 1001 |
| 2 | 10 | 10 | 1010 |
| 3 | 11 | 11 | 1011 |
| 4 | 100 | 12 | 1100 |
| 5 | 101 | 13 | 1101 |
| 6 | 110 | 14 | 1110 |
| 7 | 111 | 15 | 1111 |

# 1.6   Hardware and Networks

Once you understand what computers are and how they store information it is important to look more closely at the actual components or parts that make up a computer system.

When you hear people talk about computers they often talk about **hardware** and **software**. By hardware, they mean the electronic and mechanical parts of the computer. Computer hardware can include things such as:

• the **hard disk**, which stores programs and data,
• the **keyboard**, **CD ROM**, and the **mouse** which are used for inputting data,
• **monitors**, **printers**, and **speakers** which are output devices,
• **light pens** and **barcode readers** which are input devices, and
• **disk drives** and **modem** which can be either input or output devices.

The term **peripheral** refers to the many devices which can be attached to the computer. These peripherals often include printers, scanners, speakers, modems, and joysticks. Their primary purpose is to either provide input to, or output from the computer. Printers, for example, provide textual output from a file while barcode readers are used to scan information such as a price or part number into the computer. In later chapters we will investigate a variety of peripherals in more detail.

Here is what a standard hardware setup might look like.

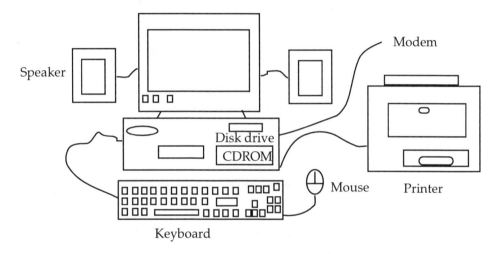

**Figure 1.4 Standard Computer Hardware Setup**

This setup includes input devices such as the mouse, keyboard, and CD-ROM and output devices such as speakers and the printer. The disk drive and modem are unique because they can be both used for both input and output. The disk drive can be used to store and retrieve files from floppy disks which can be transferred from computer to computer, while modems send and retrieve information via telephones or cable lines.

Figure 1.5 provides a simplified illustration of some of the components of the computer.

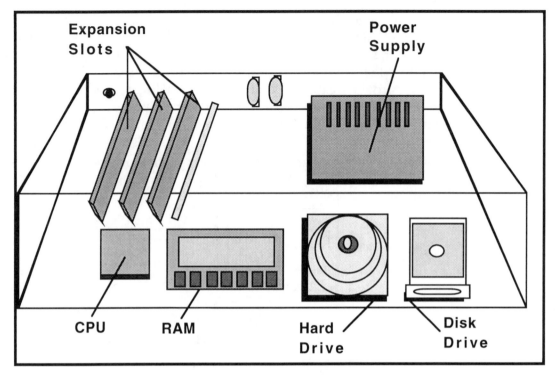

Figure 1.5 Computer Components

Many computers are also connected to **networks** which allow the computers (and their users!) to communicate and share information and resources. Networking facilitates two-way sharing of software and hardware locally or globally. Computer networks can take many forms, depending upon the type and number of computers in the network and the distance over which they must be linked. The hardware on the network may include: personal computers, mainframes, supercomputers, printers, fax machines, navigational control systems, and interactive entertainment centers. The software, however, will always include application software, desktop software, and networking operating systems.

The benefits of networking computers are enormous. Geographically remote areas can be connected to share information. Without actually transferring an entire file to all the people involved, several people can simultaneously share large files. Also, within a networked environment the information generated by a single user can be shared world-wide instantaneously.

For example, a large company with a number of sales offices in different cities can use its networked computers to maintain a single file with all of their customer information. The sales people at each office would be able to get information from this file and add information to it without having to have a separate copy of the entire file on their computers. In this way, every sales person would have access to the most up-to-date information for the entire company. The problem of keeping the separate lists in each office current would be eliminated. And finally, fewer computer resources would be needed because there would be one shared file rather than many separate files. In this way, networking enables faster, more precise communication which should translate into greater accuracy, productivity, and cost savings.

Networking also allows different types of computers to communicate. Users choose specific computers and operating systems for many reasons. For example, a particular application might be better suited for a Macintosh than an IBM PC. Networking allows users to share resources even when their systems are different.

Users on a network can also share physical resources. Many individual computers can share one scanner, printer, or other expensive piece of hardware. Sharing hardware significantly reduces the expense of running a system.

## 1.6.1   Different Kinds of Computers for Different Needs

The use of computers to perform an ever-increasing number of jobs has led to the development of various kinds and sizes of computers. The largest computers are called **supercomputers**. These computers are used primarily by government, industry, and research organizations for projects which require huge amounts of computing power, often for fast calculation purposes. Supercomputers have multiple CPUs and are known for their processing speed.

Many large businesses such as banks, airlines, insurance companies, and law enforcement agencies use **mainframe computers** to store and manipulate large amounts of information. Mainframe computers are capable of multiprocessing, that is, running many processes simultaneously. Their main advantage is the ability to store vast amounts of information and later to distribute it.

Mainframe computers are often used in a network of medium-sized computers called **minicomputers**. A minicomputer, despite its name, is a medium-sized computer. The most common computer, however, is the **personal computer**. It is also know as the **microcomputer** or **desktop computer**. This computer is designed for a single user and consists of a CPU, input/output units, and a power supply.

As more and more people are using their computers at work, at home, and on the road, **laptop** computers have become increasingly popular. These computers have been designed to provide most of the same features as a desktop or personal computer, but in a more portable size. These computers are often characterized by a smaller keyboard and a flip-top lid containing a monitor or screen.

One of the newest computers sold commercially is the **hand-held** or **palmtop computer**. These extremely small computers are often used as personal organizers, word processors, or for accessing local or global telecommunications such as **electronic mail**, commonly called **email**.

As computer power of even the smallest computers has increased, the distinctions between these kinds of computers have begun to blur, and it is important to note that the size of the computer is no longer an indication of how powerful or how fast it is.

## 1.6.2   The Silicon Chip

Computers today, regardless of what they are used for, are smaller, faster, and less expensive than they were twenty years ago. One of the main reasons for this is the development of the **silicon chip**. The importance of this technology to the computing industry can be seen in the fact the area in California where there is a high concentration of computing companies is often referred to as "Silicon Valley".

Silicon is found in common substances such as sand, but has unique properties which make it especially useful in the manufacturing of electronics equipment. While silicon alone acts as an insulator, when a line of metal is deposited on it, that metal acts as a wire **conductor** which transmits electric current. If the silicon is impregnated with certain other elements, it acts as a **semi-conductor**. These semi-conductors are used to create **transistors**. A transistor is an electronic switch that conducts electric current under certain conditions.

A series of switches and conducting wires that perform a specific function is called a **circuit** because it controls the path over which electricity can flow. A silicon chip is made up of a large number (potentially millions) of transistors which are in turn organized into circuits. Silicon chips are often called integrated circuits because each chip can contain many different circuits.

The silicon chip has also increased the speed at which computers can perform tasks, resulting in computers that perform an operation in a trillionth of a second, performing millions of calculations, or processing tens of thousands of instructions in a second.

Because silicon chips are extremely small, they can be used in many products. A silicon chip less than a centimeter (an eighth of an inch) square can store millions of bits of information and perform the work it once would have taken a room full of computers to perform. Many common products such as watches now contain silicon chips. Specialized chips are also used in many larger products such as cars, VCRs, microwave ovens, and washing machines.

Every computer from a supercomputer to a laptop computer contains silicon chips. Because modern digital computers tend to isolate the user from the actual silicon chips that control the computer's functions, each containing huge numbers of elements, very few users actually understand the underlying logic of computer chips.

# 1.7   Software

The term software refers to all of the instructions that make the hardware work. Within the computer there are many different levels of software. In this section we will briefly examine four distinct kinds of software:

- operating systems,
- programming environments, and
- applications.

### 1.7.1    Operating Systems

The **operating system** is a collection of programs that the computer uses to manage itself and use its resources efficiently. Operating systems you might have already heard of include: UNIX, Linux, Microsoft Windows™, DOS™, and MacOS™.

The operating system performs tasks such as accepting input from the keyboard and managing input and output between the computer and external devices (peripherals). Some of these devices such as printers are not part of the computer but can be used to send information to or receive information from the computer.

### 1.7.2    Programming Environments

In order to write your own program you need to use a **programming environment**. A programming environment is a set of tools that includes an **editor** for entering and changing the program, a compiler or interpreter for translating programs into a machine language that the computer can understand, and sometimes a **debugger** for locating and fixing errors.

As noted earlier in this chapter, many different programming languages have been developed, each with its own set of features. Many of these programming languages now include their own programming environments.

### 1.7.3   Applications

Software can refer to a single computer program that does one task or a collection of programs, called an **application**, that perform many of the same kinds of tasks. Some common examples of large applications include:

- computer games,
- word processors,
- graphics packages,
- virtual reality software,

- presentation software,
- web browsers,
- database management systems, and
- spreadsheets.

Computer **games** are among the most popular software applications and are available from the simplest tic-tac-toe games to highly complex role playing games with advanced graphics, animation, and sound.

**Word processing software** enables the user to create, edit, and save textual documents. Almost all word processing software provides features for editing (cut and paste) and formatting (font styles and font sizes, tab bars, and headers and footers) text. Most also include an additional set of tools such as a spell checker, grammar checker, word counter, and a thesaurus.

**Graphics applications** provide many of the same basic functions as word processors, except that they are designed for creating and manipulating images rather than text. There is a wide range of graphics packages, from simple paint programs that allow the user to create simple shapes in different colors to advanced tools that allow images to be created, modified, and displayed.

**Virtual reality** packages are programs that use computer-generated images, text, and sound to imitate real-world events. Simulation software creates a virtual environment which the user can observe and interact with. The aerospace industry, for example, uses flight simulators to test new aircraft designs before the product is released. Using simulation software to "virtually" fly the aircraft helps the designers identify and correct potential problems before the plane is built. This saves time, money, and possibly even lives. The nuclear power industry also uses simulation software to demonstrate the operations of a nuclear power plant and simulate what might happen in the event of natural disasters (such as earthquakes). In this way, simulation software can be used to test safety and emergency procedures without requiring a real emergency. Simulation software is used in many fields, such as microcomputer design, global climatic studies, agricultural research, and black-hole research.

The term **presentation software** refers to an application that helps the user organize information so that it can be used for presentations or display. These applications often provide a set of templates or example formats into which the user can insert the information she or he wishes to display. Imported text can then be formatted in a variety of different styles. Most presentation packages allow the user to import graphical images, sound, and video. If the user has access to the appropriate display hardware and software, she or he can create a computer-based presentation run from either the keyboard or a hand-held device. If no such equipment is available, the presentation can also be printed directly onto acetates (clear plastic) to be displayed using an overhead projector.

**Web browser applications** allow the user to access, view, and **download** text and graphics from the **World Wide Web**. The **Internet** is a vast and complex network of computers which provides storage space for textual and graphical information which can be shared. The term World Wide Web refers to specific kinds of files or collections of files where information is organized and displayed in **hypertext**. Hypertext is a non-linear organizational format. Rather than proceeding in a straight line from beginning to end like a book, it organizes the information in layers. In order to access the Web, users must be able to log into a computer network linked to the Internet, in other words they need an Internet account. Many large organizations such as corporations and universities provide accounts to their employees. Individuals with a home computer can also purchase an account (often on a monthly basis) from an **Internet Service Provider** (ISP) or through a telephone company or cable television provider.

**Database** applications help users store, organize, and use numbers and text. This information is usually spread out in rows and columns. Databases tend to be used for more text-rich storage such as customer information.

**Spreadsheet** applications also help users store, organize, and use numbers and text but spreadsheets usually provide more features for manipulating numbers and performing calculations and so are used for financial plans, such as budgets.

# 1.8   The Social Impact of Computers

The impact of computers on our society is profound. Many books have been written on the social aspects of technology. In this section we will briefly examine some of the positive and negative impacts of computing.

The evolution of computer hardware and software has created a revolution in our society and can in some ways be seen as the latest extension of the Industrial Revolution. During the Industrial Revolution increasing mechanization led to the growth of industry. Since industry tended to concentrate in urban (city) rather than rural (country) areas, more and more people began moving into cities to work in factories and businesses. This has also been the case with the computer revolution. Computers are now part of our everyday life and so in some subtle and not so subtle ways they affect how we work, play, and live.

## 1.8.1   Employment

One of the primary benefits of computing is that it has created thousands of new job opportunities. There is almost no industry now that does not require the skills of programmers. At the same time, the computerization of many traditional manufacturing industries, such as the auto industry, has led to the displacement of many workers. The growing use of computers has also eliminated many of the jobs formerly performed by unskilled workers or skilled tradespeople.

Increased computerization has allowed businesses, industries, and governments to streamline their operations, increase productivity, and provide services more efficiently. These improvements include easier access to goods and services such as Internet shopping, more reliable billing procedures, and faster and more detailed access to customer information. People in every profession can share information more easily. For example, scientists in different parts of the world can share their findings through email. They can also turn over the boring jobs, such as performing time-consuming calculations, to computers, thus increasing job satisfaction and improving their opportunity to find and share solutions.

At the same time, however, many people feel that computers are taking the human touch out of everything by making all our transactions so impersonal. Now, instead of dealing with people such as tellers in banks and service people at gas stations, we are dealing with machines. Instead of being people, we are personal identification numbers (pin) , social insurance numbers (SIN), and account numbers. After a while this lack of human contact becomes extremely frustrating. The mayor of the city of Toronto, for example, banned voice mail from city offices because he said it was making the people of the city feel there were no real people to help them.

## 1.8.2   Privacy

Computer telecommunications such as email have opened the windows of communication world-wide. Through email, students in Canada and students in Australia can share information about themselves and their communities, and thus come to understand each other better. Many people who may be isolated by geography or disability can find others to communicate with via a chat room or listserv. For example, deaf people from around the world use a listserv called DEAF-L to discuss issues of concern to their community and to share information about available resources.

While computer technology has made it easier for us to gather information, it has also led to invasion of people's privacy. Information about every aspect of a person's life can be collected and sold to businesses and organizations without the person agreeing or even knowing. For example, grocery stores which use optical scanners to calculate the cost of food items and let customers use bank cards to pay can collect information about what kinds of products people buy and provide that information to the people who make or advertise those products. There is also growing concern about the availability of personal information such as medical and financial records.

## 1.8.3   Access to Information

The Internet is a tool people can use to gain access to many different sources of information on any topic imaginable. One problem, however, is that some people take everything they find on the Internet at face value. They do not consider that the people who are making that information available might be ill-informed or trying to mislead.

There is a saying that "on the net, everyone is an expert". What this means is that while everyone may seem to be an expert, some people simply do not know what they are talking about. When viewing material on the Internet, it is important to determine the validity of the information. Readers should consider whether the person posting the information is likely to have the required knowledge and whether he or she might benefit from presenting false or misleading information. This does not mean that you should always trust someone of high social status, such as a university professor, while mistrusting a student. It simply means that you should always be careful to evaluate information based on its source.

There is also a debate about just how much of "the wrong kind" of information is available on the Internet. As the media have frequently reported, there is pornographic material available to those who go looking for it. For this reason many schools use some kind of blocking software on their networks to prevent students from gaining access to such information. Many companies also have very strict policies about firing employees who are caught using their office computers to download or store pornographic material.

Again, it is up to the user to access information in a responsible way. You should also keep in mind that no matter how clever you are, it is always possible for someone to track your use of a computer. Virtually every activity on a network is logged somewhere in the system and it is a relatively simple task for the network administrator to find out where you have been and what you have been doing.

## 1.8.4    Leisure Activities

For many people, computers have opened up a whole new realm of leisure activities. People can use their computers to create new computer programs, to play games, to use computer applications to master new skills, or to chat with people anywhere in the world. They can also take on-line courses. Unfortunately, like many other fascinating hobbies, computers can take over people's lives if they fall victim to computer addiction. On many university campuses, computer addiction is a major cause of failure, as students become so immersed in their hobby that they neglect their studies. Among many adults, home computers have also been known to put stress on their important relationships. Time on the computer just seems to fly by and somehow "I'll be there in ten minutes" turns into hours.

The most obvious sign of computer addiction is that addicts neglect other important aspects of their life such as family, work, friends, school, and sleep. The key to avoiding addiction is to ensure that, despite temporary indulgences, time spent at the computer is not time stolen from other important activities and people.

## 1.8.5    Illegal Activity

Like most human inventions, computers can be used in good ways and in bad ways. As computer use is increasing, so is the use of computers to commit criminal offenses. Computers are now being used to create illegal credit cards, to defraud banks, and to steal information from businesses. In this way, they have given rise to a new breed of white-collar criminals.

A new area of computer crime, called **software piracy**, involves people duplicating, using, and sharing, information (textual, graphical, and sound) and applications to which they have no right. Many people do not realize that it costs literally hundreds of thousands of dollars to create a software application. When people copy that application and share it with their friends, they rob the people who spent the time and money to develop and distribute it.

In order to try to protect themselves from software piracy, many software companies attempt to protect their products with registration codes. While such measures can prove annoying to users, they are often the only way the company can protect itself from unauthorized duplication and distribution.

Another way that software companies are fighting back is through a process called a **software audit.** If a software vendor believes that a company, organization, or institution is using its software illegally, it can demand that the company determine every single software product it uses and prove that it is using it legally (has purchased the right to use it).

Many people do not realize that it is illegal to use copyrighted material without the permission of the copyright holder. People who post images, video, or sound on their web pages without finding out who they really belong to run the risk of being charged with **copyright infringement.**

### 1.8.6 Computers: Good or Bad?

Like most objects, computers themselves are neither good nor bad, but they can be used by good or bad people to do good or bad things. As responsible human beings we all have an obligation to look carefully at how we use technology. As a caring society we need to question whether the way in which we use our tools makes the world a better place for all of us, or just a more profitable place for some and a worse place for most. Like most technologies, computers have the potential to improve life for everyone who owns one. At the same time, they have the potential to leave those who do not have access to these resources further and further behind.

# 1.9 Chapter Summary

This chapter provides an overview of the history of modern computing, including hardware, software, programming languages, and number systems. It also explores some of the current social issues in computing such as employment, privacy, and access to information.

# History of Computer Hardware

Performing arithmetic operations using mechanical calculators dates from the fifteenth century. The nineteenth century saw the design of machines not only to do calculations but to follow a sequence of instructions to control a series of arithmetic operations. Thus the programmable calculator was conceived. To communicate with the calculator, instructions and data were input as cards with holes punched in them.

In the 1940s many different electronic digital computers were developed, mostly at universities. These involved the use of vacuum tubes which were not reliable. The invention of the transistor in the early 1960s led to the design of computers that were more reliable and more powerful. Circuits containing many transistors were integrated on sheets of insulated material. Silicon chips, which could function as an insulating (non-conducting) base and, with appropriate additions, as semi-conducting parts of transistors provided for large scale integration.

# History of Programming

Computers store data and instructions as sequences of binary digits (bits). Each computer type has a repertoire of operations that it can execute directly by interpreting its coded instructions. This machine code was difficult to work with and so assembly language was developed to represent each code operation by an easy-to-remember symbolic equivalent. Assembly language then translated the instructions to machine code.

Higher level languages were developed to provide independence from machine code and make it easier for the programmer to create instructions for the computer to follow. Many higher level languages have been developed, including: FORTRAN for numerical calculation, COBOL for business applications, LISP for artificial intelligence, and LOGO for graphics no name a few.

Changes in hardware and the desire for direct user-computer interaction resulted in the development of BASIC for time-sharing large computers and Pascal for programming personal computers. Pascal incorporated the concept of structured programming. BASIC did not.

Later language developments, such as object-oriented programming, were driven by the increasing size and complexity of computer programs which made them difficult to develop and maintain.

# The Computer

The various elements of a computer, including input/output, memory and control were outlined.

# Number Systems

The relation between the decimal and binary number systems was described.

# Hardware and Networks

The range of computers from supercomputers to personal computers and their relationship in networks was described.

The silicon chip, the fundamental component of all hardware was detailed.

# Software

All computers require an operating system to permit the input and output of data and an environment for the input, editing, and translation of programs in high level languages. Application programs facilitate specialized tasks such as word processing, large data storage and manipulation, and graphics creation.

# Social Impact of Computers

While computers have displaced some workers through the automation of many routine tasks, they have also led to the creation of many new jobs.

Computers are used to store vast amounts of information. This information can be extremely useful in situations such as a medical emergency. If improperly stored and protected, however, it can also be used to invade peoples' privacy. The World Wide Web is also subject to intrusions of privacy and sometimes to fraud and theft if personal information such as credit card numbers are not properly protected.

Illegal activities such as software piracy and the creation and dissemination of computer viruses are also a danger to all computer users.

# 1.10  Technical Terms

| | |
|---|---|
| access time | control constructs |
| Ada | COBOL |
| algorithm | coding |
| Analytic Engine | control |
| application software | compiler |
| artificial intelligence | computer game |
| arithmetic logic section | computer programming |
| assembly language | computer program |
| back-up | computer screen |
| base 2 | conductor |
| base 10 | control construct |
| BASIC | copyright infringement |
| batch processing | data |
| binary notation | database |
| binary number system | decimal number system |
| binary representation | debug |
| bit | debugger |
| C++ | Difference Engine |
| central processing unit (CPU) | disk drive |
| classes | download |
| circuit | editor |

electronic mail (email)

execute

external documentation

FORTRAN

graphics package

hacker

hand-held/palmtop computer

hard disk

hardware

high-level language

hypertext

information technology

inherit

input

input device

input storage area

insulator

integrated circuit

interactive computing

internal documentation

Internet

interpreter

Internet Service Provider

invalid data

Java

keyboard

laptop

Large-scale integration

linear sequence

LISP

Logo

machine language

machine oriented

magnetic core memory

main memory

mainframe computer

maintaining

microcomputer/desktop computer

microprocessor

minicomputer

mouse

network

object oriented programming

Object Oriented Turing

object program

operating system

output

output device

output storage area

Pascal

peripheral

personal computer

place value

presentation software

primary storage

printer

problem solving

program storage

programmer

programming environment

programming language

RAM

reduced instruction-set
computing (RISC)

repetition

ROM

secondary storage device

selection

silicon

silicon chip

simulation software

software

software audit

software piracy

source program

spreadsheet

structured programming

subscript

supercomputer

switch

symbolic addressing

syntax

top-down programming

transistor

Turing

UNIX

vacuum tube

valid data

very large-scale integration
(VLSI)

virus

web browser

well-designed program

word processor

working storage space

World Wide Web

# 1.11 Exercises

1. Describe the contribution to the development of modern computers made by the following people.

   (a) Charles Babbage
   (b) Pehr George Scheutz
   (c) Herman Hollerith
   (d) Alan M. Turing
   (e) Howard T. Aiken
   (f) John W. Mauchly and J. Presper Eckert Jr.
   (g) John von Neumann
   (h) Charlotte Frose
   (i) Ada Byron
   (j) Grace Hopper

2. List the five generations of computers along with two significant features of each generation.

3. Define the following:

   (a) computer programming
   (b) programming language
   (c) syntax
   (d) debug

4. Explain two differences between machine code and assembly language.

5. List three advantages of assembly languages over machine code.

6. Differentiate between a compiler and an interpreter.

7. List five high-level programming languages.

8.  State one feature of each of the five high-level languages identified in the Exercise 7 and list the most important person(s) involved with each language.

9.  Machine code and assembly languages are both examples of "low-level languages." List five advantages high-level languages have over low-level languages.

10.  Define programming paradigm.

11.  Explain the main differences between two programming paradigms.

12.  Draw a simple model of a computer.

13.  What does the acronym CPU stand for?

14.  State the main function of the CPU.

15.  State the three main sections of the CPU.

16.  Explain the functions of each of the three sections of the CPU.

17.  Explain the significance of each of the following terms relating to computer memory.
    (a) main memory
    (b) RAM
    (c) ROM
    (d) vacuum tubes
    (e) magnetic core
    (f) silicon chip
    (g) back-up

18.  The binary number system is fundamental to really understanding how a computer functions. Explain.

19.  Explain the difference between hardware and software.

20.  List one significant feature (besides size) of each type of computer.

   (a) supercomputer
   (b) mainframe
   (c) minicomputer
   (d) personal computer
   (e) laptop
   (f) palmtop

21.  What is a silicon chip?

22.  List three features of silicon chips.

23.  List three types of software and one feature of each type.

24.  Computers can be used to obtain personal information without your knowledge. Explain.

25.  Computers have created many new job opportunities. Explain.

26.  Computers have eliminated many jobs. Explain.

# Chapter 2

# The Ready to Program with Java™ Technology Environment

In the previous chapter, we examined some of the concepts underlying programming. To start writing programs and having them executed on a computer we need to have software tools. This textbook comes with a CD containing software for developing Java programs called **Ready to Program with Java**™ **Technology**. This environment is currently available only for PCs running Windows 95 and later. The environment allows students to enter, edit, correct, and run Java programs. See Appendix G for instructions on installing and running the **Ready** software on your computer system.

**Note**: While the screen shots shown in this chapter may not correspond directly to the most recent version of the **Ready** software, the operational details will not be changed, and the instructions for use will remain accurate.

Explaining how to use the **Ready** environment requires some explanation of Java concepts. Chapter 4 provides a more complete explanation of these concepts.

# 2.1   Beginning to Use Ready to Program with Java™ Technology

Most students have had experience running computer applications such as word processors and spread sheets. This chapter assumes a familiarity with the basic use of buttons, menu bars, and clicking and dragging with a mouse.

To start the environment, click on the *Start* button at the bottom of the screen. This brings up the *Start* menu. Select the *Programs* menu item. A sub-menu appears listing the different programs installed on the machine. Select the *Ready to Program* menu item from the sub-menu. This displays another sub-menu with a single menu item, also labelled *Ready to Program*, with the program's icon (a red "e") beside it. Selecting this menu item and releasing the mouse starts up the *Ready to Program* environment.

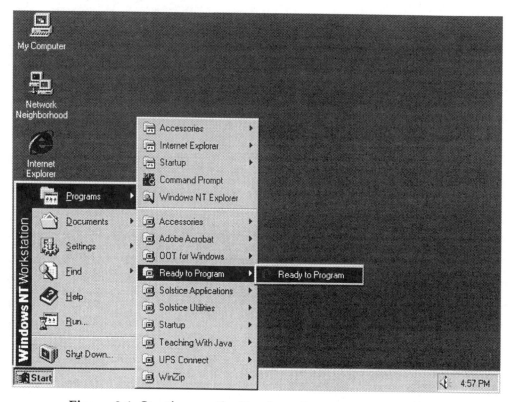

**Figure 2.1 Starting up the Ready to Program Environment**

Once **Ready** is started, a window which gives the product name and version number appears for a few seconds. It then disappears leaving an editor window. The editor window in the **Ready** environment can take one of two very similar forms, depending on whether you are using the *one-window* or the *multi-window* mode.

In *one-window* mode, all files being edited appear in a single editor window with one file visible at a time. In *multi-window* mode, each file appears in its own editor window. We will use *multi-window* mode in this chapter. Section 2.8.3 discusses the minor differences in *one-window* mode.

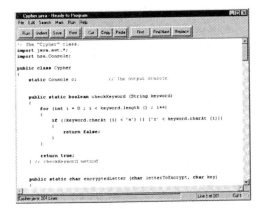

**Figure 2.2  Multi-Window Mode and One-Window Mode**

```
// The "Cypher" class.
import java.awt.*;
import hsa.Console;

public class Cypher
{
    static Console c;              // The output console


    public static boolean checkKeyword (String keyword)
    {
        for (int i = 0 ; i < keyword.length () ; i++)
        {
            if ((keyword.charAt (i) < 'a') || ('z' < keyword.charAt (i)))
            {
                return false;
            }
        }

        return true;
    } // checkKeyword method


    public static char encryptedLetter (char letterToEncrypt, char key)
    {
```

**Figure 2.3  The Editor Window**

The editor window has four basic parts:

• the menu bar,
• the button bar,
• the text area, and
• a status bar.

The menu bar contains the menus from which most of the commands to **Ready** can be issued. The button bar provides a set of shortcuts to various commonly used commands. Every command in the button bar can be found in the menus. The text area is the area where the program text is displayed. Program text is entered here. The bottom of the window contains the status bar. This is where messages are relayed from the system to you. If a message is too long for the status bar, then moving the mouse over the status bar will make a tooltip box appear showing the entire message.

# 2.2   Organization of Java Programs

A Java program consists of one or more **classes**. Each class has a name and is saved in a separate file with the same name as the class and the suffix ".java". A Java class named "BlueRect" must be saved in a file called "BlueRect.java". Thus when the chapter refers to "editing a class", this is equivalent to editing the file containing the class.

In Java there are  two distinct kinds of program: applets and applications. An applet is a Java class that inherits from *java.applet.Applet*. This is a class in the Java class library on which all applets are based. An application, however, is a Java class which contains a subprogram called *main*. In Java subprograms are called **methods** so you will often see references to a *main* method. This chapter contains only examples of creating a Java application.

Java classes can be grouped into **packages**. While this book does not discuss the creation of packages, it does use the packages that are part of the Java class library as well as a package included with **Ready** called *hsa* which contains classes used to help you write programs.

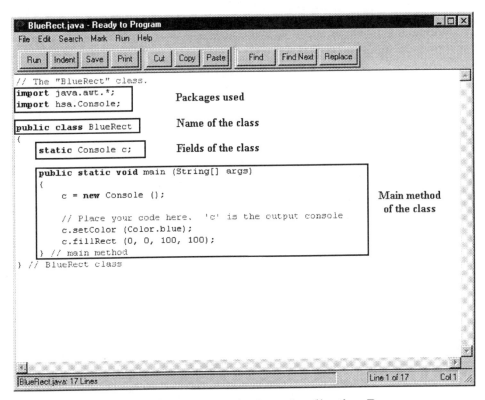

**Figure 2.4 Organization of a Java Application Program**

Java application programs follows a certain format. First there are statements indicating what packages are used by the program. This is followed by a statement indicating the name of the class. Inside the class, the fields are declared, followed by the methods in the class. Many of these lines are common to most Java programs and so even the simplest Java program will be several lines long. The **Ready** environment provides pre-built templates (called boilerplates) which contain these standard lines and other lines that are to be modified by the user. Using and editing the boilerplate allows the user to create programs more rapidly.

# 2.3   Creating a New Application

We will now look at creating a Java application program that uses the hsa *Console* class to draw a blue rectangle.

When **Ready** starts, the editor window is in the upper-left corner of the screen. To load the template for a Java application program using the *Console* class, select the *New* menu item from the *File* menu. This displays a sub-menu with a variety of templates. You can now select the *HSA Console Application Boilerplate* menu item.

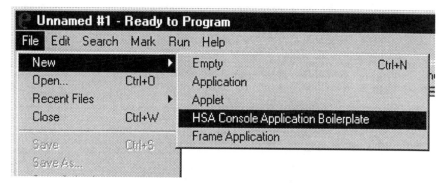

**Figure 2.5  Selecting the *HSA* Menu Item**

A dialog box asking for the name of the class appears. Enter *BlueRect*.

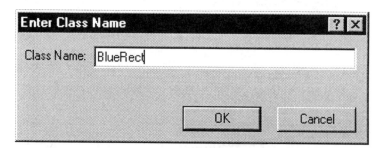

**Figure 2.6  Class Name Dialog Box**

The appropriate boilerplate text now appears in the editor window. This is a Java application program. The program, however, does not do anything. To make the program draw a blue rectangle, follow the line

```
// Place your code here. 'c' is the output console
```

with

```
c.setColor (Color.blue);
c.fillRect (0, 0, 100, 100);
```

The final program should look like this.

```
// The "BlueRect" class.
import java.awt.*;
import hsa.Console;

public class BlueRect
{
    static Console c;

    public static void main (String[] args)
    {
        c = new Console ();

        // Place your code here.  'c' is the output console
        c.setColor (Color.blue);
        c.fillRect (0, 0, 100, 100);
    } // main method
} // BlueRect class
```

Once the program has been created, it is a very good idea to save it. To save a Java class, click the *Save* button in the button bar. If the class has not been saved before, a file dialog box allowing you to specify the name of the file appears. The default name of the file is already filled in with *BlueRect.java*. It is not a good idea to change this name although you may wish to save it in a different folder using the dialog box.

It is a wise idea to save each program and its associated classes in a separate folder. This avoids the problem of having to different classes with the same name.

Once you have saved the class, you may also wish to print a copy. You can print the contents of an editor window by selecting the *Print* button from the button bar. This displays a dialog box allowing you to select from a number of options. When you click the OK button, the contents of the editor window are printed.

# 2.4   Compiling the Program

Now that you have finished editing the program and saved it, you can run it. To run a Java program, either press the *Run* button on the button bar or, as a shortcut, press the **F1** function key.

When the Run command is given, the **Ready** environment attempts to execute the Java program in the active window. To do this, it first compiles the class into Java **bytecode** which can then be run on any platform that has a Java **interpreter**. One bytecode interpreter, the IBM Java Virtual Machine, is built into **Ready**. However, the bytecode files produced by **Ready** can be executed using any Java interpreter. When a program is compiled, the result is saved in a file with the same name as the class with a ".class" suffix. For example, the *BlueRect* class will be compiled to a file called *BlueRect.class.*

You will be creating Java application programs with more than one class only one of which will have a *main* method. To run such a program, the class with the main method should be in the active window  before the *Run* command is given. To save the time taken to bring it into the active window each time you want to run the whole program, it is possible to pre-select it using the *SelectasMain* command from the *File* menu.

To do this, the class with the *main* method must first be in the active window. Once it has been selected as *main*, however, it no longer needs to be in the active window each time the *Run* command is given.

A Java class without a *main* method may not be run; you can compile it to bytecode by selecting the *Compile* command from the *Run* menu. This will show the syntax errors.  When such a class is compiled any other classes that it uses are also compiled. If try to run a class that does not have a *main* method, it will be compiled and an error message indicating that it cannot run will be displayed.

## 2.5    Errors in the Program

Errors are often detected during compilation. These are called **syntax errors** and are usually caused by typing the name of variables incorrectly, forgetting the semicolon at the end of a statement, or missing a curly brace. When a compilation is finished, if any errors are detected, the program is not executed. Instead, **Ready** displays a dialog box indicating the number of errors found and then jumps to the point in the file where the first error was detected. The line on which the error occurs is highlighted in light gray and the error itself is displayed in black. The error message is displayed in the status bar in bold.

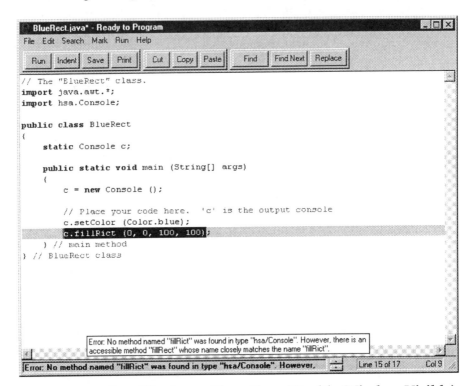

**Figure 2.7  Editor Window with an Error (Tooltip Window Visible)**

You can correct the error by editing the line. As soon as the line is modified, the error message and highlighting disappear. To go to the next error, if there is more than one, select *Find Next Error* menu item from the *Search* menu or press the F5 function key. At any point, you can press the F1 function key to compile and run the program again.

# 2.6   Running the Program

Once all the syntax errors are corrected, the program will begin executing if it has a *main* method or it is an applet. If it is not runnable, an error message will appear. Because we are using the *Console* class, a Console window appears in the upper-right corner of the screen when the *BlueRect* program runs. This window displays the output from our program. The *BlueRect* program produces a blue rectangle in the upper-left corner of the Console window. To finish with the program, we can press the *Close* button in the Console window or select *Stop* from the *Run* menu of the editor window.

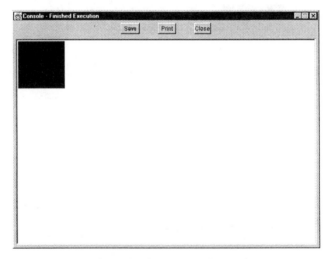

**Figure 2.8  Console Window Running BlueRect Program**

The Console window's title bar also informs the user whether the program is running, waiting for user input, or finished execution.

# 2.7   Modifying Existing Programs

**Ready** also allows you to open and edit an existing Java class. For example, if the user were to quit **Ready** by selecting *Exit* from the *File* menu and then re-enter the environment, a new empty editor window would appear. To get the *BlueRect* class again, the user selects *Open* from the *File* menu. A dialog box appears allowing the user to select the file to be opened. The user clicks on the *BlueRect.java* file name. When the file name is selected, **Ready** opens up *BlueRect* into a new window. If there was only an empty window visible, **Ready** opens the file into the empty window. The *BlueRect* class can then be edited.

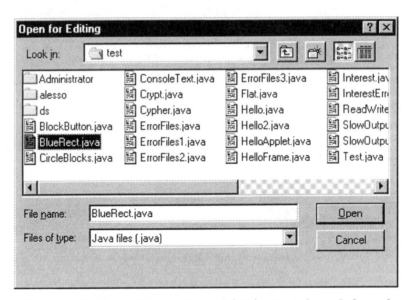

**Figure 2.9  Open Dialog Box with BlueRect.java Selected**

We will now replace the word "Blue" with "Red" using the replace command in **Ready** and then save the resulting class in *RedRect.java*. First, open up the *BlueRect* class into the editor. Then open up the *Replace* dialog box by pressing the *Replace* button in the button bar or selecting *Replace* from the *Search* menu. The Replace dialog box appears. Enter "Blue" in the *Find What* text box and "Red" in the *Replace With* text box. Then click the *Find Next* button. The selection jumps to the word "Blue" in the class on the line

      // The "BlueRect" class.

and highlights it.

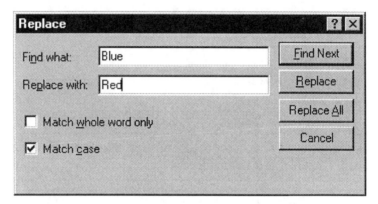

**Figure 2.10  The Replace Dialog Box**

Click the *Replace* button in the dialog box and "Blue" is replaced with "Red" and the editor jumps to the next occurrence of "Blue", which is in the line

      public class BlueRect

Continue to replace all the occurrences of "Blue" with "Red". When there are no more occurrences, **Ready** notifies you that it could not find the search string.

In order to complete the transformation of *BlueRect.java* to *RedRect.java* we also need to change the color of the rectangle it will draw from blue to red. We do this manually because *Replace* is usually case-sensitive. To make the change manually, select "blue" in the line

      c.setColor (Color.blue);

and type "red".

Once all the changes have been made, save the class in a new file by selecting *Save As* from the *File* menu. This displays a file dialog box allowing you to save the file with a new name and in a new location. If you try to save over *BlueRect.java* by clicking the *Save* button, **Ready** will warn you that you are trying to save the class *RedRect* in the file *BlueRect.java* and that this is not legal.

# 2.8    Features of Ready

## 2.8.1    Syntax Coloring

As you may have noticed, the **Ready** environment does what is called **syntax coloring**. This means that Java keywords such as **for** and **class** appear in bold face. Comments appear in green, strings in red, Java class library identifiers in black, and user identifiers in blue. You can use syntax coloring to avoid syntax errors. If a keyword is not displayed in bold face, then it is incorrectly spelled. If you forget to close the end of a multi-line comment, part of a program will appear in green because it is still part of a comment. Lastly, if an identifier from the Java class library is displayed in blue, it may be that there is a spelling error and Java does not recognize it.

## 2.8.2    Program Indentation

Properly indenting a program makes it easier to read because it makes the loops and the bodies of methods easy to see. The **Ready** environment allows the user to indent the program by clicking the *Indent* button in the button bar. This automatically indents the program in a standard indent style. It also breaks lines so that there is one statement per line.

You can also use the indenter to find missing braces. If the final brace of a program is not flush with the left side of the text area, the class is missing a closing brace. If the last two braces are flush with the left side, the class is missing an opening brace.

Using the indent feature often helps to keep your programs properly indented and more readable.

## 2.8.3    One-Window Mode

The **Ready** environment can operate in either *one-window* mode or *multi-window* mode. In **One-Window Mode**, there is only one editor window, regardless of the number of open files. A tab bar just above the text area displays the names of all the open files in the editor window. Clicking on a tab makes the corresponding file visible in the window.

To close a single file in *one-window* mode, click the close box of the inner window. Clicking the close box of the editor window closes all open files and exits the **Ready** environment, after asking for confirmation.

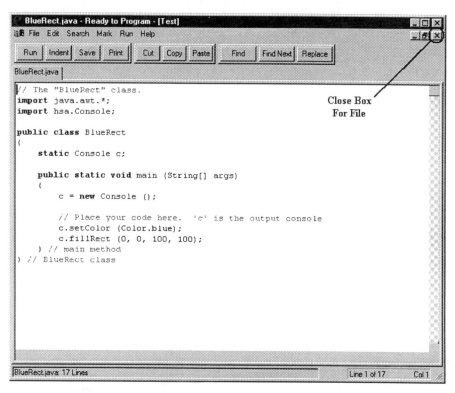

**Figure 2.11  One-Window Mode Editor Window**

## 2.9   Further Documentation

When **Ready** is installed, the **Ready to Program with Java**™ **Technology User's Guide** is also installed. To find it, you must open up the folder in which **Ready** was installed (probably C:\Program Files\Ready to Program) and then open the folder labelled *Support*. In the *Support* folder you will find a folder called *Documentation*. Opening the *Documentation* folder reveals a number of documents. If you have **Adobe Acrobat** installed (available for free at www.adobe.com), you can double click on **User's Guide.pdf** to open the Adobe Acrobat file. If you do not have Acrobat installed, then double click on **User's Guide.html** which will open your web browser and load the file.

The User's Guide contains the latest documentation and documents all aspects of the editor. It contains a more detailed tutorial and also demonstrates the creation of a Java applet.

# Chapter 3

# Programming

# 3.1    Programming and Programmers

When a programmer creates a program she or he does much more than simply sit down at a computer and begin entering commands into the keyboard. There is a whole range of activities that the programmer must do in order to create a **well-designed program**, that is, a program that reliably solves the problem it was created to solve.

Programming is the activity of:

*   Analyzing a problem to be solved.
*   Preparing a design for the steps in a set of instructions (an algorithm) that together with the data, will solve the problem.
*   Expressing the algorithm in a language that the computer can ultimately execute.
*   Ensuring that there is adequate documentation so that other people, and not just the original programmer, can understand the computer program.
*   Testing and validating the program to ensure that it will give correct results for the full range of data that it is to process.
*   Maintaining the program over time so that any changes that are needed are incorporated

Many years ago very few people knew how to program and those who did were often thought of as "gurus". Because very few people really understood computers a number of negative stereotypes began to be applied to people who did. Programmers were sometimes thought of as people, almost always males, who spent all of their time with machines and did not relate very well to other people. Like many negative stereotypes, however, this one is false.

The term **hacker** is also used to describe people who program computers but, over time, it has taken on even more negative connotations. Today the term is used to describe people who use computers to play pranks such as gaining illegal access to other people's or organizations' computers and changing data, or creating destructive computer programs called **viruses**. Computer viruses are actually hidden programs which, when downloaded by the unsuspecting user, perform unauthorized activities on any computer in which they reside. Some viruses can cause considerable damage, so many computer users run **virus checker software** to detect problems in any programs or files they load onto their computer.

Programmers come from all walks of life and programming itself can take many different forms. The field of **information technology**, which covers a wide variety of computing activities, offers many interesting and diverse career options. In truth, the only things most programmers share are their abilities to:

- solve problems,
- organize information,
- design solutions,
- express instructions in a logical sequence, and
- input them into a computer.

# 3.2   Programming Style

Often, there are two types of computer programs: programs that work but do not make sense to anyone except the person who created them, and programs that any programmer can read and understand. In the real world, no one has much use for messy, hard to read programs. As programs become bigger and more complex, they are almost always worked on by a number of different people. This means that a number of people will have to read parts of the program that they did not write. Also, over time, programs need to be changed. Often the person who changes the program is not the original programmer, but she or he still must be able to read it and understand how it works.

One of the ways to make sure that programs make sense is to follow a set of guidelines sometimes referred to as a **programming style guide**. A programming style guide provides a set of rules or expectations that every programmer must follow to ensure that all programs are clearly written and easy to fix or change. While programming style guides may be different for different workplaces, they all have certain things in common.

Quick Guide to Good Programming Style:

1.  Create a header at the beginning of every program. A header is not part of the actual program, but identifies the programmer and briefly explains what the program does. It should contain:

    • programmer's name,
    • the date,
    • the name of the saved program,
    • project (teacher's) name, and
    • a brief description of what the program does.

2.  Always include comments to explain what is happening in the program and what various parts of it do. Variables should include a brief description of how each variable is used.

3.  Use names for variables that give a good indication of what they do (for example, use "price" rather than "p").

4.  Make the structure of programs obvious by indenting the contents of loops and if-then-else structures.

One of the most important aspects of good programming style is to provide information about how the various parts of a program work within the body of the program itself. This is usually done by including **comments** at various places throughout the program. These comments are written in English but are preceded by some kind of symbol which alerts the compiler or interpreter that they are not to be read as instructions. In Java, for example, all comments are preceded by a // of /*....*/ sign. For example,

```
// This is a comment.
/* This is also a comment.
As is this line. */
```

Comments are usually placed before sections of the program to explain the purpose of the command or commands following the comment. This is especially important for long programs. The comments help the programmer to better understand the structure and purpose of the program as a whole as well as its various parts.

Efficiency is another important consideration in good programming style. An efficient program is one which meets the specified requirements, executes in the least possible amount of time, and is logically organized with clearly documented code so that it can be easily maintained.

# 3.3   The Software Development Process

Large software development projects can go through a sequence of these steps one after the other in a **software life cycle** as shown in Figure 3.1. This series of steps is sometimes called a **waterfall model** because it looks like water cascading down from one level to the next.

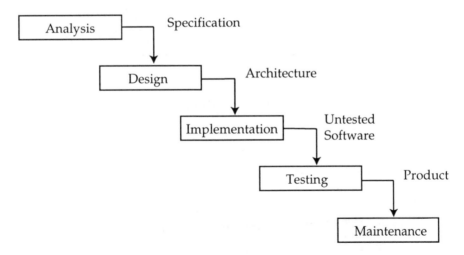

Figure 3.1 Waterfall Model of Software Development

In the early days of computing the first three parts of the programming activity were sometimes called analyzing, programming, and coding. Each of these activities might have been done by a separate person with special qualifications. Over time, however, the increasing complexity of the software being developed has required that greater emphasis be placed on the analysis of problems to be solved and the resulting design of programs and applications.

The implementation stage (once called coding because most early programs were written in machine code) has also evolved to meet the need for programs which can be understood by anyone with some knowledge of the nature of programming languages. Programmers today are much more likely to use a high-level programming language. The advantage of a high-level language is that it is easier to understand.

The waterfall model is an idealization of the programming process. In reality the process is closer to that shown in Figure 3.2.

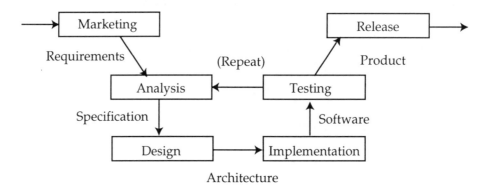

Architecture

Figure 3.2 Iterative Model of Software Evolution

There is a certain amount of backtracking in the actual evolution of a piece of software of any complexity, particularly if the software is constantly being updated.

In many ways we try to prepare programs that are self-documenting by using variable names such as *netPay* to indicate that the variable contains information concerning the net pay of an employee.

The programming language Java has a number of words called **keywords** that are used for various operations, such as **if** for selection or **while** for repetition. These have been chosen to be brief but expressive. When a programmer invents names to identify entities (**identifiers**) it is best if they are as brief as possible without sacrificing understandability. Abbreviations should be used only when they are well-understood, such as *GST* for Goods and Services Tax and *FBI* for Federal Bureau of Investigation.

Since the purpose of creating computer programs is to solve problems, before anything else, a programmer must be a problem solver. **Problem solving** is the process of breaking problems down into smaller more manageable parts. As the large problem is broken down into smaller parts, each part becomes more specific. These individual solutions to smaller problems are then combined to solve the larger problem. Problem solving is also referred to as analyzing the problem to be solved.

Once the programmer has analyzed the problem, he or she is ready to begin designing a solution. In programming, the design stage involves defining a set of instructions (called an **algorithm**) that, together with the data, will solve the problem. The next step is to express this algorithm in a programming language so that the computer can **execute** it (carry out the instructions). This stage is sometimes referred to as **coding** although this term is not as popular as it once was.

Because people other than the programmer must be able to understand, use, and often modify a program, the program must be understandable. This means ensuring that there is good documentation. There are commonly two kinds of documentation. The term **internal documentation** refers to the comments within a program that explain what the various parts do. The supplementary resources such as Reference Manuals and User's Manuals are **external documentation**. Often, an application will also provide internal **help files** that the user can access.

Once the program has been written it must be extensively tested to ensure that it performs the way it should. Testing often involves running the program with a full range of data. The programmer must also be sure to run it with both **valid data**, that is, the data the user should be inputting, and **invalid data**, that is, incorrect or unexpected data, to determine how the program will behave in as many situations as possible. When computer programs control such profound aspects of our lives as the airplanes we fly in and the machines that provide radiation to cancer patients, the results of improper or insufficient testing can be wide-ranging and catastrophic.

The programming process also involves the job of **maintaining** a program over time so that any changes that are needed are incorporated. Many businesses, for example, must frequently change or enhance their programs to make them perform new tasks or perform old tasks more efficiently.

# 3.4 Abstraction in Programs

Programs can become very complex and hard to understand and so we are constantly seeking ways to simplify them. Procedural abstraction and data abstraction are two commonly-used systems for reducing program complexity.

## 3.4.1 Procedural Abstraction

One way of making a program simpler is to divide it into a number of smaller programs or **subprograms**.

A subprogram that:

- performs some action or actions which may cause the input or output of data, or change the values of data stored in the computer's memory

is called a **procedure**.

A subprogram that:

- is given the value, or values, of some data stored in memory and yields a value

is called a **function**.

In mathematics we say $y$ is a function of $x$ and write

$$y = f(x)$$

where $x$ is the data value given to the function and $y$ is the value returned. As an example, if the square root function is given a value $x = 4$, it yields the value $y = 2$.

In this chapter we use the word procedure as a general term to include the function subprogram as well. In the C language the word **function** is used for both procedures and functions. In Java the word **method** is used for both.

For procedure-oriented programming languages certain subprograms are **predefined** so that they may be used in any program. These subprograms have been created by another programmer and placed in a **library** of subprograms available to all users. Reusing existing software components allows programmers to build on the work of others and thus speed up the programming process.

A programmer using a predefined procedure never has to read the actual procedure or even know the details of its operation, as long as she or he knows what data must be provided and what will be accomplished by it.

This is referred to as a **procedural abstraction** since we know what to expect, but do not need to know the procedure's inner workings. The details of such a procedure are **hidden**; only the **interface** to use or **call** the procedure must be known. Abstraction helps to simplify programs by providing the essential information about how to use the procedure without irrelevant details.

## 3.4.2 Data Abstraction

As programs become larger and more complex, it becomes necessary to share the task of creating a large program among a team of people. This sharing helps to ensure that the task can be completed in a reasonable amount of time. When procedural abstraction is used, often one programmer's procedure modifies the same data as another's, and the programmers must be careful about such overlapping. It seems reasonable, therefore, to isolate the procedures of each programmer or team along with the data they operate on in an airtight compartment and to **encapsulate** them in a **module** (a software object) that explicitly controls any use of its components by another module.

This is referred to as **data abstraction**. Modules that encapsulate data with the procedures that operate on the data are called **abstract data types** or ADTs.

For example, an abstract data type might be created to manage a **list** of entries that are to be kept in alphabetic order. The data in this module would be the representation of the list. There would be procedures which would allow the user of the module to add a new entry to the list, to delete an entry, to output the list in alphabetic order, and so on. These procedures, with their interfaces, are made known to a user of the module by explicitly labelling them as **public**. The way in which the data is stored in memory and the way the operations are implemented are not made available to the user. The implementation and the way the data is stored can be changed as long as the external behavior of the abstract data type remains the same.

# 3.5   Programming Paradigms

Two well known systems or **paradigms** (pronounced *paradimes*) used for creating large-scale programs are **procedure-oriented programming** and **object-oriented programming**.

## 3.5.1   Procedure-Oriented Programming

This paradigm is based on the system of designing programs in a **top-down** manner. The programmer starts by writing the specification of the problem to be solved and gradually refines the solution by breaking it into parts, each of which can in turn be broken into parts. These parts are often solved (implemented) as procedures.

Figure 3.3 is called a **structure chart**. It illustrates how the procedures activate (call) each other.

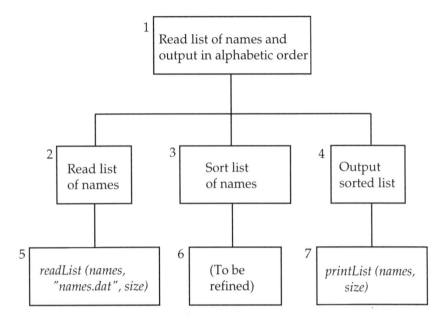

**Figure 3.3 Top-Down Programming**

This structure chart shows how a program is **refined step by step** starting at the top (1), with a statement of what is required, here sorting a list of names alphabetically. This top node in the diagram is expanded or refined into three nodes 2, 3, and 4. The computations represented by these three nodes, carried out sequentially, satisfy the top node's specification. The nodes 5, 6, and 7 are further refinements in the procedure-oriented programming language.

In procedure-oriented programming, the data upon which the various procedures operate is commonly kept centrally in a **main program** as illustrated in Figure 3.4. When one procedure is changed it may cause an effect that alters the way another procedure works if the two procedures share the same data. The data is said to be **global** to all procedures.

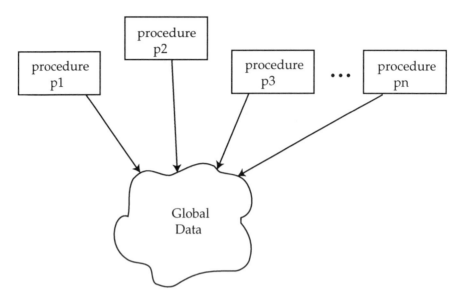

Figure 3.4 Shared Global Data in Procedure-Oriented Programming

## 3.5.2    Object-Oriented Programming

In abstract data types, data that are operated on by a set of procedures are grouped with the procedures in a module. The module encapsulates the data and procedures (methods in Java) so that no other procedures can have direct access to the data. Modules which encapsulate the data and procedures are called **objects**. These objects very often correspond to actual objects, such as a list of names with all the operations that can be performed on the list.

Creating a program as a number of objects is referred to as **object-based programming**. True object-oriented programming in a language such as Java involves a further idea – the idea of classes. The class acts as a template from which any number of similar objects called **instances** can be created. Object-oriented programming involves objects that can be **instantiated** from classes.

As well, object-oriented programming allows programmers to create a new class from an existing class. The new class extends an existing **base class**. The new class inherits data and methods from the base class. In the process of **inheritance**, additional methods may be added to those of the base class or existing methods can be changed or **overridden**. This makes the new class different from its **parent** base class, and yet saves a great deal of the original, thus reducing the effort to create the new class.

Object-oriented programming makes it convenient to reuse existing program components (classes). A language such as Java has a **library of classes** that can be used. In this way programmers do not constantly have to "reinvent the wheel". Large programs can be made from off-the-shelf components just as computers are created from basic electronic components and chips.

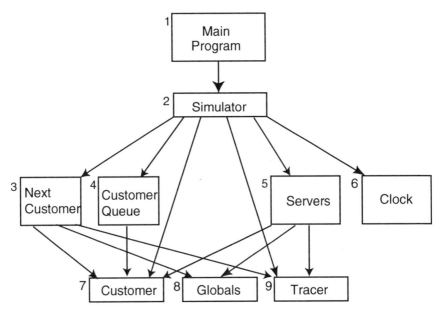

Figure 3.5 Landscape of Queue Simulator

Just as the structure of procedure-oriented programs can be represented by diagrams such as structure charts, the structure of object-oriented programs can be represented by diagrams such as **landscapes**. Figure 3.5 shows the landscape of an object-oriented program that simulates the queueing of customers in a bank. The arrows indicate the fact that some objects **import** other objects' capabilities, that is, use their methods. For example, the *CustomerQueue* object (4) uses the *Customer* object (7) but no other.

Now it is time to look more closely at the object-oriented paradigm that we will be using with Java.

# 3.6    Key Concepts in Object-Oriented Programming

There are three fundamental concepts in object-oriented programming which every Java user needs to understand. They are objects, classes, and inheritance.

## 3.6.1    Objects

An **object** is a set of data and the methods which operate on that data. In Java, an object's data are called the **fields** of the object. One example of an object might be an *Employee* object, where the object's data would be the employee's name, employee number, home address, position, hours worked, rate of pay, and income tax paid this year. The object's methods would include retrieving the employee's number, home address, position, hours worked, rate of pay, and income tax paid this year. As well, there would be methods for changing the object's data, for example, adding to the income tax total paid this year. There could also be a method to create the forms necessary to send to the government for tax purposes.

When using objects, a programmer only needs to know what the objects do, and not how they do it. In other words she or he does not need to see the data and how the methods are implemented. In this way, programmers are able to make use of objects without ever having to study the internals of these objects.

## 3.6.2    Classes

A **class** is a **template** for creating objects. From a class, you can create any number of similar objects, each of which will have its own data and an identical set of methods that apply to that data.

For example, an *Employee* class would be used as a template for creating a new *Employee* object every time an employee was added to the employee database. This employee database would consist of hundreds of *Employee* objects. Each object, when it was created (**instantiated**), would use a special method of the *Employee* class called the **constructor** method to set the data in the object appropriately for the particular employee. Once the objects were created, they would be completely separate entities.

## 3.6.3    Inheritance

**Inheritance** is a way of incorporating all of the methods and data fields from one class into another class. Then in the new class data fields and methods may then be added and existing methods changed.

For example, we might want to have a new class for employees called *PartTimeEmployee*, which could have some fields additional to those of the *Employee* class (such as the percentage of full time worked) and some additional methods (such as a method to set the percentage of full benefits the worker receives). Instead of rewriting the *Employee* class from scratch to make it into the *PartTimeEmployee* class, the *PartTimeEmployee* class will **inherit** from the *Employee* class. When one class inherits from another it keeps all the same data fields and methods of the original class. From there, we can add data fields and methods or can redefine already-existing methods of *Employee* class (for example, the calculations of taxes might be different for part time employees). In Java, if the *PartTimeEmployee* class inherits from *Employee* class, we say that the *PartTimeEmployee* class **extends** the *Employee* class.

# 3.7   Chapter Summary

This chapter has introduced numerous programming concepts and has shown two important patterns or **paradigms** for creating programs. These paradigms are especially important when programs are large.

## Steps in Programming

The process of programming can be divided into a series of steps.

- Working out the **specifications** of the problem to be solved.
- Designing an **algorithm** or set of instructions by which the problem will be solved.
- Expressing the algorithm in a high-level programming language.
- Ensuring that the algorithm (or program) is as understandably expressed as possible with additional documentation as required to make it so.
- Testing the program on a full range of data so as to eliminate errors.
- Maintaining the program by making changes as required over time.

## Procedural Abstraction

Dividing large programs into smaller subprograms simplifies them. Subprograms are of two basic types:

- **procedures** which cause actions or change values of data stored in memory, or
- **functions** which map one value or set of values into another. For example, the *sqrt* function maps a number into its square root.

To use a subprogram, the programmer needs to know what its **parameters** are to be and what action or change in values is to be expected. This information is given in its **specification** and provides an interface so that it can be used without knowing the details inside the subprogram. These details are **hidden** from the user. This abstraction simplifies the program. In Java all subprograms are called **methods**.

# Data Abstraction

Often several methods of a program share the same data and the programmer must ensure that the actions of one method do not interfere unexpectedly with the actions of another method.

The data and all the methods that can modify them may be hidden in a **module**. This **encapsulation** creates an **object** that other parts of the program can use. This encapsulation is called **data abstraction**. To use this object, other parts of the program must first **import** it. The module itself must also declare as **public** the methods that can be used.

# Object-Oriented Programming

Programming based on data abstraction is called **object-based programming** since the module corresponds to an object. True object-oriented programming requires three things: encapsulation, the concept of a class, and **inheritance**. A **class** is a **template** from which multiple **instances** of similar objects are created. For example, several objects which are lists can be created from a class called *List*.

In Java there is a large library of predefined classes. From these, objects can be instantiated. The value of having these software components available is that programs can be built from off-the-shelf components. This saves much effort, particularly in creating large programs.

# Objects, Classes, and Inheritance

Every Java user needs to understand three fundamental concepts in object-oriented programming. They are objects, classes, and inheritance.

- An **object** is a set of data and the methods which operate on that data.
- A **class** is a **template** for creating similar objects. From a class, you can create objects, each of which has its own data and an identical set of methods that apply to that data.
- **Inheritance** incorporates all of the methods and data fields from one class into another class. In the new class data fields and methods may then be added and existing methods changed.

# 3.8 Technical Terms

abstract data type

algorithm

assembly language

base class

call

data abstraction

comments

documentation

encapsulate

field of an object

keyword

identifier

import

inheritance

instantiate

invalid data

landscape

library of classes

module

parent class

predefined

procedural abstraction

procedure

procedure-oriented programming

programming style guide

step-by-step refinement

structure chart

subprogram

top-down

valid data

virus checker software

well-designed program

# 3.9    Exercises

1.    Define programming paradigm.

2.    Explain the main differences between two programming paradigms.

3.    Define the following:

(a) algorithm

(b) hacker

(c) virus

# Chapter 4

# Programming in Java

This book introduces the concepts of computer programming. Many new technical terms must be introduced. These are general terms and as such are independent of the particular programming language used. In order to really understand concepts, however, there is no substitute for writing actual programs that can be entered into a computer and executed. In this chapter we begin by introducing technical language as well as the programming language Java. These will become better understood as the book unfolds so do not worry if everything is not immediately clear.

# 4.1   What is Java?

Although in the popular press Java is most closely linked with the growing phenomena of Internet use, at its basis Java is simply an object-oriented programming language. What is special about Java, however, is that it is an object-oriented programming language that is particularly well-suited to the growing need for tools which fit the way software programmers actually work today.

The increasing size and complexity of computer programs have driven the demand for reusable, off-the-shelf programs and parts of programs that allow programmers to create large applications without constant writing from scratch. The Java class library contains an extensive collection of classes or group of classes called packages which can be imported directly into an existing program to perform a number of (often complex) tasks. This reduces programming time and the likelihood of introducing new errors (**bugs**).

Lack of standardization across hardware platforms (such as PCs or Macs), operating systems (such as Windows of Linux), and software applications has been a major stumbling block for software developers, requiring them to develop and maintain multiple versions to meet differing machine requirements. Because the Java compiler generates bytecode rather than native machine code, Java programs are platform-independent, that is, they can run on any platform that supports Java. The individual platforms must provide the software to translate the Java bytecode to machine code. This portability is also what makes Java so well-suited to use on the Internet.

Another of Java's strengths is that it has been designed to reduce the opportunity for programmers to make common programming errors. Specifically, Java eliminates **pointers**, which are a major cause of problems in C and C++ programs. It also checks array and string bounds (unlike C or C++). Together these (and other) features make Java more suitable for learning how to program than other languages.

# 4.2    Programming in Java

For many years the procedure-oriented paradigm was the usual way programs were created. Programmers trained in this tradition often find it difficult to adjust their thinking to a different paradigm such as object-oriented programming. This means that potential advantages are not achieved. It is hoped that students who learn the object-oriented approach at the same time as they learn programming may be able to learn these ideas in less time than someone who is entrenched in a different approach.

The language we will be using is the Java programming language. We will begin by looking at the concept of a method (function or procedure subprogram) in Java. After that we will examine the creation and use of classes.

To illustrate the idea of methods we will show how to use the methods of a class developed by Holt Software Associates called Console. This class allows the user to write programs that create an execution window in which a program may display graphics. Later we will see that the *Console* class can also be used to display numbers or text and permit a user to enter data of various types into this execution window.

## 4.2.1    Locating a Figure in the Console Window

The *Console* class methods can be used to draw lines, rectangles, ovals, and so on in the console window.

Any graphic figure on the screen actually consists of a number of tiny dots. These dots are called **pixels**. Because the dots are very small, when placed one after the other they appear to form a solid line.

The position and size of figures drawn in the console window must be specified as integral numbers of pixels. For example, if the center of a circle is specified as the point (150, 100), it would be 150 pixel positions to the right of the left-hand side of the window and 100 pixel positions below the top of the window. The origin of coordinates (0, 0) is at the upper-left corner of the window (see Figure 4.1).

It is not possible to specify fractions of pixels. For example, the center of the circle cannot be set at (150.5, 100.2).

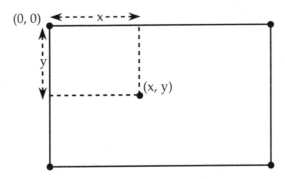

**Figure 4.1 The Console Window**

## 4.2.2   Drawing a Colored Rectangle in the Console Window

Drawing graphics requires the use of the methods that are part of the *Console* class. In the *Console* class there is a method called *fillRect* which is characterized by the **signature**

*fillRect* (**int** *x*, **int** *y*, **int** *width*, **int** *height*);

After the method's name, in parentheses, is a list of **parameters** of the method and their **data type**, which here is **int** for integer. (We make a practice of showing keywords in Java such as **int** in boldface type. We also show technical terms in boldface the first time they are used.) The explanation given with this signature is that the upper-left corner of the rectangle is at (*x*, *y*), the rectangle has a given *width* and *height*, and it is filled with the current color. The color is set by the *Console* method *setColor* whose signature is

*setColor* (*Color clr*);

The signature and the explanation of the meaning of the parameters together constitute the **specification** of the method.

In order to use these methods it is first necessary to create or instantiate a *Console* object named *c* from the *Console* class. The **program statements** that will do this are:

```
Console c;
c = new Console ();
```

It is our convention to have class names such as *Console* begin with an upper case letter. Object and method names begin with lower case letters. Notice that each statement in the program fragment is terminated by a semicolon.

The first statement **declares** that *c* will identify an object of type *Console*. The second statement actually creates the object *c*. This second statement is an **assignment statement**. In it a new object of class *Console* is assigned to the **identifier** *c*. The **new** is a keyword in Java. Each class has a special method called a **constructor** which is used to create an object that is an instance of the class. We say that the constructor method instantiates an object of the class.

The name of the constructor method is the same as the name of the class. The constructor method for this class has no parameters. When this is the case, the parentheses that follow the constructor method's name are still required but have nothing between them.

Now that we have created an instance *c* of *Console*, we are in a position to use the methods of object *c*. To use a method of object *c* we must precede the method's name by *c* followed by a dot. The two statements to draw a blue rectangle of width 50 pixels and height 100 pixels with its upper-left corner in the upper-left corner of the window are:

```
c.setColor (Color.blue);
c.fillRect (0, 0, 50, 100);
```

In the first statement the **actual parameter** (**argument**) of the *Console* method *setColor* is a constant provided by the *Color* class. Certain classes in the Java class library are usually not instantiated. The class *Color* is such a class. In this case the class' name (rather than the object's name) followed by a dot, precedes the field's or method's name.

In order to have the computer produce such a blue rectangle these statements must be incorporated into a complete program.

# 4.3   Standalone Programs in Java

In Java there are two quite different types of programs: **standalone application programs** and **applets**.

- Standalone application programs can be executed independently of an Internet browser.
- Applet programs are executed through a network browser and are capable of being shared. In applets, for security reasons, no use can be made of files of data.

Initially we will restrict our programs to standalone application programs since applets require an understanding of the Java **graphical user interface** (GUI) class library.

Here is a complete application program that draws the blue rectangle.

```java
// The "BlueRect" class.
import java.awt.*;
import hsa.Console;

public class BlueRect
{
    static public void main (String [ ] args)
    {
        Console c;
        c = new Console ();
        c.setColor (Color.blue);
        c.fillRect (0, 0, 50, 100);
    } // main method
} // BlueRect class
```

While it is probably easier to simply accept all the parts of the program that surround the four statements that instantiate the *Console* object *c* and draw the blue rectangle using the *Console* methods, a few words of explanation might be helpful. To begin, there are two **import statements** that indicate that both the **Java Abstract Windowing Toolkit** (awt) and the *Console* class of Holt Software Associates (hsa) are going to be used.

After the **import** statements there is a statement that what follows defines a *class* called *BlueRect* that is to be publically available. The **body** of the class is enclosed in curly braces { }. The opening brace is placed directly below the *p* of **public**. The closing brace is placed in the same column in the last line of the program. We think this alignment of corresponding opening and closing braces makes the program easier to understand. Often programs are written with the opening curly brace at the end of the previous line. The next line of the program

    **static public void** *main (String* [ ] *args)*

should, at this stage, be accepted as indicating that what follows is the **main method**. All *main* methods have exactly this same line. (Notice that there is no semicolon at the end.)

The body of the *main* method is enclosed in curly braces, the opening brace being written under the *s* of **static** and its matching closing brace lined up at the end of the method. The four statements that constitute the body of the *main* method are indented one level to the right of the *main* method's enclosing braces. This system of paragraphing a program makes it easier to read and understand. It is not necessary to its successful execution.

After the closing brace of the *BlueRect* class definition is a comment. This consists of any text enclosed in /* followed by */. Comments are included to document the program and to help the reader understand it. An alternative form is to begin the comment with two slashes // and end with a Return (end of line). The first line of the program uses that form of comment.

In choosing appropriate sizes for drawings it is helpful to know how large the console window is. This information is available through two *Console* class methods. The method *getWidth* has a value which is the width of the window in pixels. The method *getHeight* has a value which is the height of the window in pixels. Although there are no parameters for *getWidth* and *getHeight* their names must be followed by empty parentheses ( ). The methods *getWidth* and *getHeight* are function-type methods and each produces a value. The coordinates of the center of the window would be

(*c.getWidth*() /2, *c.getHeight*() /2)

In Java a single slash / is used for division and dividing one integer by another produces an integer value. For example,

5/2

produces the value 2, the result of division with any fractional part chopped off (**truncated**).

Changing the program *BlueRect* so that it draws a green rectangle that fills the bottom-right corner of the window would require the last two statements of the *main* method's body to be changed to

```
c.setColor (Color.green);
c.fillRect (c.getWidth() / 2, c.getHeight() / 2,
            c.getWidth() / 2, c.getHeight() / 2);
```

A list of available colors in the *Color* class can be found in the Appendix.

# 4.4   User-Defined Methods

There are a number of drawing methods that can be used in the *Console* class. So far only the *fillRect* method has been presented.

Here are some other commonly-used methods:

*drawLine* (**int** *x1*, **int** *y1*, **int** *x2*, **int** *y2*)

draws a line from the point (*x1*, *y1*) to the point (*x2*, *y2*).

*fillOval* (**int** *x*, **int** *y*, **int** *width*, **int** *height*)

draws an oval which could be enclosed in a rectangle whose upper-left corner is at (*x*, *y*) and whose width and height are given. (The rectangle is not drawn.) The oval is filled with the current color. There is a corresponding method *drawOval* that draws an oval outline. The method *drawRect* is similar to *fillRect* except that it draws the rectangle in outline. Figure 4.2 Shows an Oval Drawn using *fillOval* or *drawOval*.

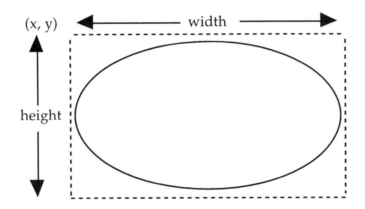

**Figure 4.2 Drawing of Oval**

## 4.4.1   Simple Examples of User-Defined Methods

The programmer can also create graphics methods that do not already exist in the *Console* class. For example, there are no methods for drawing a circle or a filled circle. The *drawOval* and *fillOval* methods of the *Console* class must be used with equal values for the parameters *width* and *height*.

We will define a method for drawing a circle of a given *radius* with its center at (*xc, yc*) in color *clr*.

```
// Method for drawing a circle.
static public void circle (int xc, int yc, int radius, Color clr)
{
    int width = radius * 2;
    int height = radius * 2;
    int x = xc – radius;
    int y = yc – radius;
    c.setColor (clr);
    c.drawOval (x, y, width, height);
} // circle method
```

Any methods used by a method labelled **static**, for example the *main* method, must also be labelled **static**. Since the *circle* method is to be available for use by other classes, it is also labelled as **public**. It does not produce a value so the keyword **void** precedes *circle* which is the method's name. The parameters follow in parentheses. These are all of type **int** except the color *clr* which is of type *Color*.

In order to use the *drawOval* method of the object *c*, the *width*, *height*, and top-left corner at (*x*, *y*) have to be computed from the parameters *xc*, *yc*, and *radius* of the *circle* method. This is done in the first four statements of the method's body. In the first statement an integer variable *width* is declared and **assigned** a value of twice the radius. The * stands for multiplication.

Because the object identifier *c* is used in this method, the declaration of *c* as of type *Console* must be outside the body of the *main* method. Since it is now to be used by **static** methods such as the *circle* method and the *main* method, it too must be labelled **static**.

Here is the entire application program for drawing a red circle with its center at the window's center, touching the top of the window.

```
//The "RedCircle" class.
import java.awt.*;
import hsa.Console;

public class RedCircle
{
    static Console c;

    static public void main (String [ ] args)
    {
        c = new Console ();
        int xc = c.getWidth() / 2;
        int yc = c.getHeight() / 2;
        int radius = c.getHeight() / 2;
        circle (xc, yc, radius, Color.red);
    } // main method

    static public void circle (int xc, int yc, int radius, Color clr)
    {
```

```
            int width = radius * 2;
            int height = radius * 2;
            int x = xc – radius;
            int y = yc – radius;
            c.setColor (clr);
            c.drawOval (x, y, width, height);
        } // circle method
} /* RedCircle class */
```

In the *main* method the *circle* method is **called** or **invoked** by the statement

   *circle (xc, yc, radius, Color.red);*

The **arguments** of the calling statement in this case have the same names as the parameters in the definition of the *circle* method but this is not necessary as long as they are in one-to-one correspondence and of compatible data types.

Figure 4.3 illustrates the structure of the program. The *main* method uses the user-defined *circle* method. The *circle* method, in turn, calls the *drawOval* predefined method of the *Console* class.

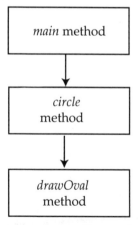

**Figure 4.3 Structure Chart of Program**

A user can create methods such as *circle* to perform a variety of tasks. For example, he or she could define a method called *ball* to create a filled circle. The *drawRect* and *fillRect* methods of the *Console* class could also be used to produce methods *square* and *block*.

## 4.4.2   A More Complicated Example

We will show how to program a method for drawing a square that is tilted relative to the console window. For this we cannot use the *drawRect* method because the *drawRect* method always produces a rectangle whose sides are parallel to the sides of the console window. Instead, we use the *drawLine* method to create a square by drawing four lines to outline the tilted square. If the four corners of square are at the points $(x1, y1)$, $(x2, y2)$, $(x3, y3)$, and $(x4, y4)$, we can write the instructions to draw the four lines as follows.

> *c.drawLine (x1, y1, x2, y2);*
> *c.drawLine (x2, y2, x3, y3);*
> *c.drawLine (x3, y3, x4, y4);*
> *c.drawLine (x4, y4, x1, y1);*

Determining the values of the coordinates of the four corners requires some knowledge of trigonometry. The first step is to define the last three points in terms of the point $(x1, y1)$, the size of the square *size*, and the angle of tilt *angle* in degrees (see Figure 4.4).

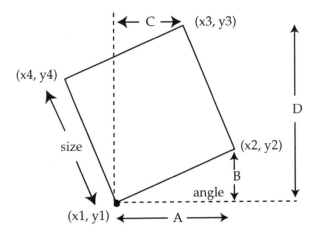

**Figure 4.4 Tilted Square**

Here is the definition of the *tiltSquare* method.

```
static public void tiltSquare (int x1, int y1, int size, int angle, Color clr)
{
    // Change angle to radians.
    double rAngle = angle * Math.PI / 180;
    // Compute four constants to help compute corners.
    final int A = (int) Math.round (size * Math.cos (rAngle));
    final int B = (int) Math.round (size * Math.sin (rAngle));
    final int C = (int) Math.round (size * Math.sqrt (2) *
                        Math.cos ((Math.PI/4) + rAngle));
    final int D =(int) Math.round (size * Math.sqrt (2) *
                        Math.sin ((Math.PI/4) + rAngle));
    // Compute corners.
    int x2 = x1 + A;
    int y2 = y1 - B;
    int x3 = x1 + C;
    int y3 = y1 - D;
    int x4 = x1 - B;
    int y4 = y1 - A;
    // Draw square.
    c.setColor (clr);
    c.drawLine (x1, y1, x2, y2);
    c.drawLine (x2, y2, x3, y3);
    c.drawLine (x3, y3, x4, y4);
    c.drawLine (x4, y4, x1, y1);
} // tiltSquare method
```

It is not necessary to follow all the details of the calculation but certain programming details should be noted. The constants *A*, *B*, *C*, and *D* are defined using the keyword **final** followed by the constant's data type, then its name, then an equal sign, then an arithmetic expression that produces its value. In this arithmetic expression the asterisk * is the multiplication sign. By convention the names of constants are expressed in upper case letters. Notice that the constant *PI* is defined in the *Math* class. The angle in radians *rAngle* is defined as a double length real number by the keyword **double** and assigned the value produced by multiplying the angle in degrees (*angle*) by *PI* and dividing by 180.

The expression

    *Math.cos (rAngle)*

is the cosine of the angle expressed in radians,

    *Math.sin (rAngle)*

is the sine of the angle expressed in radians, and

    *Math.sqrt (2)*

is the square root of 2. The three identifiers *cos*, *sin*, and *sqrt* are methods of the *Math* class that produce values.

The lines beginning with the // are **comments** to help explain what is happening in the program. These explanations are an essential part of the internal documentation of the program.

The final thing that should be noted is that each of the expressions for *A*, *B*, *C*, and *D* is enclosed in parentheses and preceded by *Math.round*. This means that the *Math* class *round* method is used to **round off** the values of each expression to the nearest integer since all values of coordinates $(x, y)$ must be integers. The *round* method of the *Math* class produces a double length integer of type **long** and, in order to assign the value to an **int** variable, the result must be **cast** as (changed to) an **int** value by preceding it by (**int**).

The *tiltSquare* method could be used in a *main* method in this way.

    *tiltSquare (c.getWidth () / 2, c.getHeight () / 2, c.getHeight () / 4,*
                  *30, Color.green);*

This would produce a green square with one corner at the center of the window, of size *getHeight*/4, tilted at an angle of 30 degrees to the horizontal.

A more interesting method called *moon* might be defined to use the *tiltSquare* method. It draws a series of tilted squares all having a common $(x1, y1)$ with angles of tilt at 10 degree intervals from tilt 0 to tilt 350. The result is a lacy circular pattern (see Figure 4.5).

Here it is.

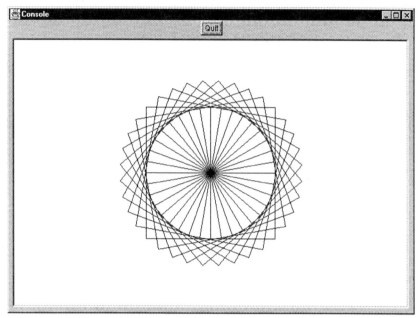

**Figure 4.5 Moon in Console Window**

```
// Method to draw a moon.
static public void moon (int xc, int yc, int size, Color clr)
{
     // Draw a series of tilted squares at intervals of 10 degrees
     // going from a tilt of 0 to a tilt of 350 degrees.
     for (int angle = 0; angle <= 350; angle = angle + 10)
     {
          tiltSquare (xc, yc, size, angle, clr);
     }
} // moon method
```

The body of this method contains a repetition construct which begins with the keyword **for** followed in parentheses by a series of three components separated by semicolons. The first component, **int** *angle* = 0, defines an integer variable *angle* that acts as the **counting index** and is initialized to zero. This part is called the **counting index initialization**.

Next is the **continuation condition:** that the value of *angle* is less than or equal to 350 expressed by *angle* <= 350. The third component is the **incrementation** of the index

   *angle = angle + 10*

The angle is increased by 10 each time the repetition is executed. So, on the first repetition the angle is 0, then on the second it is 10, on the third it is 20, on the fourth it is 30, and so on. When the angle becomes 360 the continuation condition is false and repetition ceases. This kind of repetition is called a **counted repetition.**

   The *tiltSquare* instruction in the body of the **for** repetition construct will be executed for values of *angle* going from 0 degrees to 350 degrees at intervals of 10 degrees. This will draw 36 squares at various tilts.

   The *main* method that draws a green moon centered in the center of the window would contain the statement

   *moon (c.getWidth () / 2, c.getHeight () / 2, c.getHeight () / 4, Color.green);*

   Figure 4.6 shows a structure chart to illustrate the connection between the methods.

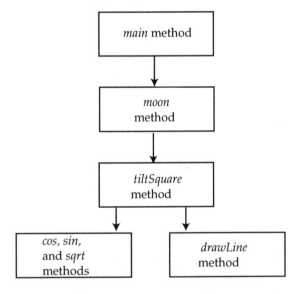

**Figure 4.6 Structure Chart for Moon Drawing**

# 4.5    The Form of Java Application Programs

In this chapter we have shown several complete Java application programs. All application programs contain a *main* method. The form of these has been:

```
//The "name-of-application" class.
import java.awt.*;
import hsa.Console;

public class name-of-application
{
    static Console c;

    static public void main (String [ ] args)
    {
        c = new Console ( );
        details of application
    } // main method

    details of any user-defined methods
} // name-of-application class
```

The *main* method is labelled as **static** as are any methods called by the *main* or any other **static** method. If methods other than the *main* method use the *Console* variable *c*, the variable is labelled **static** and is declared outside the *main* method.

Rather than repeat all these parts we will show for many applications only those parts that provide the name of the application class as a comment, the details of the particular application, and the details of any user-defined methods. The remaining parts of the program are identical for every standalone program and we will include them only for larger programs in this book. It is, however, necessary to add them each time they are not already there or the program will not run.

This sort of pattern is similar to the use in legal firms of what is called **boilerplate**, namely standard material that can be copied into a particular legal document. With a computer editor this can be a simple operation.

In the programs presented in this book different typefaces are used for different components. This is to try to make the programs easily readable and understood. Keywords of the Java language are in **boldface**; identifiers of classes, objects, methods, and variables are in *italics*; comments, digits, and quoted strings are in plainface type. In the computer all these components may be in the same typeface and in a typefont in which each character takes the same amount of space. (Many books show programs in this computer font.)

The typeface used to show the results of executing a program is the same with boldface being used to show what the user types during execution. Where output formatting is important a constant space font is used.

# 4.6   Using a Boilerplate

Many of the programs in this text are based upon a common template. The **Ready to Program with Java**™ **Technology** IDE provides a method of creating programs based on this template. To create a new class, users select **New** from the **File** menu in an editor window. This brings up a submenu with the different types of files that can be created. The user then selects **HSA Console Boilerplate**. A dialog box appears asking the user for the name of the class. Once the name has been entered the boilerplate appears in an editor window. The user can then enter the body of the program.

Here is what the empty boilerplate looks like for a class named *Example*.

```
// The "Example" class.
import java.awt.*;
import hsa.Console;

public class Example
{
    static Console c;

    static public void main (String [] args)
```

```
        {
            c = new Console ();

            // Place your program here. 'c' is the output console.
        } // main method
} // Example class
```

This class follows the form we showed where the name of application is given as *Example* and the details of application are the single line comment

// Place your program here. 'c' is the output console.

Once the program has been entered, this class should be saved as the file

*Example.java*

If there are methods other than the *main* method, these are entered after the *main* method before the closing brace of the class.

# 4.7   Chapter Summary

This chapter has introduced numerous programming concepts and has shown two important patterns or **paradigms** for creating programs. These paradigms are especially important when programs are large.

## Steps in Programming

The process of programming can be divided into a series of steps.

- Working out the **specifications** of the problem to be solved.
- Designing an **algorithm** or set of instructions by which the problem will be solved.
- Expressing the algorithm in a high-level programming language.
- Ensuring that the algorithm (or program) is as understandably expressed as possible with additional documentation as required to make it so.

- Testing the program on a full range of data so as to eliminate errors.
- Maintaining the program by making changes as required over time.

## Procedural Abstraction

Dividing large programs into smaller subprograms simplifies them. Subprograms are of two basic types:

- **procedures** which cause actions or change values of data stored in memory, or
- **functions** which map one value or set of values into another. For example, the *sqrt* function maps a number into its square root.

To use a subprogram, the programmer needs to know what its **parameters** are to be and what action or change in values is to be expected. This information is given in its **specification** and provides an interface so that it can be used without knowing the details inside the subprogram. These details are **hidden** from the user. This abstraction simplifies the program.

In Java all subprograms are called **methods**.

## Data Abstraction

Often several methods of a program share the same data and the programmer must ensure that the actions of one method do not interfere unexpectedly with the actions of another method.

The data and all the methods that can modify them may be hidden in a **module**. This **encapsulation** creates an **object** that other parts of the program can use. This encapsulation is called **data abstraction**. To use this object, other parts of the program must first **import** it. The module itself must also declare as **public** the methods that can be used.

# Object-Oriented Programming

Programming based on data abstraction is called **object-based programming** since the module corresponds to an object such as a list. True object-oriented programming requires encapsulation, the concept of a **class,** and **inheritance.** A **class** is a **template** from which multiple **instances** of objects are created. For example, several objects which are lists can be created from a class called *List*.

In Java there is a large library of predefined classes. From these, objects can be instantiated. The value of having these software components available is that programs can be built from off-the-shelf components. This saves much effort, particularly in creating large programs.

# Objects, Classes, and Inheritance

There are three fundamental concepts in object-oriented programming which every Java user needs to understand. They are objects, classes, and inheritance.

An **object** is a set of data and the methods which operate on that data.

A **class** is a **template** for creating objects. From a class, you can create objects, each of which has its own data and an identical set of methods that apply to that data.

**Inheritance** incorporates all of the methods and data fields from one class into another class. Data fields may then be added and existing methods changed.

# Graphics Methods

Methods that can be used to create graphics are encapsulated in a class called *Console* which can be imported into (made available to) any Java program. In the program an object of the class *Console* can be created (instantiated). Calling any of its methods requires the programmer to preface the method's name by the object's name, followed by a dot.

The colors used in drawing are encapsulated in the *Color* class and can be referred to by the names *red, green, blue,* and so on preceded by the class name *Color* followed by a dot.

## User-Defined Methods

The programmer can also define methods. The form of the method definition used in this chapter is

```
static public void name (parameter declaration list)
{
    body of method
}
```

Each parameter declaration consists of its data type followed by its name. The list is separated by commas.

## Structure Charts

The body of our user-defined methods contained calls to the methods of the *Console* object. A **structure chart** illustrates how the *main* method uses our *circle* method which in turn uses the *Console drawOval* method, illustrating the relationship between the *main* method, our method, and the *Console* object. Charts such as this are helpful in understanding program structure.

## Other Java Syntax

The method is only one of many Java features we have introduced in this chapter. Here are others:

- Comments can be added to a program by having a // followed on the same line by the comment and then a Return. These do not affect the execution of the program and are there to help make the program more understandable – to document it. An alternative form of a comment is to preface the comment text by /* and follow it by */.

- Constants can be defined using the keyword **final**, followed by a data type and the name or identifier of the constant, then an equal sign, then, in the example we showed, an **arithmetic expression** that gives a value to the constant.

- Arithmetic expressions have the usual mathematical symbols + for plus and – for minus. For multiplication we use *, and for division the slash /.

- In order for arithmetic expressions involving real values to have an integer value, they must be enclosed in parentheses and preceded by *Math.round*. The function *round* is predefined in the *Math* class and yields a value which is the rounded off value of its parameter. This value is of type **long**, the double length integer type. In order to change such a value to the type **int** it must be preceded by (**int**) which then **casts** it as type **int**.
- The division of two integers yields an integer. This has the effect of truncating any fractional part of the quotient.
- Other methods of the *Math* class: *sin, cos,* and *sqrt* were used in the calculation of the coordinates of the tilted square.
- The repetition construct or **for** loop was used to draw the moon. Later chapters will discuss this construct in more detail.

## The Form of Application Programs

All Java standalone applications in this book using the *Console* class have the same form as illustrated. Using the boilerplate found in the **Ready to Program with Java™ Technology** IDE saves the programmer time and effort entering a new application.

# 4.8   Technical Terms

| | |
|---|---|
| actual parameter (argument) | counting index initialization |
| algorithm | declare |
| applet | graphical user interface |
| argument | identifier |
| assigned | import statement |
| constructor | main method |
| continuation condition | parameter |
| counted repetition | pointer |
| counting index | program statement |

public                                  standalone application program

signature                               static

# 4.9   Exercises

1.  Write the method *square* with the signature

    **void** *square* (**int** *x*, **int** *y*, **int** *size*, *Color clr*)

    which when called, draws a square of *size* pixels in color *clr*. The upper-left corner of the square will be at $(x, y)$. Use the method in an application program to place a yellow square of size about one quarter of the window width with its center in the center of the window.

2.  Write the method *block* with the signature

    **void** *block* (**int** *x*, **int** *y*, **int** *size*, *Color clr*)

    which produces a filled square. Use this in an application program to draw a series of blocks of four different colors across the bottom of the window.

3.  Use a repetition construct in a program to draw a pattern of three black blocks separated by three red squares of the same size across the top of the window. Make the squares or blocks as large as will fit into the width of the window. This size will be *getWidth()*/6. **Hint:** Use this construct to draw the three black blocks:

    ```
    int size = c.getWidth () / 6;
    for (int xcorn = 0; xcorn <= 4 * size; xcorn = xcorn + 2 * size)
    {
        block (xcorner, 0, size, clr);
    }
    ```

4.  Write a program that uses the *moon* method of this chapter to draw three blue moons spaced apart and centered on the window. Choose an appropriate size for the radius of the moon.

5.  Create a circle of red balls arranged like beads on a string. To solve this problem, begin by creating a method that draws a ball of *radius*, positioned so that its center (*xc, yc*) is at the end of a stick of length *size* whose other end is at the point (*xp, yp*), and which makes an angle *angle* with the x-axis (the horizontal). Figure 4.7 shows this.

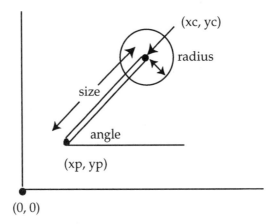

**Figure 4.7 Ball on a Stick**

The method would have the following signature.

**void** *ballOnStick* (**int** *xp,* **int** *yp,* **int** *size,* **int** *radius, Color clr*)

Note that the point in the *tiltSquare* method of this chapter (*x2, y2*) corresponds to the center of the ball.

Use the *ballOnStick* method to create a method that draws a circle of balls using the **for** repetition construct. Decide what the step size in the angle must be in order for the balls to just touch. What happens if it is smaller than this size?

# Chapter 5

# Basic Programming Language Concepts

So far we have looked at two programming paradigms: the procedure-oriented paradigm and the object-oriented paradigm and illustrated these using graphic examples. We showed how to use simple predefined classes. In addition we introduced constants, arithmetic expressions, comments, and repetition. The programming language used was Java.

Now we must begin a more systematic examination of the Java language. We will start by introducing a language for defining the Java programming language. Then the various primitive data types will be presented along with the way variables of the different types are declared, how expressions are formed, how values are assigned to variables, and output. Comments are explained as a method for documenting a program and making it more understandable.

# 5.1   Metalanguage for Defining Syntax

High-level programming languages have a formal structure that allows the computer to translate programs into instructions to implement algorithms. Just as any natural language like English has a grammar and a vocabulary, so too does a programming language like Java.

The vocabulary of Java includes words that are **reserved** by the language. These are the keywords of the language such as **if, while,** and **for.**

Java programmers also create their own words as identifiers, or names, for user-defined methods, classes, constants, and variables. There are rules for creating these identifiers.

- An identifier should be a sequence of letters, digits, and underscores beginning with a letter.
- Reserved words may not be used as identifiers.

Upper and lower case letters are distinct in keywords and identifiers. So *Tax* is distinct from *tax.* By convention we have class names begin with an upper case letter, method and variable names with a lower case letter. Constants have identifiers that are all upper case.

Extended **Backus-Naur Form** or **EBNF** grammar is a commonly-used syntax notation. It is a language that records the syntax rules, that is, rules for writing or producing acceptable statements in the Java language. EBNF is a **metalanguage** for expressing these **production rules**.

Each rule defines a **syntactic variable** such as an *identifier* in terms of other syntactic variables, and strings of characters that will ultimately form part of the Java program. These strings of characters are called **terminal tokens**. Terminal tokens in EBNF are shown in boldface type. Here is the definition of an identifier.

identifier ::= letter {letterOrDigitOrUnderScore}

In this definition the identifier is defined as being a *letter* followed by zero or more instances of *letterOrDigitOrUnderScore*. The symbol ::= means "is defined by". The curly braces {} in EBNF mean that what is enclosed can occur zero or more times. Square brackets [ ] in EBNF mean that an item is optional. This use is quite separate from the use of curly braces or square brackets in a Java program. A vertical line | means "one of". For example, the syntactic variable *letterOrDigitOrUnderScore* is defined by

letterOrDigitOrUnderscore ::= letter | digit | underscore

The syntactic variables *letter, digit,* and *underscore* are defined by these production rules containing terminal tokens (in bold):

letter ::= **a** | **b** | **c** ... | **z** | **A** | **B** | **C** ... | **Z**
digit ::= **0** | **1** | **2** ... | **9**
underscore ::= **_**

# 5.2   Primitive Data Types

The programs we introduced in Chapter 3 concentrated on graphics. To use a graphics method we had to specify the coordinates in pixels of points in a window. These were integers.

We will now consider the primitive types beyond the **int** type that are available in Java.

- There are two basic **numerical types:** the **int** type for integers, both negative and positive, and the **float** type for numbers that can have decimal points. These are often called real numbers.

- For integers there are, as well, the **byte** type (a byte is equal to 8 bits), the **short** type, and the **long** type which use one quarter, one half, and twice the number of bits as the **int** type respectively.

- For real numbers the **double** type uses twice the number of bits as the **float** type.

- Another type is the **boolean** type which has only two possible values, **true** and **false**.

- The **char** type represents a single character in **unicode**. Each unicode character is represented by 2 bytes or 16 bits.

# 5.3   Declarations of Variables

The different types of data used in a program require different amounts of space in memory to store them. In order to store data of a particular type in the computer's memory, enough space must be reserved to hold the value. This is done by including a **declaration** that establishes the identifier by which the data can be referenced and the data type of the value.

For example, to reserve space for a person's year of birth we might write

  int *yearOfBirth;*

The declaration begins with the keyword **int** which gives the data type; the identifier comes next. Notice that when an identifier is a compound word, the convention in this book is to capitalize the first letter of words other than the first word. Underscores, which are like hyphens (but not the same), could be used instead, for example,

  *year_of_birth*

Any later reference in the program to a variable must be spelled exactly the same way. If the variable is not spelled consistently, the compiler generates an error message indicating that the variable has not been declared. This happens when the identifier used and the declared identifier are not the same.

The declaration of a variable in a program must precede the use of the variable declared.

As well as allocating the proper amount of storage space in memory, the declaration of the data type of a variable establishes what operations will be possible on that variable.

# 5.4   Expressions: Arithmetic and Boolean

## 5.4.1   Arithmetic Expressions

Numbers or numerical variables of type **int**, **short**, **byte**, and **long** or **float** and **double** can be combined using the arithmetic operators +, −, *, and /. The * is for multiplication and the / for division. In an expression such as

    1.34 * 7.8 + 2 / 12.2

the multiplication (*) is evaluated first, then division (/), and finally the addition (+). When there are two operators with the same **precedence**, such as * and /, they are evaluated left to right. It is sometimes better to enclose subexpressions in parentheses to indicate the intended order of evaluation since expressions in parentheses are evaluated first. In the preceding example, the expression, written with parentheses

    (1.34 * 7.8) + (2 / 12.2)

makes the order of evaluation explicit.

When integers are combined in an expression, the result will be an integer. If there is a division operator / in an integer expression, the result is automatically truncated to be an integer. For example, 5/2 gives the result 2. It is possible to **cast** an expression such as this, that normally would yield an integer to produce a **float** result by writing

    (**float**) 5/2

This causes the 5 to be treated as a float number. If there is any float number in the expression, the result will automatically be float. The expression 3 + 6.2 gives the **float** result 9.2. If, instead, the *round* method of the *Math* class is used, the value of

> *Math.round* (3 + 6.2)

will be 9. The result is rounded to the nearest integer.

The % operator can be used to obtain the remainder on division of two positive integers. For example, the value of

> 14 % 5

is 4, which is the remainder when 14 is divided by 5. This is often referred to as the **modulo** operator.

## 5.4.2   Boolean Expressions

Boolean expressions can have only two possible values, **true** or **false**.

A Boolean expression may be a single boolean variable or consist of a **comparison**. A simple comparison has the form

> expression comparison-operator expression

To be compared, the values of the two expressions must be of the same or compatible data types, that is, both numbers.

The comparison operators are:

| Symbol | Meaning |
|--------|---------|
| == | equal to |
| != | not equal to |
| > | greater than |
| < | less than |
| >= | greater than or equal to |
| <= | less than or equal to |

Boolean variables, or comparisons can be combined using the boolean or **logical** operators && for **and**, and || for **or**. If two boolean expressions are combined using the operator && then both expressions must be true before the compound expression is true. If they are combined using the || operator then at least one of the two must be true before the compound expression is true.

Here is a boolean expression which will test whether an exam mark submitted is a number between 0 and 100.

   $0 <= mark$ && $mark <= 100$

The value is **true** if *mark* occurs in this range.

## 5.5   Assignment Statements

The value of an expression can be stored in a variable in memory. The variable must have been declared and its data type must be the same or compatible with the data type of the expression. This is done using an **assignment** statement. The assignment statement has the form

   variable = expression;

To illustrate, here is an application program that uses the assignment statement. It is presented as a program fragment that must be placed as the body of a *main* method in the *BoilerPlate* class defined in Chapter 1.

Here is the boilerplate for a Java program. The details of an application can be placed into the boilerplate to produce a complete application program.

```
import java.awt.*;
import hsa.Console;

public class name-of-application
{
    static Console c;
```

```
static public void main (String [ ] args)
{
    c = new Console ( );
    details of application
}
details of any user-defined methods
} /* name-of-application class */
```

Here is the program fragment that provides the "details of application".

```
int hoursWorked;
double payRate;
double totalPay;
hoursWorked = 40;
payRate = 21.50;
totalPay = hoursWorked * payRate;
c.println ("Totalpay = " + totalPay);
```

A real numerical constant like 21.50 is of type **double** and cannot be assigned to a variable of type **float**. A **float** value could, however, be assigned to a variable of type **double**.

In the last statement the **string constant** in double quotes causes the value of *totalPay* to be converted to a string and concatenated to it. The + here is the **concatenation operator** not the addition operator. When the list of output items in a *print* or *println* statement begins with a string constant, this conversion of subsequent items to strings takes place. For example, the statement

```
c.println ("Here are two integers " + 2 + 3);
```

will produce the output

```
Here are two integers 23
```

To produce a space between the 2 and 3 another string constant consisting of a space surrounded by quotes is required as in this statement:

```
c.println ("Here are two integers " + 2 + " " + 3);
```

Integer values can be assigned to **float** or **double** variables but the converse is not true unless the **float** or **double** value is cast as an integer. For example,

> **int** *hoursWorked*;
> *hoursWorked* = (**int**) 12.3;  //Converts 12.3 to 12.

Here is a boolean example of an assignment statement.

> **boolean** *correct*;
> *correct* = 7 < 10 || 5 > 7;
> *c.println* (*correct*);

The boolean variable *correct* will have the value **true** stored in it since the expression assigned to it is true. In evaluating a compound expression, such as that on the right-hand side of the assignment statement here, if the first of the two boolean expressions separated by the || determines the value of the whole expression by being true, the evaluation is short circuited and the second boolean expression is not even evaluated. Similarly with the && operation, if the first expression is false, the second is not evaluated.

The && operator has higher precedence than the || operator.

## 5.5.1 Initializing Variables in their Declarations

An assignment statement can be combined with a declaration to give a variable its initial value. For example,

> **int** *sum* = 0;

declares a variable *sum* and sets its value as 0.

## 5.5.2 Constants

Some values stored in memory called **constants** remain the same throughout the execution of a program.

A constant must be initialized in its declaration. Declaring it as a constant with the keyword **final** before its data type means that its value cannot be changed. Any subsequent attempt to assign a value to a constant is a violation of its definition.

For example,

**final double** *INTEREST_RATE* = 7.5;

defines the constant *INTEREST_RATE*. By convention, constants are given identifiers of upper case letters.

## 5.5.3    Syntax of Assignment Statements

The syntax of the assignment statement expressed in EBNF is

assignment-statement ::= variable = expression;

Notice that the symbol = is a terminal token in the assignment statement, but the symbol ::= is a symbol in the EBNF metalanguage. The data type of the expression after the = must be the same or compatible with the data type of the variable or else a syntax error will be reported and execution terminated. An integer-valued expression is compatible with a real variable but not the reverse.

## 5.5.4 Variable Names on Both Sides of an Assignment Statement

The assignment statement is not an equation as is obvious when an assignment contains the same variable identifier on both sides. For example, these statements might appear in a program.

**int** *sum* = 1;
*sum* = *sum* + 1;

Here *sum* is given an initial value of 1 in its declaration. In the assignment, the expression on the right-hand side is evaluated to give the value 2. This value is then assigned to the variable *sum*. This gives *sum* the value 2 after the execution of the assignment statement.

This sort of assignment occurs frequently in programs and can be written in abbreviated form as

*sum* += 1;

A still shorter form of this particular assignment statement is

*sum ++;*

Similarly the assignment

*sum = sum * 10;*

can be written in short form as

*sum *= 10;*

The assignment

*sum = sum - 1;*

can be written as either

*sum −= 1;*

or

*sum −−;*

Here is an example program that uses assignment statements to produce the value of multiplying the integers between 1 and 5 together (5 factorial).

```
// The "ProductOfIntegers" class
// Computes the product of the first five integers.
int number = 1;
int product = number;
number++; // number has value 2
product = product * number;
number++; // number has value 3
product = product * number;
number++; // number has value 4
product = product * number;
number++; // number has value 5
product = product * number;
c.println ("Product of first 5 integers is " + product);
```

The output of these instructions would be

Product of first 5 integers is 120

We will see later how this result can be programmed more simply with a repetition construct.

## 5.6  Output Statements

The hsa *Console* class provides the *print* or *println* methods for producing output. When a string is output it may consist of a series of string constants and other data types concatenated using the + operator. In general, each output item is output by a single statement. To output two items requires two output statements. If the *print* method is used these are on the same line. If two calls to the *print* method are given, such as in

```
c.print (15);
c.print (12);
```

the result is 1512. The items are both on the same line and there are no blanks output between the items. The *print* statement continues the output on the current output line. The statements

```
c.println (15);
c.println (12);
```

produce these two lines of output.

```
15
12
```

The method *println* causes a Return after its output.

Boolean values are output as *true* or *false*. For example,

```
c.println (7 > 2);
```

produces the output *true*.

By default a call to *print* or *println* sends output to the screen.

## 5.6.1   Output Formatting

As previously noted, the space around an output item can be controlled by outputting an accompanying **string constant**.

For example, the statements

```
int mark = 86;
c.print ("Here is a mark ");
c.println (mark);
```

result in this output.

Here is a mark 86

The blank after "Here is a mark" causes a space before the value of *mark*. The same result could be obtained by the single statement

c.println ("Here is a mark " + *mark*)

The + sign here causes the *mark* to be converted to a string and concatenated to the string constant. In statements of this sort a string should be the first output item in a list separated by the concatenation operator. For example, the statement

c.println (2 + 3 + " is five");

produces the output

5 is five

whereas the statement

c.println ("Twenty-three is " + 2 + 3);

produces the output

Twenty-three is 23

Another way to control the format of an output item is to follow its name or value by a **format item**. The format item is either an integer or an integer variable. The value of the format item controls the size of the field in which the output item is displayed. Numerical items are right justified in the field. For example, the statements

*c.print* (35, 6);
*c.print* (12, 3);
*c.println* (2, 3);

would result in this output. The blank spaces are represented by the symbol Δ.

ΔΔΔΔ3 5Δ12ΔΔ2

The first item output is in a field of size 6 spaces and is at the right-hand side of the field. This leaves four blanks to the left of it. The second item is in a field of size 3 which gives one blank to the left of the 12. The third item has two blanks to the left of the 2. Because the third statement is a *println*, the line is ended.

A **float** or **double** number is output with the decimal place and as many as sixteen digits to the right of the decimal point. Trailing zeros in decimal places are omitted. For example,

*c.println* ((**double**) 5/16, 12);

would result in the output

ΔΔΔΔΔΔ0.3125

All digits after the fourth decimal place are zeros. Note that the decimal point takes one of the spaces. Another easy way of getting the effect of casting an integer value as a **double** value is to add a decimal point after it.

The output of real numbers can be messy unless the number of decimal places is controlled. To control the number of decimal places output, as would be required in outputting a bank balance in dollars and cents, a second format item can be provided for a **float** or **double** value. For example,

*c.println* ((**double**) 5/3, 6, 2);

would produce the output

ΔΔ1.67

Here two decimal places are output and the value is rounded.

Very large or very small real values are output in **exponent form**. For example, 1.3E7 is the exponent form for 13 million. For string values, the string is output left justified in its field. For example, the statements

> *c.print* ("Balance", 10);
> *c.println* ("Interest", 10);

would produce the output

```
BalanceΔΔΔInterestΔΔ
```

Output formatting is very useful for producing neat tables of results. We will now look at an example of using output formatting.

When a bank computes the interest on a bank account, it stores the new account balance to the nearest cent. Here are the instructions that will do this and prove, by outputting, that the new balance is indeed stored to the nearest cent.

```
// The "NearestCent" class
// Computes bank balance to nearest cent.
double balance = 210.38;
double intRate = 3.25;
int interestInCents;
interestInCents = (int) (balance * intRate + .5);
c.println (interestInCents, 5);
balance = balance + (double) interestInCents / 100;
c.println ("Balance ");
c.println (balance, 10, 2);
c.println (balance, 12, 4);
```

The output for these statements is

```
ΔΔ684
```

```
Balance
```

```
ΔΔΔΔ217.22
```

```
ΔΔΔΔ217.2200
```

By outputting two more decimal places of balance in its second output statement, the program shows that the next figures are zeros.

## 5.7    Comments in Programs

Internal documentation is an essential element of good program design. Parts of a program used to document the program are called comments. Comments may be placed anywhere in a program between other statements or on the same line after a statement. In one form the comment is preceded by // and terminated by the end of the line. The other form of a comment is to precede it by /* and follow it by */. In this form the comment may continue over any number of lines.

Here is an example showing a comment going over several lines.

```
/* Here is an example of a comment
that goes over several lines of
a program. */
```

The other form for a comment would look like this:

```
// Here is an example of a comment
// that goes over several lines of
// a program.
```

We tend to use the second form more frequently. Notice that in either case there are no semicolons at the end of the lines although, in fact they would do no harm. The first type of comment is perhaps more prone to error since if the closing */ were omitted the comment would just run on and on. Lines in a program can be temporarily deleted by prefacing them with //. This changes them to a comment.

# 5.8    Chapter Summary

This chapter has introduced a number of basic concepts of programming. The primitive data types were presented along with the form of expressions of the various types.

## Metalanguage for Syntax Definition

To define the syntax in a programming language we could use natural language such as English. Often, however, definitions in natural language are relatively easy to understand but not precise enough. Instead a formal language is introduced to define the programming language. This acts as a **metalanguage. Extended Backus-Naur Form** or **EBNF** is a metalanguage commonly used in computer science for describing a programming language.

**Syntax variables** such as **identifiers** are defined in terms of other syntactic entities and **terminal tokens**. To **produce** a syntactically correct program in a particular programming language we use these definitions, or **production rules**, replacing each syntactic variable by its definition until only terminal tokens remain.

## Primitive Data Types and Declarations

The primitive data types of Java include: **byte, short, int,** or **long** for integers, **float** or **double** for real numbers, and **boolean**. A variable is declared as of one of these types by writing a **declaration** such as

    int *age;*

A declaration starts with the data type followed by the identifier of the variable. The variable must be declared before it can be used.

## Arithmetic Expressions

Numbers, both real and integer, or numerical variables can be combined using the **arithmetic operators** to form arithmetic expressions. The order of evaluation in expressions is:

*   expressions in parentheses,

- the multiplication and division operators * and /,
- the addition and subtraction operators + and −, and
- operations with the same precedence are evaluated from left to right in the expression.

Integers can be assigned to real variables but real numbers may not be assigned to integer variables.

Integer division always results in an integer. Any fractional part is truncated.

The % operator produces the remainder on integer division. It is called the **modulo operator.**

## Boolean Expressions

A Boolean expression can be:

- a boolean variable,
- a comparison,
- comparisons or boolean variables compounded by using the boolean or logical operators: && (for **and**) and || (for **or**), or
- boolean expressions in parentheses.

The comparison operators are >, <, ==, <=, >=, and !=.

In a compound expression, each individual comparison or boolean variable is evaluated left to right. If the left value immediately determines the value of the compound, the remaining evaluation is **short circuited** and not done. For example, in the compound expression

    7 < 9 || 8 > 5

the fact that 7 is less than 9 will cause the whole expression to be true no matter what the next comparison might yield.

## Assignment Statements

The value of an expression can be assigned to a variable using the form

variable = expression;

The value of the expression must be the same as, or compatible with, the data type of the variable. An integer expression can be assigned to a real variable but not the converse.

Initial assignments of values to variables can occur in their declarations. For example,

int *sum* = 0;

The expression assigned to a variable can contain the same variable. For example,

*sum* = *sum* + 2;

means that the value stored in *sum* is increased by 2 and stored back in *sum*. A short form for this assignment is

*sum* += 2;

The particular short form

*sum* ++;

is the same as

*sum* += 1;

and

*sum* −−;

is the same as

*sum* −= 1;

## Output Statements

Output statements use the *print* or *println* method of the *Console* class with an output item as a parameter. By default these methods place the output item in a **field** that is just large enough to hold it. A *println* statement causes a new line after the output item is output.

To control the format of output the values can be interspersed with the output of string constants that have extra blanks preceding or following them. Several output items that begin with a string constant can be concatenated using the + operator. Items that are numerical or boolean values are converted to strings.

Another way to control the format is to follow the single **output item** in a *print* or *println* statement by a **format item** which is separated from it by a comma. This controls the size of the field used for output. Numbers are right justified in their field. Strings are left justified. Real numbers can have the number of decimal points output controlled by following the first format item by a comma and a second format item. Very large or very small numbers appear in **exponent form**.

## Comments

Comments can be placed between or at the end of statements to make a program understandable. They may begin with // and end at the end of the current line. They may alternatively be preceded by /* and followed by */. Variables and constants should not require comments since the names chosen for identifiers should explain their contents. Comments are not followed by semicolons.

# 5.9   Technical Terms

actual parameter (argument)

assignment statement

boolean type

char type

comparison

concatenation operator

constant

declaration

double type

Extended Backus-Naur Form (EBNF)

exponent form

float type

format item

logical operator

long type

int type

metalanguage

modulo operator                          reserved word

numerical type                           string constant

precedence                               syntactic variable

production rule                          terminal token

# 5.10 Exercises

1.  Which of these identifiers is syntactically correct?

    a)  *sum*

    b)  *3rdPage*

    c)  *two+two*

    d)  *Fixed_Price*

    e)  *high-level*

2.  The arithmetic expression

    $$3 * 5 + 7 - 2/6$$

    has a value 21.666.... What value would be computed? Write the same expression with all parentheses included.

    What are the values of the following expressions?

    (a)  $3 * ((5 + 7) - 2)/6$
    (b)  $3 * 5 + (7 - 2)/6$
    (c)  $((3 * 5) + 7 - 2)/6$

3.  Write a program that computes the interest on a bank balance to the nearest cent and stores the result in a variable called *newBalance*. Prove that the new balance is stored to the nearest cent by an output instruction that prints *newBalance* with three decimal places. Test the program using a variety of values assigned to the balance and the interest rate.

4.  What is output by the following statements involving boolean expressions?

    ```
    c.println ( 5 > 3 && 7 > 9 || 6 < 8);
    c.println ( 2 < 6 && 5 < 10 && 7 > 3);
    ```

5.  What is output by this program segment?

    ```
    int sum = 0;
    for (int count = 1; count <= 10; count ++)
    {
        c.println ("sum = " + sum + " count = " + count);
        sum += 1;
    }
    c.println ("sum = " + sum);
    ```

    What would be the output if the incrementation part of the for were *count += 2*? See what happens if an attempt is made to output *count* in the last *println* statement.

# Chapter 6

# Input of Data

In the programs so far there has been no input of data. The output was produced by graphic statements in the program such as *drawLine* or by the output statements *print* and *println*. In this chapter, we will be looking at the various ways of inputting data. Input statements will be shown for input from the keyboard, the standard input device, or from a file. Ways to input numerical data and string data will be discussed and programs that involve repetition are presented for inputting sequences of similar data items. As well, methods of generating data for purposes of testing programs, and ways to analyze numerical data statistically are given.

# 6.1   Entering Programs

Programs can be directly entered using the editing environment of the computer. This allows programs to be created in the input window by typing on the keyboard. They can be edited to correct typing errors, then run. If the instructions in a program are not syntactically correct, syntax errors are reported. These syntax errors must be corrected, using the editor of the environment, before the program is run again. When the program gets past the stage where there are syntax errors, that is, to the **execution phase**, the output can be examined to see if it is what is expected.

At this stage the errors that remain are usually semantic errors. What the programmer wanted and what was actually produced were not the same. For example, the program might have a statement to *drawLine* instead of a *drawRect* statement. Such errors in meaning can only be detected by examining the output and so are not reported to the user by the compiler. Semantic errors are corrected by editing the program in the same way as syntax errors are corrected.

Just as the keyboard is used to input the program and any editing changes, it is also the **standard input** device for entering the data on which the program operates. The program itself must contain one or more statements to read or input the data from the keyboard. We will now show how input of various data types can be accomplished using Java standard input and afterwards how it is done using methods of the *Console* class.

# 6.2   Standard Input and Output

Java provides a way of reading input from the standard input device (the keyboard) and writing to the **standard output** device (the screen) but its built-in facilities for this are quite primitive. They provide the ability to read in either single characters or entire lines of data from the keyboard but there is no built-in facility to read any other data types, for example integers and booleans.

The facilities for output are somewhat better. All of Java's primitive data types can be output directly. There are, however, no methods for printing numbers into fixed-length fields or with a specified number of decimal places.

In later sections, we use Holt Software's *Console* class. This class has methods for reading in all of Java's primitive data types directly and for outputting data into fixed-length fields. The *Console* class also has facilities for doing basic graphics. This means that you only need to read the rest of this section if you want a better understanding of doing input and output without the hsa *Console* class.

Reading from standard input uses a predefined object called *System.in*. This is an object of class *InputStream*. An *InputStream* can only read in single characters. To be useful, *System.in* must be converted to a *DataInputStream*, from which an entire line of input can be read at a time. The statement

*DataInputStream stdin* = **new** *DataInputStream* (*System.in*);

performs the conversion. Once this is done, the *readLine* method is used to read a line of input from the standard input device.

The *System.out* object's *print* and *println* methods send data to the standard output device. The *print* and *println* methods take an item of any Java primitive data type or a *String* object as an argument. The *print* method outputs the item to the standard output without following it with a Return. The *println* method outputs the item following it with a Return. The statement

*System.out.print* (*s*)

outputs a string *s* not followed by a Return while

*System.out.println (i)*

outputs an integer *i* followed by Return.

Here is a small application program using standard input to read a name and standard output to repeat it.

```
// The "EchoName" class.
// Asks for your name and echoes it back.
import java.awt.*;
import java.io.*;

public class EchoName
{
    static public void main (String [ ] args) throws IOException
    {
        String name;
        DataInputStream stdin = new DataInputStream (System.in);
        System.out.println ("Please type your name: ");
        name = stdin.readLine ();

        // Output the reply.
        System.out.println ("Your name is \"" + name + "\"");
    } // main method
} /* EchoName class */
```

In the *EchoName* class,

> *DataInputStream stdin = new DataInputStream (System.in);*

converts *System.in* into the *DataInputStream* object *stdin* from which entire lines from standard input can be read. The next line writes the message "Please type your name" to standard output (the screen) to prompt for a name. As the user types a name it is echoed on the screen. The program then reads an entire line of input from standard input into *name* (not including the end-of-line character at the end). The last few lines of the *main* method display the result.

The *main* method header has the words

> **throws** *IOException*

in it. This phrase must be used whenever a DataInputStream is used.

# 6.3   Input of Numerical Data

The most common and simplest form of input used in programs is by reading lines. A line is a series of characters terminated by Return (the enter key).

A line that represents an integer consists of an optional sign (+ or −) followed by one or more digits. For example, −375 and 258 are integers. When Java standard input is used, the line of characters representing an integer must be parsed and converted to a numerical value. This is a complicated process and, for this reason, we use the methods of the *Console* class to handle input and output. Applications using the Console class must have the form illustrated in the *BoilerPlate* class shown here.

```
import java.awt.*;
import hsa.Console;

public class name-of-application
{
    static Console c;

    static public void main (String [ ] args)
    {
        c = new Console ( );
        details of application
    } /* main program */

    details of any user-defined methods
} /* name-of-application class */
```

Now, here are the details of the body of a *main* method that inputs an integer. It is to be part of the *NextYear* class.

```
// The "NextYear" class.
// This tells you how old you will be next year.
int age;
c.print ("Please enter your age: ");
age = c.readInt ();
c.print ("Your age next year will be ");
c.println (age + 1);
```

Notice that the way the *Console* method *readInt* is used is different from the way the *println* or *print* methods are used. The method *readInt* here yields a value that is assigned to the variable *age*. The method has no parameters but must be followed by parentheses with nothing between them.

In terms of the classification of methods as either functions or procedures the *print* or *println* methods are procedures: they cause output, whereas the *readInt* method is a function: it has a value.

Whenever input is expected from the user, the program should assist the user by outputting an input **prompt**. The prompt in this program is:

Please enter your age:

Because the *print* instruction rather than *println* is used for the prompt, the cursor remains at the end of the prompt, just after "age:", waiting for the user's input. Notice that the prompt message has a space after it. At this stage the user enters his or her age and presses Return. The Return signals the computer that the input is complete. The user can also correct an input error by backspacing and retyping the value before pressing Return.

Here is a sample *Console* execution window from the program.

Please enter your age: **21**
Your age next year will be 22

The user's input 21 is shown in boldface type. On the computer screen there is no difference in appearance between what the computer outputs and what is echoed on the screen as the user types input data.

Real numbers are entered in the same way as integers, except that they may contain a decimal point. Here is a program that calculates the area of a floor. The real numbers are of type **double**.

```
// The "FloorArea" class.
// Find the area of a floor given its length and width.
double len, width;
c.print ("Enter length in meters ");
len = c.readDouble ();
c.print ("Enter width in meters ");
width = c.readDouble ();
c.print ("Area is ");
c.print (len * width);
c.println (" square meters");
```

We can also combine the last three statements into a single statement this way.

```
c.println ("Area is " + len * width + " square meters");
```

The + sign indicates that the value of *len * width* is to be converted to a string and concatenated to the other two strings.

When two or more variables such as *len* and *width* are of the same data type they can be declared in a single statement, listed separated by commas, as in "**double** *len, width*;".

# 6.4    Input of String Data

String data can be read as lines using the *Console* class method *readLine*. Here is a program segment that inputs a line of characters, namely a string, and echoes it. Compare this with the *EchoName* class (section 6.2).

```
// The "NameInOut" class.
// Read a name and output it.
String name;
c.println ("Please enter your full name");
name = c.readLine ();
c.println ("Your name is \"" + name + "\"");
```

Here is a sample console execution window.

> Please enter your full name
> **Bill Gates**
> Your name is "Bill Gates"

Again the user's input is in boldface type.

In the *println* statement that outputs the name there are three components: a string constant which acts as a label, a string variable *name*, and another string constant. The label indicates what the output represents. At the end of the labelling string constant that is enclosed in double quotes are the characters \". This indicates that a double quote mark is wanted in the labelling string itself. In the program the name is joined to the label string, then a second double quote is concatenated to result in a quote following the name.

The backslash \ is used with other special characters like a double quote as well. To get a backslash itself in a string two backslashes are required. The statement

> *c.println* ("Here is a backslash character \ \ ");

would produce the output

> Here is a backslash character \

The meaning of the + operator is very different when it is used with strings. While with numerical values the + operator indicates addition, with strings it means to concatenate, or join end to end. We say the operator + is **overloaded**, that is, used with different meanings in two different contexts. The statement

> *c.println* (4 + 5);

would output the integer 9. Here the + is interpreted as the addition operator.

# 6.5    Input of Sequences of Data

One of the most common operations in computing is to read a sequence of data items of the same type. This requires the repetition of the input operation.

## 6.5.1    Counted Repetition

Suppose the average of a series of 10 exam marks is to be calculated. Here is a program segment that does this.

```
// The "TenAvg" class.
// Compute the average of 10 marks.
int mark;
int sum = 0;
c.println ("Enter 10 marks one to a line");
for (int count = 1; count <= 10; count ++)
{
    mark = c.readInt ();
    sum += mark;
}
c.println ("Average of 10 marks is " + (double) sum /10);
```

The repetition construct which begins with the keyword **for** is called a **counted loop** or a **for** statement. In parentheses following the **for** are three components separated by semicolons. These are

- the declaration and initialization of the counting index,
- the continuation condition, and
- the incrementing of the counting index.

The counting is recorded in the **counting index** *count* and has a **range** from 1 to 10. The index *count* will start with a value 1 and then each time the **body** of the loop is executed it is increased by 1. This continues until the 10th time through the body at which point *count* has a value 11 and the loop terminates. The instruction after the loop body is then executed. To see the value of *count* on each repetition insert a *c.println (count);*

statement inside the loop.

In order that the average will be output as a real number, with decimal places, the variable *sum* is cast as **double** by having the keyword **double** placed in parentheses ahead of it. The average otherwise would be truncated since both *sum* and 10 are integers.

The usual style for writing a loop is to indent the statements in the loop's body a few spaces from the column where the body's enclosing curly brace is located. This is known as paragraphing or pretty printing the program. The final output statement concatenates the label "Average of 10 names is" to the output value using the + operator. The output value is automatically converted to a string then concatenated.

The program that was presented is not very general; it works only with a sequence of 10 marks. To make it more general, the number of marks in the sequence could be input along with the actual sequence. Here is a modified version of the program segment which asks the user for the number of marks, reads them in and prints the average.

```
// The "HowManyAvg" class.
// Compute average of a sequence of marks.
int howMany, mark;
int sum = 0;
c.print ("How many marks are there? ");
howMany = c.readInt ();
c.println ("Enter "+ howMany + " marks one after the other");
for (int count = 1; count <= howMany; count++)
{
    mark = c.readInt ();
    sum += mark;
}
c.println ("Average of " + howMany + " marks is " +
    (double) sum /howMany);
```

Again the various output items in the final *println* statement are concatenated using the + operator.

This program is an example of processing each data item as it is read. Although the programs in this chapter do not check for bad input, if the user entered a real number in reply to the prompt

How many marks are there?

in this program, a run-time error would be reported and execution terminated.

## 6.5.2   Conditional Repetition

A sequence of data items can be processed by a different kind of repetition construct called a **while** statement. Here, reading and processing continues until a data item is entered that is a **signal** or **sentinel** to stop the processing, rather than having a predetermined number of data items. This type of repetition is called a **conditional loop**; repetition continues until a certain condition becomes false.

For example, here is a program segment that reads a sequence of words until it reads the sentinel word "stop". When it encounters the word it stops the repetition. The fact that the sentinel word is "stop" has nothing to do with what happens. If the sentinel word was "banana" repetition still would stop but the user might not see clearly why this happened.

```
// The "LastLetter" class.
// Read a sequence of words and output the last letter
// of each word until the sentinel is read.
String word;
final String SENTINEL = "stop";
c.println ("Enter a sequence of words, end with " + SENTINEL);
// Words must have at least one letter.
word = c.readLine ();
while (! word.equals (SENTINEL))
{
    c.println ("Last letter of " + word + " is " +
        word.charAt (word.length () − 1));
    word = c.readLine ();
}
c.println ("This is the end of the sequence");
```

As with the sequence of numbers, each line is input and then processed before the next line is input. Note that the input statement for strings is *readLine* rather than *readInt* which is for integers. The repetition construct begins with the keyword **while**. Action of the loop stops when the word input is equal to the sentinel. The continuation condition

(!*word.equals* (*SENTINEL*))

is a boolean expression which is either true or false. The exit from the loop occurs when it is false. The condition uses the *equals* method of the *String* class. The exclamation mark means **not**. As well, the methods of *charAt* and *length* of the *String* class are used in the output statement. These three methods of the *String* class will be explained in more detail in Chapter 8.

# 6.6   Input from a File

So far all the input has been from the keyboard, which is the standard input device. This allows the program to read data directly from a user. In many cases, however, programs are required to receive data input from a file. Reading data from a file or writing data to a file is possible in application programs but not possible in applets.

To read data from a file, the program must establish a connection to the particular file that is to be read. This is done in this example by statements which open a stream called *input* from the file named *fileName*.

```
BufferedReader input;
input = new BufferedReader (new FileReader (fileName));
```

Here is an example program which asks the user to enter the name of the file where the data to be read is stored and then reads and processes the data. Each positive integer in the file is on a separate line. The program reads a line at a time using the *readLine* method and parses it to change it to an integer. The program reads positive integers until *input.readLine* () returns **null** (indicating the end of file has been reached) and then finds the average of the integers.

```
// The "FileAvg" class.
// Input a sequence of integers entered originally one to a line
// from a file whose name is to be read in from the keyboard
// and find their average.
String fileName, line;
int number;
int sum = 0, count = 0;
c.println ("What is the name of the file of integers? ");
fileName = c.readLine ();
BufferedReader input;
input = new BufferedReader (new FileReader (fileName));
line = input.readLine ();        //Read a line of characters.
while (line != null)             //File is terminated by a null.
{
    number = Integer.parseInt (line);   //Change to an integer.
    count ++;
    sum += number;
    line = input.readLine ();    //Read next line.
}
c.println ("Average of " + count + " numbers is " + (double) sum/count);
```

Notice that *input* is declared to be an object of class *BufferedReader*. If the opening operation is not successful, the program execution will be stopped. We say that this class is capable of **throwing an I/O exception**. When this is the case, the words

**throws** *IOException*

must be added to the *main* method's header.

The *BufferedReader* class is part of the *java.io* package. To use the class (and the other file reading and writing classes in this chapter) the package must be imported into the class, just as *hsa.Console* and *java.awt* were imported into the previous classes. This is done by adding the line

**import** *java.io.*;*

to the other import statements in the class.

Each integer is recorded as a line of characters and is parsed and changed to an integer by the statement

*number = Integer.parseInt (line);*

Reading and writing a file is similar to using the Java standard input and output *System.in* and *System.out*.

# 6.7   Output to a File

Data produced as the output of a program can be output to a file. Output of data to a file is similar to input from a file except that the class for output is *PrintWriter* (or *PrintStream*) if text form output is wanted. The *PrintWriter* class is connected to *FileWriter* by the chaining of objects. To output to a text file, the *print* and *println* methods are used, just as in the *Console* class.

Here is a program that writes the odd integers from 1 to 361 in text form to a file that is named by the user.

```
// The "OddInts" class.
// Produce a file of data consisting of the odd integers
// from 1 to 361 inclusive.
PrintWriter output;
String fileName;
c.println ("What is the name of the file for the integers? ");
fileName = c.readLine ();
output = new PrintWriter (new FileWriter (fileName));
for (int number = 1; number <= 361; number += 2)
{
    output.println (number);
}
// Close file.
output.close ();
```

The statement

```
output.println(number);
```

outputs *number* as a string of characters followed by a Return. A null string is automatically placed at the end of the file.

If a file is to be read again after it has been output, it should be closed. This allows the file to be opened again as input later in the program if required. At the end of execution of a program all files are automatically closed so that the file in this example need not have been closed. Note that once again, *main* must be modified to indicate that it can throw an *IOException*, and the *java.io* package must be imported.

Files may also be kept in binary form. The use of binary output of files will be discussed in Chapter 15.

Here is a program that inputs text stored in a file named *"poem.dat"* and outputs the same text to a file called *"poem2.dat"* with the lines numbered.

```
// The "NumberLines" class.
// Read the file named "poem.dat" line by line
// and output the lines, numbered, to a file named "poem2.dat".
String text;
int lineCount = 0;
BufferedReader input;
PrintWriter output;
input = new BufferedReader (new FileReader ("poem.dat"));
output = new PrintWriter (new FileWriter ("poem2.dat"));
text = input.readLine ();
while (text != null)
{
    lineCount ++;
    output.println (lineCount + "  " + text);
    text = input.readLine ();
}
output.close ();
```

When the *readLine* method reaches the end of file, it returns a **null**. To see the result of the program's action, the file "poem2.dat" can be brought into the editor of the environment.

# 6.8 Generated Data

Often a large amount of data is required to test programs. This is particularly true if the data is being analyzed statistically. Rather than try to input vast quantities of data through the keyboard, it is possible to produce or generate the data artificially for testing purposes.

The *random* method of the *Math* class is very useful for generating simulated data. A real randomly-chosen value between 0 and 1 (but not including 1) can be generated and assigned to the variable *randomReal* by these statements.

```
double randomReal;
randomReal = Math.random ();
```

To produce a random integer, say between 1 and 6 suitable for the result of a cast of a die (one of a pair of dice), we could use these statements.

```
int die;
die = (int) (Math.random () * 6) + 1;
```

By multiplying a real random number between 0 and 1 by 6 we produce a real number between 0 and 6 (but not including 6). When this is cast as an integer, as it is by preceding it by (**int**), the real value is truncated, leaving a random integer between 0 and 5 inclusive. By adding 1 the result becomes a random integer between 1 and 6 inclusive.

Here is a program that produces a file called "dice", simulating the throw of two dice 300 times.

```
// The "DiceData" class.
// Simulate the throw of two dice 300 times
// and store the generated data in file "dice".
int die1, die2, roll;
PrintWriter output;
output = new PrintWriter (new FileWriter ("dice"));
for (int count = 1; count <= 300; count ++)
{
```

```
die1 = (int) (Math.random () * 6) + 1;
die2 = (int) (Math.random () * 6) + 1;
roll = die1 + die2;
output.println (roll);
}
output.close ();
c.println ("Simulated data of 300 throws now in file 'dice' ");
```

# 6.9   Statistical Analysis of Data

One way of characterizing a sequence of numbers is to compute their **average** value. Another commonly-used statistical characteristic is the **variance**. This is defined as the mean (average) of the square of the differences between each data item and the average value. The variance measures the extent to which individual numbers differ from the average. If there are $n$ data items each of which will be called $x_i$ their average is produced by the formula

$$\text{average} = \bar{x} = \frac{1}{n}\sum_{i=1}^{n} x_i$$

where the $\Sigma$ means to add up the individual values $x_i$ for $i$ going from 1 to $n$.

The variance is defined as

$$\text{variance} = \frac{1}{n}\sum_{i=1}^{n}\left(\bar{x} - x_i\right)^2$$

This can be rewritten as

$$= \frac{1}{n}\sum_{i=1}^{n}\left(\bar{x}^2 - 2\bar{x}x_i + x_i^2\right)$$

This shows that the variance can be computed as the average of the squares of the $x_i$ minus the average value squared.

Here is a program to compute the mean and variance of the generated data for the dice throws stored in the file "dice".

```
// The "DiceStats" class.
// Compute the mean and variance for the simulated dice throws
// in file "dice" prepared by the data generation program.
int roll;
int count = 0, sum = 0, sumOfSquares = 0;
String line;
BufferedReader input;
input = new BufferedReader (new FileReader ("dice"));
line = input.readLine ();
while (line != null)
{
    roll = Integer.parseInt (line);
    count ++;
    sum += roll;
    sumOfSquares += roll * roll;
    line = input.readLine ();
}
double average = (double) sum/count;
double variance = (double) sumOfSquares/count – average * average;
c.println ("Average=" + average + " Variance=" + variance);
```

# 6.10  Chapter Summary

This chapter discusses the input of data from the keyboard, which is the **standard input** device, and from files. As well, the output of data to files is presented.

## Entering Programs

Programs are entered using the environment editor. Syntax errors are reported at compilation time and corrections can be made. When there are no errors, the program can be run. If results do not match what is expected, the program must contain semantic errors. These errors must be found and corrected.

# Input of Data

Java provides a way of reading data from the standard input device (the keyboard). There are no built-in facilities for reading primitive data types. Only single characters or entire lines can be input. This is done using a predefined object *System.in* of the *InputStream* class. *InputStream* provides only for the reading of single characters. To achieve the reading of entire lines, *System.in* must be converted to a *DataInputStream* with the statement

*DataInputStream stdin =***new** *DataInputStream (System.in);*

which provides the *readLine* method.

Input and output is through a system console window. Input is echoed as it is entered.

The hsa *Console* class was devised to make input and output of data much simpler. The methods of the hsa *Console* class permit the input and output of all primitive data types. Moreover, output can be formatted.

## Input of Sequences of Data

Many computer applications involve the input of a sequence of data of the same data type. This requires the use of a repetition construct in the program. There are two basic types of repetition constructs.

• In the **counted loop** an **index** changes incrementally as each data item is input. The form of this construct is:

**for** (index declaration and initialization; continuation condition;
    index incrementation)
{
    body of **for** loop
}

The body of a **for** loop consists of the statement or statements in curly braces. The usual style is to indent the body a few spaces from the beginning and ending braces of the construct. This **paragraphing** makes the program easier to understand. If the body contains only one statement the curly braces are not necessary but can be used nevertheless. For consistency, we tend to use them in many cases where the body has only one statement.

- In the **conditional loop** used in this chapter, data items are processed until a continuation condition becomes false. Then control exits from the loop to the statement after the loop's enclosing curly brace. The loop begins with the keyword **while** followed by a **continuation condition** in parentheses.

## Input from a File

To read **text data** from a file, an *input* object of class *BufferedReader* is instantiated by a statement such as

*input = **new** BufferedReader (new FileReader (fileName));*

All output to a text file is as strings of characters. Files of strings are terminated by **null**.

## Output to a File

To write text data to a named file, an object of type *PrintWriter* is declared and instantiated by chaining to a class *FileWriter* by statements of this type

*PrintWriter output;*
*output = **new** PrintWriter (**new** FileWriter (fileName));*

## Generated Data

Instead of preparing files of data from actual problems, large quantities of data can be automatically generated. This can be done using the method *random* from the *Math* class. These values are uniformly distributed, meaning that if many values were generated, there would result approximately the same number of each of the possible subranges of values. A program that produces simulated data for throws of two dice was shown.

## Statistical Analysis of Data

A program was shown for computing the **average** and **variance** for a sequence of numerical data items stored in a file. These statistical measures are useful in understanding how data is distributed among possible values.

# 6.11  Technical Terms

| | |
|---|---|
| average | range |
| conditional loop | sentinel |
| counted loop | signal |
| counting index | standard input |
| execution phase | standard output |
| null | throwing an I/O exception |
| overloaded | variance |
| prompt | |

# 6.12  Exercises

1. Write a program that creates a table of the even integers and their squares. The columns of the table should be properly labelled. Arrange that the values of integers go from 10 to 360. Store this table in a file called "squares". Now, in the same program, read the file "squares" and add a third column which is the square root of the *squares* column. Store the output in the file "table2". Using the environment editor, examine the file "table2" to see how closely the first and third columns agree.

2. Write a program that generates a student's exam mark out of 100 by producing 10 random numbers ranging from 0 to 10 and adding them. Output the sequence of 10 marks and their average.

3. A series of marks for an examination is to be averaged. Write a program that first asks the user to enter the number of marks in the series then generates this number of marks by the method shown in Exercise 2. Test it for the extreme cases where the number is 0 or 1.

4. Prepare a file called "exammark" of 100 generated exam marks using the method of exercise 2, that is, where each mark is a sum of 10 random integers between 0 and 10. Find the average and variance of the marks stored in the file "exammark".

# Chapter 7

# Control Constructs

So far we have introduced many of the basic concepts of programming: primitive data types, assignment statements, input and output statements, and comments. In this chapter we will look at **structured statements.** These **constructs** can change the flow of execution of a program from a linear sequence of execution of statements to either **repetition** or **selection.** We have already made simple use of some of these **control constructs,** namely repetition, which includes both the counted **for** loop and the **conditional while** loop. In this chapter we will examine the loop constructs in more detail, and present several selection constructs.

# 7.1   Structure within Methods

Within the methods of a program there are groups of statements that form substructures. These are the control constructs. The three basic kinds of control constructs are:

- **Linear Sequence** where statements are executed one after the other in the order in which they are written.
- **Repetition** where a group of statements is to be executed repeatedly.
- **Selection** where one group of statements is selected for execution from a number of alternatives, depending on a test upon data.

The realization that all algorithms could be expressed in terms of using these three basic control constructs appeared in the early 1970s and formed the basis of what is known as structured programming. Before that time, the structure of programs could be quite complex and trying to follow the sequence of execution in a program was like untangling a plate of spaghetti. It was therefore the custom to provide charts along with the program to show the sequence of execution or **flow of control.** Figure 7.1 shows the **flow chart** for a program with nested **while** loops.

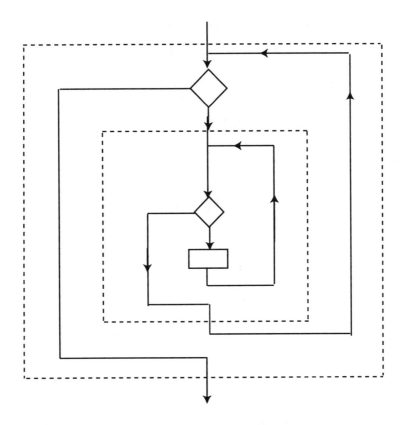

**Figure 7.1 Flow Chart of Nested While Loops**

Dotted lines forming a box surround each loop, one nested inside the other. There is a single flow line entering each box and a single line leaving. This would be true for any of the three basic control constructs.

Flow charts are not really necessary in structured programs. High-level languages were developed to make it easy to use the three basic control constructs, which when used exclusively, make it impossible to create "spaghetti programs".

Programmers now use **structure charts** or landscapes. These charts express the relationships and the **flow of data** among objects and methods, rather than flow of control.

# 7.2   Repetition Constructs

We have already introduced the two basic repetition constructs: the counted **for** loop and the conditional **while** loop. In this section we will provide a more detailed description of these kinds of repetition.

## 7.2.1   The Counted Loop

In Java, the counted loop begins with the keyword **for**. The body of the loop is enclosed in curly braces. It is thus easy to spot the **scope** or extent of the loop. To make it even easier, the style in writing programs is to indent the **body** of the loop. This is called paragraphing or pretty printing the loop structure.

The syntax of a **for** construct is:

```
for (index declaration and initialization;
        continuation condition; incrementation statement)
{
        body of repetition
}
```

Note that the three components in parentheses after the **for** are separated by semicolons and that the line does not have a semicolon after the right parenthesis. The index is sometimes called the **control variable** or **counter**.

In most of the counted loop examples we have shown so far, no particular use is made of the **index** of the loop except to count the number of times the loop has been repeated. Within the scope of the loop, its value can be used in the statements of the loop body. Its value should not be altered however.

Here is an example program to compute the sum of the squares of integers from 1 to 100 inclusive.

```
// The "SumSquares" class.
// Compute the sum of the squares of integers from 1 to 100.
int sum = 0;
for (int number = 1; number <= 100; number ++)
{
    sum += number * number;
}
c.println ("Sum of squares of numbers from 1 to 100 is " + sum);
```

Here the index *number* is used to calculate the square to be added to the sum. Notice that the index *number* is declared as an integer variable. It has a scope that is the extent of the loop construct and it is not known outside the loop. To ask for the output of *number* outside the loop would result in a syntax error.

The amount by which the index changes on each repetition is controlled by the incrementation statement. If, in the previous example, only the sum of the squares of the odd numbers was wanted, the first line of the construct would be

```
for (int number = 1; number <= 100; number +=2)
```

Here the index *number* would be in turn 1, 3, 5 ... 99. If the increment 2 were added to 99 it would be 101, which would exceed the upper limit of the **range**, so the last iteration happens with *number* set to 99.

An endless loop can be achieved by using the **for** loop with blank initialization, continuation, and incrementation as in

```
for (;;)
```

The semicolons separating the three blank components remain.

Here is an example of a program that computes the value of the product of successive integers beginning with the highest requested down to the lowest requested.

```
// The "ProductofSuccessiveIntegers" class.
// Computes the product of integers from highest to lowest.
int highest, lowest;
c.println ("Enter the highest integer");
highest = c.readInt ();
c.println ("Enter the lowest integer");
lowest = c.readInt ();
int product = 1;
for (int count = highest ; count >= lowest ; count—)
{
    product = product * count;
    c.println ("Product is " + product);
}
```

Here the counting index count is being decreased by 1 on each repetition.

## 7.2.2   The Conditional Loop

There are two forms of the conditional repetition. One is referred to as a **while** construct and it has this form:

```
while (continuation condition)
{
    statements of while construct
}
```

The other is referred to as a **do** construct and it has this form.

```
do
{
    statements of do construct
}
while (continuation condition);
```

The difference between these two is where the continuation condition is tested. In the **while** the continuation condition is tested at the beginning and in the **do** it is tested at the end. Notice that in the **do** loop there is a semicolon after the continuation condition.

If there is only one statement in the body of a **for, while,** or **do** construct. then it need not be enclosed in curly braces. In this book, however, for consistency we usually use braces even if there is only one statement.

It is possible to write programs using just conditional loops and no counted loops. Here is an example where a conditional loop does the same thing as a counted loop. The problem is similar to one we solved before using a counted loop: to sum the squares of the first 100 integers.

```
// The "Sum100" class.
// Sum the first 100 integers.
int sum = 0;
int number = 1;
while (number <= 100)
{
    sum += number;
    number ++;
}
c.println ("Sum of first 100 integers is " + sum);
```

In this example the index *number* is declared as an integer and initialized to 1 outside the loop. Inside the loop, at the beginning, the *index* number is tested to see if it has reached the upper limit of the range. At the end of the loop's body the index *number* is increased by 1. The counted loop does these operations:

- setting the initial value of the index,
- testing to see if it has reached its upper limit, and
- increasing it by 1 on each iteration.

The counted loop is definitely convenient, but not essential.

The principal difference between the **while** and **do** constructs is that the **while** loop can be executed zero times but the **do** loop must be executed at least once. We will show more examples of the **while** loop in later sections of this chapter.

An infinite conditional loop can be obtained using the starting expression

**while**(true)

After we look at the selection construct we will show how this can be combined with the **break** statement to permit an exit from within the body of the conditional loop rather than at the beginning of end.

## 7.2.3   Testing of Loops

It is important to make sure that a loop produces the desired results. The loop should be tested to see that the program works properly when the loop body is executed zero times, once, a typical number of times, and where an attempt is made to have it execute an inappropriate number of times.

As an example, consider a program that uses a conditional loop to find the sum of the first *n* integers, where the user enters the value *n*.

```
// The "SumInts" class.
// Find the sum of the first n integers.
int n;
c.println ("Enter a positive integer or 0");
n = c.readInt ();
int sum = 0;
int number = 0;
while (number < n)
{
    number ++;
    sum += number;
}
c.println ("Sum of first " + n + " integers is " + sum);
```

Values of *n* should be tested for at least 0, 1, 10, and −2. The program should be run for these values and the results checked against known answers. It is helpful that we know the answer is given by the formula

$$n (n + 1) / 2$$

where *n* must be a positive integer. The result could be calculated by hand if a formula were not available.

In testing programs with loops it is often helpful to insert an output statement in the body of the loop to print the value of the index of a counted loop or the variables that are changing on each iteration. This can be removed when the program is working properly.

# 7.3    Basic Selection Constructs

The basic form of the **if** selection construct is:

```
if (condition)
{
      statements of if clause
}
else
{
      statements of else clause
}
```

The condition is evaluated and, if it is true, the sequence of statements in the **if clause** is executed. Alternatively, if the condition is false, the sequence of statements of the **else clause** is executed. Only one of the two alternative sequences is executed, depending on the truth or falsity of the condition. The condition is, of course, a boolean expression. If there is only one statement in a clause it need not be surrounded by curly braces.

Here is an example in which a selection construct is nested in a repetition construct.

```
// The "PassFail" class.
// Read a sequence of exam marks and indicate whether each mark
// is a pass or fail.
// The sequence of marks is terminated by a sentinel –1.
int mark;
final int SENTINEL = –1;
c.println ("Enter marks of exams, end with " + SENTINEL);
mark = c.readInt ();
while (mark != SENTINEL)
{
      if (mark >= 50)
      {
            c.println ("The mark " + mark + " is a pass");
      }
      else
      {
            c.println ("The mark " + mark + " is a failure");
```

```
        }
        mark = c.readInt ();
    }
c.println ("The end");
```

Notice that the first mark must be read outside the **while** construct since it must be tested in the continuation condition. The next mark is read on each repetition at the end of the body of the **while** construct.

Here is a sample execution window for this program.

```
Enter marks of exam, end with –1
68
The mark 68 is a pass
35
The mark 35 is a failure
–1
The end
```

When the sentinel is read, the statement following the **while** construct would be executed. In the program the sentinel is labelled **final** in its declaration. This means its value is constant and cannot be changed.

If there is nothing to be done in the **else** clause of a selection then the keyword **else** is omitted and the selection becomes either executing the **if** clause, or doing nothing. Here is an example.

```
// The "PassPercent" class.
// Compute the percentage of pass marks in a sequence of exam marks.
int mark;
final int SENTINEL = –1;
c.println ("Enter marks of exams, end with " + SENTINEL);
int countOfPasses = 0;
int countOfMarks = 0;
mark = c.readInt ();
while (mark != SENTINEL)
{
    countOfMarks ++;
    if (mark >= 50)
    {
        countOfPasses ++;
    }
```

```
        mark = c.readInt ();
}
c.print ("Percentage passed is ");
c.print ((double) (countOfPasses * 100) / countOfMarks);
c.println ("%");
```

Selection can be made among more than two alternatives. A three-way selection is done using one **if...else...** construct nested inside a second.

Here is an example of a three-way selection where people riding buses are classified by age as: students (12 years old or less), adults, or seniors (65 years old or more).

```
// The "BusFare" class.
// Read sequence of ages counting
// the number of students, seniors, and adults.
final int SENTINEL = -1;
int student = 0, adult = 0, senior = 0;
c.println ("Enter ages, end with " + SENTINEL);
int age;
age = c.readInt ();
while (age != SENTINEL)
{
    if (age >= 65)
        senior ++;
    else
        if (age <= 12)
            student ++;
        else
            adult ++;
    age = c.readInt ();
}
c.println ("senior=" + senior + " adult=" + adult + " student=" + student);
```

In the loop a second **if...else...** construct is nested in the **else** clause of the first **if...else...**. Since an **if...else...** construct is considered to be a single statement, the nested **if...else...** does not require curly braces.

In each of the previous examples **while** loops were used. In the continuation condition of each, a variable's value was compared to a sentinel. In order for this condition to be evaluated at the beginning of the execution, an initial value of the variable had to be read in outside the loop. Then, at the end of the loop, a new value of the variable in the condition was read in. The statements that did this were identical: one outside the loop and one inside. There is an alternate form of a conditional loop that makes use of the **if** and **break** statements. This can provide an **exit** from the loop anywhere between the beginning and end.

Here is a program equivalent to the last example using the **if** and **break** statements.

```
// The "BusFare2" class.
// Read sequence of ages counting the number of students,
// seniors, and adults.
final int SENTINEL = –1;
int student = 0, adult = 0, senior = 0;
int age;
c.println ("Enter ages, end with " + SENTINEL);
while (true)
{
    age = c.readInt ();
    // Test exit condition.
    if (age == SENTINEL)
        break;
    if (age >= 65)
        senior ++;
    else if (age <= 12)
        student ++;
    else
        adult ++;
}
c.println ("senior = " + senior + " adult = " + adult + " student = "
        + student);
```

Rather than testing a continuation condition involving a variable at the beginning of the **while** loop, this form of the **while** loop uses the continuation condition **true**. This means that the loop would keep running endlessly unless there were an **exit condition** somewhere inside the loop's body. The exit here is

> **if** (*age* == *SENTINEL*)
>     **break**;

Note that the **exit condition** is the opposite of the continuation condition. The **break** statement gives control to the statement following the loop's body if the exit condition is true. In other words, execution then continues from the statement following the loop's body.

This variation means that conditional loops can be written with an exit anywhere that is convenient, rather than being restricted to the beginning, as in the ordinary **while** loop, or the end in the **do** loop. Notice that this simplifies the program.

In writing this version of the program a slightly different kind of paragraphing was used for the nested **if...else** statements. When there are many layers of nesting, this format prevents the program listing from "drifting" to the right. We have not used curly braces since the **if** and **else** clauses consisted of only single statements.

The **continue** statement is similar to the **break** statement except that rather than going to the statement following the loop, as **break** does, it merely goes to the end of the loop body.

# 7.4   Flow Charts

Producing correct programs requires programmers to understand flow of control. Although paragraphing of programs makes it unnecessary to draw a diagram showing the flow of control through a program, producing a diagram for each of the basic control constructs can be very helpful.

A sequence of instructions can be represented by a box with an arrow entering the box and an arrow leaving it (see Figure 7.2).

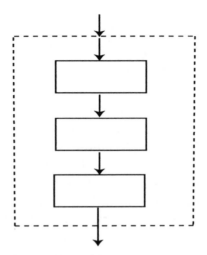

**Figure 7.2 Flow Chart of Sequence**

A **while** conditional repetition construct can be represented by the diagram in Figure 7.3. When the continuation condition is true, the remaining statements of the loop are executed and control returns to the beginning of the loop. When the continuation condition is false, control leaves the construct.

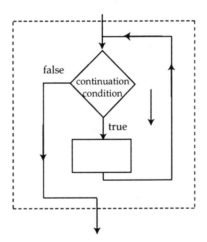

**Figure 7.3 Flow Chart of While Conditional Repetition**

A two-way selection can be represented by the diagram in Figure 7.4.

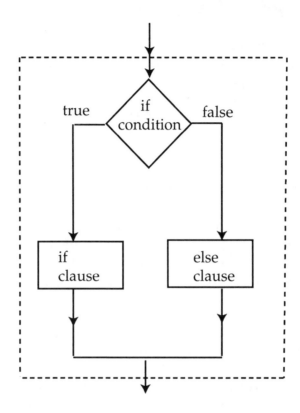

Figure 7.4 Flow Chart of Two-way Selection

Around each of the basic diagrams there is a dotted box. There is only one entry point into each box and one exit point from each box.

Any one of the three constructs can be nested inside the box of another construct. For example, the if clause of a selection may have a sequence nested in it. Any one of the boxes of the sequence may, in turn, contain a repetition construct. One of the boxes of the repetition may contain another repetition construct, and so on. The flow chart of Figure 7.1 shows one loop nested inside another.

# 7.5   Tracing Execution

In trying to write programs that are correct, it is very helpful to simulate the action of the computer and follow the sequence of execution of the statements. As the process proceeds, the user records the values of variables that are changed after any statement that changes their values. As well as variables, the values of any **for** loop indexes are recorded.

This process of tracing is usually done on paper away from the computer and is known as **desk-checking** a program. The hope is to spot any errors and eliminate them before the program is run on the computer.

In programming a loop, a common error is to have one too many, or one too few, repetitions. These are called **off-by-one errors**. Loops should be traced with data that tests extreme conditions.

Frequently a programming environment contains a **debugging** facility that executes the statements one after the other at slow speed or at a one-statement-at-a-time pace. The values of the variables and indexes are displayed as the process goes on. For a debugging facility to be useful, the programmer must already have a good idea of what to expect at each stage so that when an error occurs, it can be spotted and the error corrected. Quick fixes at the keyboard often prove disastrous so that a little forethought is, in the end, the best course of action.

# 7.6   Another Selection Construct

Any multi-way selection can be programmed using nested **else ...ifs** but under certain circumstances there is a possible alternative. This is the **switch** or **case construct**.

Here is an example program fragment that assigns a letter grade to exam marks. If there are several case values that require the same action, these cases can be listed, separated by colons, before the action required.

```
// The "LetterGrades" class.
// Produce letter grades from marks for test.
int A = 0, B = 0, C = 0, D = 0, F = 0;   //These are not constants.
int mark;
c.println ("Enter marks end with –1");
mark = c.readInt ();
while (mark != –1)
{
    switch (mark)
    {
        case 8: case 9: case 10:
            A ++;
            break;
        case 7:
            B ++;
            break;
        case 6:
            C ++;
            break;
        case 5:
            D ++;
            break;
        case 0: case 1: case 2: case 3: case 4:
            F ++;
            break;
        default:
            c.println ("Mark is incorrect, enter again");
            break;
    }
    mark = c.readInt ();
}
c.println ("A = " + A);
c.println ("B = " + B);
.. and so on
```

In the **switch** construct the statements in each **case** clause are not enclosed in curly braces. If the **break** statement is omitted then the statements of the following alternative are also executed. The **default** clause must be the last alternative and is executed when no earlier match occurs.

When several cases have the same requirements, the different cases are separated by colons preceding the statements that are to be executed. In the example, this is equivalent to having no statements in the **case 8** clause or the **case 9** clause. Since there is no **break** statement, the statements of the **case 9** clause are executed. Thus all three cases: 8, 9, and 10, have the statements of **case** 10 executed.

Here is another example program using the **switch** construct. It is somewhat simpler since each input produces a different response. In the previous example a grade of F could be produced with any one of 5 different marks. This program displays a menu to the user of possible inputs: 1 - sing, 2 - cry, and so on.

```java
// The "Respond" class.
// Choose a response.
import hsa.Console;

public class Respond
{
    public static void main (String [] args)
    {
        Console c = new Console ();
        int command;

        while (true)
        {
            c.print ("Choose from 1–sing, 2–cry, 3–laugh, 4–stop: ");
            command = c.readInt ();

            if (command == 4)
                break;

            switch (command)
            {
                case 1:
                    c.println ("La la la");
                    break;
                case 2:
                    c.println ("Boo hoo");
                    break;
                case 3:
```

```
                    c.println ("Ha ha ha");
                    break;
                default:
                    c.println ("I don't understand");
                    break;
            }
        }
    } // main method
} /* Respond class */
```

It is also possible to use single characters rather than integers as the **case** labels. For example, this program asks the user to enter a number to indicate the selection and then executes the **switch** statement using that number. The programmer could instead have written the program to accept a single character. This would require changing the **switch** statement and the statement which reads the input. The program might then display this menu.

```
    c.print ("Choose from 's' - sing, 'c' - cry, 'l' - laugh, 'f' - finish: ");
```

Then the individual cases are labelled as **case** 's', **case** 'c', and so on. Note that the single character labels are in single quotes and each one must be different.

Here is an example program where constants, such as LEFT_VOTE, that have integer values are used to identify the different cases. This perhaps makes the program easier to understand. Java only allows integers or single characters as case labels.

```
// The "Voting" class.
import hsa.Console;

public class Voting
{
    static final int LEFT_VOTE = 1;
    static final int MIDDLE_VOTE = 2;
    static final int RIGHT_VOTE = 3;

    public static void main (String [] args)
    {
```

```
Console c = new Console ();
int vote;
int left = 0, middle = 0, right = 0;
final int SIGNAL = -1;

c.println ("Vote 1 for Left, 2 for Middle, 3 for Right, end with " +
    SIGNAL);

while (true)
{
    c.print ("Enter vote: ");
    vote = c.readInt ();

    if (vote == SIGNAL)
        break;

    switch (vote)
    {
        case LEFT_VOTE:
            left++;
            break;
        case MIDDLE_VOTE:
            middle++;
            break;
        case RIGHT_VOTE:
            right++;
            break;
        default:
            c.println ("Invalid vote");
            break;
    }
}
c.print ("Left", 8);
c.print ("Middle", 8);
c.println ("Right", 8);
c.print (left, 8);
c.print (middle, 8);
c.println (right, 8);
} // main method
} /* Voting class */
```

# 7.7   Checking Input Data

Runtime errors occur in programs if input data is not appropriate and preparation in the program has not been made for such inappropriate or bad data. In the *LetterGrades* class program, if the user enters an integer that is not in the range 0 and 10 or the sentinel −1, the **default** option of the **switch** statement gives the user the error message

> Mark is incorrect, enter again

We say that such a program is forgiving − that the user has a second chance to enter appropriate data rather than having execution stop.

This would not work however if, by mistake, the user entered the letter *B* instead of the mark 7. An **exception** would be thrown when the statement

> *mark = c.readInt ();*

was executed and the system attempted to interpret *B* as an integer and failed. An error message would appear and execution would stop.

Handling such exceptions is possible in Java with a little more programming. This technique of handling bad data is based on the fact that any input data, whether an integer, a real number, or a string, can be read as a string by *readLine*, without causing an exception. After it has been read in as a string, it can be parsed to see if it is an integer (**int**) or a real number (**float** or **double**). In the *letterGrades* class program a variable *markStr* would be declared as a *String* and the statement

> *mark = c.readInt ();*

would be replaced by these statements

```
while (true)
{
    try
    {
        String markStr = c.readLine ();
        mark = Integer.parseInt (markStr);
        break;
    }
```

```
catch (NumberFormatException e)
{
    c.println ("Bad mark, try again");
}
}
```

The input statement

```
markStr = c.readLine ();
```

is in a **while** (**true**) loop where the exit occurs with the **break** if the string *markStr* can be successfully parsed as an integer. The attempt to read and parse it is preceded by the keyword **try**, and parsing occurs in the statement

```
mark = Integer.parseInt (markStr);
```

In this statement the *parseInt* method of the *Integer* class tries to produce an integer from the string *markStr*. If it succeeds, it exits from the **while** loop at the **break**. If it throws an exception, the instructions in the **catch** clause are executed. The **catch** statement has a parameter that specifies the type of exception that is being caught, which in this case is a *NumberFormatException*.

In Java there are different kinds of exceptions that can be caught and **exception handling** is extremely important in software that is to be user friendly and able to cope with errors made by the user without having them stop execution.

In the *LetterGrades* class program the input statement

```
mark = c.readInt ();
```

occurs twice, once just before the **while** and again at the end of the loop body. If we leave the loop this way the "forgiving input loop" must be included twice. It is perhaps simpler to use the form

```
while (true)
{
    forgiving input loop
    if (mark = -1) break;
    switch statement
}
```

# 7.8   Common Programming Errors

Many of the simplest programming errors involve semicolons. These are:

- Forgetting the semicolon after a statement.
- Using a semicolon after the header of

  a **do** or **while** loop,

  an **if** condition, or

  a **switch** construct.
- Using a semicolon after a closing curly brace.

Other errors involve the use of curly braces. Common ones are:

- Omitting curly braces when there is a single statement in an **if** or **else** clause or in a **for** loop and later adding another statement without adding the curly braces.
- Forgetting a closing curly brace particularly when constructs are nested and two curly braces are required, one after the other.

Common errors in **switch** constructs are:

- Not using a colon after the case label.
- Not repeating the keyword **case** before each value of the label when a number of values share the same statements.
- Forgetting to include the **break** as the last statement of each alternative except when it is specifically intended that the next alternative also be tested.

Common errors in **for** loops are:

- Forgetting to include the data type of the index variable in its declaration and initialization.
- Having the continuation condition count one too few or one to many executions by confusing the relations <= and < or > and >=.
- Not using semicolons between the initialization, continuation, and incrementation components.
- Attempting to change the value of a counting index inside the body of the loop.

- Attempting to output the value of a loop's index outside the body of the loop.

Common errors in conditional loops are:

- Forgetting the parentheses around the continuation condition.
- Forgetting to initialize any variable in the continuation condition of a **while** loop outside the loop itself.
- Forgetting to alter the value of a variable in the continuation condition inside the loop so that it changes from one iteration to the next.
- Forgetting that the body of a **do** loop will be executed at least once.
- Forgetting the semicolon after the continuation condition of a **do** loop.

Common errors in selection constructs are:

- Forgetting the parentheses around the condition.
- Forgetting the relationship of the **if**s and **else**s when selections are nested. An **else** always belongs to the nearest **if** preceding it in the program.

# 7.9   Chapter Summary

## Control Constructs

This chapter discusses the structure within methods. Ultimately all methods can be created out of three basic **control constructs**:

- **linear sequence** where statements are executed one after the other,
- **repetition** where certain statements are repeatedly executed for a fixed number of times (**counted repetition**), or until some condition is false (**conditional repetition**), and
- **selection** where one sequence of statements is selected from alternative sequences depending on a condition.

# Flow Charts

The **flow of control** in the execution of a method can be represented by a **flow chart**. Diagrams of this sort were prevalent before structured programming became the accepted style for programs. At that time, many programs had complicated sequences of execution of their instructions. These programs were referred to as "spaghetti" programs.

The control structure of structured programs can be easily followed by reading the program itself, without a supplementary flow chart, particularly if the body of each construct is indented to indicate its **scope**.

The flow charts of the three basic control constructs: sequence, repetition, and selection were shown.

# Repetition Constructs

Of the two basic repetition constructs, the **conditional loop** is the primary one in that a **counted loop** can be programmed using a conditional loop, whereas the reverse is not possible. Counted loops begin with the keyword **for**. Following the **for** in parentheses are three components separated by semicolons. These are:

- the declaration and initialization of the index,
- the continuation condition, and
- the increment of the index on each execution of the loop.

The value of the index can be used in statements inside the loop but is not available outside the loop.

Conditional loops may begin with the keyword **while** followed in parentheses by the continuation condition. The body of the loop is in curly braces. The other form of the conditional loop begins with the keyword **do** and ends with **while** followed in parentheses by the continuation condition followed by a semicolon.

A variation of the conditional loop, where an exit is achieved at any place inside the body of the loop, can be done using the header

**while (true)**

and having within the body the statement

**if** (exit condition) **break;**

## Selection Constructs

The form of the basic selection construct is:

```
if (condition)
{
    statements of if clause
}
else
{
    statements of else clause
}
```

If the condition following the **if** is true, the statements of the **if** clause are selected and executed; if false, the statements of the **else clause** are executed. If there are no statements in the **else** clause, the keyword **else** is omitted.

The basic selection is a two-way choice between two alternatives. To achieve multi-way selection, nested **if...else** constructs are used for additional alternatives.

## Tracing Execution

Following the sequence of execution of the statements for a variety of input data helps produce correct programs even before they are run. This process, called **desk checking** or **tracing**, helps the programmer find errors. The process of finding and fixing errors is called **debugging**.

Often programmers are tempted to run a program immediately on the computer and fix errors without much thought. This often prolongs the process of producing a correct program.

When tracing loops, extreme values of the test data should be tested. If a sequence of data items is to be processed, sequences of length 0 and 1 should be checked.

## The Switch Construct

Multi-way selection can be achieved using a **switch** or **case construct**. The keyword **switch** is followed by a selection expression whose possible values of the selection expression correspond to the values following the keyword **case** in a sequence of alternatives in the form

> **case** value of selection expression : statements for this alternative

If two selection expression values require the same consequences, they are listed, separated by colons, each preceded by the keyword **case**. After the statements of an alternative, the statement

> **break**;

must appear unless it is intended that the statements of the next case also be executed.

The selector variable can be an integer or a character. The final alternative can have no values of case following the keyword **default**. It is executed if the case selector expression`s value does not equal any case value of the other cases.

**Switch** structures are often used where a **menu** of alternatives is displayed for a user to make a selection.

## Checking Bad Data

If data of the wrong data type is entered by a user, a runtime error will stop execution. If all data is read as string data, no error occurs.

A program can be designed to handle bad numerical data by reading it as a string and parsing it. The reading and parsing is preceded by the keyword **try** and, if the parsing throws a *NumberFormatException*, it can be caught by a **catch** clause. This can output an error message and allows the user to attempt to enter an appropriate data type. The **try** and **catch** are enclosed in a loop which is exited when the data is appropriate.

# 7.10 Technical Terms

| | |
|---|---|
| case construct | flow of control |
| catch statement | flow of data |
| control variable | index |
| counter | linear sequence |
| debugging | off-by-one error |
| desk checking | scope |
| do construct | selection |
| exception handling | structure chart |
| exit condition | switch construct |
| flow chart | while construct |

# 7.11 Exercises

1. A sequence of integers is stored in a file called "ages". Write a program to find the range of ages present, that is the difference between the oldest and the youngest.

2. Write a program to show how a mortgage on a house will be paid off (amortized) over a certain number of years given the amount of the mortgage, the proposed annual payment, and the annual interest rate charged.

   Prepare a table showing the amount of interest and capital paid in each year, and the final balance owing at the year's end. Label the columns of the table. Show also the total interest paid during the amortization.

3.  Federal income tax is charged at these rates:

    17% on the first $29,590 of taxable income,

    26% on the next $29,590 of taxable income, and

    29% on any income in excess of $59,180.

    Write a program to compute the tax for any taxable income submitted by the user. Have the program work for a series of taxpayers until a negative taxable income is entered.

4.  Simulated data representing exam marks out of 100 can be prepared by generating each mark as the sum of marks of 10 questions each out of 10. Generate a mark for each question as a random integer from 0 to 10. The exam marks so generated will not be uniformly distributed, as the integers generated by a single call to *random*, but will be close to a normal or Gaussian distribution (sometimes referred to as a Bell curve). Prepare a file of simulated data representing a class of 200 students and call it *examdata*.

5.  Write a statistical analysis program. It is to read the file *examdata* prepared in the previous exercise and determine the percentage of the class that would get various grades: A (80 or over), B (70-79), C (60-69), D (50-59), and F (below 50). Have it tabulate these statistics. Run this analysis program again using, as input, a file of simulated data of uniformly distributed exam marks. Compare the results with those that are closer to a Bell curve.

# Chapter 8

# Strings

In Java there are only a few primitive data types: those pertaining to numbers both integer and real, the boolean type, and two not mentioned so far: **char** and **byte**. One data type that is often primitive in other programming languages is the string data type. In Java the string is an abstract data type and a string variable is implemented as an object through the *String* class.

# 8.1   The String Data Type

The string data type is used for strings of characters such as names, addresses, phone numbers, and so on. For example, the string "elephant" contains eight characters. In a Java string the positions of the characters are numbered beginning at 0. In the zeroth position is the letter "e" in the first position is the letter "l", and so on. The **length** of the string is 8. This string

"148 O'Reilly St."

has 16 characters; the blanks and punctuation marks are characters. Each character is represented in Unicode which is 16 bits in length. The first 8 bits are the same as the ASCII code representation of a character.

As shown in Chapter 5, a string of characters in quotation marks (a string constant) can be output by a statement such as

*c.println* ("Here is a string of characters");

In an output statement it is possible to concatenate string constants and numbers using the + operator. In fact, the number is automatically converted to a string.

The conversion of objects to *String* objects is done by calling the *toString* () method of the object to be converted. Most Java class library objects support the *toString* () method. You can add a *toString* () method to your own classes to allow them to be converted to strings automatically. This is recommended because it makes debugging easier and is helpful to others using your class. Primitive data types, like **int** or **boolean** are automatically converted to strings when concatenated to other strings.

# 8.2   Declaring String Objects

In Java a string is an object. Declaring an object as a string requires use of the *String* class. For example, to declare a string object called *word* with the string "Charles" stored in it, these statements are required.

> *String word;*
> *word* = **new** *String* ("Charles");

This creates an object of *String* class called *word*. The string "Charles" is stored in *word*. A string constant such as "Charles" is automatically changed to a *String* object so that these can be abbreviated to the statement

> *String word* = "Charles";

The *String* class has a number of commonly-used methods. For example, the *substring* method can be used to extract a portion of a string object. There are two forms of the substring method. For the *String* object *word*

> *c.println (word.substring* (3));

produces the output

> *rles*

the substring of "Charles" starting at character position number 3 to the end of the string (the character positions start numbering at zero).

Alternatively, two actual parameters can be provided to the *substring* method. For example, the statement

> *c.println (word.substring* (2, 4));

produces the output

> *arl*

These are the characters in positions numbered 2 to 4 inclusive. The *String* class *length* method will provide the number of characters in the string. For example,

   *c.println (word.length ());*

produces the output 7, the length of the string "Charles". The *length* method has no parameters but empty parentheses must be included.

   The expression

   *c.println (word.substring (word.length () – 1 ));*

can be used to find the last character in a string. This character is in position *word.length () – 1*. The substring with one parameter goes from that character to the end of the string. Attempting to ask for a substring beyond the end of the string produces an **exception**. For example, the statement

   *c.println (word.substring (5, 8));*

produces an exception since the *word* has character positions only from 0 to 6. This kind of exception need not be notified in the *main* method's header as an *IOException* must be by adding **throws** *IOException*, but it will cause execution to stop.

   The *String* method *charAt* can be used to find the character at any string position. For example the statement

   *c.println (word.charAt (0));*

produces the output C, the first character in the string.

   Since a string constant such as "Charles" is automatically a *String* object, it can be used in any of the expressions where *word* is used with the same result. For example

   *c.println ("Charles".charAt (0));*

produces the output C.

   Here is an example program that reads in a word and outputs the characters of the word in reverse order.

```
// The "ReverseLetters" class.
// Reverses the letters in an input word.
String word;
c.print ("Enter a word: ");
word = c.readLine ();
for (int count = word.length () – 1 ; count >= 0 ; count– –)
{
    c.print (word.charAt (count));
}
c.println ();
```

A later example will show how the word with the reversed letters can be stored in the computer.

# 8.3   Concatenation of Strings

The concatenation operator + can be used in string expressions. Another way to concatenate two *String* objects to create a new *String* object, is to use the *String* class method *concat*. For example,

```
String s1 = "sea";
String s2 = "shore";
String s3 = s1.concat(s2);
c.println (s3);
```

results in the output

*seashore*

Notice that string *s1* and *s2* are not changed. After a string is assigned a value it cannot be changed.

Here is another example of concatenation which shows how a first and last name can be concatented in reverse order with the last name first. In this example the name is stored in this form.

Byron, Ada

```
// The "FullName" class.
// Combines first and last names.
String firstName = "Ada";
String lastName = "Byron";
String fullName = lastName + ", " + firstName;
c.println (fullName);
```

Here the *concat* method could not be used.

# 8.4   Replacing Characters in Strings

Individual characters in a string object can be replaced by other characters to create a new *String* object. For example, this program fragment

```
String s1 = "Mississippi";
String s2 = s1.replace('i', 'e');
c.println (s2);
c.println (s1);
```

produces the output

```
Messesseppe
Mississippi
```

Again notice that string *s1* is not changed.

Every occurrence of the character 'i' is replaced by the character 'e'. Single character constants like 'i' have single quotes around them. A single character is of primitive data type **char**. String constants like "our" have double quotes.

A special version of character replacement is obtained using the *String* class methods *toUpperCase* or *toLowerCase*. For example, if this statement were added to the previous program fragment

```
c.println (s1.toLowerCase());
```

the output would be

```
mississippi
```

Any upper case character is changed to a lower case one where possible. If the statement

   *c.println (s1.toUpperCase ());*

were added the output would be

   MISSISSIPPI

Lower case characters are changed to upper case where possible.

# 8.5   Searching for Patterns in Strings

The *String* class methods *indexOf* and *lastIndexOf* are useful in finding string patterns in other strings. For example, the program fragment

   *String vowels* = "aeiou";
   *c.println (vowels.indexOf ((**int**) 'i'));*

produces the output 2, the character position of the letter *i* in the *vowels* string. When the string pattern sought contains only one character, the character is in single quotes and must be cast as an integer. For a string pattern of more than one character, the pattern is enclosed in double quotes and is not cast as an integer. For example

   *c.println (vowels.indexOf ("eio"));*

produces the output 1, which is the position of the beginning of the substring "eio" in the string "aeiou". If the pattern is not in the string, the output is −1.

The last occurrence of the pattern in a string can be obtained using the method *lastIndexOf*.

The first occurrence of the pattern in the string starting at index *start* is found using the *indexOf* method with two parameters in this form

   *indexOf (String* pattern, **int** start)

Here is a program that reads a series of words ended by "*" and removes all the vowels in each word.

```
// The "Squish" class.
import hsa.Console;

public class Squish
{
    public static void main (String [] args)
    {
        Console c = new Console ();
        String word, newWord;
        final String VOWELS = "aeiouAEIOU";

        c.println ("Enter a series of words one to a line, end with '*' ");
        while (true)
        {
            word = c.readLine ();
            if (word.equals ("*"))
                break;
            newWord = "";
            for (int i = 0 ; i < word.length () ; i++)
            {
                if (VOWELS.indexOf (word.charAt (i)) == -1)
                {
                    newWord = newWord + word.charAt (i);
                }
            }
            c.println ("Word without vowels is " + newWord);
        }
    } // main method
} /* Squish class */
```

Here is an example execution of the *Squish* class.

Enter a series of words, end with '*'.
**elephant**
lphnt
**bicycle**
bcycl
**Extreme**
xtrm
*

The string *newWord* has the value initialized to the null string outside the **for** loop. Inside the loop it is assigned a new value whenever the character is not a vowel.

Here is a program to find the number of occurrences of a character in a string. When a character of type **char** is used instead of a string, it must be cast as an **int**.

```
// The "Occurs" class.
String word = "Mississippi";
int count = 0;
int index = 0;
int where;
char ch = 'i';
for (;;)
{
    where = word.indexOf ((int) ch, index);
    if (where != −1)
    {
        count ++;
        index = where + 1;
    }
    else
        break;
}
c.println ("There are "+ count + " occurrences of "
                + ch + " in the word " + word);
```

The **for** loop has null initialization, continuation, and incrementation so that a seemingly endless **for** loop would be produced. The exit occurs when the **else** clause is executed, that is, when *where* equals −1 and the **break** statement is executed. An endless **while** loop can be produced using **while (true)**.

# 8.6   Comparing Strings

Strings can be compared using the *String* class methods *equals, equalsIgnoreCase*, and *compareTo*. The boolean expression

   *s1.equals* (s2)

is true if *s1* and *s2* are strings of the same length and they have the same characters in the same sequence. Comparison of equality of strings ignoring the case of characters is obtained using the method *equalsIgnoreCase*. For example, this program fragment

```
String s1 = "Peter";
String s2 = "peter";
c.println (s1.equalsIgnoreCase(s2));
```

produces the output *true*.

Here is a program fragment that reads words until the word "stop" is entered and outputs each word a character at a time, one to a line.

```
// The "Spelling" class.
// Output the letters of words that are input.
String word;
word = c.readLine ();
while (!(word.equals ("stop")))
{
    for (int count = 0; count < word.length (); count ++)
    {
        c.println (word.charAt (count));
    }
    word = c.readLine ();
}
```

Notice that the *String* class does not have a *notEquals* method so that the exclamation mark indicating the *not* unary operator is used in front of the boolean expression

*word.equals* ("stop")

Here is a similar program fragment that reads words until the word "last" is entered and tests whether or not the word contains the letter "s".

```
// The "Ess" class.
import hsa.Console;

public class Ess
{
    public static void main (String [] args)
    {
        Console c = new Console ();
        String word;

        c.println ("Enter words, onto a line, end with \"last\"");
        while (true)
        {
            c.print ("Enter word: ");
            word = c.readLine ();
            if (word.equals ("last"))
                break;
            if (word.indexOf ('s') != -1)
                c.println (word + " contains an 's' ");
            else
                c.println (word + " does not contain an 's' ");
        }
    } // main method
} /* Ess class */
```

Notice that to include "last" in the quoted prompt each double quotation mark had to be preceded by a backslash \. We could instead have used single quotes around the sentinel in the prompt, namely as 'last'. The words must be entered one to a line since they are being read by the *readLine* method of the console.

Strings can be put into sequence, normally in alphabetic order, using the *compareTo* method. If *s1* and *s2* are string objects that have been instantiated with string values the expression

    s1.compareTo (s2)

has a value 0 if the values of *s1* and *s2* are equal, is negative if *s1* is less than (comes before alphabetically) *s2*, and positive if *s1* comes after *s2*. The sequencing depends on the Unicode value of the characters. Capital (upper case) letters have different values than little (lower case) letters.

This program uses the *compareTo* method to find the alphabetically last of a series of names. The case of the names is to be ignored in determining the one that is alphabetically last.

```
// The "LastInList" class.
// Output the alphabetically last of a series of names,
// ended by a sentinel name.
String name, sentinel, last;
c.println ("What is the sentinel name? ");
sentinel = c.readLine ();
c.println ("Enter names, end with " + sentinel);
name = c.readLine ();
last = name.toLowerCase ();
while (! (name.equals (sentinel)))
{
    if (last.compareTo (name.toLowerCase ()) < 0)
    {
        last = name.toLowerCase ();
    }
    name = c.readLine ();
}
c.println ("Alphabetically last name is " + last);
```

An execution window for this program might be

> What is the sentinel name?
> **Yahoo**
> Enter names, end with Yahoo
> **Dog**
> **cat**
> **Zebra**
> **Lion**
> **unicorn**
> **Yahoo**
> Alphabetically last name is zebra

If only the sentinel is entered the final line would be

> Alphabetically last name is yahoo

Notice that the sentinel itself has been converted to lower case. The method *toLowerCase* is used so that it will not matter if some names are capitalized.

# 8.7   The StringBuffer Class

When a *String* object has been initialized its contents cannot be altered. The *StringBuffer* class, however, can be used to create strings whose actual contents can be changed. For example, this fragment

```
StringBuffer s1;
s1 = new StringBuffer ("Hello");
s1.append (" there");
c.println (s1);
```

produces the output

> Hello there

It is not correct to write the first two lines as

```
StringBuffer s1 = "Hello"
```

since "Hello" is a *String* object and cannot be assigned to initialize a *StringBuffer* object.

The *StringBuffer* class method *append* can be used to concatenate a string to the end of the present contents of the *StringBuffer* object.

Here is an example where a word is read in and the letters reversed to determine whether or not the string is a **palindrome** (a word or phrase that is the same backwards as forwards). It is assumed that all the letters are lower case (no capital letters).

```
// The "Palindrome1" class.
// Determines whether or not a word is a palindrome
// by reversing the letters.
String word;
c.println ("Enter a word");
word = c.readLine ();
StringBuffer reverse = new StringBuffer ();
for (int count = word.length () – 1; count >= 0; count--)
{
    reverse.append (word.charAt (count));
}
if (word.equals (reverse.toString ()))
    c.println ("The word " + word + " is a palindrome");
else
    c.println ("The word " + word + " is not a palindrome");
```

In the example it is assumed that all the letters in *word* are in lower case. A palindrome test normally should ignore the case of letters, so that a word such as *Madam* is a palindrome.

The *Palindrome1* class program could be made to do this by replacing the test

   **if** (*word.equals* (*reverse.toString* ()))

by the test

   **if** (*word.toLowerCase* ().*equals* (*reverse.toString* ().*toLowerCase* ()))

This unusual looking boolean expression is understood by noting that the method *toLowerCase* applies to a *String* object and yields a value that is a *String* object. This is known as a **cascaded method call** and is evaluated from left to right after the part in parentheses is evaluated.

You can always use *String* objects instead of *StringBuffer* objects by repeatedly creating new *String* objects with the changed contents. This, however is slower and wastes computer memory.

There are several methods of the *StringBuffer* class besides the *append* method that are useful.

- The *charAt* (**int** *n*) method has a value that is the character of the contents at index *n*.
- The *setCharAt* (**int** *n*, **char** *ch*) method sets the character at position *n* to *ch*.
- The *setLength* (**int** *n*) method sets the length of the buffer to *n*.
- The *toString* () method converts the *StringBuffer* object to a *String* object.
- The *insert* (**int** *n*, *arg*) method converts its second argument, which can be a primitive data type or any object that has a *toString* method, and inserts it into the present string in the buffer starting at character position *n*.

For example, this program fragment

```
StringBuffer s = new StringBuffer ("How   it is ");
s.insert (3, 7 > 6);
c.println (s.toString ());
```

would produce the output

How true it is

The boolean expression 7 > 6 has a value *true* which is converted to a string and inserted into the contents of *s* starting at position 3 which is after the first blank following *How*. Notice that there are two blanks after the word "How" in the program fragment.

# 8.8    The StringTokenizer Class

The *StringTokenizer* class is part of the *java.util* package. In order to use it

import *java.util.*;*

must be at the beginning of the program.

This class is principally used to divide a line of text into its tokens, where a token is a series of characters separated from its neighbors by **white space** and where white space consists of blanks, end of lines, or tabs.

In this example, a line of text will be read in and its tokens output one to a line and counted. It uses several methods of the *StringTokenizer* class: *countTokens* to find the number of tokens in the line, *nextToken* to find the next token in the line, and *hasMoreTokens* to determine when the last token of the line has been processed.

```
// The "WordsInLine" class.
// Read a line of text and output tokens one to a line.
String line;
c.println ("Enter a line of text");
line = c.readLine ();
StringTokenizer words = new StringTokenizer (line);
c.println ("Number of tokens in line is " + words.countTokens ());
c.println ("The words in line are: ");
while (words.hasMoreTokens ())
{
    c.println (words.nextToken ());
}
```

Here is a sample execution.

Enter a line of text
**How now brown cow**
Number of tokens in line is 4
The words in line are:
How
now
brown
cow

Here is a program called *Purge* that reads words from a file called "script" and outputs all of the four-letter words in the script to a file called "censor". The complete program is shown here since, as with all uses of reading from and writing to files, we must use the *java.io* and *java.util* libraries. The *main* method header must also include "**throws** *IOexception*".

```
// The "Purge" class.
import java.io.*;
import java.util.*;
import hsa.Console;

public class Purge
{
    public static void main (String [] args []) throws IOException
    {
        BufferedReader script;
        PrintWriter censor;
        script = new BufferedReader (new FileReader ("script"));
        censor = new PrintWriter (new FileWriter ("censor"));
        String word;

        while (true)
        {
            String line = script.readLine ();
            if (line == null)
                break;
            StringTokenizer words = new StringTokenizer (line);
            while (words.hasMoreTokens ())
            {
```

```
                    word = words.nextToken ();
                    if (word.length () == 4)
                    {
                        censor.println (word);
                    }
                }
            }
        script.close ();
        censor.close ();
    } // main method
} /* Purge class */
```

# 8.9   Text Processing

One of the important uses of computers is to process text. It is possible to format the text so that each line begins in a certain column and ends in a certain column. We say it is both left and right justified. Another common form is to have text left justified but leave the right side "ragged". Words are added to the line until the addition of the next word would produce a line longer than a fixed maximum.

Here is a program that reads a file named "text" and outputs a file named "ragged" with a ragged right side whose lines are as long as possible but no longer than a user-specified maximum length. The complete application program is shown here because some changes from the usual form are needed.

```java
// The "Justify" class.
import java.awt.*;
import java.io.*;
import java.util.*;
import hsa.Console;

public class Justify
{
    static Console c;

    static public void main (String [] args) throws IOException
```

```
{
    c = new Console ();
    // Reformat text in file "text" in ragged right style so that the
    // number of characters in the line is limited to a given
    // maximum. Store the revised text in file "ragged".
    int maxLength;
    c.println ("What is the maximum length of line? ");
    maxLength = c.readInt ();
    String inputLine;
    StringTokenizer inline;
    StringBuffer outline = new StringBuffer ();
    String infileName, outfileName;
    c.println ("What is the name of the input file? ");
    infileName = c.readLine ();
    BufferedReader input;
    input = new BufferedReader (new FileReader (infileName));
    c.println ("What is the name of the output file? ");
    outfileName = c.readLine ();
    PrintWriter output;
    output = new PrintWriter (new FileWriter (outfileName));
    inputLine = input.readLine ();
    int lineLength = 0;
    while (inputLine != null)
    {
        inline = new StringTokenizer (inputLine);
        while (inline.hasMoreTokens ())
        {
            String token = inline.nextToken ();
            if (lineLength + token.length () <= maxLength)
            {
                outline.append (token + " ");
                lineLength += token.length () + 1;
            }
            else
            {
                output.println (outline);
                lineLength = token.length () + 1;
                outline = new StringBuffer (token + " ");
            }
        }
        inputLine = input.readLine ();
    }
```

```
        // Print remaining partial line and close file.
        output.println (outline);
        output.close ();
    } // main method
} /* Justify class */
```

Notice that to the standard boilerplate we have added the line

> **import** *java.io.\*;*

and that the *main* method has

> **throws** *IOException*

added to the header. These changes are necessary when a program is reading from a file and writing to a file. Because the *StringTokenizer* class is to be used, the line

> **import** *java.util.\*;*

is also added.

As a second example of text processing, here is a program that eliminates the punctuation marks in a text. This program requires the examination of the characters in each line to see if the character is a punctuation mark. If it is not, the character is appended to the output line. The same changes in the standard boilerplate are necessary as in the previous program.

```
// The "RemovePunctuation" class.
// Eliminate all the punctuation marks from the file
// "text" and store the result in "text2".
final String PUNCTUATION = ",.:;'?!()\ "";
String inline;
StringBuffer outline = new StringBuffer ();
BufferedReader input;
input = new BufferedReader (new FileReader ("text"));
PrintWriter output;
output = new PrintWriter (new FileWriter ("text2"));
inline = input.readLine ();
while (inline != null)
{
```

```
    for (int index = 0; index < inline.length (); index++)
    {
        if (PUNCTUATION.indexOf (inline.charAt (index)) == –1)
            outline.append (inline.charAt (index));
    }
    output.println (outline);
    outline.setLength (0); // Set outline to have no characters.
    inline = input.readLine ();
}
output.close ();
```

Computers can also be used to help to translate from one language to another. This is done all the time with computer programming languages. The Java programs that you write are translated into the bytecode language by the Java compiler. Each computer platform must then interpret the bytecode language to its own machine code. To show how computers do translations, we will look at an example program that translates English text into Pig Latin.

Pig Latin is a very simple language sometimes used by adults to baffle little children, much as parents spell words to prevent them from being understood by the young. The translation rules from English to Pig Latin are very simple: each word that begins with a vowel has *way* added to the end of it; each word that begins with a consonant has the consonant moved to the end of the word and then has *ay* added. For example, the word "it" becomes "itway" and "girl" becomes "irlgay".

Here is the translation program. The original English text is in a file and the Pig Latin translation is written to a file. The names of these files must be supplied by the user. (Because files are involved we have included the complete program.)

```
// The "PigLatin" class.
import java.io.*;
import java.util.*;
import hsa.Console;

public class PigLatin
{
    public static void main (String [] args) throws IOException
```

```
        {
                Console c = new Console ();
                String fileName;
                BufferedReader inFile;
                PrintWriter outFile;

                c.print ("Enter the name of the file where the English is stored: ");
                fileName = c.readLine ();
                inFile = new BufferedReader (new FileReader (fileName));

                c.print ("Enter the name of the file for the Pig Latin: ");
                fileName = c.readLine ();
                outFile = new PrintWriter (new FileWriter (fileName));

                c.close ();

                String word;
                while (true)
                {
                        String line = inFile.readLine ();
                        if (line == null)
                                break;
                        StringTokenizer words = new StringTokenizer (line);
                        while (words.hasMoreTokens ())
                        {
                                word = words.nextToken ();
                                if ("aeiouAEIOU".indexOf (word.charAt (0)) != –1)
                                {
                                        outFile.print (word + "way ");
                                }
                                else
                                {
                                        outFile.print (word.substring (1) + word.charAt (0) +
                                                "ay ");
                                }
                        }
                }
                inFile.close ();
                outFile.close ();
        } // main method
} /* PigLatin class */
```

# 8.10  Chapter Summary

In Java (unlike many programming languages not including C) strings are objects of a *String* class rather than being of a primitive data type.

## The String Data Type

In a string the character positions are numbered from 0 to the length of the string minus 1. A string of length 8 has character positions 0, 1, 2, ..., 7. Strings can be concatenated using the + operator. In an output statement a string can consist of the concatenation of string constants, strings, and other primitive data types. If the string or string constant precedes the primitive data types they are automatically converted to strings. Objects can also be concatenated by using their *toString* methods.

A string constant is automatically created as a *String* object so that rather than declaring and initializing a string *word* by the statement

> *String word* = **new** *String* ("Charles");

the statement

> *String word* = "Charles";

is sufficient.

## String Methods

There are a number of *String* class methods.

- The *length* method yields the number of characters in a string. For example,

  > *word.length* ()

  has a value that is the length of the *String* object *word*. There are no parameters for *length* but it has empty parentheses after it.

- The *substring* method has two forms. The value of

  *word.substring* (5)

  is the substring of *word* from the character in position 5 to the end of the string in *word*. In the other form,

  *word.substring* (5, 7)

  is the substring of word from character position 5 to character position 7 inclusive.
- The *charAt* method is used when a substring of only one character is wanted. For example,

  *word.charAt* (5)

  has a value that is the character of *word* at position 5.

In all these methods, using a character position outside the range of the *String* object produces an exception.

- The *concat* method is used to concatenate (join) two string objects to create a new string object. For example,

  *word1.concat* (*word2*)

  has a value that is a string object with the value of *word2* concatenated after the value of *word1*. This is the same as

  *word* + *word2*

- The *replace* method is used to replace characters or substrings in a *String* object by other characters or substrings to create a new *String* object. A string constant of a single character has single quotes.
- The *toUpperCase* method creates a *String* object that has the value with all characters changed to upper case. For example, if *word* is a *String* object whose value is *Madam*, then

  *word.toUpperCase* ()

  is a *String* object with value MADAM.

- The *toLowerCase* method is similar, but converts the characters in the string to lower case.

## Searching for Patterns in String Objects

- The *indexOf* method is used to find a pattern in another string. For example, the statements

   *String word* = "even";
   *c.println (word.indexOf* ("ve"));

  will produce the output 1 which is the position of the first of the string "ve" in "even". If the pattern being searched for is a single character it must be cast as a type **int**. The search may also be begun at any character position. For example, these statements

   *String word* = "occurrences";
   *c.println (word.indexOf* ((**int**) 'c', 2));
   *c.println (word.indexOf* ((**int**) 'c', 3));

  produce the output

   2
   8

- The *lastIndexOf* method is used to find the position of the last occurrence. In these last two methods, if there is no occurrence a value −1 is returned.

## Comparing Strings

A number of *String* class methods are useful in comparing the values of two *String* objects.

- The *equals* method yields a boolean value that is true for the expression

   *word1.equals (word2)*

  if the *String* object *word1* has the same characters in the same sequence and is the same length as has the *String* object *word2*.

- The *equalsIgnoreCase* method is the same as *equals* except that the case of the letters (upper or lower) does not matter.

- The *compareTo* method has a value for the expression

    *word1.compareTo (word2)*

of 0 if the two are equal, −1 if the value of *word1* is less than that of *word2*, and +1 if the value is greater. The comparison is done on the basis of the Unicode values of characters which preserves alphabetic ordering. Upper and lower case letters have different Unicode values.

## The StringBuffer Class

Once a *String* object is initialized, its value cannot be changed. The *StringBuffer* class is useful when changes are required. It is declared and instantiated by a statement such as

　　*StringBuffer s1 =* **new** *StringBuffer* ("OK");

Since "OK" is a *String* object and not a *StringBuffer* object the constructor must be used. Here are some methods of the *StringBuffer* class.

- The *length* method is similar to that for the *String* class. It has a value of the current length.
- The *append* method is used to append any *String* object to the current value of the *StringBuffer* object. If *line* is a *StringBuffer* object and *word* is a *String* object, the expression

    *line.append (word)*

is the *StringBuffer* object with the word appended to it. Other primitive data types are automatically converted to *String* objects when appended.

## The StringTokenizer Class

This class is useful for breaking a line of text into **tokens**, that is a sequence of characters surrounded by **white space**, where white space consists of blanks, tabs, or Returns. The *StringTokenizer* methods include:

- the *countToken* method which has a value equal to the number of tokens in the line,

- the *nextToken* method which finds the next token in the line, and
- the *hasMoreTokens* method which indicates whether the line has more tokens.

These methods are useful in text processing.

# 8.11  Technical Terms

cascaded method call                          palindrome

char data type                                token

exception                                     white space

# 8.12  Exercises

1. Write a program to read text from a given file and reformat it so that the lines are no longer than a given maximum length. Instead of having it left justified with a ragged right have it right justified with a ragged left. Store the result in a file called "right", as well as displaying it on the screen.

2. Write a program to read lines of text from a file called "right" and center each line in a space that is 80 characters wide. Display the result on the screen and store it in the file called "center".

3. Write a program to read a line of text and change the spelling of words ending in "or" to end in "our".

4. Write a program to generate the values for car license plates that consists of three capital letters, chosen at random, followed by a space and then three digits chosen at random.

# Chapter 9

# Methods

As programs grow larger it is important to subdivide them into subprograms each of which is easy to create and easy to understand. In this way the complexity of larger programs is controlled.

Historically subprograms were of two basic types: functions and procedures.

- A function subprogram produced a value.

- A procedure subprogram caused one or more actions.

In a structured programming language such as Pascal or Turing, subprograms were clearly separated into these two types. In the language C, all subprograms are referred to as functions. In Java all subprograms are called methods. All Java methods must belong to a class. The methods of a class provide a way for the user of an object instantiated from the class to manipulate the instance variables of the object. This chapter examines Java methods in detail.

# 9.1   Kinds of Methods

One of the most important facts about methods is that, in order to use one, all that must be known about it is its signature and,

- if it is a function-type method, what value it produces,

- if it is a procedure-type method, what action or actions it produces.

As with C, function-type methods in Java can have **side effects**, that is, they produce actions as well as having a value.

To illustrate the two types of methods we will refer to the methods that we have used all along: the methods of the *Console* class.

The method *fillRect* will be used as an example of a procedure-type method. Its signature is

*fillRect* (**int** *x*, **int** *y*, **int** *width*, **int** *height*)

In the signature, after the method's name in parentheses, is a list of its parameters and their data types. The list is separated by commas. The specification is completed by adding that the action produced by this method is to draw a rectangle with its upper-left corner at the point with coordinates (*x*, *y*) and having the given *width* and *height*. The rectangle is to be filled with the current drawing color. The current color is set by another *Console* method called *setColor* whose signature is

    *setColor (Color clr)*;

# 9.2   Calling a Method in a Program

To call or invoke the use of the *fillRect* method in a program, **actual parameters** or arguments must be provided corresponding to the **formal parameters** of the signature. For example, this statement could be included in a program (assuming a *Console* object *c* has been instantiated first).

    *c.fillRect (0, 0, 50, 100)*;

When executed, the statement would produce a filled rectangle whose upper-left corner is at the origin of coordinates (0, 0) and which is 50 pixels wide and 100 pixels high. The rectangle would be green if the rectangle-drawing statement were preceded by this statement

    *c.setColor (Color.green)*;

The color *green* is a constant of the *Color* class and is used as the argument of the *setColor* method.

In any call to a method the name of the object to which the method belongs precedes the method's name and is separated from it by a dot.

In the last statement, *setColor* is a method of object *c*. The call to a procedure-type method acts like a statement in the program. For example, the call to the procedure-type method *setColor* changes the current color for drawing to *green*.

In any call to a method there is always a one-to-one correspondence between the formal parameters of its signature and the actual parameters or arguments of the call to the method. For example, here is the correspondence for *fillRect*.

| data type | parameter | argument |
|-----------|-----------|----------|
| int | *x* | 0 |
| int | *y* | 0 |
| int | *width* | 50 |
| int | *height* | 100 |

The data types of corresponding parameters and arguments must also agree.

As an example of a function-type method, we will use the *readInt* method of the *Console* class. Here is a program fragment that uses the *readInt* method to read in an integer.

```
int number
number = c.readInt ();
```

There are no parameters for the *readInt* method but parentheses are still necessary.

# 9.3   Defining a Method

If a method is to be used outside the class in which it is defined, it must be declared as **public** in the class. If it is a function-type method, the data type of the value returned by the function follows the keyword **public**. If it is a procedure-type method, the keyword **void** is used in this position instead. After these keywords comes the signature of the method. For example, the *fillRect* method would be defined by this **header:**

**public void** *fillRect* (**int** *x*, **int** *y*, **int** *width*, **int** *height*)

After this header comes the **body** of the method surrounded by curly braces.

Here is the complete definition of a function-type method called *square* that will produce a value which is the square of its single integer parameter.

```
// Method to produce the square of an integer.
static public int square (int number)
{
    return number * number;
} // square method
```

This function-type method *square* has the data type of the value returned, namely **int**, after the keyword **public**. It has one parameter called *number* which is also of data type **int**. All function-type methods have the keyword **return** followed by the value that is to be returned in their body.

Here is a program that uses this *square* method. In this case, we show the entire application program, including the boilerplate, so that the relationship between the *main* method and the *square* method of the enclosing *TableOfSquares* class is clear.

```
// The "TableOfSquares" class.
import java.awt.*;
import hsa.Console;

public class TableOfSquares
{
    static Console c;

    // Main method to print the squares of numbers from
    // 1 to 10.
    static public void main (String [] args)
    {
        c = new Console ();
        for (int value = 1; value <= 10; value ++)
        {
            c.println ("Square of " + value + " = " + square (value));
        }
    } // main method

    // Method to produce the square of an integer.
    static public int square (int number)
    {
        return number * number;
    } // square method
} /* TableOfSquares class */
```

Because both *main* and *square* are methods of the *TableOfSquares* class, when *square* is called in *main*, contrary to the usual practice, the method's name is not preceded by an object or class name with a dot.

In the call to *square* in *main* the argument *value* is in correspondence with the method's parameter *number*. Both are of **int** data type.

## 9.3.1   Labelling Methods and Variables as Static

The *main* method is always declared **static** because the class in which it resides is not instantiated. For *main* to call methods contained in this class, those methods must be labelled **static**. A static method is called a **class method**.

Some classes in the Java class library, for example the *Math* class, are never instantiated. All of its methods must in fact be labelled as **static**. To call such a method, the class name, followed by a dot precedes the method's name. For example,

**double** *sqrtOfTwo = Math.sqrt* (2);

calls the square root method *sqrt* of the *Math* class.

In most classes the methods are not labelled as **static**. (These non-static methods are called **object methods**.) Before a method of a non-static class can be used, the class must first be instantiated to create an object of the class. For example, using the *println* method of the *Console* class requires a statement such as

*Console c =* **new** *Console* ( );

to instantiate an object of this class. Using the method *println* of this object requires the object's name followed by a dot and then the method's name. For example,

*c.println* ("Hello there");

Variables can also be labelled as **static**. Usually, if a variable of a class is not labelled **static**, when the class is instantiated to create an object, the object has a copy of that variable. When a method of that object is then called, it uses the copy particular to that object. Such variables are called **object** or **instance variables**.

If a variable in a class is labelled **static**, it is created only once when the class is first **loaded** (assembled into the program). It is called a **class variable**. When a method of an object instantiated from that class is called, any reference to that variable is to the class variable and not to a copy in the object.

# 9.4   Access to Instance Variables

The idea of an object is that the data and the methods that have access to that data are encapsulated so that no outside object can have access to the data except by using the object's methods. This protects the data from unintentional interference by methods of an outside object.

Encapsulation has the advantage that the user of an object need not know how the data is being stored or the details of implementation of the methods. These details could be changed as long as the specifications of the methods remained constant.

The definition of the details is contained in the class. For example, we have *Console* class methods and *String* class methods that we know how to use but have no idea how they are implemented. To use the methods of a class we must create an **instance** of the class. The class serves as a template or pattern for creating objects of the class. The variables (data) of the object are called instance variables and the methods of the object are called object or instance methods. In general, only the instance methods of an object are available to another object. The instance variables are not; they are accessible only to the instance methods of their own object.

Because the instance variables are part of the encapsulation with the instance methods, the instance methods have direct access to them and there is no need to pass them as parameters to the methods. In a sense, the instance variables are **global variables** that are limited to a single object.

# 9.5   Scope of Identifiers

In Java, identifiers can only be used after they are defined. An identifier is defined by:

- declaring it in a variable declaration statement,
- declaring it as the index variable in a **for** statement,
- declaring it as the name of a method or class, or
- declaring it as the name of a parameter to a method.

The **scope** of an identifier is that part of the program where the identifier is known and can be used.

- **Scopes defined by syntactic constructs:** In general, an identifier is known from the point where it is introduced until the end of the enclosing construct.
- **Global identifiers:** Identifiers defined in the class as variables, constants, or methods are known to any contained method and are said to be local to the class.
- **Control variables for iterations:** An identifier introduced as the index of a **for** loop can be used in the body of the **for** loop but not outside. It is local to the **for** loop.
- **Structured statements:** An identifier introduced in a declaration inside the body of a structured statement, such as **for, while,** or **if,** can be used until the end of that body. It is local to the body.
- **Redefining is prohibited:** An identifier cannot be redefined in a scope where it is known. For example, it is not legal to write a declaration of a variable $m$ in a scope where $m$ is already defined, or to use the variable $i$ as the index of a **for** loop in a scope where $i$ is already defined.
- **Methods:** A method introduces a new scope. The name of the method is always known in the body of the method and in any other method belonging to the same class. If the method is declared as **public** it is known to any object that imports its class.

- **Reusing identifiers**: Names of parameters and local identifiers inside a method can be the same as names used in the class scope. The identifier is being reused. If it were not possible to reuse identifiers, the programmer writing a method would need to know all of the global identifiers in the class where the method would be used. If a reused identifier appears in a statement inside the method, it is the local identifier (parameter, variable, or constant) that is meant. To use a global variable with the same name, the programmer must first use the keyword **this** followed by a dot.

- **Imported identifiers**: Identifiers used inside a method but not defined there in either the formal parameter list or in a local definition, are global to the method. These identifiers must be defined in the containing class.

- **Imported identifiers cannot be redefined**: The rule for importing and the rule prohibiting redefining taken together mean that if an identifier from the class is used in a method, that identifier cannot subsequently be redefined in the method.

Understanding the scope of identifiers is an important aspect of ensuring that your programs will actually work the way you expect them to. In the next section we will look at various ways of testing programs.

# 9.6    Testing of Programs

Computer programs are complicated and difficult to construct, and as a result they are often not correct. Errors in programs are traditionally called **bugs**. Most programs, especially those of any complexity, have bugs in them. Although in theory it is possible to prove programs correct, the proof process is difficult and is not usually carried out.

It is still important, though, to gain confidence in a program. Programs should be tested to determine how well they conform to their specifications. It is often pointed out that testing can only show errors, not their absence. This is because any interesting program will accept many different inputs, it can go through many different states, produce many different outputs, and it can end in many different states. Testing can only examine a limited number of these situations. Nonetheless, testing is important. Given the opportunity to fly in an airplane that has had its flight control software tested, and another that has not had its software tested, a wise person will choose the one with the tested software.

Testing can be done in many ways.

In **blackbox testing** the tester has the specification of the program (often an informal description of what the program is to do) but not the text of the program itself. The program is like a black box whose internals cannot be examined. By trying out appropriate samples of data values, the tester attempts to determine if the program meets its specification.

In **whitebox testing** the tester has the specification and also the text of the program. This means that a more detailed and thorough job of testing can be done. For example, knowing how the program is constructed, the tester can ensure that each statement in the program is executed (each loop, and each branch of each selection statement). Further, by examining the text of the program the tester can see how different parts of the program depend on each other, and can ensure that each significantly different internal state of the program is entered at least once in a set of tests. It is also generally useful to test the limit conditions of programs (the ends of ranges of allowed values, lists of the minimum and maximum specified size, and so on).

One way to test a method is to write a small *main* method, called a **driver**, that provides the environment needed by the method, and that calls the method with different sets of values provided for the parameters.

# 9.7    Tracing of Methods

Another way to understand a method is to trace its execution. This is done by making a table that corresponds to the state of the computation, and changing the values in the table to reflect the progress of the computation. For example, here is a method to test whether the first few integers are primes.

A prime is any number that is greater than or equal to 2, and that is divided evenly only by itself and by 1. Thus, 2 is a prime number because it can be divided evenly only by itself and by 1. Since every other even number can be divided by 2, no other even number can be prime. Also, 3 is a prime number because it can be divided evenly only by itself and by 1. Similarly, 5 and 7 are prime. But 6 and 9 are not a prime because they can be divided evenly by 3.

In the *checkPrime* method the number *n* is divided by a sequence of factors going from 2 up to the integer less than the square root of *n*. If no factor up to this point divides it evenly, it is prime. We need not search for a factor larger than the square root of *n* because, if it exists, the other factor in the product must be less than the square root and we would have found it.

```
// The "TestPrime" class.
// Tests whether the integers from 2 to 10 are prime.
import hsa.Console;

public class TestPrime
{
    static public void main (String [] args)
    {
        Console c = new Console ();
        for (int number = 2; number <= 10; number ++)
        {
            c.println ("" + number + "," + checkPrime (number));
        }
    } // main method
```

```
// Method to test whether integer is prime or not.
static public boolean checkPrime (int n)
{
    double sqrtr = Math.sqrt (n);
    int factor = 2;
    while (factor <= sqrtr && n % factor != 0)
    {
        factor ++;
    }
    return factor > sqrtr;
} // checkPrime method
} /* TestPrime class */
```

The program produces this output.

```
2, true
3, true
4, false
5, true
6, false
7, true
8, false
9, false
10, false
```

The state of the program at the beginning of the first time through the loop is

*where* : *main* (first time into loop)
*values* :
*number* = 2

The state is shown as a line indicating the point *where* in the execution that is being represented, followed by a list of variables with their values. When a method is called, the name of the method, the values of its parameters, local variables, and constants are added to the state. As soon as the method has been entered in this program, the state is

*where* : *main* (first time into loop)
*values* :
*number* = 2

> *where : checkPrime* (*entry*)
> *values :*
>     *n* (from *number*) = 2

The method creates a new scope so it is shown as a new *where* with its own set of variable values. Notice that the parameter *n* is explicitly tied to *number*, the variable that was passed as the corresponding actual parameter. Tracing proceeds in this manner for *number* going from 2 to 10.

A trace table like this allows programmers to manually mimic the execution of a program. It is often valuable to build such a table, especially if a program is behaving in unexpected ways.

# 9.8   Function Methods

The concept of a function in mathematics is that it yields a precise value for a given parameter or set of parameters. Many of the commonly-used **mathematical functions** are methods defined in the *Math* class of the Java class library. For example, *Math.cos* (*x*) and *Math.sin* (*x*) produce the cosine and sine of the angle *x* in radians.

Some mathematical functions have two parameters, for example

   *Math.min* (10.2, 9.8)

has a value 9.8, the minimum of its two parameters. The *Math* method *max* produces a value that is the maximum of its two parameters.

Some methods have no parameters. For example, the *Console* method *getWidth* has a value that is the width in pixels of the currently-active window. Although there are no parameters, a call to *getWidth* must have empty parentheses following its name.

A function-type method definition is similar to that of a procedure-type method definition. Here are the main differences.

•   The signature of a function-type method has the data type of the value that the method produces rather than the keyword **void** just before the name of the method. This name is followed by the parenthesized list of parameters.

- The body of the function-type method has a **return** statement at the end. The value produced by the method follows the keyword **return**.

We will now create a function-type method called *again* that will have a value that is a string with a string pattern repeated a given number of times.

```
// Method to produce a repeated string pattern n times.
static public String again (String pattern, int n)
{
    StringBuffer repeat = new StringBuffer ();
    for (int count = 1; count <= n; count ++)
    {
        repeat = repeat.append (pattern);
    }
    return repeat.toString ();
} // again method
```

A driver *main* method might use these statements to test this method. (Remember to add the boilerplate.)

```
// The "TestAgain" class.
for (int lineNumber =1; lineNumber <= 5; lineNumber ++)
{
    c.println ("" + lineNumber + " "+ again ("*", lineNumber));
}
```

The output for this would be

```
1 *
2 **
3 ***
4 ****
5 *****
```

Here is a complete program which contains a function-type method *roundCent* that produces the value to the nearest cent of its **double** integer parameter *amount*. Notice that the parameter is first multiplied by 100 then rounded to be an integer. If, for example, the *amount* were 98.3276, the result of the multiplication would be 9832.76. This is rounded to the integer 9833. This integer value is then divided by 100.0 which would yield 98.33. This is the correct value of *amount* rounded to the nearest cent. If the integer had been divided by 100 rather than 100.0 it would have produced an incorrect answer. Because dividing an integer by an integer always results in an integer, dividing by 100 would have produced an incorrect value of 98.

In the *main* driver method to test the method *roundCent*, the values of *balance*, *interestRate*, and *interest* are all declared as **double** since numbers with decimal points will be read in. All such numbers are categorized as **double** rather than **float**.

```java
// The "Interest" class.
import hsa.Console;

public class Interest
{
    public static void main (String [] args)
    {
        Console c = new Console ();
        double balance, interestRate, interest;

        c.print ("Enter balance: ");
        balance = c.readDouble ();
        c.print ("Enter current interest rate: ");
        interestRate = c.readDouble ();
        interest = roundCent (balance * interestRate / 100);
        balance += interest;
        c.println ("New balance = " + balance);
        c.println ("Interest = " + interest);
    } // main method.

    public static double roundCent (double amount)
    {
        return Math.round (amount * 100) / 100.0;
    } // roundCent method
} /* Interest class */
```

# 9.9   Method Overloading

Here is another example of a function-type method. This method has a value that is the number of times a pattern occurs in a string of characters. Its header is

**public int** *occurrences (String pattern, String text)*

The resulting value will be the number of times the *pattern* string occurs in the *text* string. The method *occurrences* will use the *String* class method *indexOf*. In the *String* class there are several versions of the *indexOf* method. These differ from each other in that their parameter lists are different. We say the method *indexOf* is overloaded. One such variation of *indexOf* has this header

**public int** *indexOf (String pattern)*

and a call to this particular method in the method *occurrence* would be made this way

*text.indexOf (pattern);*

Its value would give the string position of the first occurrence of the *pattern* in *text*.

Another form of the *String* method *indexOf* has this header

**public int** *indexOf (String pattern,* **int** *index);*

Here the value of the method *indexOf* is the position of the first occurrence of the *pattern* starting at the position *index* of the string. In either version, if the pattern is not present, the result −1 is returned. This second version of the *String* method *indexOf* will be used in the method *occurrences.*

```
// Method to find number of occurrences of pattern in text.
static public int occurrences (String pattern, String text)
{
    int count = 0, index = 0;
    while (text.indexOf (pattern, index) != -1)
    {
```

```
        count ++;
        index = text.indexOf (pattern, index) + pattern.length ();
    }
    return count;
} // occurrences method
```

In a driver *main* method the statement

```
// The "TestOccur" class.
c.println (occurrences ("is" , "Mississippi"));
```

produces the output 2.

Another example of an overloaded method is the *println* () method of the *Console* class which can take a variety of different data types as its argument.

# 9.10  Recursive Methods

Often a method uses other methods while computing the result required by its specification. Sometimes a method can be defined so that it uses itself on a smaller version of the problem. We say a definition is recursive when the thing being defined is used in the definition.

**Recursive** definitions are common in mathematics. Any series in which a term is defined using the values of earlier terms in the series is a recursive definition. For example, the sum of the first $n$ integers can be defined as the value of $n$ plus the sum of the first $n - 1$ integers. This example was used in the previous chapter.

Here is a recursive function-type method to compute this sum.

```
//Recursive method to compute the sum of the first n integers.
static public int sum (int n)
{
    if (n <= 1)
        return n;
    else
        return n + sum (n -1);
} // sum method
```

Notice that the method *sum* is defined with a body that uses the method *sum* on a smaller version of the problem (summing a smaller number of integers in this case). It is this use of the name *sum* inside the body of the method *sum* that makes the function recursive.

A method that has a recursive definition will result in several copies of the method's parameters and variables being used when the program is executed. Consider what happens when this statement in the *main* method uses the method *sum*.

> c.println (sum (3));

When *main* applies the method *sum* to the value 3, the result will be a chain of calls of the method. To compute the sum of the first 3 integers, the sum of the first two integers is needed, and to compute that sum it is necessary to compute the sum of the first integer. A trace table might look like this:

> *where : main* (in *println* statement)
> values : (none)

> *where : sum* (in second **return** statement)
> values : (none)
> $n = 3$

> *where : sum* (in second **return** statement)
> values :
> $n = 2$

> *where : sum* (in first **return** statement)
> values :
> $n = 1$

The third and last call is about to return the value 1, which will be used to compute the value 3 in the second call, which will be used to compute the value 6 in the first call, which will be printed by the *main* method.

Many definitions can be recast in recursive terms. Some computer scientists believe that recursion is a more natural way to think about many computations than is iteration. Other computer scientists believe that recursion is a useful way to think, but they avoid recursive programs because recursion requires more method calls. Since method calls take time and space, these people prefer to write iterative versions of algorithms so that the execution will be faster and smaller. In general, it is probably appropriate to use recursive methods when the data values being processed are most naturally and easily defined in recursive ways. Sometimes recursive algorithms are very inefficient, even if they are easy to write. Recursion is a tool that requires careful use.

Here is a recursive definition of the reverse of a string. Later in the chapter there will be another definition that is not recursive, and these two versions can be compared. An attractive feature of this one is its simplicity, but an unattractive feature of it is that for a string containing $n$ characters it requires $n$ method calls.

```
// Method to find reverse of string word recursively.
static public String reverse (String word)
{
    if (word.length () <= 1)
        return word;
    else
        return reverse (word.substring (1)) + (word.charAt(0));
} // reverse method
```

Here is another example of a recursive definition. The number of occurrences of a character in a string can be defined recursively: it is either 0 or 1, depending on whether the first character is the desired character or not, plus the number of occurrences in the remainder of the string. This will seem like a strange definition to many readers. It is perhaps more natural to think of this method iteratively.

# 9.11  An Example Using Methods

The various features of methods that have been described will now be used to determine whether a string is a palindrome. As mentioned in Chapter 8, a palindrome is a string that reads the same forwards and backwards. The string "radar" is a palindrome but "sonar" is not. Usually blanks and punctuation are ignored in palindromes, and the difference between upper case and lower case letters is also ignored. This means that the phrase "A man, a plan, a canal: Panama." is a palindrome.

A simple way to determine if a string is a palindrome is to compute the reverse of the string, and then compare it to the original string. Here is a function that computes the reverse of a string. Unlike the previous definition of the *reverse* function, this one is iterative.

```
// Iterative method to find reverse of string.
static public String reverse (String word)
{
    StringBuffer back = new StringBuffer ();
    for (int i = word.length () – 1; i >= 0; i ––)
    {
        back = back.append (word.charAt (i));
    }
    return back.toString ();
} // reverse method
```

This function could be used to determine if a simple string like "radar" or "sonar" is a palindrome, but it cannot be used when a string contains blanks, punctuation, or upper case letters. To deal with the more general case it is necessary to have a function that will remove the blanks and punctuation from a string. We will call a string containing characters other than letters "dirty". This function, called *clean*, will remove all of these extra characters.

```
// Method to clean punctuation and white space out of string.
static public String clean (String s)
{
    String dirt = ",.:;()!'\\* ";
    StringBuffer t = new StringBuffer ();
    for (int i = 0; i < s.length (); i++)
    {
        if (dirt.indexOf (s.charAt (i)) == −1)
            t.append (s.charAt (i));
    }
    return t.toString ();
} // clean method
```

It is still necessary to deal with upper case letters. One simple approach is to create a string that has all the upper case letters replaced by their lower case equivalents. The next method produces a string that contains only lower case letters from a string that contains both upper case and lower case letters. (Although we use it in this example, the *lowerCase* method is not actually necessary because the *String* class in Java provides a built-in method for changing the case of characters. This built-in method is called *toLowerCase*.)

```
// Method to change string so it contains only lower case letters.
static public String lowerCase (String s)
{
    StringBuffer t = new StringBuffer ();
    char ch;
    for (int i= 0; i < s.length (); i ++)
    {
        ch = s.charAt (i);
        t = t.append (Character.toLowerCase (ch));
    }
    return t.toString ();
} // lowerCase method
```

These three methods can now be put together to produce a method that will determine whether a string is a palindrome when punctuation and letter case are ignored.

```
// Method to use methods reverse, clean, and lowerCase to
// test palindrome.
static public boolean testPalindrome (String s)
{
    String t = lowerCase (clean (s));
    return t.equals (reverse (t));
} // testPalindrome method
```

Here is a *main* method to test these methods. It reads in three strings.

```
// The "PalindromeTest" class.
// Test method testPalindrome.
String text;
for (int count =1; count <= 3; count ++)
{
    c.println ("Enter a line of text");
    text = c.readLine ();
    c.println ("" + text + "  " + testPalindrome (text));
}
```

Here is a sample execution window.

> **Madam, in Eden I'm Adam**
>     Madam, in Eden I'm Adam true
> **radar**
>     radar true
> **Hello**
>     Hello false

# 9.12 Function Methods with Side Effects

In mathematics a function has the property that it yields a specific value for a given parameter (or set of parameters). For example, the function that determines the square root of a number such as 16 always gives the same value when its parameter is 16.

In mathematical notation we can write $\sqrt{9}$ and be certain that this always represents the value 3. In Java we can write *Math.sqrt* (9) to compute the same value.

This unchanging nature of the value of a function, once the parameters are fixed, allows normal mathematical reasoning to be applied to functions. For example,

$$2 \times \sqrt{9} = \sqrt{9} + \sqrt{9}$$

or, more generally,

$$2 \times f(x) = f(x) + f(x)$$

If a function did not always return the same value for a given parameter, this would not be true and reasoning about functions would become very difficult.

It is possible in Java to write function-type methods that do not behave like mathematical functions. A function is not well-behaved if it makes any changes to the program in which it is called.

Changes made to the calling program by a function are called **side effects**. Side effects complicate mathematical reasoning and logic.

Here is an example of a benign side effect. Suppose a programmer wants to keep track of the number of times that a method is used. If a function contains an important part of the work to be done in a program, counting the number of times the method is called might give very helpful information to a user who is experimenting with the program.

# 9.13  A Case Study Involving Methods

In this case study we will work through the development of a program using the procedure-oriented programming paradigm. Unlike the object-oriented programming paradigm which involves the use of programs that have classes in addition to the *main* method, the procedure-oriented paradigm involves the use of a single class containing a *main* method which calls other methods. In Java, this procedure-oriented approach can perhaps more accurately be referred to as method-oriented.

This case study will illustrate the procedure-oriented programming paradigm using top-down development and step-by-step refinement (as described in Chapter 3) to design a program to encrypt and decrypt messages using an alphabet cypher. The first step in the design process is to have a clear specification of the problem to be solved.

## 9.13.1   Specification of Problem to be Solved

Our task is to write a Java application program to encrypt and decrypt messages. The program should ask for the message and the key word used in the alphabet cypher and encode or decode the message.

In an alphabet cypher every letter in the message is translated a certain number of letters forward. In the 'b' cypher, all of the letters 'a' are translated to 'b's, 'b's to 'c's, 'c's to 'd's and so on. In the 'r' cypher, 'a's are translated to 'r's, 'b's to 's's and so on. Letters translated beyond the end of the alphabet are wrapped to the beginning. In the 'y' cypher 'a' is translated to 'y', 'b' to 'z' and 'c' to 'a'. In the 'f' cypher, for example

> Who are you?

becomes

> Bmt fwj dtz?

Capital letters are translated using the corresponding capital letter of the cypher. For example here 'w' is translated to 'b' and a 'W' is translated to 'B'.

A more complicated version of this cypher uses a key word. The first letter of the message is translated using the first letter of the key word. The second letter of the message is translated using the second letter of the key word and so on. When there are no more key word letters, the translation cycles back to the beginning.

For example, if the key word is "help", the message "Who are you?" is translated as follows:

'W' is translated using the 'h' cypher
'h' is translated using the 'e' cypher
'o' is translated using the 'l' cypher

and so on. The advantage of this cypher is that identical letters in the message do not necessarily translate as having identical letters in the encoded message. To decrypt the message, the user must have the encrypted message and the keyword and reverse the process.

## 9.13.2   Design of the User Interface

We begin out top-down solution to the problem by designing the user interface. This interface is fairly simple since the program can use a text base interface to ask users whether they want to encrypt or decrypt a message or whether they want to quit the program. The *hsa* Console class can be used to provide simple input and output. The *main* method's loop will ask the user for his or her choice (encrypt, decrypt, or quit).

## 9.13.3   Program Design

We have chosen a design based on the method-oriented paradigm. In general there are two reasons to use methods. One is because the same block of code is to be used at several different locations in the program. The second reason is that using methods also helps to make the program easier to understand and cuts down on the number of bugs. Since methods can be changed and tested independently, they also make programs easier to maintain, fix, and improve over time.

### 9.13.4   Stepwise Refinement

While no technique is guaranteed to produce a good program, a straightforward problem such as the alphabet cypher lends itself well to stepwise refinement. Here are the stages required to develop a solution.

First we examine the *main* method which accepts the commands encrypt, decrypt, or quit from the user and carries out the required action. Before writing the *main* method in Java, we describe it in a form of English often called **pseudocode** which is half way between English and an actual programming language.

Here is the pseudocode version of the *main* method.

```
main
    loop
        get command from user
        if command = 1 then encrypt a message,
        else if command = 2 then decrypt a message
        else if command = 3 then quit loop
    end loop
```

The obvious next step is to create methods to "encrypt a message" and to "decrypt a message". The methods do not need parameters because the message and keyword are entered within the methods themselves. We label these two methods **public static void *encrypt* ()** and **public static void *decrypt*.** Each of these two methods should ask for the message to be encrypted/decrypted, ask for the key word used to encrypt/decrypt the message and then encrypt/decrypt the message.

Here are the methods in pseudocode.

```
encrypt
    get message from user
    get key word from user
    calculate encrypted message
    output encrypted message

decrypt
    get encrypted message from user
    get key word from user
    calculate decrypted message
    output decrypted message
```

Asking for user input and displaying output is straightforward. However, calculating the encrypted and decrypted message is not trivial. We refine that step by making two more methods. These methods have as parameters the message to be encrypted or decrypted and the key word. Given that we want them to produce the encrypted or decrypted message, we make them function-type methods that return a *String*. We label these two methods **public static** *String encryptedMessage* (*String message, String keyword*) and **public static** *String decryptedMessage*.

To encrypt a message, we go through each letter of the message and encrypt it using the specified letter of the key word. The logic for this is

> *encryptedMessage*
>> set the encrypted message string to the empty string
>> for each letter in the message
>>> calculate the encrypted letter from the letter in the
>>>> message and the appropriate letter of the key word
>>> add the encrypted letter to the end of the encrypted message
>>>> string
>> return the encrypted message string

The *decryptedMessage* method is similar.

The next refinement is to look at *encryptedMessage* and decide that the calculation of the encrypted letter would make a good method. We name it *encryptedLetter*. In general, if a calculation is somewhat complicated, then it is a good candidate to be in a method by itself. We will call these methods *encryptedLetter* and *decryptedLetter*

The refinement now looks like this:

> *encryptedMessage*
>> set the encrypted message string to the empty string
>> for each character in the message
>>> encrypted character = *encryptedLetter* (message character,
>>>> key word character)
>>> add the encrypted character to the end of the encrypted
>>>> message string
>> return the encrypted message string

The *encrypt* method now looks like this:

*encrypt*
>get message from user
>get key word from user
>encrypted message = *encryptedMessage* (message, key word)
>output encrypted message

The methods for decryption are:

*decryptedMessage*
>set the decrypted message string to the empty string
>for each character in the message
>>decrypted character = *decryptedLetter* (message character,
>>    key word character)
>>add the decrypted character to the end of the decrypted
>>    message string
>return the decrypted message string

*decrypt*
>get encrypted message from user
>get key word from user
>decrypted message = *decryptedMessage* (message, key word)
>output decrypted message

## 9.13.5  Further Refinement - Encrypting a Letter

When doing a calculation on a character, such as shifting a letter forward or backward in the alphabet, it is usually necessary to convert the letter to an integer, do the shifting calculation on it, and then transform it back into a character. This done by casting the letter *ch* which is a **char** to an **int**.

**int** *i* = (**int**) *ch*;

To transform the integer back to the character we cast it to a **char** using this statement:

**char** *ch* = (**char**) *i*;

For example, to encrypt a letter using the 'd' cypher, you transform the character to an integer, add 3 to the value and then transform it back to a character. However, if the value exceeds the value of 'z' after you have added 3, then you subtract 26 to bring the value back in the range 'a' .. 'z'. Note that a lower case letter must be checked for exceeding 'z', an upper case letter checked for exceeding 'Z' and any non-letter character is not transformed at all. For example, to encrypt 'Y' in the 'd' cypher, you would convert it to an integer (89), add three (92), realize that the result is greater than the value for 'Z' (90) and subtract 26 for a result of 66 which is the character 'B'.

The *encryptedLetter* method first converts the key word letter into a value. The key word letter value is 0 for 'a', 1 for 'b', and so on. This value is calculated by subtracting the integer value of 'a' from the integer value of the key word letter.

The method checks them to see if the message character is a lower case letter. If it is, it adds the key word value to the integer value of the message character, compares it with 'z' and if it exceeds the value of 'z', it subtracts 26. If the message character is upper case, it adds the key word value to the integer value of the message character, compares it with 'Z' and if it exceeds the value of 'Z', it subtracts 26. If the message character is neither upper case or lower case, it returns the user character. This means, for example, that spaces and punctuation marks are not encrypted.

Note that in all this we are assuming that the key word contains only lower case letters.

Here is the next refinement for *encryptedLetter*.

*encryptedLetter*
    key word letter value = integer value of key word letter – (**int**) 'a'
    if message letter between 'a' and 'z', then
        encrypted letter code = integer value of message character +
            key word letter value
        if encrypted letter code > (**int**) 'z' then
            Subtract 26 from encrypted letter code
        return (**char**) encrypted letter code

        else if message letter between 'A' and 'Z', then
            encrypted letter code = integer value of message character +
                key word letter value
            if encrypted letter code > (**int**) 'Z' then
                Subtract 26 from encrypted letter code
            return (**char**) encrypted letter code
        else
            return message letter

The *decryptedLetter* method is much the same as *encryptedLetter* except the key word letter value is subtracted rather than added. For lower case encrypted letters the comparison is made as to whether the letter is less than 'a' and if it is, 26 is added.

The last refinement that we will examine is an error check. The solution expects the key word to be all lower case and devoid of punctuation, spaces, and so on. To guarantee this, the "get key word from user" in *encrypt* and *decrypt* is replaced with

        loop
            get key word from user
            if *checkKeyword* (keyword)
                exit loop
            put error message
        end loop

where the *checkKeyword* method is

    *checkKeyword*
        for each character in key word
            if not a letter
                return **false**
        return **true**

All that is left at this point is to put it all together and translate the refinement into a Java program.

## 9.13.6   The Java Program

Here is the Java program for the *Cypher* class.

```java
// The "Cypher" class.
import java.awt.*;
import hsa.Console;

public class Cypher
{
    static Console c;            // The output console

    public static boolean checkKeyword (String keyword)
    {
        for (int i = 0 ; i < keyword.length () ; i++)
        {
            if ((keyword.charAt (i) < 'a') || ('z' < keyword.charAt (i)))
            {
                return false;
            }
        }

        return true;
    } // checkKeyword method

    public static char encryptedLetter (char letterToEncrypt, char key)
    {
        int keyCode = (int) key - (int) 'a';
        int encryptedLetterCode;

        if (('A' <= letterToEncrypt) && (letterToEncrypt <= 'Z'))
        {
            encryptedLetterCode = (int) letterToEncrypt + keyCode;
            if (encryptedLetterCode > (int) 'Z')
            {
                encryptedLetterCode -= 26;
            }
            return (char) encryptedLetterCode;
        }
```

```
    else if (('a' <= letterToEncrypt) && (letterToEncrypt <= 'z'))
    {
        encryptedLetterCode = (int) letterToEncrypt + keyCode;
        if (encryptedLetterCode > (int) 'z')
        {
            encryptedLetterCode -= 26;
        }
        return (char) encryptedLetterCode;
    }
    else
    {
        return letterToEncrypt;
    }
} // encryptedLetter method

public static String encryptedMessage (String message, String keyword)
{
    int keywordLetter = 0;
    StringBuffer answer = new StringBuffer ();

    for (int i = 0 ; i < message.length () ; i++)
    {
        char ch = encryptedLetter (message.charAt (i),
            keyword.charAt (keywordLetter));
        keywordLetter = (keywordLetter + 1) % keyword.length ();
        answer.append (ch);
    }
    return answer.toString ();
} // encryptedMessage method

public static void encrypt ()
{
    String message, encryptedMessage, keyword;

    c.println ();

    c.println ("Message Encryptor");
    c.println ();

    c.print ("Message to encrypt: ");
    message = c.readLine ();
    // Keep looping until we get a legal keyword
```

```
        while (true)
        {
            c.print ("Keyword: ");
            keyword = c.readLine ();
            if (checkKeyword (keyword))
                break;
            c.println ("The keyword must be all letters and all lower case");
        } // while

        encryptedMessage = encryptedMessage (message, keyword);
        c.println ("The encrypted message is: " + encryptedMessage);
        c.println ("——————");
} // encrypt method

public static char decryptedLetter (char letterToDecrypt, char key)
{
    int keyCode = (int) key – (int) 'a';
    int decryptedLetterCode;

    if (('A' <= letterToDecrypt) && (letterToDecrypt <= 'Z'))
    {
        decryptedLetterCode = (int) letterToDecrypt – keyCode;
        if (decryptedLetterCode < (int) 'A')
        {
            decryptedLetterCode += 26;
        }
        return (char) decryptedLetterCode;
    }
    else if (('a' <= letterToDecrypt) && (letterToDecrypt <= 'z'))
    {
        decryptedLetterCode = (int) letterToDecrypt – keyCode;
        if (decryptedLetterCode < (int) 'a')
        {
            decryptedLetterCode += 26;
        }
        return (char) decryptedLetterCode;
    }
    else
    {
        return letterToDecrypt;
    }
} // decryptedLetter method
```

```
public static String decryptedMessage (String message, String keyword)
{
    int keywordLetter = 0;
    StringBuffer answer = new StringBuffer ();

    for (int i = 0 ; i < message.length () ; i++)
    {
        char ch = decryptedLetter (message.charAt (i),
            keyword.charAt (keywordLetter));
        keywordLetter = (keywordLetter + 1) % keyword.length ();
        answer.append (ch);
    }
    return answer.toString ();
} // decryptedMessage method

public static void decrypt ()
{
    String message, decryptedMessage, keyword;

    c.println ();

    c.println ("Message Decryptor");
    c.println ();

    c.print ("Message to decrypt: ");
    message = c.readLine ();
    // Keep looping until we get a legal keyword
    while (true)
    {
        c.print ("Keyword: ");
        keyword = c.readLine ();
        if (checkKeyword (keyword))
            break;
        c.println ("The keyword must be all letters and all lower case");
    } // while

    decryptedMessage = decryptedMessage (message, keyword);
    c.println ("The decrypted message is: " + decryptedMessage);
    c.println ("————————");
} // decrypt method
```

```
public static void main (String [] args)
{
    c = new Console ();

    while (true)
    {
        String command;

        c.println ("Enter a command");
        c.println (" 1 .. Encrypt a message");
        c.println (" 2 .. Decrypt a message");
        c.println (" 3 .. Quit");
        c.println ();
        c.print ("Enter a command: ");

        command = c.readLine ();

        if (command.equals ("1"))
        {
            encrypt ();
        }
        else if (command.equals ("2"))
        {
            decrypt ();
        }
        else if (command.equals ("3"))
        {
            break;
        }
    } // while
} // main method
} // Cypher class
```

# 9.14  Chapter Summary

## Types of Methods

The complexity of large programs can be controlled by subdividing them into interacting objects. In turn, objects are kept simple by creating subprograms called **methods** within the object.

Methods of a class provide a way for the user of an object instantiated from the class to manipulate the instance variables of the object.

Historically subprograms have been of two types. These two types are still evident in the methods of object-oriented programs. They are:

- function-type methods that produce a value, and
- procedure-type methods that cause one or more actions.

A function-type method is called by using its name in an expression. A procedure-type method is called by using it as a statement in the program that is calling it.

## Defining Methods

The **call** to a procedure-type method is like an additional statement available for writing programs in Java.

A procedure-type **declaration** has this syntax.

```
static public void method-name (formal parameter list)
{
    body of method
}
```

A **parameter list** is:

List of data type and parameter names, separated by commas

The parameters declared in the method declaration are **formal parameters**. The names of the parameters must be distinct, and different from the method's name.

A procedure-type method is called with a **call statement.**

> method-name (list of actual parameters)

The actual parameters supplied in the call statement are also called **arguments.** The actual parameters are in a one-to-one correspondence with the formal parameters. The data types of the actual parameters must match, or be compatible with, the data types of the formal parameters.

Execution of a procedure-type method is from the beginning to the end of its body, unless an explicit **return** statement causes earlier termination. A **return** is seldom used in a procedure-type method but is always present at least once in a function-type method followed by the value being returned.

A function-type method is defined by

> **static public** data-type method-name (formal parameter list)

and called by using its name, followed by the actual parameter list in parentheses, in an expression.

## Local Identifiers, Global Identifiers, and Parameters

Methods can receive information from the program that calls them through their parameters or through **global identifiers**. Global identifiers are those identifiers that are declared outside of the method and are known in the class where the method is defined.

**Local identifiers** are those identifiers defined within the method. The names of parameters are local to the method, as are names that are introduced in the body of the method.

## Testing of Programs

Testing increases confidence that a program meets its specification.

**Whitebox testing** takes advantage of the structure of the program. Tests should exercise every statement in the program, the limiting cases for data values, and every significantly different internal state.

**Blackbox testing** uses only the specification of a program and thus cannot take advantage of knowledge about how the program is built.

## Tracing of Programs

A program can be traced by creating a table that shows the state at any instant, and then mimicking by hand the actions of the program as it changes the machine's state.

## Recursive Methods

Sometimes a method can be defined so that it uses itself on a smaller version of the problem. A definition is **recursive** when the name being defined is used in the definition.

A method that has a recursive definition will result in several copies of the method's variables and parameters being used when the program is executed.

Many definitions can be recast in recursive terms. Some computer scientists believe that recursion is a more natural way to think about many computations than is iteration. Other computer scientists believe that recursion is a useful way to think, but they avoid recursive programs because recursion requires more method calls. Recursion is a tool that requires careful use.

Iterative and recursive methods were compared in testing whether or not a string was a palindrome.

A simple way to determine if a string is a palindrome is to compute the reverse of the string and then compare it to the original string.

A palindrome can also be defined in a recursive manner. A string is palindrome if the first and last characters are the same, and the remainder of the string is also a palindrome.

# 9.15  Technical Terms

| | |
|---|---|
| actual parameter | mathematical function |
| blackbox testing | object method |
| class method | object variable |
| class variable | recursive |
| driver | side effect |
| formal parameter | static method |
| global variable | void |
| header | whitebox testing |
| instance variable | |

# 9.16  Exercises

1. Write a procedure-type method called *compound* that has as parameters an amount of money deposited in the bank and an annual compound interest rate, and produces a table of values of the balance after each year for 10 years. Be sure that the annual balance is kept to the nearest cent. Write a driver program and test the method.

2. Write a procedure-type method called *inputInteger* that will ask for the input of an integer and store it in the variable that is its only parameter in such a way that, if a real number or string is input, the procedure does not halt execution but simply asks the user to try again.

3. Write a function-type method called *phoneList* that accepts as a parameter a name that consists of a first and last name, and returns a value that is the last name then the first with a comma between. For example, if the value stored in *name* before calling the method was "Veena Guru" the value produced by the method would be "Guru, Veena".

4. When a person is buying a house that has a cost $c$, the money available is a combination of savings $s$, plus a mortgage loan amount $m$, that can be obtained. The financial institution from which the mortgage loan is to be obtained will establish some borrowing limit $b$, based on a consideration of the person's salary, credit history, and so on. Write a method to compute $m$ in terms of $c$, $s$, and $b$. Use the *Math* methods *max* and *min*.

5. Write an implementation of the function-type method based on the recursive definition of a palindrome that accepts strings containing upper case letters, punctuation, and blanks. The upper case letters are to be converted to lower case, and the punctuation and blanks are to be ignored.

6. Write a recursive function-type method to compute the alphabetically first character in a string. For the string "recursive", the function should return the value "c".

7. Write a non-recursive function-type method to perform the same computation as in the previous exercise.

8. A string is a palindrome if the front half is a mirror image of the back half. To say this another way, a string is a palindrome if, for each character in the front half of the string, that character is the same as the character in the mirror image position in the back half of the string.

   This definition suggests another iterative way of checking if a string is a palindrome. Write a method that determines if a string is a palindrome by using a **for** statement that examines each character in the front half of the string and compares it with the character in the mirror image position in the back half of the string.

Produce two versions of your function. In the first version, assume that the string to be checked contains only lower case letters. In the second version, assume that the string can contain upper case letters, punctuation, and blanks. The upper case letters are to be converted to lower case, and the punctuation and blanks are to be ignored.

9.  Does the method *checkPrime* return the proper result for the values 2 and 3? Use tracing to explain your answer.

10. The *Cypher* class encrypts and decrypts words using the first letter of the keyword for the first character in the message, the second letter for the next character, and so on. In this example the keyword is "code".

    | | |
    |---|---|
    | Message: | `Is this a test? Yes` |
    | Key word string: | `codecodecodecodecod` |

    This means that when the user enters a message to decrypt, the spacing and punctuation must be exactly right or the message will not decrypt properly. Modify the *Cypher* class by having the place in the key word only increased when used to encrypt a letter.

    | | |
    |---|---|
    | Message | `Is this a test? Yes` |
    | Key word string: | `co deco d ecod eco` |

11. A great deal of information can be derived from a message's word breaks, punctuation, and letter case. Modify the *Cypher* class so that it outputs the encrypted message without any punctuation in blocks of five letters, all in lower case.

    | | |
    |---|---|
    | Message | `Is this a test? Yes` |
    | Key word string: | `codecodecodecodecod` |
    | Encrypted: | `Kg xjwv c wiuh? Asv` |
    | Modified: | `kgxjw vcwiu hasv` |

# Chapter 10

# Classes and Inheritance

In Java all programs are classes, but not all classes are programs. A standalone application program is a class that contains a *main* method, and may, or may not, contain other methods. An applet is a class that extends the class *Applet*. It contains a number of standard methods including a *paint* method. Neither one of these two classes is used as a template to create objects.

In this chapter we look at the more general idea of a class, how objects are instantiated from it and how new classes can be produced from it by inheritance.

# 10.1  Objects and Abstract Data Types

As programs become larger, controlling interference between parts becomes more difficult. Interference can be minimized by isolating all methods that share common variables and encapsulating them in an object, along with the shared variables. When this is done, no other part of a program needs to be concerned with how the data is stored in the object. Only those methods inside the object are involved. In this sense the data is abstracted and we speak of the whole as an abstract data type or ADT.

Of course, one object in a program must communicate with other objects or it would not be a single program, just a group of separate, smaller programs. This communication occurs when one object uses methods of another object. This is known as **message passing**. For any object to use a method encapsulated in another object, several things are necessary.

- The object using another object's method must have imported the other class to which the other object belongs either explicitly or implicitly.
- The method that is used must have been declared **public**.

In Java, objects are instantiated from classes which act as templates for their creation.

Whenever changes are made in the way an object stores data or the way that its methods are implemented, assuming their signatures and what they accomplish remain unchanged, other objects using objects instantiated from the class need not be altered. By this means, unwanted interference between objects in a larger program can be prevented, without having to keep each class unchanged.

# 10.2 Using a Class

We will begin by looking at an object instantiated from a class from the outside, as any other object or *main* method using it would, and see how it can be used. For example, consider a class called *Turtle* that can be used to instantiate objects to produce line drawings.

To visualize the object, think of a turtle that is set at a certain position on the screen and pointed in a certain direction. As the turtle moves, it traces a line on the screen. It always moves in a straight line unless its direction is changed. It can turn a certain angle to its left or to its right. It can also move without leaving a trace.

Here is the list of the public methods of the *Turtle* class with their signatures. These angles are in degrees and measured in a counterclockwise direction from a horizontal line pointing right, just as they are in mathematics.

| Signature | Behavior |
|---|---|
| setColor (**Color** clr) | Set color of trace. |
| setPosition (**int** x, **int** y) | Place turtle at (x, y). |
| setAngle (**int** angle) | Point turtle at angle to horizontal. |
| move (**int** distance) | Move distance in pointing direction. |
| turnLeft (**int** angle) | Turn angle to turtle's left from present pointing direction. |
| turnRight (**int** angle) | Turn angle to turtle's right from present pointing direction. |
| showTrace () | Cause trace to show. |
| hideTrace () | Stop trace from showing. |

If the constructor method of the Turtle class with no parameters except the *Console* name is used, the position of the turtle is initialized to be the center of the window. Its angle is set to zero, that is, pointing directly to the right side of the window. Its color is set to black and the trace is set to show.

The position and angle of the turtle are initialized to other values when the object is instantiated by the *Turtle* class constructor whose signature is

Turtle (*Console c*, **int** *x*, **int** *y*, **int** *angle*);

Here is a *main* method that uses the *Turtle* class to draw a red square of size 30 pixels with its upper-left corner at the center of the console window. (Do not forget the boilerplate.)

```
// The "RedSquare" class.
// Draw a red square of size 30 pixels with its upper-left corner
// at the center of console window.
// Instantiate object t and set color.
Turtle t;
t = new Turtle (c);
t.setColor (Color.red);
t.move (30); // Draw first side.
t.turnRight (90);
t.move (30); // Draw second side.
t.turnRight (90);
t.move (30); // Draw third side.
t.turnRight (90);
t.move (30); // Draw fourth side.
```

Classes in a class library can be grouped into packages. Since the *Turtle* class is stored as part of the package named *hsa.book* it is imported by the statement:

**import** *hsa.book.*;

Here is a shorter *main* method to draw a red square.

```
// The "RedSquare2" class.
// Draw a red square using repetition.
Turtle t;
t = new Turtle (c);
t.setColor (Color.red);
for (int side = 1; side <= 4; side ++)
{
    t.move (30);
    t.turnRight (90);
}
```

This program leaves the turtle pointing in its original direction, to the right, whereas the previous longer program leaves it pointing up.

It is possible to create a drawing using the *Turtle* class that is the same as would be produced by the *moon* graphic created in the first chapter. Here is the *main* method to do this.

```
// The "DrawMoon" class.
// Draws a moon at center of console window
// of radius 60 pixels and color green.
Turtle t;
t = new Turtle (c);
t.setColor (Color.green);
for (int square = 1; square <= 36; square ++)
{
    for (int side = 1; side <= 4; side ++)
    {
        t.move (60);
        t.turnRight (90);
    }
    t.turnRight (10);
}
```

After each square is drawn the turtle is turned right an angle of 10 degrees so that the following square is tilted at an angle of 10 degrees to the one just drawn. After the 35th square is drawn, this turns the turtle so that it is pointing along the horizontal to the right side of the window. This program is simpler than the one requiring a tilted square method shown in Chapter 4.

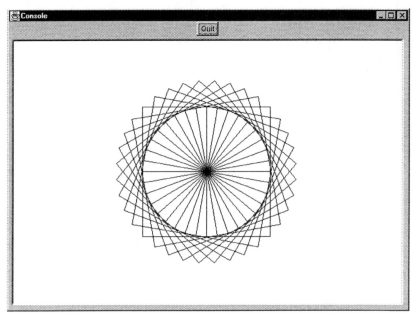

Figure 10.1 Output from Execution of DrawMoon.

# 10.3 Creating the Turtle Class

We will now look at how the *Turtle* class itself is implemented. Using the class requires no knowledge of its implementation. The instantiated class encapsulates both data and methods. Methods that are to be available to be used by other objects are labelled **public**. The data and methods used only by other methods of the class are labelled **protected**. The data (or instance variables) record the current position of the turtle, the direction that it is pointing, its current color, and whether or not the trace is currently showing.

Here is the *Turtle* class.

```
// The "Turtle" class.
import java.awt.*;
import hsa.Console;

public class Turtle
{
    protected Console c;
    protected int x, y, angle;
    protected boolean showing = true;
    protected Color clr = Color.black;

    // Constructor for default initial values of position and angle.
    public Turtle (Console c)
    {
        this.c = c;
        x = c.getWidth () / 2;
        y = c.getHeight () / 2;
        angle = 0;
    } // Default Turtle constructor.

    // Alternate constructor.
    public Turtle (Console c, int x, int y, int angle)
    {
        this.c = c;
        this.x = x;
        this.y = y;
        this.angle = angle;
    } // Alternate Turtle constructor.

    // Other methods of Turtle class.

    public void setColor (Color clr)
    {
        this.clr = clr;
    } // setColor method

    public void setPosition (int x, int y)
    {
        this.x = x;
        this.y = y;
    } // setPosition method
```

```java
    public void setAngle (int angle)
    {
        this.angle = angle;
    } // setAngle method

    public void turnLeft (int turnAngle)
    {
        angle += turnAngle;
        angle = angle % 360;
    } // turnLeft method

    public void turnRight (int turnAngle)
    {
        angle -= turnAngle;
        angle = angle % 360;
    } // turnRight method

    public void showTrace ()
    {
        showing = true;
    } // showTrace method

    public void hideTrace ()
    {
        showing = false;
    } // hideTrace method

    public void move (int distance)
    {
        int newx, newy;
        double rAngle = (angle * Math.PI) / 180;
        newx = (int) Math.round (x + Math.cos (rAngle) * distance);
        newy = (int) Math.round (y + Math.sin (rAngle) * distance);
        if (showing)
        {
            c.setColor (clr);
            c.drawLine (x, y, newx, newy);
        }
        x = newx;
        y = newy;
    } // move method
} /* Turtle class */
```

The method *move* is slightly more complex than the other methods but is perhaps easily understood by examining Figure 10.2. Notice that

$$\sin (rAngle) = dy / distance$$
$$\cos (rAngle) = dx / distance$$

and

$$newx = x + dx$$
$$newy = y - dy$$

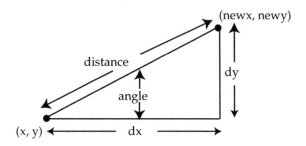

Figure 10.2 Geometry of a Move

It might be better if $x$, $y$, and *rAngle* were maintained as real variables and rounded only when a method is called, to avoid cumulative error due to rounding at each turn.

# 10.4  Instantiating Two Objects from a Class

Here is a *main* method that uses two turtles to draw two spirals, one in orange and the other in cyan. Each spiral begins at the center of the screen but the orange turns to the right, and the cyan to the left.

```
// The "TwoSpirals" class.
// Instantiate two turtles from Turtle class.
// Draw spirals in opposite directions with turtle in two different colors.
Turtle turtle1, turtle2;
```

```
turtle1 = new Turtle (c);
turtle2 = new Turtle (c);
// Set turtle1 to draw in cyan.
turtle1.setColor (Color.cyan);
// Set turtle2 to draw in orange.
turtle2.setColor (Color.orange);
// Set turtle1 to start pointing to upper-left.
turtle1.turnLeft (120);
// Set turtle2 to start pointing to upper-right.
turtle2.turnLeft (60);
// Draw two spirals simultaneously.
for (int distance = c.getWidth () /4; distance > 1; distance --)
{
    turtle1.move (distance);
    turtle1.turnLeft (70);
    turtle2.move (distance);
    turtle2.turnRight (70);
}
```

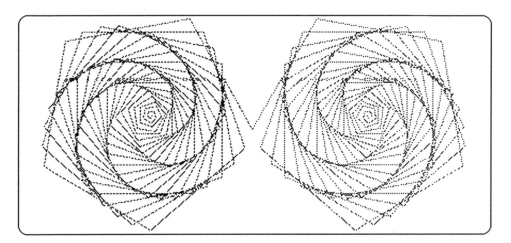

**Figure 10.3 Output from Execution of Two Turtles Drawing.**

In each spiral, after a line is drawn, the turtle is turned by an angle of 70 degrees, to the left for the first turtle and to the right for the second. The distance moved on each leg of a spiral decreases by one pixel from the initial value of *getWidth* / 4, which is one-quarter of the window's width, down to zero.

# 10.5 Method Overloading

In the *Turtle* class definition there are two methods named *Turtle*. These are each constructor methods. When a turtle object is instantiated using the constructor with one parameter, as by *Turtle* (*Console c*), the first version is used. The turtle is set to the default position of the center of the screen, pointing to the right.

The second version has, as well, parameters for the coordinates of the starting position and starting angle. This allows the user to begin drawing at another point in the window and pointing in another direction. In either case the turtle is set to showing the trace and drawing in black. In the second version of the constructor there must be a distinction between the parameters of the constructor *x*, *y*, and *angle* and the class variables *x*, *y*, and *angle*. To differentiate them, the keyword **this** identifies the variables that belong to the object itself. Thus the statement

   **this**.*x* = *x*;

assigns to the instance variable *x* the value of the parameter *x*.

When two or more methods have the same identifier, as the two versions of the constructor method *Turtle* have here, we say the method is overloaded. Which version is to be used depends on the parameters provided. It is possible to have methods of a class other than the constructor method overloaded but this is not done.

Many classes in the Java library provide a variety of constructor methods. No two of these can have the same number and data type of parameters or they could not be distinguished from one another. If no constructor method is provided for a class, the initial values of instance variables are automatically default values.

# 10.6  Creating a New Class by Inheritance

It is possible to create a new class based on an old one by modifying it in various ways. New methods can be added or existing methods changed.

We will change the class *Turtle* by allowing control of the width of the line that is traced by the turtle. This means we must add an additional class variable called *lineWidth* that can be changed from its default initialized value of 1 pixel by the operation

*setLineWidth* (**int** *width*)

where *width* is the new line width. We must also change the existing method *move* to draw a line of the proper width. It, in turn, will use a new method that is added, but not made public, called *drawFatLine*. This method creates a fat line by drawing a ball of radius half the line width at points along the line, close enough together to create the effect of a solid line, somewhat like a ballpoint pen.

Here is the new class.

```
// The "FatTurtle" class.
// For drawing graphics with a variety of line widths.
// This class extends the Turtle class.
import hsa.Console;
import hsa.book.*;

public class FatTurtle extends Turtle
{
    // Add a new variable.
    protected int lineWidth;

    // Only one version of constructor provided.
    public FatTurtle (Console c)
    {
        super (c);
        // Use default setting for other variables defined in Turtle class.
        lineWidth = 1;
    } // FatTurtle constructor
```

```
// Add a new method to set LineWidth.
public void setLineWidth (int newWidth)
{
    lineWidth = newWidth;
} // setLineWidth method

// Draw a filled ball of radius and center at (x, y)
// in the current color.
protected void drawBall (int xc, int yc, int radius)
{
    int diameter = radius * 2;
    int x = xc – radius;
    int y = yc – radius;
    c.fillOval (x, y, diameter, diameter);
} // drawBall method

// Add method drawFatLine.
protected void drawFatLine (int x1, int y1, int x2, int y2)
{
    // Line drawn by moving a ball point pen whose ball
    // is half line width.
    // Line drawn at x values of ball separated by DX which
    // is half the radius.
    // Constants used in calculation.
    final double LEN = Math.sqrt (((x2 – x1) * (x2 – x1)) + ((y2 – y1)
                        * (y2 – y1)));
    final double SINA = (y2 – y1) / LEN;
    final double COSA = (x2 – x1) / LEN;
    final int RADIUS = (lineWidth / 2) + 1;
    final double DX = RADIUS * COSA / 2;
    final double DY = RADIUS * SINA / 2;
    // Set position to draw first ball's center at (x1, y1).
    double xpos = x1;
    double ypos = y1;
    // Draw series of balls along line from (x1, y1) to (x2, y2).
    do
    {
        drawBall ((int) Math.round (xpos), (int) Math.round (ypos),
            RADIUS);
        xpos += DX;
        ypos += DY;
```

```
        }
        while (Math.sqrt ((x2 – xpos) * (x2 – xpos) + (y2 – ypos) * (y2 – ypos))
                >= RADIUS / 2);
    } // drawFatLine method

    // This method overrides the move method of the Turtle class.
    public void move (int distance)
    {
        double rAngle = angle * Math.PI / 180;
        final int newx = (int) Math.round ( x + Math.cos (rAngle) * distance);
        final int newy = (int) Math.round ( y + Math.sin (rAngle) * distance);
        if (showing)
        {
            c.setColor (clr);
            if (lineWidth == 1)
                c.drawLine (x, y, newx, newy);
            else
                drawFatLine (x, y, newx, newy);
        }
        x = newx;
        y = newy;
    } // move method
} /* FatTurtle class */
```

Notice that it is not necessary to repeat the methods of *Turtle* that are unchanged. The only new variable added is *lineWidth*. The only new method made public is *SetWidth*. The new method *move* overrides (replaces) the old version of *move*. If the width is given as 1 pixel, the *Console* method *drawLine* is used. If the width has been set at another value then the new method *drawFatLine* is used.

## 10.6.1  Using the Modified Class

Here is a *main* method that uses the *FatTurtle* class to draw concentric fat circles with centers at the center of the window. The circles will each be made up of 36 short straight lines. A yellow circle will have a radius of *getWidth/* 6 and *lineWidth* of 10 and a green circle radius *getWidth* / 4 and *lineWidth* of 20 pixels.

```
// The "FatCircles" class.
// Use FatTurtle class to draw concentric circles.
FatTurtle turtle1, turtle2;
turtle1 = new FatTurtle (c);
turtle2 = new FatTurtle (c);
turtle1.setLineWidth (10);
turtle2.setLineWidth (20);
turtle1.setColor (Color.yellow);
turtle2.setColor (Color.green);
// Set the x position of each turtle at its own radius from the center
// of the window pointing up.
// Compute some constants.
final int XC = c.getWidth () / 2;
final int YC = c.getHeight () / 2;
final int RADIUS1 = c.getWidth () / 6;
final int RADIUS2 = c.getWidth () / 4;
final int STEPANGLE = 10;
final double STEPANGLERADIANS = STEPANGLE * 2 * Math.PI / 360;
final int DISTANCE1 = (int) Math.round (RADIUS1 *
        STEPANGLERADIANS);
final int DISTANCE2 = (int) Math.round (RADIUS2 * STEPANGLERADIANS);
turtle1.setPosition (XC + RADIUS1, YC – DISTANCE1 / 2);
turtle2.setPosition (XC + RADIUS2, YC – DISTANCE2 /2 );
turtle1.turnLeft (90);
turtle2.turnLeft (90);
for (int direction = 0; direction <= 360; direction += STEPANGLE)
{
    turtle1.move (DISTANCE1);
    turtle1.turnLeft (STEPANGLE);
    turtle2.move (DISTANCE2);
    turtle2.turnLeft (STEPANGLE);

}
```

Figure 10.4 Output from Execution of FatCircles

# 10.7  Class Hierarchy

When one class extends another class the parent or base class is called the **superclass**; the one that inherits from it is the **subclass**.

A subclass may not inherit any variables or methods of the superclass that are labelled as **private**. But it may inherit any labelled as **protected**. That is why we have labelled so many of the variables as **protected**. They cannot be used by another class outside the hierarchy in either case. An object of a subclass "**is an**" object of the superclass. But the reverse is not true. The object of a superclass is not an object of the subclass.

Structured Java data types such as strings and arrays are objects, as are those that we create such as record types or node types for a **linked list**. They are used by reference. All these classes are extensions of the superclass *Object*. It is thus possible, for example, to create a *List* class for maintaining a list that has data of type *Object*. Since all non-primitive data types are *Object*s the same *List* class could be used for many different structured data types.

There exist, as well, a number of classes called **type wrapper classes**, one for each of the primitive data types: *Integer* for **int**, *Float* for **float**,

*Boolean* for **boolean,** and so on. In this way primitive data types can be adapted to a class written for *Objects*.

In this chapter we showed a *Turtle* class which we extended to *FatTurtle*. The *Turtle* class is the superclass, the *FatTurtle* is the subclass. Sometimes, in setting up a class hierarchy, the superclass has one or more methods which have no body. Such methods are labelled **abstract,** as is also the class itself. An **abstract class** cannot be used to instantiate any objects. It is used only to be the superclass of a number of different subclasses. Any object instantiated from one of the subclasses "is an" object of the superclass and thus can be referred to as such.

An abstract class can contain methods including constructors that have a body and these can be used in any subclass. Such a constructor is referred to by the keyword **super** rather than by the name of the superclass itself.

# 10.8  Chapter Summary

This chapter extends the ideas of classes introduced in the first chapter and shows how one class may inherit from another class.

## Abstract Data Types

In programming it is common that several methods access the same variables. If one method is changed, this can affect the other methods in unexpected ways. For this reason, it is useful to encapsulate the data and methods that share the data into an object. This forms an abstract data type since other objects of the program need not be concerned with how that data is stored. Only those methods encapsulated with the data need be concerned.

Other objects may use the methods in the object provided that the signatures and behavior of the encapsulated methods are known to the user. This usage is called **message passing**. Variables that make up the encapsulated data are accessed by the object's methods as global variables and are not passed explicitly as parameters to its own methods.

## Using an Object

One object, the user object, may use another object's (the used object) methods under these conditions.

- The user object must **import** the used object.
- The used object must declare the method to be used as **public**.

## The Turtle Object

An example is provided of an object that is useful for making line drawings. The object is a turtle that can be placed at any point in the window, pointed in a certain direction, and moved in a straight line in that direction. It can be turned to its left or right and the next line drawn. It can be arranged that the line shows or not, so discontinuous line drawings are possible. To use the turtle, the signatures and behaviors of its methods must be known, but the mechanism of implementation need not be known.

The data that is encapsulated with these methods record: the current position, angle of pointing, color, and whether or not the trace is to show for the turtle.

Each method call in the user program must be of the form

Name-of-object.method-name (arguments);

## Classes

To use a class, an object must be declared as belonging to the class by a declaration such as

class-name object-name;

This next assignment allocates space for an instance of this class.

object-name = **new** class-name (arguments);

Depending on what arguments are supplied, the appropriate constructor method of the class is executed to set initial values of the instance variables. If no arguments are provided, default values are used. Each object created from the same class must have a different identifier. If two objects from the same class are instantiated in the program the name identifies which object is referred to.

We used a *Turtle* class and instantiated two turtles and drew lines with each "simultaneously". (Actually only one turtle at a time was drawing.)

## Creating a New Class by Inheritance

One of the benefits of using classes is that a class can be modified easily to:

- add new data (instance variables),
- add new methods, and
- modify existing methods.

Defining such a modified class requires an addition to the header at the beginning of the class definition of the form

> **extends** name-of-original-class

Any new instance variables are then defined and any new methods added. If an existing method is to be modified, its complete new definition must appear. This new definition will **override** the old definition which may no longer be used in the new class.

If the same identifier is used for a method's parameter as for an instance variable, in the body of the method the instance variable's name is preceded by the keyword **this** followed by a dot.

## 10.9  Technical Terms

abstract class                                    subclass

linked list                                       superclass

message passing                                   type wrapper classes

protected

## 10.10    Exercises

1. Instantiate an object from the *Turtle* class and use its methods to write a method to draw a square with its upper-left corner at (*xc*, *yc*) and of size *size* in color *clr*. The signature of this procedure will be

   *square* (**int** *xc*, **int** *yc*, **int** *size*, *Color clr*);

   It must, of course, be a part of a program that imports the *Turtle* class. Now write a program that uses *square* to draw 100 random-sized red squares, located with upper-left corners at random points in the window.

2. Using the Turtle class, write a method to draw a moon similar to that drawn in this chapter with a center at (*xc*, *yc*) made up of squares of size *size* in color *clr*. The signature of the *moon* method should be

   *moon* (**int** *xc*, **int** *yc*, **int** *size*, *Color clr*);

   Draw 20 moons of random size at random points in the window.

3.  Use an object instantiated from the *Turtle* class to draw a simple house with a peaked roof and a window as shown in Figure 10.5.

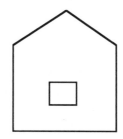

**Figure 10.5 Picture of House**

Make the house drawing into a method and use it in a *main* method to draw a row of houses across the bottom of the window. Modify the program to draw a series of such rows. Arrange that as the rows move from the bottom to the top of the window the houses get smaller, to create the illusion of distance.

4   Use the class *FatTurtle* to instantiate three turtles to draw in the three primary colors: blue, yellow, and red. Start each turtle at a different spot on the screen then have each make 25 moves of distance 5 pixels randomly in one of the four directions: left or right, up or down. Have them move "simultaneously", that is, the blue making one random move, then the yellow, then the red.

5.  Use the class *FatTurtle* to create a window with horizontal stripes. Have 10 stripes filling the window and alternate the colors from one stripe to the next. Make this into a method that will produce alternating stripes of any two colors with the number of stripes filling the window specified as a parameter. The signature of the method is

    *stripes* (**int** *number, Color clr1, Color clr2*);

6.  Use the class *FatTurtle* to instantiate two turtles, one of which will draw horizontal stripes, the other the same number of vertical stripes. Program the two turtles to draw "simultaneously", the first in red and white, the second in green and yellow.

7. Use the class *FatTurtle* to write a method to draw regular polygons of *n* sides in lines of *width* with the center at (*xc*, *yc*) and size (distance from center to any vertex) *size*. Its signature would be

   *polygon* (**int** *xc*, **int** *yc*, **int** *size*, **int** *width*, *Color clr*);

   Use the method *polygon* to approximate a circle by using as large a number of sides *n* as practical.

8. Create a class called *TurtleDash* that inherits from the *Turtle* but which draws all lines as interrupted (dashed) lines rather than continuous lines. Use the class to instantiate a turtle and draw a blue dashed square of size *getHeight / 4*.

# Chapter 11

# Applets and Graphical User Interfaces

An applet is a Java program that can be sent over the **Internet** and run under **World Wide Web browsers** such as **Netscape's Navigator™**. Applets provide access to the Graphical User Interface (GUI) features of Java. Moreover, applets with a GUI can be run on many different **computer platforms**; they are **portable**. The GUI interface elements may, however, be slightly different from one platform to another. In this chapter we will look at how to create applets with graphical user interfaces.

# 11.1 The Structure of an Applet

All applets are classes that inherit from the class *Applet* so that each must import the *Applet* class with the statement

> **import** *java.applet.Applet;*

The *Applet* class has a number of methods and these are often overridden by new versions of the methods in the new subclass applet.

Here are the methods.

- *init* which acts like a class constructor to initialize values of instance variables or set up GUI components. It is called automatically when the applet is run.
- *start* which initializes some of the more advanced features such as concurrent executions or complex animation.
- *paint* which is called once, after *init* completes or again any time a *repaint* method is called. Output of text or drawings is performed in *paint* using the object *g* instantiated from the *Graphics* class.
- *stop* which is called when execution is finished to perform any termination required.
- *destroy* which cleans up after the applet is removed from memory.

The applets we will be showing will only override the *init* and *paint* methods of the Applet class. By default, the other methods listed above will be the ones inherited from the *Applet* class which, in fact, do nothing. There is one more standard Applet method.

- *action* which is perhaps the most interesting applet method. It is used so that a program can communicate with the various actions of the program's user, such as entering input, and clicking or dragging the mouse.

The three standard Applet methods *init, paint,* and *action* will be discussed in detail. Applets can contain other user-defined methods which are called by any of the standard methods.

The **Ready to Program with Java™ Technology** IDE has an applet boilerplate. This boilerplate defines the *init* and *paint* methods. To create a class based on the applet boilerplate, the user selects **New** from the **File** menu in the editor window and then selects **Applet Boilerplate** from the submenu. A dialog box appears so the actual name of the class can be entered.

Here is the class created with the name *ExampleApplet*.

```
// The "ExampleApplet" class.
import java.applet.*;
import java.awt.*;

public class ExampleApplet extends Applet
{
    // Place the instance variables here.

    public void init ()
    {
        // Place the body of the initialization method here.
    } // init method

    public void paint (Graphics g)
    {
        // Place the body of the drawing method here.
    } // paint method
} // ExampleApplet class
```

# 11.2 Applets with No Input

We will begin looking at the details of applets by restricting our attention to very simple applets. The first program outputs the first four lines of "Mary had a little lamb". (This, we believe, is not under copyright.)

Here is the applet. It has no *init* method.

```
// The "Rhyme" class.
import java.applet.Applet;
import java.awt.*;

public class Rhyme extends Applet
{
    public void paint (Graphics g)
    {
        g.drawString ("Mary had a little lamb", 20, 25);
        g.drawString ("Its fleece was white as snow", 20, 40);
        g.drawString ("And everywhere that Mary went", 20, 55);
        g.drawString ("The lamb was sure to go", 20, 70);
    } // paint method
} /* Rhyme class */
```

The *Rhyme* applet imports the *Applet* class and the *awt* package from which it is using the *Graphics* class. An object *g* of the *Graphics* class is automatically instantiated by having *g* as a standard parameter of the *paint* method.

The *drawString* method of the *Graphics* class is used to place the string constant on the screen, starting at coordinates (20, 25). Each subsequent line of the rhyme has a 15 pixels larger value of *y*. This spaces the lines of the rhyme.

Since *paint* is a procedure-type method it has the keyword **void** before its name.

After compiling the applet it is necessary to produce a **Hypertext Markup Language** (HTML) file to place the applet in a browser for execution (browsers read text files). The *HTML* file for this applet, for example, is:

```
<HTML><BODY>
    <APPLET CODE = "Rhyme.class" WIDTH=300 HEIGHT=100>
    </APPLET>
</BODY></HTML>
```

Classes such as *Rhyme* are compiled into files with an extension *.class* on their names. The width and height of the area of output for the applet in pixels (the applet's display area) is specified in the *HTML* file. The *HTML* file begins with the **tag** <HTML> and ends with </HTML>. The applet itself has the tag <APPLET> and is terminated by </APPLET>.

Figure 11.1 shows the result of executing the program.

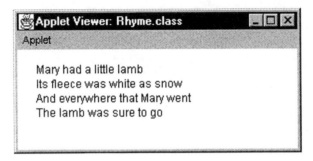

**Figure 11.1 Output of Rhyme Applet**

Here is another example of an applet that draws 18 blocks in a circle around the center of the screen. It has two function-type methods that calculate the sine and cosine of angles in degrees. ($2\pi$ radians = 360 degrees). Java only has built-in methods to calculate the sine and cosine of angles in radians. The methods are not be labelled **static** because they are used by the non-static method *paint*.

```
// The "CircleBlocks" class.
// Draws 18 blocks in a circle.

import java.applet.*;
import java.awt.*;

public class CircleBlocks extends Applet
{
```

```java
    public static final int BLOCK_SIZE = 10;

    public double sind (int angleInDegrees)
    {
        double angleInRadians;

        angleInRadians = angleInDegrees * Math.PI / 180;

        return Math.sin (angleInRadians);
    } // sind method

    public double cosd (int angleInDegrees)
    {
        double angleInRadians;

        angleInRadians = angleInDegrees * Math.PI / 180;

        return Math.cos (angleInRadians);
    } // cosd method

    public void paint (Graphics g)
    {
        int midx = getSize ().width / 2;
        int midy = getSize ().height / 2;
        int radius = Math.min (midx, midy) - BLOCK_SIZE;

        g.setColor (Color.red);

        for (int angle = 0 ; angle < 360 ; angle += 20)
        {
            int xpos = (int) (midx + sind (angle) * radius);
            int ypos = (int) (midy + cosd (angle) * radius);

            g.fillRect (xpos - BLOCK_SIZE / 2, ypos - BLOCK_SIZE / 2,
                        BLOCK_SIZE, BLOCK_SIZE);
        }
    } // paint method
} // CircleBlocks class
```

The *paint* procedure first calculates the position of the center of the applet drawing surface and stores it in *midx* and *midy*. To do this it calls the *getSize* method which is part of the *Applet* class. The *getSize* method returns a *Point* object which contains two fields *width* and *height*. Thus the width of the applet drawing surface is *getSize ().width* and the height is *getSize ().height*. The radius of the circle that the blocks are to be drawn in is calculated using the shorter of the screen width and height with the block size subtracted.

The **for** statement cycles the angle from 0 to 360 in 20 degree increments. Each time through the loop, it calculates the center of the block to be drawn and then uses *g.fillRect* to draw the block. Remember that in Java the first of the two parameters passed to *fillRect* is the upper-left corner of the block. To get *xpos* and *ypos* to be the center of the block, we subtract half the block size from the upper-left corner coordinates.

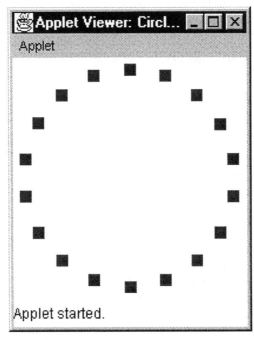

Figure 11.2 Output of CircleBlocks Applet

# 11.3  Applets with User Input and Output with GUI

We will now consider an example of an applet with input as well as output. This next applet program accepts input, in this case the user's age, in a box on the screen and then, when Return is pressed, outputs the bus fare that the user must pay. The fare is $2.00 for adults, $1.00 for seniors, and $.50 for children under 12 years of age.

In addition to the standard applet methods *init* and *action* a user-defined method *fare* is used to perform the actual calculation. The age of the customer is entered into a box in the applet. This box is a graphical user interface (GUI) component of the class *TextField*. The box is labelled with the user prompt by a component of the *Label* class.

Here is the applet program.

```
// The "BusFare3" class.
import java.applet.Applet;
import java.awt.*;

// Class to output bus fare given age.
public class BusFare3 extends Applet
{
    Label prompt;      // Declare user prompt.
    TextField input;   // Declare input box.
    int age;           // Declare input variable.

    // Sets up GUI components.
    public void init ()
    {
        prompt = new Label ("Enter age then press Return");
        input = new TextField (5);
        // Place label and text field on applet.
        add (prompt);
        add (input);
    } // init method
```

```
// Respond to action of user's input.
public boolean action (Event e, Object o)
{
    age = Integer.parseInt (o.toString ());
    showStatus ("$" + fare (age)); // Show fare.
    input.setText (""); // Clear entry box.
    return true; // Shows action responded to.
} // action method

// Method to compute fare from age.
public String fare (int age)
{
    if (age < 12)
        return "0.50";
    else if (age >= 65)
        return "1.00";
    else
        return "2.00";
} // fare method
} /* BusFare3 class */
```

This program uses two GUI components:

- a *Label* to indicate what is to be entered into the input box, and
- a *TextField* to hold the input.

The *Label* is given the identifier *prompt* and the *TextField* the identifier *input*.

In the *init* method the prompt *Label* is instantiated with a string constant and the input *TextField* instantiated as having spaces for up to 5 characters. The label and text field are not placed on the screen until the two *add* lines are executed.

In the *action* method there are two standard parameters: *e* of type *Event* and *o* of type *Object*. The *action* method returns a value **true** when the action has been carried out.

The *Event* argument *e* is normally used to decide what event has occurred. In this example there is only one possible event, namely the pressing of Return after entering the value for *age*, so *e* is not used explicitly in the *action* method. If a number of different actions are possible then the *e* must be examined to see which one has actually occurred.

Figure 11.3 shows the results of running the program.

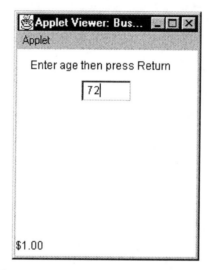

**Figure 11.3 Output of BusFare3 Applet**

The *Object* argument *o* will contain the contents of the text field when the Return key has been pressed. The text field input is transformed into a string using the *toString* method and must then be parsed by the *parseInt* method of the *Integer* class so that it can be assigned to *age* which is an **int** variable.

The *setText* method of the *TextField* class is used to display a null string in the field. This clears the text field so that another value of *age* can be entered. The result of the fare calculation provided by the method *fare* is displayed in the **status bar** at the bottom of the web browser window. The status bar's position varies with the browser being used. To display the result, the value of *fare*, which is a *String* type, must be shown as the argument of the *showStatus* method of the *Applet* class.

Here is an example of an applet that uses a button. The *BlockButton* applet draws a randomly place block on the screen in response to a button press. The *init* method of the applet creates the button and then places in on the applet drawing surface using the *add* method.

```
// The "BlockButton" class.
// Draws blocks in response to button pushes.
import java.applet.*;
import java.awt.*;

public class BlockButton extends Applet
{
    public boolean action (Event e, Object o)
    {
        Graphics g = getGraphics ();

        g.setColor (Color.green);
        g.fillRect ((int) (Math.random () * getSize ().width),
                (int) (Math.random () * getSize ().height), 20, 20);

        return true;
    } // action method

    public void init ()
    {
        Button button = new Button ("Draw Block");
        add (button);
    } // init method
} // BlockButton class
```

When the button is pressed by the user, the Java Virtual Machine calls the *action* method. In this example, because we know there is only one component, we do not need to check which component caused the *action* method to be called. The *action* method calls the applet's *getGraphics* to obtain the applet's drawing surface. Unlike the *paint* method, the *action* method does not have a *Graphics* object to draw upon. Once this is done, the drawing color is set to green and *fillRect* is called with a randomly upper-left corner. Once again we use *getSize* ().*width* and *getSize* ().*height* to obtain the size of the applet's drawing surface. Note that *fillRect* expects integers for its parameters, so we must convert the random coordinates into integers before passing them into *fillRect*.

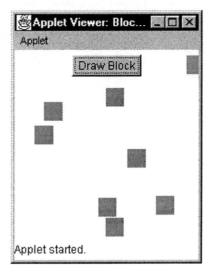

Figure 11.4 Output of BlockButton Applet

# 11.4 Applets with Multiple GUI Components

So far we have introduced the idea of the GUI components *TextField* and *Label*. In this section we will look at another GUI component, the **button.** A button is a box with a label in it that can be clicked by the mouse to trigger an event.

We will illustrate this with an example where there is one text field to enter an integer labelled "Input integer", two buttons one labelled "Square" the other "Cube", and a second text field labelled "Output". If an integer is entered into the input field and the button "Square" clicked, the square of the integer is displayed in the output field. If "Cube" is clicked the cube of the integer appears in the output field.

Figure 11.5 shows this applet.

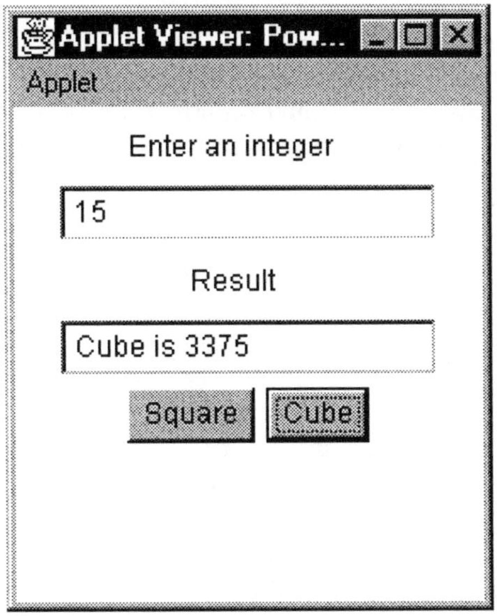

Figure 11.5 Output of the Powers Applet

Here is the applet program.

```
// The "Powers" class.
import java.applet.Applet;
import java.awt.*;

// Class to produce either a square or cube of an integer.
public class Powers extends Applet
{
    Label enter;
    TextField input;
    int number;
    Label result;
    TextField output;
    Button square;
    Button cube;

    // Set up GUI components.
    public void init ()
```

```
    {
        enter = new Label ("Enter an integer");
        input = new TextField (20);
        result = new Label ("Result");
        output = new TextField (20);
        square = new Button ("Square");
        cube = new Button ("Cube");
        add (enter);
        add (input);
        add (result);
        add (output);
        add (square);
        add (cube);
    } // init method

    // Respond to action of user.
    public boolean action (Event e, Object o)
    {
        number = Integer.parseInt (input.getText ());
        if (e.target instanceof Button)
        {
            if (e.target == square)
                output.setText ("Square is " +
                    Integer.toString (square (number)));
            else if (e.target == cube);
                output.setText ("Cube is " + Integer.toString (cube (number)));
            return true;
        }
        return true;
    } // action method

    // Method to compute square.
    public int square (int number)
    {
        return number * number;
    } // square method

    // Method to compute cube.
    public int cube (int number)
    {
        return number * number * number;
    } // cube method
} /* Powers class */
```

Each labelled button is created by a single statement that both instantiates and labels the button. The *target* of an event is the graphical user interface component that the user activated. If *button1* is clicked, this target is equal to *button1*.

# 11.5  Layout of GUI Components

The GUI components *Label*, *TextField*, and *Button* have, by default, been placed in the applet's display area in the order in which they are added, starting at the top left and going to the right. When no more components can be placed in the same line, the components are placed on the next line and so on. This default layout is called *FlowLayout*.

Layout can also be controlled using other **layout managers**. The programmer chooses the layout manager using the *setLayout* method of the *Container* class. A container is an area where the GUI components can be laid out. A **panel** is such a container.

There can be a number of panels in the applet's display area and each panel is placed in the applet using *FlowLayout*. In the statement that sets the layout of the panel, the space between components (horizontal gap) and the space between the component and the upper and lower edges of the panel (vertical gap) can also be set. The panel's size depends on the sizes of the components it contains and the gap sizes.

Here is an applet that has two panels. The first panel is on the top of the applet. The label in that panel is left justified in accordance with the layout specified for the panel. The second panel is at the bottom of the applet. The label in that panel is centered.

```
// The "PanelTest" class.
import java.applet.Applet;
import java.awt.*;

public class PanelTest extends Applet
{
    private Panel p1, p2;
```

```
    private Label label1, label2;

    public void init ()
    {
        p1 = new Panel ();
        p2 = new Panel ();
        p1.setLayout (new FlowLayout (FlowLayout.LEFT, 20, 10));
        label1 = new Label ("This label is on left");
        p1.add (label1);
        p2.setLayout (new FlowLayout (FlowLayout.CENTER, 5, 30));
        label2 = new Label ("This label is centered");
        p2.add (label2);
        p1.setBackground (Color.red);
        p2.setBackground (Color.blue);
        setLayout (new BorderLayout ());
        add ("North", p1);
        add ("South", p2);
    } // init method
} /* PanelTest class */
```

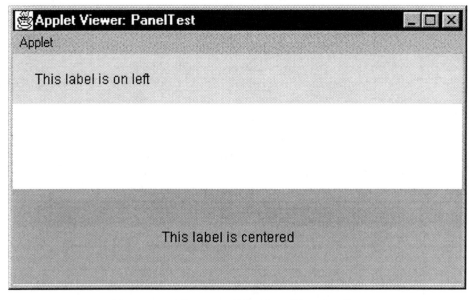

Figure 11.6 Output of the PanelTest Applet

Figure 11.6 shows the result of running this program. Notice that the labels are first added to their containers (the panels) and then the panels are added to the applet. In the *setLayout* method for *p1*, 20 is the horizontal gap and 10 the vertical gap. In order to see the differences in the two panels, this applet should be run with a display area of width 400.

In the layout manager, called *BorderLayout*, components are placed in the applet's display area in five areas: *North, South, East, West,* and *Center*, each area having one component in it. For example, the statement

*add* ("North", *P1*);

adds the panel *P1* in the *North* area and

*setLayout* (**new** *BorderLayout* ());

sets the applet's layout manager to *BorderLayout*.

# 11.6  Other GUI Components

The *Checkbox* GUI component allows the programmer to create a box on screen which can be used to elicit an "on or off" response from the user. The **check box** has only two states: checked or not checked. By default, when the box is instantiated, it is not checked. If the box is clicked at any time its state is changed from checked to unchecked, or vice versa.

For example, check boxes can be used to control type face. In this textbook some words are in italics, some in bold face, and some in italic-bold face. Others are in plain face. Since a face cannot be both plain and italic we cannot have three check boxes (plain, bold, and italic) that could be checked independently. We could, however, have two check boxes: one italic and one bold.

A *Font* object must be instantiated by a statement such as

   *f* = **new** *Font* ("SansSerif", *Font.PLAIN*, 24);

which controls the text font. This statement sets the font name to "SansSerif" (a sans serif type), the font style to plain, and the point size of the font to 24 points. The *TextField* method *setFont* is used to set the font of a text field *name* to the font *f* with the statement

   *name.setFont* (*f*);

Here is the applet for controlling the text style of text displayed in a text field.

```
// The "TextCheckbox" class.
import java.applet.Applet;
import java.awt.*;

public class TextCheckbox extends Applet
{
    private TextField name;
    private Checkbox boldFont, italicFont;
    private Font f;

    public void init ()
    {
        name = new TextField ("My name", 10);
        boldFont = new Checkbox ("Bold");
        italicFont = new Checkbox ("Italic");
        f = new Font ("SansSerif", Font.PLAIN, 24);
        name.setFont (f);
        add (name);
        // Check boxes are by default initialized to unchecked.
        add (boldFont);
        add (italicFont);
    } // init method

    public boolean action (Event e, Object o)
    {
        int box1, box2;
        if (e.target instanceof Checkbox)
```

```
        {
              // Read state of Bold box.
              if (boldFont.getState () == true)
                  box1 = Font.BOLD;
              else
                  box1 = Font.PLAIN;
              // Read state of Italic box.
              if (italicFont.getState () == true)
                  box2 = Font.ITALIC;
              else
                  box2 = Font.PLAIN;
              f = new Font ("SansSerif", box1 + box2, 24);
              name.setFont (f);
        }
        return true;
    } // action method
} /* TextCheckbox class */
```

Figure 11.7 shows the result of running this program.

Figure 11.7 Output of the TextCheckbox Applet

Radio buttons are similar to check boxes except that only one of a group of buttons can be clicked at a time. Radio buttons must be grouped into a *CheckboxGroup*.

Here is an applet to demonstrate radio buttons that change the type style of printing in a text field.

```java
// The "FontButtons" class.
import java.applet.Applet;
import java.awt.*;

public class FontButtons extends Applet
{
    private TextField name;
    private CheckboxGroup style;
    private Checkbox sansSerif, serif, monoSpaced;
    private Font f;

    public void init ()
    {
        name = new TextField ("My name", 15);
        f = new Font ("SansSerif", Font.PLAIN, 14);
        name.setFont (f);
        add (name);
        style = new CheckboxGroup ();

        // Check SansSerif radio button only to start.
        sansSerif = new Checkbox ("SansSerif", style, true);
        serif = new Checkbox ("Serif", style, false);
        monoSpaced = new Checkbox ("Monospaced", style, false);
        add (sansSerif);
        add (serif);
        add (monoSpaced);
    } // init method

    public boolean action (Event e, Object o)
    {
        String fontName;
        if (e.target instanceof Checkbox)
        {
```

```
            if (sansSerif.getState () == true)
                fontName = "SansSerif";
            else if (serif.getState () == true)
                fontName = "Serif";
            else
                fontName = "Monospaced";
            f = new Font (fontName, Font.PLAIN, 14);
            name.setFont (f);
        }
        return true;
    } // action method
} /* FontButtons class */
```

Figure 11.8 shows the result of running this program.

Figure 11.8 Output of the FontButtons Applet

# 11.7 Graphics Using Applets

So far, we have been able to draw graphics using the *hsa Console* class. Most of these same graphics methods can be used with the *Graphics* class. Graphics are drawn on a GUI component of the *Canvas* class. The size of the canvas must be set using the *resize* method of the *Component* class. If a canvas *c* is instantiated by

> *Canvas c = **new** Canvas ();*

it can be set to be 200 pixels wide and 150 pixels high by the statement

> *c.resize (200, 150);*

Here is an applet to draw 10 blue balls of radius 20 pixels each at random locations on a canvas of width 250 pixels and height 275 pixels.

```
// The "Random" class.
import java.applet.Applet;
import java.awt.*;

public class Random extends Applet
{
    final int WIDTH = 250;
    final int HEIGHT = 275;
    final int RADIUS = 20;
    int xCenter, yCenter;

    public void paint (Graphics g)
    {
        Canvas c = new Canvas ();
        c.resize (WIDTH, HEIGHT);
        for (int count = 1; count <= 10; count ++)
        {
            xCenter = (int) (Math.random () * (WIDTH – 2 * RADIUS)) +
                RADIUS;
            yCenter = (int) (Math.random () * (HEIGHT – 2 * RADIUS)) +
                RADIUS;
            drawBall (g, xCenter, yCenter, RADIUS, Color.blue);
```

```
        }
    } // paint method

    public void drawBall (Graphics g, int x, int y, int radius, Color clr)
    {
        g.setColor (clr);
        g.fillOval (x – radius, y – radius, 2 * radius, 2 * radius);
    } // drawBall method
} /* Random class */
```

Figure 11.9 shows the result of running this program in an applet display area of width 260 and height 300.

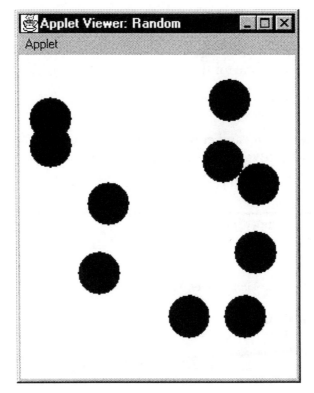

Figure 11.9 Output of the Random Applet

# 11.8  Simple Animation

It is possible to simulate the motion of objects by drawing an object in one position, erasing it, then redrawing it in a nearby location over and over. To demonstrate this process, we will create an applet that draws a red ball at a random position on a canvas then moves it step-by-step by a distance $dx$ in the $x$-direction and $dy$ in the $y$-direction. When the ball reaches the boundary of the canvas it is bounced off the border. When it reaches the top or bottom boundary the $y$-increment ($dy$) is reversed. When it reaches either side boundary its $x$-increment ($dx$) is reversed.

The drawing and redrawing is done here in the *action* method. In this method, there is no automatic instantiation of an object of the *Graphics* class as there is in the *paint* method because of its parameter.

This is done for the canvas *display* with the statements

```
Graphics displayG;
displayG = display.getGraphics ();
```

If the drawing and erasing of the ball occurs too rapidly the animation is not effective so a time wasting method called *delay* is included.

Here is the applet.

```
// The "Bounce" class.
import java.applet.Applet;
import java.awt.*;

public class Bounce extends Applet
{
    final int WIDTH = 250;
    final int HEIGHT = 275;
    Button bounce = new Button ("Bounce Ball");
    Canvas display = new Canvas ();

    public void init ()
    {
        super.init ();
        setLayout (new BorderLayout ());
```

```
        add ("North", bounce);
        display.resize (WIDTH, HEIGHT);
        add ("Center", display);
} // init method

public boolean action (Event e, Object o)
{
    final int RADIUS = 20;
    Graphics displayG;
    int x, y, dx, dy;
    displayG = display.getGraphics ();
    displayG.setColor (Color.white);
    displayG.fillRect (0, 0, WIDTH, HEIGHT);
    displayG.setColor (Color.black);
    displayG.drawRect (0, 0, WIDTH, HEIGHT);
    x = (int) (Math.random () * (WIDTH – 2 * RADIUS)) + RADIUS;
    y = (int) (Math.random () * (HEIGHT – 2 * RADIUS)) + RADIUS;
    drawBall (displayG, x, y, RADIUS, Color.red);
    dx = 1;
    dy = 1;
    for (int i = 0; i < 1000; i ++)
    {
        drawBall (displayG, x, y, RADIUS, getBackground ());
        x += dx;
        y += dy;
        if (x <= RADIUS | | x >= WIDTH – RADIUS)
            dx = –dx;
        if (y <= RADIUS | | y >= HEIGHT – RADIUS)
            dy = –dy;
        drawBall (displayG, x, y, RADIUS, Color.red);
        delay (10000); // Wastes time to produce delay.
    }
    Font f = new Font ("Serif", Font.BOLD, 72);
    displayG.setColor (Color.blue);
    displayG.setFont (f);
    displayG.drawString ("Done! ", WIDTH / 2 – 80, HEIGHT / 2);
    return true;
} // action method
```

```
public void drawBall (Graphics g, int x, int y, int radius, Color clr)
{
    g.setColor (clr);
    g.fillOval (x – radius, y – radius, 2 * radius, 2 * radius);
} // drawBall method

public void delay (int howLong)
{
    // This wastes time.
    for (int i = 1; i <= howLong; i ++)
    {
        double garbage = Math.PI * Math.PI;
    }
} // delay method
} /* Bounce class */
```

The result of running the applet is difficult to show since it is a moving graphic. The HTML to run the applet should specify a width 260 and a height 300 to accomodate the size of the drawing area used by this applet.

# 11.9  A Case Study Using GUIs and Graphics

We will now look at an example that combines many of the GUI and graphic concepts presented earlier in this chapter.

## 11.9.1  Problem Specification

Write a Java applet that allows the user to draw a single oval or a square of a predefined size. The user should be able to select whether the shape is drawn in red, green, or blue and whether the shape should be filled in or outlined.

## 11.9.2   User Interface – Component Selection

Much of the work in this problem involves the design of the user interface. Solving this problem requires a group of controls and a drawing surface upon which the shape is drawn.

We want a shape drawn in response to a user command. The GUI component most closely associated with a user command is a button. When the user presses a button "something should happen". In this case, the applet will have three buttons: one to draw a rectangle, one to draw an oval, and one to clear the screen.

We must also allow the user to select the color of the shape to draw. Since we do not act upon the color that the user selects until the draw command is given, a button is not the appropriate GUI element for color selection. The shape can have only one color at a time so that the selection of colors is mutually exclusive. This is best achieved with a group of the alternative GUI elements called "radio buttons".

The final GUI component will control whether the shape is drawn filled or outlined. Because we have two mutually exclusive options here, we have a choice of components. We could again choose radio buttons labelled "filled" and "not filled", or use the check box GUI component instead. In general, a check box is used when the result of not selecting the check box is obvious. Here the box would be labelled "Filled". Two radio buttons would be used when the options are not obvious and both need to be labelled. For example, if a piece of text must either be bold or italic, we would use radio buttons since "not bold" does not necessarily mean italic in the mind of the user.

Once the control components have been decided upon, the drawing surface must be determined. Areas used to draw on are generally a Java *Canvas*. We will set a specific size for the *Canvas* drawing surface within the program. If the HTML that calls the applet does not specify a large enough applet drawing surface to contain the size of the canvas we choose, parts will not be visible. We will therefore draw a border around the *Canvas* to alert the user as to the location where any requested shape will appear.

### 11.9.3   User Interface – Placement of Components

Once the components have been decided upon, they need to be placed in the applet. It usually makes sense to group all of the control components in one location. In this case, we will place all the control components on the left side of the applet and the shape drawing area (*Canvas*) on the right side of the applet. Because the command components are most important to the user, we place the three buttons at the top of the control area. We place the rest of the components at the bottom of the control area. In general, a radio button group should be stacked vertically. In this case, we will place the radio buttons on the left and the check box on the right.

Once the layout has been decided we need to create panels to enable Java to place the components where we want them. We will use border layouts within each panel as they are easy to use.

The control components and the drawing surface form a layout. The control components appear on the left (west) side and the shape display appears on the right (east). The controls panel is then further subdivided into a buttons panel and an options panel. The buttons appear above (north) and the rest of the components appear below (south). The buttons are placed in the button panel. We stack them one over the other by placing them in another border layout (north, center, and south).

The radio buttons and check box form the options panel which is further subdivided. The radio buttons are placed on the left (west) and the check box on the right (east). Finally, the radio buttons are stacked vertically in the north, center, and south positions of another border layout. Figure 11.10 shows how the layout panels are nested within each other. This nesting of panels allows for the development of complicated layouts.

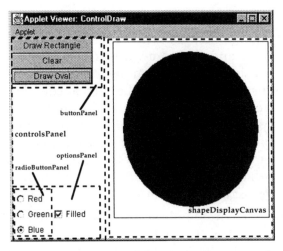

Figure 11.10 Output of the ControlDraw Applet

## 11.9.4 The Program

Our program has three parts. One part creates the control components, the second part places the components and the third draws the shapes when the user presses a button. These three parts could be further subdivided using methods, but each of these parts is simple enough that little would be gained by subdivision.

First we declare the GUI components and create them in the class header. The components must be fields if we are to access them in more than one method. As an alternative, the components could be declared in the class header and created in the *init* method.

The components are then placed into the applet in the *init* method since they only need to be laid out once when the applet first runs. Each panel is declared and its layout type specified. We do not need to declare the panels as fields since we will not be referring to them later. The GUI components are then laid out in their panels.

The *action* method is called whenever the user presses a button. We check to see if the button is pressed (remember that the component that caused the action is specified by the *target* field of the *Event* object). Because we are going to be drawing, we also need a *Graphics* object. Because we are drawing to the *Canvas* we need the *Graphics* object associated with that *Canvas*. This is achieved using the *getGraphics ()* method. When any of the buttons is pressed, we erase the *Canvas* and then draw a box just inside its borders. If we are drawing a shape (rather than just clearing the drawing area), we then get the current color. We get the current color by calling the *getState ( )* method of each of the radio buttons until we find the button that is currently selected. We then set the drawing color of the *Graphics* object to the appropriate color. We then determine whether the filled check box is set using *getState ()* and use either a *draw* method (*drawRect* or *drawOval*) or a *fill* method (*fillRect* or *fillOval*) as appropriate to draw the shape just inside the border.

Note that we do not act when the user selects a radio button or the check box. Java automatically updates the check boxes and radio buttons for us. We only need to check the state of the button when a drawing command is given. It is important, however, that our *action* method return **false** if a non-button component is selected so that Java can handle it automatically.

Here is the *ControlDraw* applet.

```java
// The "ControlDraw" class.
import java.applet.Applet;
import java.awt.*;

public class ControlDraw extends Applet
{
    // Class header
    final int WIDTH = 250;
    final int HEIGHT = 275;
    Button rect = new Button ("Draw Rectangle");
    Button clear = new Button ("Clear");
    Button oval = new Button ("Draw Oval");
    CheckboxGroup colorGroup = new CheckboxGroup ();
    Checkbox red = new Checkbox ("Red", colorGroup, true);
    Checkbox green = new Checkbox ("Green", colorGroup, false);
    Checkbox blue = new Checkbox ("Blue", colorGroup, false);
    Checkbox filled = new Checkbox ("Filled", true);
    Canvas shapeDisplayCanvas = new Canvas ();
```

```
public void init ()
{
    super.init ();
    // Insert code to initialize the applet here.
    setLayout (new BorderLayout ());
    Panel radioButtonPanel = new Panel ();
    radioButtonPanel.setLayout (new BorderLayout ());
    Panel optionsPanel = new Panel ();
    optionsPanel.setLayout (new BorderLayout ());
    Panel buttonPanel = new Panel ();
    buttonPanel.setLayout (new BorderLayout ());
    Panel controlsPanel = new Panel ();
    controlsPanel.setLayout (new BorderLayout ());
    radioButtonPanel.add ("North", red);
    radioButtonPanel.add ("Center", green);
    radioButtonPanel.add ("South", blue);
    optionsPanel.add ("West", radioButtonPanel);
    optionsPanel.add ("East", filled);
    buttonPanel.add ("North", rect);
    buttonPanel.add ("Center", clear);
    buttonPanel.add ("South", oval);
    controlsPanel.add (buttonPanel, "North");
    controlsPanel.add (optionsPanel, "South");
    add ("West", controlsPanel);
    shapeDisplayCanvas.resize (WIDTH, HEIGHT);
    add ("East", shapeDisplayCanvas);
} // init method

public boolean action (Event e, Object o)
{
    Graphics displayG;
    int x, y, dx, dy;
    displayG = shapeDisplayCanvas.getGraphics ();
    displayG.setColor (Color.black);
    if (e.target == rect)
    {
        displayG.clearRect (0, 0, WIDTH, HEIGHT);
        // Erase previous drawing.
        displayG.drawRect (5, 5, WIDTH - 10, HEIGHT - 10);
        if (red.getState ()) displayG.setColor (Color.red);
        else if (green.getState ()) displayG.setColor (Color.green);
        else displayG.setColor (Color.blue);
```

```
            if (filled.getState ())
            {
                displayG.fillRect (20, 20, WIDTH – 40, HEIGHT – 40);
            }
            else
            {
                displayG.drawRect (20, 20, WIDTH – 40, HEIGHT – 40);
            }
            return true;
        }
        else if (e.target == clear)
        {
            displayG.clearRect (0, 0, WIDTH, HEIGHT);
            displayG.drawRect (5, 5, WIDTH – 10, HEIGHT – 10);
            return true;
        }
        else if (e.target == oval)
        {
            displayG.clearRect (0, 0, WIDTH, HEIGHT);
            displayG.drawRect (5, 5, WIDTH – 10, HEIGHT – 10);
            if (red.getState ()) displayG.setColor (Color.red);
            else if (green.getState ()) displayG.setColor (Color.green);
            else displayG.setColor (Color.blue);
            if (filled.getState ())
            {
                displayG.fillOval (20, 20, WIDTH – 40, HEIGHT – 40);
            }
            else
            {
                displayG.drawOval (20, 20, WIDTH – 40, HEIGHT – 40);
            }
            return true;
        }
        return false;
    } // action method
} /* ControlDraw class */
```

# 11.10    Chapter Summary

## Applets

Applets are Java programs that can be run under a **browser** and shared through the **World Wide Web**. Java applets are portable from one computer platform to another. Each applet program is a class that extends the Applet class. The Applet class has a number of standard methods that can be overridden. The standard methods used in the applets we created are:

- *init* which acts as a class constructor,
- *paint* which is used to output text and graphics, and
- *action* which is used to detect and act upon the user's actions such as the Return after input of data or the clicking of a mouse.

Other user-defined methods can be included in the applet. These are used by the standard methods which are executed automatically when the applet is run, just as the *main* method of an application program is executed. The *init* method is executed first, then the *paint* method, and then the *action* in response to the user.

Each applet must have an *HTML* file placed in the browser. The size of the applet's display area is specified in the *HTML* file.

## Applets with Input and Output and GUI

GUI components called *TextFields* can be labelled using the GUI component *Label*. These *Labels* indicate to the user what is to be entered into the text field. The *TextFields* provide textual input to applets. After entry, when Return is pressed, the *action* method converts the input to a string and then parses it to yield the appropriate data type of the input. The output could be placed in a second *TextField* but is often shown in the **status bar** at the bottom of the web browser window. All input and output must be a string of characters.

## Applets with Multiple GUIs

In addition to actions that can be created by pressing Return after input in a text field, actions can be created using *Button* components. An example is shown which has an input text field and two buttons labelled "Square" and "Cube" that cause either the square or cube of the number in the text field to be displayed in an output text field depending on which of the buttons is clicked. The *Event* argument *e* of the action method is examined by *e.target* to determine which button was pushed. The action of pressing Return after input is ignored. Only the pressing of a button is responded to.

## Layout of GUI Components

The default layout of GUI components is left to right across the top of the applet until a line is filled. When one line is filled a new line is started. This is called *FlowLayout*.

A different **layout manager** can be selected using the *setLayout* method of the *Container* class. An applet can be divided into **panels** each of which can have its own layout. The panels themselves are also laid out in the applet.

*BorderLayout* is another layout manager which places a component in one of five areas of the container (panel or applet) namely: *North, South, East, West,* and *Center*. The *add* statement identifies the component area.

## Other GUI Components

**Check boxes** can be created as *Checkbox* components. Boxes yield a value of checked or unchecked (true or false) and their value is changed from one to the other by clicking.

A group of check boxes can be used to identify a number of mutually-compatible alternatives. Groups of boxes which are used with mutually-exclusive alternatives are called **radio buttons**. Only one of the group may be checked at a time. Check boxes used as radio buttons must be grouped explicitly into a *CheckboxGroup*.

## Graphics Using Applets

All the graphics methods implemented in the *Console* class are available through the *Graphics* class which is instantiated automatically in the *paint* method. Graphics are drawn on a *Canvas* whose size is specified in the applet using the *resize* method of the *Canvas* class.

## Simple Animation

Motion of objects can be simulated by a series of still graphics where the object is placed in slightly different places on the canvas in each successive graphic. Between each, the image must be erased before it is redrawn. A **delay** between drawing and erasing can control the speed of animation.

If drawing is to be done in the *action* method rather than in the *paint* method, a *Graphics* object must be explicitly instantiated for it.

## Complex Graphical User Interfaces

An example was given showing an interface with buttons, a check box, a set of radio buttons laid out in several panels, as well as a canvas for showing graphics of different kinds and in different colors depending on user input. A good layout is not easily achieved.

# 11.11 Technical Terms

| | |
|---|---|
| button | layout manager |
| checkbox | portable |
| Hypertext Markup Language (HTML) | status bar |
| | void |
| Internet | World Wide Web browser |

# 11.12    Exercises

1. Write an applet that will produce a table showing the balance in a bank account at the end of each year if an interest rate of 10% a year is credited at the end of each year. In the table show the year, starting in 1998 when $1,000.00 is deposited, the interest for the year, and the balance at the end of the year for 10 years. You will need to display the output using the *drawString* method of the *Graphics* class.

2. Write an applet which produces the same table as Exercise 1 but asks the user to enter the starting year, the initial deposit, the interest rate, and the number of years the table is to display. You will need to create labelled *TextFields* for each input item and a button to initialize the calculation once the data has been entered.

3. Write an applet with a panel containing two buttons, one labelled "Ball" and the other "Block", and a canvas on which either a ball or a square block is drawn depending on which button is clicked. Arrange to erase the previous drawing each time a button is clicked.

4. Modify the applet of Exercise 3 to have a second panel with radio buttons to control the color of the ball or block drawn.

5. Test the *BorderLayout* manager by adding buttons labelled "North" on the north position, one labelled "East" in the east position, and so on. Repeat the exercise using two panels, one in the north position and one in the south position.

6. Test the *FlowLayout* default manager by adding several text fields of different lengths in the applet. Change the lengths of the fields to see what happens.

7. Create an applet to show the animation of red circles radiating from the center of a canvas until they touch the border of the canvas, then starting again from the center.

8. Change the applet of Exercise 7 so that you do not erase the circle as it moves out but when it reaches the border and starts over from the center.

9. Write an applet to show the animation of a ball starting at the center of its canvas and moving randomly in any of the four directions: north, south, east, and west by a small amount until it reaches the border of the canvas, then starting over. Try not erasing the image so as to produce a zigzag trail.

10. Modify the applet of Exercise 9 so that the color of the ball changes randomly among three different colors, each time it starts from the center. Follow the animation for 10 starts from the center.

11. Write an applet to control the type font with check boxes to indicate bold or italic, radio buttons to choose the type style, radio buttons to choose the point size, and a text field to contain the text whose font is to be controlled.

# Chapter 12

# Creating Web Pages with HTML

One of the main features of the Java programming language is its ability to have its applets operate through the Internet on the World Wide Web. Through this means, Java programs can be shared. Java applets are executed over the Internet by being part of a **web page**. These applets can then be used in a variety of ways, for example accessing databases and managing systems remotely. Applets can also used to incorporate animated illustrations into a web page. In this chapter we will look at how web pages are created and how Java applets are included in them.

# 12.1 The Hypertext Markup Language

Anyone with access to the Internet can download web pages to their computer. A page may consist of text and illustrations or pictures. The text itself is often laid out with headings and divided into paragraphs. Some words may be in bold type, some in italics, and so on. If the same web page were downloaded to a different computer platform, the appearance of the page might be quite different. For example, words that are in a bold typeface might appear underlined.

In order to make a web page displayable on a variety of computer platforms, the text of the page must be marked by special symbols to indicate how the text should appear. This requires a common markup language that is understood by all computer platforms. Each different platform type must have a **markup language interpreter** in much the same way as it has a Java bytecode interpreter.

The common markup language used on the Internet is the Hypertext Markup Language (HTML). We have already seen how an HTML file is created for a Java applet. We will now look at the markup language **tags** that are needed to format text by creating headings, paragraphs, typefaces, and so on.

# 12.2  Markup Tags

HTML is for the most part a **semantic markup language**, that is, the tags indicate the meaning of a particular piece of text. Most of the tags appear as a pair. All tags are enclosed in angle brackets. This distinguishes them from the actual text. For example, to indicate that the piece of text

Markup Tags

is to be a major heading, the text is preceded by the tag <H1> and followed by the end tag </H1>. This indicates that the text is to be a type 1 heading, that is, the most important heading. We record this in the HTML file as

<H1> Markup Tags </H1>

The form for this type of tagged element is

<tag-name> text </tag-name>

The particular appearance of this heading might be different on different computer platforms but it will remain a heading.

The web browser determines how a particular tagged text is displayed. While HTML is designed to permit appropriate display in a wide variety of environments, most of our references will be for Netscape's Navigator™ or Microsoft's Internet Explorer™.

A piece of tagged text is called an **element**. For example,

<H2> Purpose of Tags </H2>

is an element that will produce a heading of type 2. The text of a type 2 heading is generally smaller than that of a type 1 heading, so the type 2 heading can be used as a sub-heading.

Tags are case-insensitive so instead of <H2> we could write <h2>.

# 12.3 HTML Documents

An **HTML document** is the complete file that is made accessible to the web server. The document begins with the tag <HTML> and ends with the end tag </HTML>. The document is divided into a **header** (not to be confused with a heading) and a **body**. The header is marked by the tag <HEAD> and ended by the tag </HEAD>. The user can also choose to include a title to be displayed in the title bar of the browser. For example, the file

```
<HTML>
<HEAD>
<TITLE>
A Blank Page
</TITLE>
</HEAD>
</HTML>
```

produces a blank window with the title "A Blank Page" in the title bar.

To produce text in the window itself, we precede the text by the tag <BODY> and end it by </BODY>. Here is an example.

```
<HTML>
<HEAD> <TITLE> A Short Example </TITLE> </HEAD>
<BODY> Here is some text </BODY>
</HTML>
```

This creates a window with "A Short Example" in the title bar and the words "Here is some text" in the window.

The spacing of an HTML file has no effect on what is produced. It can be entered on separate lines, or all run together. When the browser displays text, it condenses the white space between words to a single space no matter how many spaces are present. There are, however, tags which can be used to have the browser display the text exactly as typed (see Section 12.4 for more information).

For an HTML document to be accessible, it must be placed on a computer running a web server. The web server makes files placed in certain directories accessible to the Internet. When a web user enters the web address of the HTML document, the web server sends a copy of the document to the user's local web browser. The web browser then displays the document in the browser's window.

# 12.4  HTML Tags for Formatting Text

We have already mentioned the tag for creating headings. There are six levels of headings: H1, H2, H3, H4, H5, and H6, in decreasing order of importance. Here is an example of an HTML document.

```
<HTML>
<BODY>
    <H1> The Main Heading </H1>
    <H2> The First sub-heading </H2>
        <P> Text of first sub-heading
    <H2> A Second sub-heading </H2>
        <P> Text of second sub-heading
</BODY>
</HTML>
```

This might produce the result shown in the browser window of Figure 12.1.

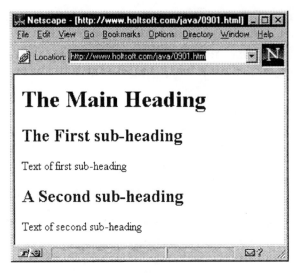

Figure 12.1 Result of Running HTML File

The text under each heading is preceded by the **paragraph tag** <P>. There is no end tag for a paragraph; the paragraph is ended when a new paragraph or heading tag is encountered. Normally, displayed text within a paragraph continues until it reaches the end of the browser window line, at which time a new line is begun. The start of a new line can be controlled by inserting a break tag <BR> in the text. The <BR> tag does not have a corresponding end tag. For example, the text

```
<HTML>
<BODY>
    <P> Mary had a little lamb. <BR> Its fleece was white as
        snow. <BR> And everywhere that Mary went <BR> The
        lamb was sure to go.
</BODY>
</HTML>
```

would be displayed as

```
Mary had a little lamb.
Its fleece was white as snow.
And everywhere that Mary went
The lamb was sure to go.
```

Notice that the end-of-lines in the entry text are ignored.

Preceding the text by the tag <CENTER> and following it by </CENTER> centers text in the window rather than left justifies it.

The typeface used by individual parts of a text can be controlled by the following tags, each of which requires a corresponding end tag.

```
<B> for Bold
<BIG> for Big
<BLINK> for Blinking text (Netscape only)
<I> for Italic
<SMALL> for Small
<U> for Underline
<EM> for Emphasis
```

How these are interpreted depends on the particular computer platform used to display the text.

Certain tags we have presented can have **attributes**. Normally a paragraph is left justified. The <P> tag, however, can have an attribute that controls whether the paragraph is left or right justified. The tag

<P ALIGN="right">

causes the paragraph to be right justified. The quoted part of the attribute ALIGN="right" is case sensitive, unlike the tags themselves, and must be entered as shown.

The alignment of headings allows both "right" and "center". For example,

<H1 ALIGN="center"> Here is a Heading </H1>

produces a first level heading centered in the browser window. By default, headings are left justified.

With the <BODY> tag, attributes can control the background color and text color. For example,

<BODY BGCOLOR="red">

causes the background of the browser window to be red. The entry

<BODY TEXT="blue">

causes the text of the browser window to be displayed in blue. The colors available by name are the same as for the Java *Color* class.

The tag <HR> can be used to create a horizontal line (a rule) across the page.

A long quotation presented in a text without quotation marks around it can be indented from the rest of the text using the <BLOCKQUOTE> tag.

Lists can be formatted, unnumbered, with some sort of bullets indicating the individual entries using the <UL> tag. For example, the HTML text

```
<HTML>
<BODY>
    <H3> Here is an unordered list of colors </H3>
    <UL> <LI> red <LI> green <LI> blue </UL>
</BODY>
</HTML>
```

produces the output of Figure 12.2.

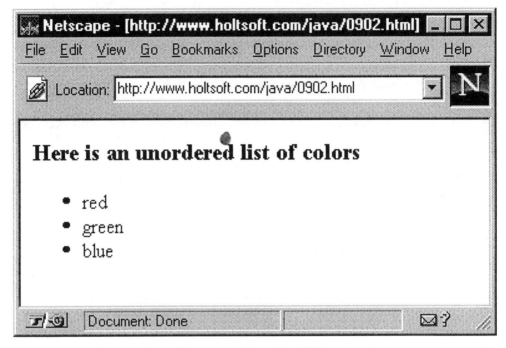

Figure 12.2 Unordered List

The <LI> tag precedes each list entry and does not have a corresponding end tag.

An ordered list, in which the entries are "numbered" in some way, can be created using the <OL> tag which has, as an attribute, the type of the "number".

The type may be:

"a" for little letters a, b, c, etc.
"A" for capital letters A, B, C, etc.
"1" for numerals 1, 2, 3, etc.
"i" for lower case Roman numerals i, ii, iii, etc.
"I" for upper case Roman Numerals I, II, III, etc.

The HTML text

```
<HTML>
<BODY>
    <H3> Here is an ordered list of colors </H3>
    <OL TYPE="a"> <LI> red <LI> green <LI> blue </OL>
</BODY>
</HTML>
```

produces the output of Figure 12.3.

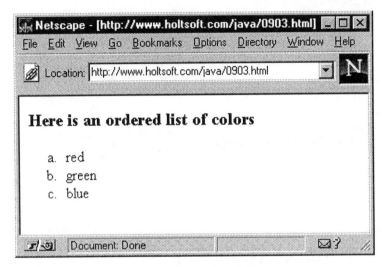

Figure 12.3 Ordered List

A list element can also contain a list. In this way, lists can be nested inside other lists.

Text can be kept in the exact format that it is typed in by using the <PRE> tag. For example, the HTML text

```
<HTML>
<BODY>
    <PRE>
        The boy stood on the burning deck
        Eating peanuts by the peck.
    </PRE>
</BODY>
</HTML>
```

will maintain the format. The text is usually then monospaced as in Figure 12.4. The <PRE> tag is often used to display ASCII text in columns.

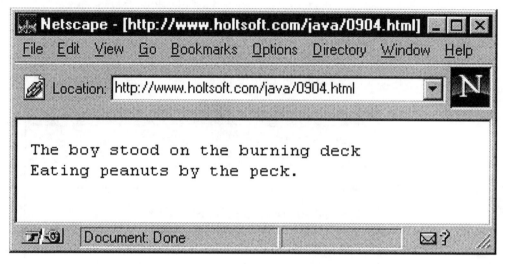

Figure 12.4 Text Displayed in Original Format

# 12.5  Linked Web Pages

While it is possible to organize a series of web pages in a linear form (like the pages of a book) they are usually organized as hypertext. This means that the pages are connected in such a way that a reader can move from one page to another using **links** that are embedded in the text itself. The user simply clicks the mouse on one of the links and is automatically moved to the new destination designated by the link. For example, a web page might represent the front page of a newspaper. If the lead article continues on another page, the reader clicks the hypertext link at the bottom of the article on the front page and the link automatically brings up the page with the remainder of the article.

To make an element in the text into a link to another page, or to another location in the same page, the element must be marked with the <A> or **anchor tag**. An **anchor element** cannot contain other tags with the exception of a <BR> or an <IMG> tag. (The <IMG> tag, used for displaying images, will be explained later in more detail.)

To allow an anchor element to point to another location, it must have an HREF attribute. This stands for Hypertext REFerence. When the jump is to another web page, this attribute gives the web address of the new destination. If the jump is to another location on the same page the HREF is to a named location on that same page.

The web address of any document is called its **Universal Resource Locator (URL)**. The document may be, for example, an HTML file or a picture. The format of a URL is the web **protocol**, namely *http* followed by a colon and two slashes, the machine name followed by a slash, then the path of the document. This path is not necessarily a directory path on the machine where the file resides; it is up to the web server software to interpret the path as it sees fit.

It is common to have a directory called *public* or *html* in the user's home directory for storing files that are to be available to the web. The URL for such a file then is

    http://machine-name/~user-name/file-name

The web server interprets this URL to return the file given by *file-name* from *user-name*'s *public* directory. If the URL contains only a file name, then it refers to a file on the same machine, in the same directory as the web page.

If a word such as "difficulties" on a web page is to be a link to another web page it is marked up in this way

    <A HREF=URL-of-other-web-page> difficulties </A>

It is common for words or phrases that can act as links to other locations to be displayed in a distinguishing color. Many systems have anchor elements displayed in blue, whereas other text is in black. This tells the reader what elements can be clicked.

If the programmer wants to create a link from one location to another on the same page, the link is marked up in this way.

<A HREF="#destination-name"> difficulties </A>

To specify the link's destination, the programmer marks up the text at the destination as follows.

<A NAME="made-up-name-of-destination"> text-at-destination </A>

The text at the destination of a link is not displayed in any distinguishing way.

When a jump occurs in the same web page, the page is scrolled so the destination text is moved to the top of the browser window.

# 12.6  Tables in Web Pages

Tables are often used in web pages. A table is prefaced by a <TABLE> tag. This tag has an attribute to align the table by

ALIGN="alignment"

where alignment can be "left", "right", or "center" (default "left"). The attribute

BORDER="width"

controls the width of the border drawn between elements of the table. The attribute

CELL PADDING="padding"

controls the space in pixels between the contents of the cell and the border (default = 1). The attribute

CELL SPACING="width"

is the width of the dividing line between cells (default = 2). The size of the table is controlled by the attribute

WIDTH="table-width"

If the table width is followed by a percent sign (%), the table is sized to be a certain percentage of the window's width.

In specifying a table, the rows are marked by the <TR> tag. Within a row each entry is marked as a header by the <TH> tag or as an element of data by the <TD> tag.

Here is the HTML for a simple multiplication table. The column headings are the multipliers, the row headings are the multiplicands, and the data entries are their products. The top-left corner entry is an * to indicate "multiplication".

Here is the HTML for a times table.

```
<HTML>
<BODY>
   <TABLE BORDER="1">
      <TR>
         <TH>*
         <TH>1
         <TH>2
         <TH>3
         <TH>4
      </TR>
      <TR>
         <TH>1
         <TD>1
         <TD>2
         <TD>3
         <TD>4
      </TR>
      <TR>
         <TH>2
         <TD>2
         <TD>4
         <TD>6
         <TD>8
      </TR>
      <TR>
         <TH>3
         <TD>3
```

```
            <TD>6
            <TD>9
            <TD>12
        </TR>
        <TR>
            <TH>4
            <TD>4
            <TD>8
            <TD>12
            <TD>16
        </TR>
    </TABLE>
</BODY>
</HTML>
```

This produces the table of Figure 12.5.

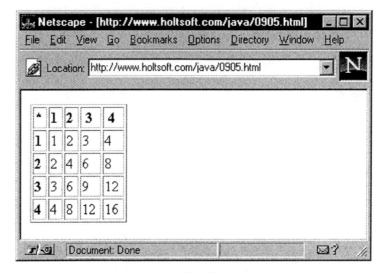

**Figure 12.5 Multiplication Table**

The <TR>, <TD>, and <TH> tags can have attributes. These attributes include the

ALIGN="alignment"

attribute where *alignment* is "left", "right", or "center" and the

VALIGN="vertical-alignment"

attribute where *vertical-alignment* is "top", "middle", or "bottom". If an ALIGN or VALIGN attribute is given for <TR> it becomes the default for the entire row unless overridden.

For the <TD> and <TH> tags, a given cell can occupy more than one row or column. The attributes

```
ROWSPAN="number-of-rows"
COLSPAN="number-of-columns"
```

control the number of rows or columns the cell occupies.

Here is an example of the multiplication table with additional rows and columns to illustrate these attributes.

```
<HTML>
<BODY>
<TABLE BORDER>
    <TR>
        <TH COLSPAN="2" ROWSPAN="2" ALIGN="center"
                        VALIGN="middle">*
        <TH COLSPAN="2" ALIGN="center">1-2
        <TH COLSPAN="2" ALIGN="center">3-4
    </TR>
    <TR>
        <TH>1
        <TH>2
        <TH>3
        <TH>4
    </TR>
    <TR>
        <TH ROWSPAN="2" VALIGN="middle">1-2
        <TH>1
        <TD>1
        <TD>2
        <TD>3
        <TD>4
    </TR>
    <TR>
        <TH>2
        <TD>2
        <TD>4
        <TD>6
```

```
            <TD>8
      </TR>
      <TR>
          <TH ROWSPAN="2" VALIGN="middle">3-4
          <TH>3
          <TD>3
          <TD>6
          <TD>9
          <TD>12
      </TR>
      <TR>
          <TH>4
          <TD>4
          <TD>8
          <TD>12
          <TD>16
      </TR>
   </TABLE>
   </BODY>
   </HTML>
```

Figure 12.6. shows the results. Note that if no width is specified with the BORDER attribute, a default width is used.

Figure 12.6 Modified Multiplication Table

# 12.7  Images in Web Pages

Many web pages incorporate pictures and diagrams along with text. Most web browsers have the ability to display images in two formats, **GIF** or ".gif" (Graphics Interchange Format) and **JPEG** or ".jpeg" (Joint Photographic Expert Group). The GIF format is suited to storing computer graphics. The JPEG format is used to store compressed photographs.

To include images, the basic format is

    <IMG SRC="url">

where *url* is the URL of the image to be displayed. No <IMG> end tag is used. Attributes of the <IMG> tag are

    ALT="string"

where *string* is the text to be displayed if the image itself cannot be displayed. This happens if the user has turned off image loading to save time in downloading a web page or is displaying the page in an environment incapable of displaying graphics (such as a text terminal). By custom, the *string* is enclosed in square brackets to indicate that it is an alternate to the actual image.

Other <IMG> attributes control the size of the image. They are

    HEIGHT="image-height"
    WIDTH="image-width"

If the image in the file has a different size than is given by these two attributes, it is scaled up or down to fit. Providing the height and width of the image permits the browser to lay out the page before the image itself is downloaded. This saves time in downloading web pages.

The image can be aligned by the attribute

    ALIGN="alignment"

where *alignment* is either "left" or "right".

The text flows around an image. If the image is left justified, the text appears on the right and vice versa. When this wrapping occurs, the text is very close to the image. The attributes:

        HSPACE="horizontal-space"
        VSPACE="vertical-space"

can be used to create more space around the image. They control the horizontal and vertical space between the image and the text.

An image can also be used as an anchor element so that clicking it will lead to another web page. This is done by placing the image specification inside an <A> tag. For example,

<A HREF="Next-Page.html"> <IMG SRC="Next.gif" ALT=" [Next Page] ">
</A>

allows the image displayed from the file *Next.gif* to point to the web page in the HTML file *Next-Page.html*.

The <CENTER> tag is used to center an image. For example, the following HTML draws the picture in sunset.jpeg.

        <CENTER>
            <IMG SRC="sunset.jpeg" ALT=" [Picture of sunset] ">
        </CENTER>

In such a case, text is not wrapped around the image.

# 12.8  Applets in Web Pages

To embed an applet in a web page we use the <APPLET> tag as in

<APPLET CODE="url" WIDTH="width" HEIGHT="height">

where *url* is the web address of the applet *class* file. It includes the *.class* extension. The *width* and *height* define the space the web browser reserves for the applet (the applet's display area). The ALT attribute may be included to show text that is to be displayed if the applet cannot be run. This can happen if the browser does not support Java, or Java has been turned off in the preferences of the browser. The applet element must end with the </APPLET> end tag.

The applet element can also contain PARAM elements. These are parameters passed to the applet. The form of these parameters is

<PARAM NAME="name" VALUE="value">

Within the applet *class* definition, a parameter is read using the *getParameter* method of the *Applet* class in the form

getParameter ("parameter-name")

This function-type method returns a *String* object corresponding to the *value* associated with the *parameter-name* or **null**.

As an example, we will show an applet called *ScrollingText* that moves text horizontally in the applet's display area. The actual text to be scrolled might be specified in an HTML file such as:

<APPLET CODE="ScrollingText.class"
                    HEIGHT="100" WIDTH="500">
<PARAM NAME="message" VALUE="Display this! ">
</APPLET>

Inside the applet named *ScrollingText*, the value of the parameter could be read in its *init* method as shown here.

```
public void init ()
{
    message = "Scrolling Example";
    if (getParameter ("message") != null)
    {
        message = getParameter ("message");
    }
}
```

Since a value of the *message* parameter is provided in the HTML, the message "Display This!" will be used. If no value is provided for the parameter, the *init* method will use a value of *message*

"Scrolling Example"

By using parameters, the programmer can create more general applets whose behavior can be modified by changing the HTML that calls the applet rather than changing the Java program itself.

There is no direct way of changing the width and height of the applet unless the applet creates a *Frame* object of the desired size. Within an applet, the assigned width and height of the applet can be determined using the methods of the *Applet* class

> *size ().width*
> *size ().height*

These methods are used in the *ScrollingText* applet to center text horizontally.

To create the illusion of scrolling to the left, the text is first drawn, then erased, and redrawn starting in a position slightly to the left of its previous starting point. The delay necessary in animation before the text is erased and redrawn is achieved using the *Thread.sleep* (20) method. This produces a delay of 20 milliseconds. This *Thread* method is not explained in this book but may be used instead of putting in a time wasting loop as we have in other animation examples.

Here is the *ScrollingText* applet.

```
// The "ScrollingText" class.
import java.applet.*;
import java.awt.*;

public class ScrollingText extends Applet
{
    // The default message to be scrolled.
    String message = "Scrolling Example";
    static final int SIZE = 40;       // The font size of the message.
    static final int SPEED = 5;       // The speed that it is scrolled.

    // Read parameter "message" from HTML.
    public void init ()
    {
        // Get the message from a parameter, if available.
        if (getParameter ("message") != null)
        {
            message = getParameter ("message");
```

```
        }
    } // init method

    public void start ()
    {
        Font font = new Font ("Serif", Font.BOLD, SIZE);
        Graphics g = getGraphics ();
        int fontHeight = getFontMetrics (font).getAscent ();
        int appletWidth = size ().width;
        int appletHeight = size ().height;
        int x = 0;
        // Set the y location of text so that message is centered vertically.
        int y = (appletHeight + fontHeight) / 2;

        show ();
        g.setFont (font);

        while (true)
        {
            // Draw the message twice in order to get the impression
            // of scrolling off the left edge.  (See Figure 12.7.)
            g.setColor (Color.black);
            g.drawString (message, x, y);
            g.drawString (message, x - appletWidth, y);

            // Pause 40 milliseconds.
            try { Thread.sleep (40); }
            catch (InterruptedException e) { }

            // Erase the message in the previous location.
            g.setColor (getBackground ());
            g.drawString (message, x, y);
            g.drawString (message, x - appletWidth, y);

            // Change the location scrolling it to the left. When the
            // location moves off the left edge, move it to the right edge.
            x -= SPEED;
            if (x < 0)
                x = appletWidth;
        }
    } // start method
} /* ScrollingText class */
```

Figure 12.7 illustrates the scrolling of the message "Scrolling Example". The text in hollow letters is outside of the applet's display area and does not show.

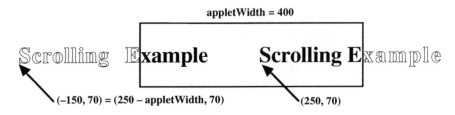

Figure 12.7 Explanation of Scrolling Text

# 12.9  An Example Web Page with Applets

We will now create a web page containing a number of attention-getting applets which use animation.

The applet called *ScrollingText* creates a moving banner for the company name "Frank's Used Cars!". This animation continues for as long as the web page is displayed.

The web page also uses a more complicated applet which bounces the message "Special Deals!" around in the applet's display area. The message starts out with the font size of 6 points. Every time the message hits a wall the font size increases by one point. When the text can no longer fit in the space allocated for the applet, it is displayed centered in the applet's display area. The entire process begins again when a user clicks the applet display area.

The colors of the background and of the bouncing text can be controlled by parameters in the HTML for the applet.

In the applet, the *start* method is executed immediately after the *init* method and is used to perform the animation.

Figure 12.8 shows the text "Bouncing Text Class" in various locations as it hits the borders of the applet display area. The direction of the bounce is shown as well as the coordinates of the beginning of the text at the time of the bounce.

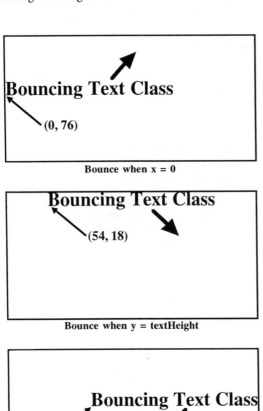

appletWidth = 331
appletHeight = 161
textWidth = 221
textHeight = 18

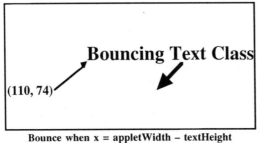

Figure 12.8 The BouncingText Applet

Here is the *BouncingText* class.

```
// The "BouncingText" class.
import java.applet.*;
import java.awt.*;

public class BouncingText extends Applet
{
    // The default message to be "bounced".
    String message = "Bouncing Text Class";
    Color textColor = Color.black;  // The default color of the message.
    boolean finished = false;// Whether the text is finished "bouncing".
    int size;                       // The current size of the text.

    // Read parameter "message" from HTML.
    public void init ()
    {
        // Read the "message" parameter.
        if (getParameter ("message") != null)
        {
            message = getParameter ("message");
        }

        // Read the "color" parameter.
        if (getParameter ("color") != null)
        {
            String textColorString = getParameter ("color");
            if (textColorString.equalsIgnoreCase ("red"))
                textColor = Color.red;
            else if (textColorString.equalsIgnoreCase ("green"))
                textColor = Color.green;
            else if (textColorString.equalsIgnoreCase ("blue"))
                textColor = Color.blue;
            else if (textColorString.equalsIgnoreCase ("yellow"))
                textColor = Color.yellow;
            else if (textColorString.equalsIgnoreCase ("cyan"))
                textColor = Color.cyan;
            else if (textColorString.equalsIgnoreCase ("white"))
                textColor = Color.white;
            else if (textColorString.equalsIgnoreCase ("black"))
                textColor = Color.black;
        }
```

```
    // Read the "bgcolor" parameter.
    if (getParameter ("bgcolor") != null)
    {
        String textColorString = getParameter ("bgcolor");
        if (textColorString.equalsIgnoreCase ("red"))
            setBackground (Color.red);
        else if (textColorString.equalsIgnoreCase ("green"))
            setBackground (Color.green);
        else if (textColorString.equalsIgnoreCase ("blue"))
            setBackground (Color.blue);
        else if (textColorString.equalsIgnoreCase ("yellow"))
            setBackground (Color.yellow);
        else if (textColorString.equalsIgnoreCase ("cyan"))
            setBackground (Color.cyan);
        else if (textColorString.equalsIgnoreCase ("white"))
            setBackground (Color.white);
        else if (textColorString.equalsIgnoreCase ("black"))
            setBackground (Color.black);
    }
} // init method


// Handle event of mouse button pressed down.
// Restarts bouncing.
public boolean mouseDown (Event e, int x, int y)
{
    finished = false;
    start ();
    return true;
} // mouseDown method


// If the text is finished "bouncing" (finished is true), then the
// paint method draws the message in the specified size in the middle
// of the applet's area.
public void paint (Graphics g)
{
    if (finished)
    {
        // Create the font and get width and height of the message.
        Font font = new Font ("Serif", Font.BOLD, size);
        int textWidth = getFontMetrics (font).stringWidth (message);
        int textHeight = getFontMetrics (font).getAscent ();
```

```
        // Set the font and color.
        g.setFont (font);
        g.setColor (textColor);

        // Draw the message in the center of the applet's space.
        g.drawString (message, (size ().width – textWidth) / 2,
            (size ().height + textHeight) / 2);

    }
} // paint method

// The start method "bounces" the text. It starts by erasing the
// applet's space and then setting the font to size 6. The main
// loop moves the message one pixel in the specified direction until
// the message meets an edge. It then changes the direction of
// travel of the message and increases the size of the message by
// one point. It exits the loop when the message is too large to
// fit in the applet's space.
public void start ()
{
    Font font;                          // The current font of the message.
    Graphics g = getGraphics ();    // The graphics context of the applet.
    int appletWidth = size ().width;     // The applet's width.
    int appletHeight = size ().height;   // The applet's height.
    int x, y;           // The lower-left corner of the text message.
    int dx, dy;             // The direction of travel of the message.
    int textWidth = 0;      // The width of the text.
    int textHeight = 0;     // The height of the text.

    show ();        // Must be called for applet graphics to be visible.

    // Erase the applet's drawing surface.
    g.clearRect (0, 0, size ().width, size ().height);

    // Set x, y to be the lower-left corner of the drawing surface.
    x = 1;
    y = appletHeight – 1;

    // Set dx, dy to move text diagonally upwards and to the right.
    dx = 1;
    dy = –1;
```

```
// Set the initial size for the message.
size = 6;

// Create the font and get the message's current height and width.
font = new Font ("Serif", Font.BOLD, size);
textWidth = getFontMetrics (font).stringWidth (message);
textHeight = getFontMetrics (font).getAscent ();

// If the message is too long or tall to be bounced, exit now.
if ((textWidth >= appletWidth) || (textHeight >= appletHeight))
{
    finished = true;
    repaint ();
    return;
}

// Set font and color and draw the string in the initial position.
g.setFont (font);
g.setColor (textColor);
g.drawString (message, x, y);

// The font grows one point in size every time it hits a side
// until it no longer fits in the applet's space.
while (true)
{
    // Erase previous text by drawing the message in the previous
    // location in the applet's background color.
    g.setColor (getBackground ());
    g.drawString (message, x, y);
    g.drawRect (x, y - textHeight, textWidth, textHeight);

    // If the text is at an edge, increase the size of the text.
    if ((x <= 0) || (y < textHeight) || (x > appletWidth - textWidth)
        || (y >= appletHeight))
    {
        int oldTextWidth = textWidth;

        size++;
```

```
// Create font and get message's new height and width.
font = new Font ("Serif", Font.BOLD, size);
textWidth = getFontMetrics (font).stringWidth (message);
textHeight = getFontMetrics (font).getAscent ();

// Set the new font.
g.setFont (font);

// If the message no longer fits, break out of the loop.
if ((textWidth >= appletWidth) ||
    (textHeight >= appletHeight))
{
    finished = true;
    break;
}

// Did we hit the left edge?
if (x <= 0)
{
    dx = -dx;
}
// Did we hit the right edge?
else if (x > appletWidth - oldTextWidth)
{
    dx = -dx;
    // Change x so entire message fits in applet's space.
    x = appletWidth - textWidth;
}

// Did we hit the bottom edge?
if (y >= appletHeight)
{
    dy = -dy;
}
// Did we hit the top edge?
else if (y < textHeight)
{
    dy = -dy;
    // Change y so entire message fits in applet's space.
    y = textHeight;
}
}
```

```
        // Modify the text's location by the current direction of travel.
        x += dx;
        y += dy;

        // Draw the message in the new position.
        g.setColor (textColor);
        g.drawString (message, x, y);

        // Sleep for 20 milliseconds. Without the pause, the message
        // moves too quickly and flashes terribly because it is
        // spending more time erased than visible.
        try { Thread.sleep (20); }
        catch (InterruptedException e) { }
    }

    // After the loop, reduce the size of the text by three points and
    // call the paint routine to place the message in the center of the
    // applet's drawing surface.
    size -= 3;
    repaint ();
  } // start method
} /* BouncingText class */
```

Note that the *paint* method is called whenever the applet needs to be painted. This method does nothing unless the text has stopped bouncing, in which case *finished* is set to true. If *finished* is true it gets the height and width of message and draws the message centered in the applet's display area.

Here is the HTML for the web page. It contains a table as well as the two applets we have shown.

```
<HTML>
<HEAD>
    <TITLE>Frank's Used Cars!</TITLE>
</HEAD>
<BODY>
    <CENTER>
```

```
<APPLET CODE="ScrollingText.class" WIDTH=500
                                    HEIGHT=100>
    <PARAM NAME="message"
                    VALUE="Frank's Used Cars!">
    </APPLET>
</CENTER>

<HR>

<H1>Get them cheap!</H1>
<B>Frank's Used Cars!<B> provides cheap cars for the masses.
These cars have been driven only a few hundred thousand
miles and are as good as new. <EM>Most still have their
original steering wheels!</EM> And many still have brakes.
Some even come with their original owners! Learn the car's ins
and outs with the person who should know.
<P> Come one, come all and pick up your cheap car at
<B>Frank's Used Cars!</B>

<HR>

<CENTER>
    <APPLET CODE="BouncingText.class" WIDTH=500
                                      HEIGHT=100>
        <PARAM NAME="message"
                        VALUE="Special Deals!">
        <PARAM NAME="color" VALUE="blue">
        <PARAM NAME="bgcolor" VALUE="yellow">
    </APPLET>
</CENTER>

<HR>

<CENTER>
    <TABLE BORDER>
    <TR ALIGN="center">
        <TH>
        <TH>Without Steering Wheels or Brakes
                (Handyman Special!)
        <TH>With Steering Wheel
        <TH>With Brakes
        <TH>With Both (Deluxe!)
    </TR>
```

```
        <TR ALIGN="center">
            <TH>1958 Anblaster Mystique
            <TD>$500
            <TD>$1000
            <TD>$1200
            <TD>$7500
        </TR>
        <TR ALIGN="center">
            <TH>1972 Postal Truck
            <TD>$1500
            <TD>$2000
            <TD>$2400
            <TD>$8500
        </TR>
        <TR ALIGN="center">
            <TH>1986 Bullet Special<BR>(+$200 for hole removal)
            <TD>$1800
            <TD>$2600
            <TD>$2900
            <TD>$9800
        </TR>
        </TABLE>
        With original driver, add $300.
        <BR>
        <EM>
            Original driver is not covered by the warranty.
        </EM>
        <BR>
        <SMALL><SMALL>
            Then again, neither is the car.
        </SMALL></SMALL>
    </CENTER>
</BODY>
</HTML>
```

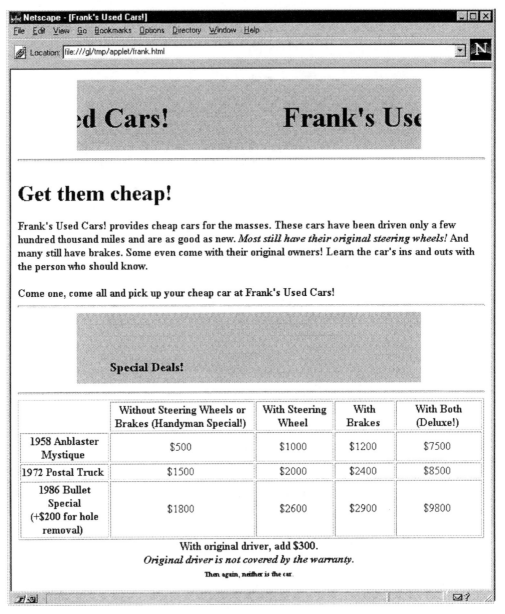

Figure 12.9 The Web Page

# 12.10     Chapter Summary

Java and the Internet are closely connected. Java applets can be shared over the Internet and can be incorporated into web pages to provide attention-getting animated components. This chapter discussed how web pages can be created and how applets can be included in them.

### Hypertext Markup Language (HTML)

Since web pages must be able to be downloaded to a variety of computer platforms, the text of the pages must be marked with tags to describe how the text is to be displayed, for example: when a new paragraph is to begin; what is to be a heading; and so on. A web page is often more than one of a series of pages that can be examined linearly. It is usually a **hypertext** that allows the reader to move from one point in the text, the **link**, to another point, quite often on a different page, called the **destination**. In this way persons scanning the page can find out more information about a particular item that interests them. **Tags** must be incorporated in the marked up web page to permit this hypertext property.

### Markup Tags

Markup tags must be distinctive from the text that will ultimately appear on the web page. To accomplish this, all tags are enclosed in angle brackets. Each tag type has a name. For example, a tag for a major heading has the **tag name** H1. For a less important heading, a sub-heading, the tag name might be H2.

Many tags come in pairs that bracket the text controlled by the tag. The end tag has the same tag name as the beginning tag except that it has a slash (/) in front of the name. The form for bracketed tag pairs is

<tag-name> web text </tag-name>

The actual appearance of a web page element on a computer screen can vary from one computer platform to another, but the meaning is preserved. For example, a heading might appear in bold face on one computer platform and underlined on a different one.

## HTML Documents

An HTML document is a file that is made accessible to a web server. It is bracketed by the <HTML> .. </HTML> tags. A document may have a header bracketed by the <HEAD> .. </HEAD> tags. The header is displayed in the browser title bar. The text to be shown in the browser window is bracketed by the <BODY> .. </BODY> tags. In the text, line breaks and white space are reduced to a single space.

## Formatting Text

Headings in text are bracketed by heading tags. Six levels of importance of heading tags are H1, H2, .. H6.

Paragraphs begin with the <P> tag with no corresponding end tag. Line breaks can be included using the <BR> tag. Text to be displayed without change must be bracketed by the <PRE> .. </PRE> tags.

Text typeface can be controlled by tags: <B> for Bold, <BIG> for Big, <I> for Italic, <SMALL> for Small, and <U> for Underline, each of which must have corresponding end tags.

## Tag Attributes

Certain tags can have attributes. These can control alignment, justification, background color, text color, and so on. The part of an attribute given in quotes is case sensitive. For example, the <BODY> tag can be written with this attribute.

<BODY TEXT="blue">

The corresponding end tag does not have the attribute.

Both ordered and unordered lists can be included in web pages.

## Linking Web Pages

To have web pages connected as **hypertext** rather than a series linearly ordered pages, it is necessary to have elements of the text act as **links** to other web pages or to other points in the same page. Links are bracketed by the <A> .. </A> **anchor tags**. Links to another page must have an anchor tag that has an attribute that specifies where the other page is located, that is its **Universal Resource Locator** or URL. Links to the same page give the named destination.

Link elements are usually displayed in a different color from the rest of the text. Links are often in blue. Clicking on the link displays the destination page.

## Tables in Web Pages

The format of tables can be controlled by a number of tags to indicate rows and columns.

## Images in Web Pages

Both photographs and graphics can be included in web pages using the <IMG> tag. The <IMG> tag has various attributes to control image type and alignment with text.

## Applets in Web Pages

Applets can be included in a web page by using the <APPLET> tag in HTML code. The width and height of the space for the applet (the applet's display area) are specified using the WIDTH and HEIGHT attributes of the <APPLET> tag.

A useful additional feature mentioned here is the inclusion of a parameter tag <PARAM> in the applet. This allows the user to include a value for the parameter that is then read by the applet using the *getParameter* method of the Applet class.

## Web Page

In this chapter we have included the full HTML document to draw a web page that includes a table and two applets showing animations. These are shown in detail.

# 12.11    Technical Terms

anchor element

anchor tag

attribute

body

element

GIF

header

HTML document

JPEG

markup language interpreter

paragraph tag

protocol

semantic markup language

Universal Resource Locator (URL)

web page link

# 12.12    Exercises

1. Create the HTML to produce a web page that is similar to the title page of this chapter.

2. Create the HTML to produce a web page that is similar to the first summary page of this chapter. Arrange that the title page of Exercise 1 have links to the first two entries of the summary page for the first two sections of the chapter: 12.1 and 12.2.

3. Change the web page for "Frank's Used Cars" so that the bouncing sign is "Drive a Wreck" and is in cyan-colored letters.

4. Change the HTML of the applet to provide the color in which the scrolling text is to be displayed and change the applet code to get the value of the color parameter.

# Chapter 13

# Arrays

Data can also be structured so that the set of values to be used in a class or method is not just a collection of things with unique names. The relationships among data values in a computation can be made clear by organizing the values into structures. This chapter introduces arrays as one of the mechanisms that Java provides for structuring data values.

# 13.1  Lists as Arrays

Related data values can be grouped together and isolated from other data values in a program in several different ways.

One way is to make an **array of variables** of the same type. This array has a single name, and an individual **element of the array** is selected by giving an **index value** that uniquely identifies it.

This is a familiar idea from mathematics. A sequence of terms can be represented by a variable $t$. A particular term in the sequence can be represented by an expression such as $t_i$ where $i$ is the index value of the term. Values of the sequence can be defined and used in expressions like this.

$$t_{n+1} = k \times t_n$$

An array in Java is a group of variables that are all of the same type, and that can be referenced using a single name together with an index. The array must be declared. The declaration gives the array's name, the data type of the elements of the array, as well as the range of values to be used as its index. Here is an array declaration.

**int** $a$ [] = **new int** [10];

The declaration makes $a$ the name of an array of integers. The array contains 10 elements, which can be accessed using the index values 0 through 9 inclusive. The individual element in array $a$ with index $i$ is written as $a[i]$ rather than in the mathematical form $a_i$. The index of an array element is sometimes referred to as a **subscript** because of the mathematical notation.

The array declaration can also be written in a slightly different form namely

int [] *a* = **new int** [10];

One of the simplest uses of an array is for storing a **list of values**. As an example, we will look at a problem where a random list of ten positive integers between 1 and 1000 is to be generated, and then printed with each value expressed as a fraction of the largest value in the list. Our program to solve this problem will have three parts. First the values are generated and stored in an array. Second the array is searched to find the largest value. Third the values in the array are output, with their values divided by the largest value.

Here is the program. As usual the boilerplate is omitted.

```
// The "Normalize" class.
// Normalize each element in list of 10 random integers
// dividing it by the largest integer in the list.
final int SIZE = 9;
int list [] = new int [SIZE + 1];
// Generate random value for list.
for (int i = 0; i <= SIZE; i ++)
{
    list [i] = (int) (Math.random () * 1000) + 1;
}
// Find largest value in list.
int largest = list [0];
for (int i = 1; i <= SIZE; i ++)
{
    if (list [i] > largest)
        largest = list [i];
}
// Output normalized values.
for (int i = 0; i <= SIZE; i ++)
{
    c.print (i, 3);
    c.println ((double) list [i] / largest, 7, 2);
}
```

The program will produce output of this nature.

```
0    0.98
1    0.76
2    0.90
3    0.68
4    0.74
5    0.31
6    1.00
7    0.50
8    0.29
9    0.42
```

Notice that the array declaration uses a named constant *SIZE* rather than the integer 9. This name is used to control each of the three iterations in the program. It is good style to use named constants so that readers can see the meaning of the bounds for iterations. More important, the program can be easily changed to work with a different size of array. Only the definition of the constant *SIZE* need be changed.

## 13.1.1  Frequency Distribution

As a second example that uses arrays, consider the problem of determining how many times each value occurs in 1000 throws of two dice, and printing a table of the accumulated results. This is called a **frequency distribution**. An array can be declared to store the counters for all the possible throws.

Since the array elements here are to be counters, each one must be initialized to zero. This happens automatically when an array of integers or reals is declared.

Here is the *DiceTest* class.

```
// The "DiceTest" class.
// Count the frequency of the 11 different values of the
// throw of two dice 1000 times.
int freq [] = new int [11];
// Note freq [0] contains the number of throws with value 2.
int die1, die2, roll;
for (int times = 1; times <= 1000; times ++)
```

```
    {
        die1 = (int) (Math.random () * 6) + 1;
        die2 = (int) (Math.random () * 6) + 1;
        roll = die1 + die2;
        freq [roll – 2] ++;
    }
    // Frequency distribution.
    for (int i = 0; i < 11; i ++)
    {
        c.println ("Throw of " + (i + 2) + " occurred " + freq [i] +" times");
    }
```

Perhaps the program would be easier to understand if the array *freq* had been declared to have 13 elements and *freq* [2] contained the number of times a 2 was rolled and so on. This means *freq* [0] and *freq* [1] would not be used.

## 13.1.2  A Class for Maintaining a List of Names

A class can be particularly useful for maintaining data structures such as a list of names. By implementing a list as a class called *NameList*, a name can be added to the list, a name can be deleted from the list, or the list can be printed.

The list of names encapsulated in the class is stored in an array. Each of the operations of the class is written as a method that manipulates the array.

When a value is added, it goes at the end of the list. A value can appear more than once in the list.

Before a value is deleted, its position in the list must be determined. This is done by moving along the list from the first element and examining each element until the value is found. Once the value to be deleted has been found, the last value in the list can be stored in the position of the value to be deleted and the list can be shortened. Because the last value in the list moves forward into the position of the value being deleted, the values in the list do not maintain their order as deletions occur. Only the first occurrence of a repeated name is deleted.

Here is the *NameList* class which implements a list of names. This class must be instantiated to create a list.

```
// The "NameList" class.
import hsa.Console;

public class NameList
{
    final int MAX = 10;
    // Declare variables.
    String list [] = new String [MAX];
    int size = 0;
    Console c;

    // Constructor.
    public NameList (Console c)
    {
        // All elements of integer list set to zero automatically.
        this.c = c;
    } // NameList constructor

    // Add a name to list.
    public void insert (String name)
    {
        size ++;
        list [size - 1] = name;
    } // insert method

    // Delete a name from list.
    public void delete (String name)
    {
        int i = 0;
        while (!name.equals (list [i]))
        {
            i ++;
        }
        // Place last name in list at the deletion point.
        list [i] = list [size - 1];
        size --;
    } // delete method
```

```
        // Output list of names.
        public void printList ()
        {
            c.print (" [");
            for (int i = 0; i < size – 1; i ++)
            {
                c.print (list [i]);
                c.print (",");
            }
            if (size > 0)
                c.print (list [size – 1]);
            c.println ("]");
        } // printList method
} /* NameList class */
```

Here is a client application program that uses an object of this class, reads commands from a user, and manipulates the object using the object's methods.

```
// The "UseNameList" class.
// This is a main method to test the class NameList.
// Instantiate an object of NameList class.
NameList names = new NameList (c);
c.println ("Commands you can give after the prompt");
c.println ("i to insert a name");
c.println ("d to delete a name");
c.println ("p to print the list");
c.println ("q to quit");
while (true)
{
    char command;
    c.print (">"); // Prompt for command.
    command = c.readLine ().charAt (0);
    if (command == 'q') break;
    switch (command)
    {
        case 'i':
            String newName;
            c.print ("Enter name to insert: ");
            newName = c.readLine ();
```

```
            names.insert (newName);
            break;
        case 'd':
            String oldName;
            c.print ("Enter name to delete: ");
            oldName = c.readLine ();
            names.delete (oldName);
            break;
        case 'p':
            names.printList ();
            break;
        default:
            c.println ("This is an incorrect command try again");
            break;
    }
}
```

Here is a sample output.

```
Commands you can give after the prompt >
 i to insert a name
 d to delete a name
 p to print the list
 q to quit
>i
Enter name to insert: Hercule Poirot
>i
Enter name to insert: Jane Marple
>i
Enter name to insert: Hercule Poirot
>i
Enter name to insert: Nero Wolfe
>p
[Hercule Poirot, Jane Marple, Hercule Poirot, Nero Wolfe]
>d
Enter name to delete: Hercule Poirot
>p
[Nero Wolfe, Jane Marple, Hercule Poirot]
>q
```

## 13.1.3  Computing Prime Numbers

With arrays it is possible to write very interesting and subtle programs. For example, an array can be used to determine a list of all the prime numbers up to some given value.

The general idea for this algorithm originated with a Greek mathematician named Eratosthenes who developed an algorithm now called the **sieve of Eratosthenes**. It works like this. First, make a list of all the integers from 2 up to some limit, such as 20.

$$2,3,4,5,6,7,8,9,10,11,12,13,14,15,16,17,18,19,20$$

Values in the list can be marked, meaning that they are not prime. In the beginning, no values are marked.

Starting at the left end of the list, find the next value that is not marked. It is a prime number. But all multiples of it are not prime, so they can be marked. Since the first value in the list is 2, it is considered to be prime. All multiples of 2 are not prime, and are marked.

$$2,3,\overline{4},5,\overline{6},7,\overline{8},9,\overline{10},11,\overline{12},13,\overline{14},15,\overline{16},17,\overline{18},19,\overline{20}$$

The next unmarked value after 2 is 3, so it too is prime. All multiples of 3 can then be marked. Some of them, such as 6, have already been marked.

$$2,3,\overline{4},5,\overline{6},7,\overline{8},\overline{9},\overline{10},11,\overline{12},13,\overline{14},\overline{15},\overline{16},17,\overline{18},19,\overline{20}$$

The value 4 is skipped over now, because it has been marked. The next unmarked value 5 is a prime. All of the multiples of 5 need to be marked. As it turns out, all of them have been marked so the list remains the same. The value 6 is skipped (it is marked). The value 7 is prime but all its multiples have been marked. In fact, there are no more marks to be added to the list. All of the values that are unmarked are primes.

Eratosthenes' algorithm can be implemented in a direct way using an array. It is not necessary to store the integers themselves, because they are determined by their index in the list. Instead, it is only necessary to store an indication of whether a value has been marked. The boolean data type is sufficient for this purpose. The array *isPrime* contains a boolean value for each integer. If the boolean value ends up being true, the integer corresponding to the index is prime, otherwise the integer is not prime (it is a multiple of some smaller integer). We will not use the two elements of *isPrime* with indexes 0 and 1 so that the array index is the actual integer being tested.

Here is the *FindPrimes* class.

```java
// The "FindPrimes" class.
// Find prime numbers using Erastosthenes' sieve.
int size;
c.println ("Enter maximum value to test");
size = c.readInt ();
// Declare array isPrime.
boolean isPrime [];
isPrime = new boolean [size + 1];
// A boolean array is automatically initialized to false.
// Initialize array elements as true.
for (int i = 2; i<= size; i ++)
{
    isPrime [i] = true;
}
// Multiples of a prime are not prime.
for (int i = 2; i <= size; i ++)
{
    if (isPrime [i]) // This value is prime.
    {
        for (int j = 2 * i; j <= size; j += i)
        {
            isPrime [j] = false;
        }
    }
}
c.println ("Between 2 and " + size + " the primes are");
final int valuesPerLine = 10;
int valuesPrinted = 0;
for (int i = 2; i <= size; i ++)
{
    if (isPrime [i])
    {
        c.print (i, 5);
        valuesPrinted ++;
```

```
        if (valuesPrinted % valuesPerLine == 0)
            c.println ();
    }
}
if ((valuesPrinted % valuesPerLine) != 0)
    c.println ();
```

The program produces this output for an input value of 500.

```
Enter maximum value to test: 500
Between 2 and 500 the primes are:
    2    3    5    7   11   13   17   19   23   29
   31   37   41   43   47   53   59   61   67   71
   73   79   83   89   97  101  103  107  109  113
  127  131  137  139  149  151  157  163  167  173
  179  181  191  193  197  199  211  223  227  229
  233  239  241  251  257  263  269  271  277  281
  283  293  307  311  313  317  331  337  347  349
  353  359  367  373  379  383  389  397  401  409
  419  421  431  433  439  443  449  457  461  463
  467  479  487  491  499
```

# 13.2 Related Lists

Sometimes several kinds of values need to be kept together. For example, to keep a list of books in a library it may be necessary to record the author and title of each book. There are many other pieces of information that could be kept as well.

This can be done by keeping arrays that are conceptually related to each other: the first entry in the author list corresponds to the first entry in the title list, and so on. Although there is nothing explicit in the declarations to show that the lists are related, the program treats them as related; every time an author is used, the corresponding title is also used.

A book list can be maintained using the same algorithms as were used earlier for maintaining a list of names. Notice that when a book is inserted in the list, both the author and title values are inserted.

Similarly, when a book is deleted from the list, both an author and a title are deleted. The class *BookList* is very similar to the class *NameList*.

Here is the *BookList* class which implements a list of up to 10 authors and titles. This class must be instantiated to create a list.

```java
// The "BookList" class.
// A class to maintain a list of authors and titles.
import hsa.Console;

public class BookList
{
    // Declare variables.
    final int MAX = 10;
    String author [] = new String [MAX];
    String title [] = new String [MAX];
    int size = 0;
    Console c;

    // Constructor.
    public BookList (Console c)
    {
        // All elements of author and title array set to null automatically.
        this.c = c;
    } // BookList constructor

    // Add a book to the list.
    public void insert (String name, String book)
    {
        size ++;
        author [size – 1] = name;
        title [size – 1] = book;
    } // insert method

    // Delete a book from the list.
    public void delete (String name, String book)
    {
        int where = 0;
        while (true)
        {
```

```
            if (author [where].equals (name) && title [where].equals (book))
                break;
            where ++;
        }
        // Put the last item in bookList in position where.
        author [where] = author [size − 1];
        title [where] = title [size − 1];
        size −−;
    } // delete method


    // Print list of books.
    public void printList ()
    {
        for (int i = 0; i < size; i ++)
        {
            c.println ("  " + author [i] + "/ " + title [i]);
        }
    } // printList method
} /* BookList class */
```

Here is the driver application program that manipulates the class. It is similar to the driver for *NameList*.

```
// The "UseBookList" program.
// A main method to test the class BookList.
// Instantiate an object of BookList class.
BookList books = new BookList (c);
c.println ("Commands you can give after the prompt >");
c.println ("i insert a book into the list");
c.println ("d delete a book from the list");
c.println ("p print the list of books");
c.println ("q quit");
while (true)
{
    char command;
    c.print ("> "); // Prompt for command.
    command = c.readLine ().charAt (0);
    if (command == 'q') break;
    switch (command)
    {
```

```
         case 'i':
             String newAuthor, newTitle;
             c.print ("Enter author to insert: ");
             newAuthor = c.readLine ();
             c.print ("Enter title to insert ");
             newTitle = c.readLine ();
             books.insert (newAuthor, newTitle);
             break;
         case 'd':
             String oldAuthor, oldTitle;
             c.print ("Enter author to delete: ");
             oldAuthor = c.readLine ();
             c.print ("Enter title to delete: ");
             oldTitle = c.readLine ();
             books.delete (oldAuthor, oldTitle);
             break;
         case 'p':
             books.printList ();
             break;
     }
}
```

Here is a sample output from this program.

```
     Commands you can give after the prompt >
      i  insert a book into the list
      d  delete a book from the list
      p  print the list of books
      q  quit
     >i
     Enter author to insert: Elizabeth George
     Enter title to insert: A Great Deliverance
     >i
     Enter author to insert: Minette Walters
     Enter title to insert: The Ice House
     >i
     Enter author to insert: Elizabeth George
     Enter title to insert: Playing For the Ashes
     >p
       Elizabeth George / A Great Deliverance
       Minette Walters / The Ice House
       Elizabeth George / Playing For the Ashes
     >q
```

# 13.3 Declaration of Arrays

In Java a one-dimension array is declared by placing empty square brackets after the array's name. The declaration

int *marks* [];

indicates that *marks* is to be an array of integers. An alternative declaration is

int [] *marks*;

In Java, an array is an object and must be instantiated. The statement

*marks* = **new int** [12];

instantiates the array *marks* to be an array of 12 elements. The individual elements are named *marks* [0], *marks* [1], *marks* [2] ... *marks* [11].

All arrays know their own length. The integer expression

*marks.length*

gives the length for the array *marks*. Notice that there are no empty parentheses after *length*.

The size of the array can be read in when the program is executed. When this happens, the array is dynamic. Here is an example of a dynamic array.

```
c.println ("Enter size of array");
int size;
size = c.readInt ();
int marks [];
marks = new int [size];
```

Initial values are automatically assigned to arrays. Elements of numeric arrays are all set to zero. Boolean arrays are set to **false**. Arrays of objects, such as strings, are set to **null**.

Initial values can be assigned at the time of declaration. For example, the single statement

> int [] *number* = {1, 3, 5, 7, 9};

establishes an array of 5 elements where *number* [0] has the value 1, *number* [1] has the value 3, and so on. The array is fully created and initialized.

Here is an example program that reads in a one-dimensional array of prices whose size is first input, followed by the actual list of prices.

```
// The "PriceList" class.
// Reads an array of prices.
// The length of the list is to be input.
double [] price;
c.print ("How many prices in the list? ");
int count = c.readInt ();
price = new double [count];
for (int i = 0 ; i < count ; i++)
{
    c.print ("Price for item " + (i + 1) + ": ");
    price [i] = c.readDouble ();
}

// Add statement to process array.
```

# 13.4 Two-Dimensional Arrays

Arrays can have more than one dimension. The two-dimensional array is useful for storing tables of information. A table contains rows and columns of entries. Each entry is of the same data type. To declare a two-dimensional array of integers called *table* we use the statement

> int *table* [] [];

This integer array can be instantiated to have 10 rows and 5 columns by the statement

> *table* = new int [10] [5];

Here is a program segment that will compute a table of powers of the integers from 1 to 10. The columns will correspond to powers 1, 2, 3, 4, and 5. This means the integers 1 to 10 will be in column 1, their squares in column 2, their cubes in column 3, and so on.

```
// The "Powers2" class.
// Compute a table of powers of integers from 1 to 10.
int table [] [];
table = new int [10] [5];
for (int i = 0; i < 10; i ++)
{
    table [i] [0] = i + 1;
    for (int j = 1; j < 5; j ++)
    {
        table [i] [j] = table [i] [j – 1] * ( i + 1);
    }
}
// Print table.
for (int i = 0; i < 10; i++)
{
    for (int j = 0; j < 5; j ++)
    {
        c.print (table [i] [j], 7);
    }
    c.println ();
}
```

This is the output of the program.

|    |     |      |       |        |
|----|-----|------|-------|--------|
| 1  | 1   | 1    | 1     | 1      |
| 2  | 4   | 8    | 16    | 32     |
| 3  | 9   | 27   | 81    | 243    |
| 4  | 16  | 64   | 256   | 1024   |
| 5  | 25  | 125  | 625   | 3125   |
| 6  | 36  | 216  | 1296  | 7776   |
| 7  | 49  | 343  | 2401  | 16807  |
| 8  | 64  | 512  | 4096  | 32768  |
| 9  | 81  | 729  | 6561  | 59049  |
| 10 | 100 | 1000 | 10000 | 100000 |

# 13.5 Methods With Array Parameters

An element of an array can be passed as a parameter to a method in the same way that a primitive variable can be passed.

Entire arrays can also be passed as parameters. Since the array is an object, the parameter is a **reference to the array**. The signature of the subprogram must contain a specification of the array type.

Here is an example where an array is passed to a method to be initialized. This method initializes an array of *size* elements to random integers between 1 and 10.

```
// A method to initialize the first size elements of an array
// to random integers between 1 and 10.
static public void initialize (int a [], int size)
{
    for (int i = 0; i < size; i ++)
    {
        a [i] = (int) (Math.random () * 10) + 1;
    }
} // initialize method
```

```
// This method prints the first n elements of an array of integers.
static public void printArray (int a [], int n)
{
    for (int i = 0; i < n; i ++)
    {
        c.println (a [i]);
    }
} // printArray method
```

Here is a driver program to test these two methods.

```
// The "RandTest" class.
// A main method to test the methods initialize and printArray.
int howBig;
c.print ("Enter size of array ");
howBig = c.readInt ();
```

```
int array [];
array = new int [howBig];
initialize (array, howBig);
printArray (array, 5);
```

In the method *initialize*, all the elements of the array are initialized. Sometimes only part of the array whose size is declared in the *main* method is to be used in a method. When this is true, an additional parameter must be passed to the method to indicate how much of the array is to be used. The call to the *printArray* method prints only the first 5 elements of the array. The entire array can be printed by making the second parameter have the value *howBig*.

The number of elements in an array that are to be processed in a method need only be given as a parameter if that number is different from the size of the array declared. If it is the same, within the body of the method the array method *length* can be used to find the actual value of the number of elements in the array. This is similar to the method *length* for the *String* class except that here no parentheses are needed.

Here is part of a class that sums the values of an array.

```
// A method to compute the sum of all the values of an integer array.
static public int sumArray (int a [])
{
    int sum = 0;
    for (int i = 0; i < a.length; i ++)
    {
        sum += a [i];
    }
    return sum;
} // sumArray method
```

Here is a driver *main* method to test this method.

```
// The "TestSumArray" class.
// A main method to test the method sumArray.
int list [];
list = new int [10];
for (int i = 0; i < 10; i ++)
{
    list [i] = i + 1;
}
c.println ("Sum of elements of list = " + sumArray (list));
```

Here is another example of a method with an array parameter shown together with the *main* driver method to test the method. The method *maxArray* is a function-type method whose value is the largest element in the array that is its parameter. Again, the *length* method is used to find the length of the array. This is possible because the number of elements in the array is the same as the length declared when it is instantiated, namely 5.

```
// The "Best" class.
import hsa.Console;

public class Best
{
    public static void main (String [] args)
    {
        Console c = new Console ();
        int [] mark = new int [5];

        c.println ("Enter five marks");
        for (int i = 0 ; i < 5 ; i++)
            mark [i] = c.readInt ();
        c.println ("The best mark is " + maxArray (mark));
    } // main method

    public static int maxArray (int [] list)
    {
        int biggest = list [0];

        for (int i = 1 ; i < list.length ; i++)
        {
```

```
                    // The following two lines could be replaced by:
                    //    biggest = Math.max (biggest, line [i]);
                    if (list [i] > biggest)
                        biggest = list [i];
                }
            return biggest;
        } // maxArray method
    } /* Best class */
```

# 13.6 Searching

Arrays are often used to store information that will be used many times. Sometimes it is important to know whether a value is in a list, for example checking to see if a person is authorized to use some service (such as gain entry to a secure area). Sometimes it is important to find information associated with a key, as in looking up a name in a telephone directory in order to retrieve the associated telephone number.

The search program earlier in the chapter worked with a list of names in arbitrary order. Often, however, it is more useful to maintain lists that are sorted. A list is sorted in ascending order if each value in the list is no larger than the one that comes after it in the list.

When a list is sorted there is more work involved when inserting or deleting values if the order is to be maintained. Think of the list as being laid out from left to right. Before a value can be inserted, the appropriate location for it must be found in the list; then the value in that location, together with all the values to the right of that location, must be shifted to the right to make room for the new value. Before a value can be deleted, its location must be found in the list; then all the values to the right of that location must be shifted to the left.

Only one element of an array can be manipulated at a time. To shift a part of a list left or right, the values must be shifted one at a time. To shift to the right, the last element must be moved to the right and the previous element must then be moved into the vacated position, and so on. To move to the left, the first element must be moved to the left and the second element must then be moved into the vacated position, and so on.

The methods that maintain a sorted list can be used to override the previously-written methods in the *NameList* class. Here are the *insert* and *delete* methods that maintain a sorted list, as part of a new class called *SortedList*.

```java
// A class that keeps list sorted called SortedList.
import hsa.Console;

public class SortedList extends NameList
{
    // Constructor for SortedList.
    public SortedList (Console c)
    {
        super (c);    // Call NameList's constructor.
    } // SortedList constructor

    // Override insert method of NameList.
    public void insert (String name)
    {
        int i = 0;
        while (i < size && (name.compareTo (list [i]) > 0))
        {
            i ++;
        }
        // Shift the remaining items to make room.
        for (int j = size; j >= i + 1; j --)
        {
            list [j] = list [j - 1];
        }
        size ++;
        list [i] = name;
    } // insert method
```

```
// Override delete method of NameList.
public void delete (String name)
{
    int i = 0;
    while (!name.equals (list [i]))
    {
        i ++;
    }
    // Shift remaining items down.
    for (int j = i; j < size – 1; j ++)
    {
        list [j] = list [j + 1];
    }
    size ––;
} // delete method
} /* SortedList class */
```

Because the list of values is now maintained in sorted order, the output from the driver program will look like this.

```
Commands you can give after the prompt >
i  insert a name into the list
d  delete a name from the list
p  print the list of names
q  quit
>i
Enter name to insert: Hercule Poirot
>i
Enter name to insert: Jane Marple
>i
Enter name to insert: Hercule Poirot
>i
Enter name to insert: Nero Wolfe
>p
[Hercule Poirot, Hercule Poirot, Jane Marple, Nero Wolfe]
>d
Enter name to delete: Hercule Poirot
>p
[Hercule Poirot, Jane Marple, Nero Wolfe]
>q
```

Notice that the names are sorted by their first letters, so *Hercule* Poirot comes alphabetically before *Jane* Marple.

Each of the two methods *insert* and *delete* must first search in the list: either to find a location where a new value is to be placed, or to find a location from where a value is to be deleted. The searching can be separated out into a method that both other methods can use.

Here is another class that implements a sorted list.

```
// The "SortedList2" class.
// A class to keep list sorted that uses a separate find method.
import hsa.Console;

public class SortedList2 extends NameList
{
    // Constructor for SortedList2.
    public SortedList2 (Console c)
    {
        super (c);  // Call NameList's constructor.
    } // SortedList2 constructor

    // A new method find used by insert and delete methods.
    protected int find (String name)
    {
        int where = 0;
        while (where < size && list [where].compareTo (name) < 0)
        {
            where ++;
        }
        return where;
    } // find method

    // Override insert method of NameList.
    public void insert (String name)
    {
        int locationToInsert = find (name);
        // Shift the remaining items over to make room.
        for (int j = size; j >= locationToInsert + 1; j --)
        {
            list [j] = list [j - 1];
        }
        size ++;
```

```
        list [locationToInsert] = name;
    } // insert method

    // Override delete method of NameList.
    public void delete (String name)
    {
        int location = find (name);
        if (location < size && list [location].equals (name))
        {
            // Shift remaining items down.
            for (int j = location; j < size -1; j ++)
            {
                list [j] = list [j + 1];
            }
            size --;
        }
        else
        {
            c.println ("Name " + name + " is not in list");
        }
    } // delete method
} /* SortedList2 class */
```

The search method used here is called **sequential search** because it examines the locations one after the other sequentially. The *insert* and *delete* methods have been changed to use this common method.

While sequential search is effective, it is not efficient. The fact that the values are sorted can be exploited to make searching faster. The **binary search** technique works by dividing a sorted list of values in two parts (hence binary) at each step, and retaining only half of the values for further consideration. The search algorithm is given a list of sorted values, together with a value to be found (or a location in which the value will be placed, if the value is to be inserted).

At each step the search proceeds like this: examine the value in the middle of the list; if it is larger than the value being searched for, discard the right half of the list, but if the value in the middle is smaller, discard the left half of the list. When the list being searched is reduced to a single entry, either the value has been found, or the place where it is to be inserted has been found.

The class *FastSortedList* includes an implementation of the binary search algorithm.

```
// The "FastSortedList" class.
// An extension of SortedList2 with a binary search method for find.
import hsa.Console;

public class FastSortedList extends SortedList2
{
    // Constructor for FastSortedList.
    public FastSortedList (Console c)
    {
        super (c);  // Call SortedList2's (and thus NameList's) constructor.
    } // FastSortedList constructor

    // This method overrides the find method SortedList2.
    protected int find (String name)
    {
        int first = 0;
        int last = size – 1;
        while (first != last && last > 0)
        {
            int middle = (first + last) / 2;
            if (name.compareTo (list [middle]) <= 0)
            {
                // Name lies in first half or not in list.
                last = middle;
            }
            else
            {
                // Discard first half (including middle).
                first = middle + 1;
            }
        }
        int where = first;
        if (where < size && list [where].compareTo (name) < 0)
            where ++;
        return where;
    } // find method
} /* FastSortedList class */
```

# 13.7  Efficiency of Algorithms

Some algorithms run much faster than others. The speed of an algorithm depends upon many factors including the speed of the underlying computer, the quality of the compiler that translates it to machine language, and the skill of the programmer. Beyond these factors, in many cases there is a fundamental reason why one program will always run faster than another. This reason has to do with how many times the parts of the algorithm are executed as a function of the size of the input to the algorithm.

It can be shown that the time required for a binary search is essentially a constant $k_1$ times the *log* of the number $n$ of items to be searched.

Time for binary search = $k_1 \, log \, n$

The time required for a sequential search of the same list is essentially a constant $k_2$ times $n$.

Time for sequential search = $k_2 \, n$

The sizes of the constants $k_1$ and $k_2$ depend on the things we have mentioned, such as the computer, the compiler, and the programmer. However, as $n$ increases, $log \, n$ grows much more slowly than $n$, so for large enough $n$, eventually it will be true that

$k_1 \, log \, n < k_2 \, n$

This implies that for long lists, the time for a binary search will be less than the time for a sequential search, no matter what values we have for constants $k_1$ and $k_2$.

## 13.7.1  Sequential Search Time

A sequential search inspects each item in a list to see if the item matches the input key (see Figure 13.1). If the key matches the item, the inspection loop terminates.

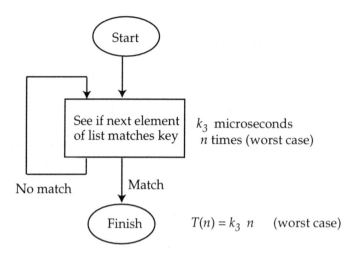

**Figure 13.1 Timing Analysis for Sequential Search**

There are a fixed number of things to be done in each loop iteration so we can conclude that each iteration takes a fixed amount of time, which we will take to be $k_3$ microseconds. (We have used microseconds as our unit for time. Other units, such as seconds, can be used as well.) On average, if the key is randomly chosen from a set of $n$ distinct elements and the list contains these same elements in a random order, there will be $n/2$ iterations. From this we can conclude that the best, average, and worst times to execute a sequential search are:

$$T_{best}(n) = k_3 \qquad \text{Best time}$$
$$T_{avg}(n) = k_3\, n / 2 \qquad \text{Average time}$$
$$T_{worst}(n) = k_3\, n \qquad \text{Worst time}$$

We ignore the time taken to start up (or to finish) the algorithm, on the grounds that this time will be small compared to the total time of the algorithm when $n$ is large.

The average time can be useful for predicting the time for the search. We usually concentrate on the worst time for two reasons. First, it is often easier to determine the worst time. Second, the worst time is useful if we need to put a bound on the time a program will take.

## 13.7.2  Binary Search Time

A binary search repeatedly discards halves (and sub-halves and so on) of a list until only one element remains. This is illustrated in Figure 13.2.

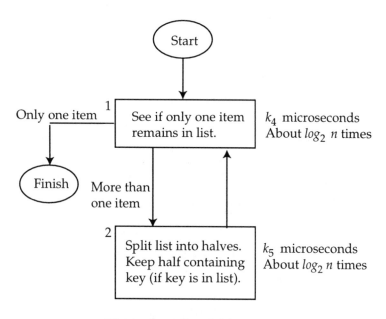

$$T(n) \text{ is about } (k_4 + k_5) \, log_2 \, n$$

**Figure 13.2 Analysis of Running Time for Binary Search**

Each test to see if the list has been reduced to a single element consumes a fixed amount of time, which we will take to be $k_4$ microseconds (see Figure 13.2). Each split, together with discarding half of the list, consumes a fixed amount of time, which we take to be $k_5$ microseconds. If the original list is 8 long, we will have to split 3 times:

Split down to size 4
Split down to size 2
Split down to size 1

The number of splits is equal to $log_2 8$ because, if $n$ is a power of 2,

$$log_2 n = \text{number of times to divide } n \text{ by 2 until } n \text{ is } 1$$

**Table of Powers of 2**

| $n$ | $2^n$ | | $n$ | $2^n$ |
|---|---|---|---|---|
| 0 | 1 | | 10 | 1024 = 1K |
| 1 | 2 | | 11 | 2K |
| 2 | 4 | | 12 | 4K |
| 3 | 8 | | 13 | 8K |
| 4 | 16 | | 14 | 16K |
| 5 | 32 | | 15 | 32K |
| 6 | 64 | | 16 | 64K |
| 7 | 128 | | 17 | 128K |
| 8 | 256 | | 18 | 256K |
| 9 | 512 | | 19 | 512K |
| 10 | 1024 = 1K | | 20 | 1024K = 1M |
| $log_2 n$ | $n$ | | $log_2 n$ | $n$ |

**Table of Logarithms Base 2 of $n$**

Figure 13.3 Powers of 2 and Logarithms Base 2

Figure 13.3 is both a table of powers of 2 and a table of logarithms of 2. For example, reading the fourth line of the table from left to right, we get $2^3 = 8$. Reading that same line from right to left, we get $log_2 8 = 3$. The value of $2^{10} = 1024$ is often written in computer literature as K for kilo, because it is very close to the value 1000. Similarly, $2^{20}$ is often written as M for mega.

Returning to our analysis of binary search, if $n$ is a power of 2, that is, if $n$ is one of 1, 2, 4, 8, 16, 32, etc., the number of times to execute each of boxes 1 and 2 in Figure 13.3 will be $log_2 n$.

# 13.8 Chapter Summary

## Lists as Arrays

A list of data values of the same type can be stored in an array. The values are accessed using a single name together with an integer-valued index.

The **sieve of Eratosthenes** is an algorithm that uses a list of boolean values to determine which integers are **prime numbers**.

## Related Lists

Sometimes values of different data types need to be kept together. This can be done by keeping related values in arrays that are conceptually in parallel. For example, a list of books can be kept as two related lists: an array of authors and an array of titles.

## Declaration of Arrays

A **one-dimensional array** declaration indicates the type of the elements of the array, as well as the acceptable values for the index used with the array name. These statements instantiate an integer array of 12 elements.

```
int a [];
a = new int [12];
```

The elements of the array have indexes running from 0 to the length of the array minus 1. The length of the array is available from the expression *a.length*. The element of an array *a* with index value *i* is referred to as *a* [*i*]. Arrays can have their sizes determined at the time that the program is run. These are called **dynamic arrays**.

## Tables as Arrays

Arrays with two dimensions can be used to represent tables. A two-dimensional **array** integer $b$ is defined by a declaration of the form

int $b$ [] []

The element of array $b$ whose first index is $i$ and second $j$ is referred to as $b[i]$ $[j]$.

## Methods With Array Parameters

Arrays can be passed as parameters to methods. The signature of the method must contain a specification of the array type.

## Searching

Sequential searching examines the values in a list from first element to last to find a value being searched for, or a place to insert a new value if the list is sorted. **Binary searching** examines the middle value of a sorted list, discarding either the part of the list before the middle value, or the part after the middle value, at each step. The process continues until a single element remains. Either this is the sought value or the value is not in the list.

## Efficiency of Algorithms

An algorithm that takes input, such as a list, of size $n$ is said to run in time $T(n)$, that is, the running time depends in some way on the number of elements $n$. Usually the worst case time is of interest and $T(n)$ is taken to mean $T_{worst}(n)$.

# 13.9  Technical Terms

anchor element                          list of values

array of variables                      prime number

binary search                           reference to an array

element of the array                    sequential search

frequency distribution                  sieve of Eratosthenes

index value

# 13.10    Exercises

1.  Modify the "Normalize" program that generates the random numbers so that the largest value is found in the same loop that generates the list of random values.

2.  The program to find primes can be improved in several ways. One improvement results from using an array to store a boolean value only for the odd integers (since every even integer larger than 2 is not prime) and to treat 2 as a special case. This means that the $i$th array entry corresponds to the integer $2i+1$. A program that incorporates this improvement could look for primes over twice as large a range with a given amount of memory. Modify the program to store a boolean value only for odd integers.

3.  Make the prime number program more efficient by combining the iteration that marks values with the iteration that prints unmarked values.

4.  Write a program that reads a list of names from a file and outputs the list with any duplicates removed.

5.  Write a program to read an unordered list of integers. The list is to be printed in ascending order. Keep an associated list that marks those values that have been printed. The program should use an iteration to find the smallest unmarked value, print it, and mark it.

6. Extend the class definition for *BookList* to include a method called *printAuthors* that prints the list with each author being listed once, and all of the books by that author indented under the author's name.

7. A two-dimensional array of characters can be used to store a picture if the blank is used for background and an asterisk is used for non-blank parts. Write a class for pictures that has two methods. The first method should put a horizontal line into the picture; the method will have the coordinates of the endpoints as parameters. The second method will output a picture.

8. Extend the class from the previous exercise to allow a rectangle to be inserted into a picture.

9. Extend the class from the previous exercise to allow a circle to be inserted into a picture.

# Chapter 14

# Advanced Object Oriented Concepts

In earlier chapters we used many of the constructs of object-oriented programming, including objects and classes. In Chapter 10 we introduced the concept of inheritance, showing how new classes can be created by extending existing classes.

In this chapter we will further develop the concept of inheritance using abstract classes. An abstract class defines a signature for some of its methods but does not provide their implementation. We will also discuss Java interfaces, which allow classes to inherit behavior from more than one source.

# 14.1  Separate Classes for Drawing Shapes

To illustrate the power of inheritance we will first show three separate classes for drawing shapes that have a great deal of code that is similar. These classes are called *Rectangle, Oval,* and *Triangle.* We will then show how programming these three classes can be simplified by having each of them inherit from a common **base** class (also called **ancestor** class or **superclass**) called *Shape.*

Each of these three classes has public methods to *show* the shape, *hide* the shape, and *move* the shape to a new location on the graphic surface. Each also has protected methods to *draw* the shape and to *erase* the shape which are called by the *show, hide,* and *move* methods. A *paint* method also calls the *draw* method and is used whenever a *paint* or *repaint* method is called in a *Frame* or *Applet.*

Here is the *Rectangle* class.

```
// The "Rectangle" class.
// This class handles rectangles on a graphics surface. Once created, they
// can be moved, hidden, and shown again.

import java.awt.*;

public class Rectangle
{
```

```
protected Component surface; // The surface to draw on.
protected int x, y; // The x, y location of the upper–left corner.
protected int rectWidth, rectHeight; // The rectangle's width and height.
protected boolean visible = false; // Is the shape currently visible.
protected Color color = Color.red; // The color of the shape.

// Create a rectangle that is to be drawn on the surface (which should
// be either an Applet or a Frame).
public Rectangle (Component surface, int x, int y, int rectWidth,
    int rectHeight)
{
    this.surface = surface;
    this.x = x;
    this.y = y;
    this.rectWidth = rectWidth;
    this.rectHeight = rectHeight;
    show ();
} // Rectangle constructor

// If the shape is not already visible, make it visible.
public void show ()
{
    if (!visible)
    {
        draw ();
        visible = true;
    }
} // show method

// If the shape is visible, hide it.
public void hide ()
{
    if (visible)
    {
        erase ();
        visible = false;
    }
} // hide method

// Redraw the shape if it is visible.
public void paint ()
{
```

```
        if (visible)
        {
            draw ();
        }
    } // paint method

    // Move the shape to a new location.
    public void move (int x, int y)
    {
        if (visible)
        {
            erase ();
            this.x = x;
            this.y = y;
            draw ();
        }
        else
        {
            this.x = x;
            this.y = y;
        }
    } // move method

    // Draw the shape.
    protected void draw ()
    {
        Graphics g = surface.getGraphics ();
        g.setColor (color);
        g.fillRect (x, y, rectWidth, rectHeight);
    } // draw method

    // Erase the shape.
    protected void erase ()
    {
        Graphics g = surface.getGraphics ();
        g.setColor (surface.getBackground ());
        g.fillRect (x, y, rectWidth, rectHeight);
    } // erase method
} /* Rectangle class */
```

The *Rectangle* class uses the *fillRect* method of the *Graphics* class of the Java class library. The parameters *x* and *y* specify the coordinates of the upper-left corner of the rectangle. The dimensions of the rectangle are *rectWidth* and *rectHeight*. The rectangle is oriented parallel to the coordinate axes. Remember that the origin of coordinates in any graphics surface is in the upper-left corner. The drawing surface can be either of an *Applet* or a *Frame* class so the more general superclass *Component* is used as the object type of *surface*.

Here is the *Oval* class.

```java
// The "Oval" class.
// This class handles ovals on a graphics surface. Once created, they
// can be moved, hidden, and shown again.

import java.awt.*;

public class Oval
{
    protected Component surface; // The surface to draw on.
    protected int x, y; // The x, y location of the center of the oval.
    protected int xRadius, yRadius; // The x and y radius of the oval.
    protected boolean visible = false; // Is the shape currently visible.
    protected Color color = Color.blue; // The color of the shape.

    // Create an oval that is to be drawn on the surface (which should
    // be either an Applet or a Frame).
    public Oval (Component surface, int x, int y, int xRadius, int yRadius)
    {
        this.surface = surface;
        this.x = x;
        this.y = y;
        this.xRadius = xRadius;
        this.yRadius = yRadius;
        show ();
    } // Oval constructor

    // If the shape is not already visible, make it visible.
    public void show ()
    {
        if (!visible)
```

```
    {
        draw ();
        visible = true;
    }
} // show method

// If the shape is visible, hide it.
public void hide ()
{
    if (visible)
    {
        erase ();
        visible = false;
    }
} // hide method

// Redraw the shape if it is visible.
public void paint ()
{
    if (visible)
    {
        draw ();
    }
} // paint method

// Move the shape to a new location.
public void move (int x, int y)
{
    if (visible)
    {
        erase ();
        this.x = x;
        this.y = y;
        draw ();
    }
    else
    {
        this.x = x;
        this.y = y;
    }
} // move method
```

```
// Draw the shape.
protected void draw ()
{
    Graphics g = surface.getGraphics ();
    g.setColor (color);
    g.fillOval (x – xRadius, y – yRadius, 2 * xRadius, 2 * yRadius);
} // draw method

// Erase the shape.
protected void erase ()
{
    Graphics g = surface.getGraphics ();
    g.setColor (surface.getBackground ());
    g.fillOval (x – xRadius, y – yRadius, 2 * xRadius, 2 * yRadius);
} // erase method
} /* Oval class */
```

The *Oval* class uses the *fillOval* method of the *Graphics* class. The first two parameters specify the coordinates of the upper-left corner of the rectangle that just encloses the oval. The next two parameters give the length and width of the enclosing rectangle. The *xRadius* is half the width of the oval and *yRadius* is half its height. The center of the oval is at $(x, y)$.

Here is the *Triangle* class.

```
// The "Triangle" class.
// This class handles equilateral triangles on a graphics surface. Once
// created, they can be moved, hidden, and shown again.

import java.awt.*;

public class Triangle
{
    protected Component surface; // The surface to draw on.
    protected int x, y; // The x, y location of lower–left corner.
    protected int sideLength; // The length of a side of the triangle.
    protected boolean visible = false; // Is the shape currently visible.
    protected Color color = Color.green; // The color of the shape.
```

```
// Create an equilateral triangle that is to be drawn on the surface
// (which should be either an Applet or a Frame).
public Triangle (Component surface, int x, int y, int sideLength)
{
    this.surface = surface;
    this.x = x;
    this.y = y;
    this.sideLength = sideLength;
    show ();
} // Triangle constructor

// If the shape is not already visible, make it visible.
public void show ()
{
    if (!visible)
    {
        draw ();
        visible = true;
    }
} // show method

// If the shape is visible, hide it.
public void hide ()
{
    if (visible)
    {
        erase ();
        visible = false;
    }
} // hide method

// Redraw the shape if it is visible.
public void paint ()
{
    if (visible)
    {
        draw ();
    }
} // paint method
```

```
// Move the shape to a new location.
public void move (int x, int y)
{
    if (visible)
    {
        erase ();
        this.x = x;
        this.y = y;
        draw ();
    }
    else
    {
        this.x = x;
        this.y = y;
    }
} // move method

// Draw the shape.
protected void draw ()
{
    Graphics g = surface.getGraphics ();
    int [] xp = new int [3];
    int [] yp = new int [3];
    xp [0] = x;
    yp [0] = y;
    xp [1] = x + sideLength / 2;
    yp [1] = (int) (y - Math.sqrt (3.0) / 2.0 * sideLength);
    xp [2] = x + sideLength;
    yp [2] = y;
    g.setColor (color);
    g.fillPolygon (xp, yp, 3);
} // draw method

// Erase the shape.
protected void erase ()
{
    Graphics g = surface.getGraphics ();
    int [] xp = new int [3];
    int [] yp = new int [3];
    xp [0] = x;
    yp [0] = y;
    xp [1] = x + sideLength / 2;
```

```
        yp [1] = (int) (y − Math.sqrt (3.0) / 2.0 * sideLength);
        xp [2] = x + sideLength;
        yp [2] = y;
        g.setColor (surface.getBackground ());
        g.fillPolygon (xp, yp, 3);
    } // erase method
} /* Triangle class */
```

The *Triangle* class uses the *fillPolygon* method of the *Graphics* class. The *fillPolygon* method has, as parameters, two arrays *xp* and *yp* which give the list of coordinates of the vertices of the polygon. The third parameter gives the number of vertices in the polygon, which in this case is 3. Figure 14.1 shows the orientation of the triangle which is an equilateral triangle with one vertex at $(x, y)$.

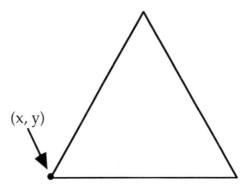

**Figure 14.1 The Triangle Drawn by the *Triangle* class.**

The class *ShapeTest*, which extends the *Applet* class, is an applet program that draws 10 shapes of random sizes and locations in the applet display area. In the *init* method of the applet, the type of shape (rectangle, oval, or triangle) is chosen randomly. The array *shapes* is an array of NUM_SHAPES *Objects* and defines the shape objects to draw. There is, as well, a related array of NUM_SHAPES integers called *shapeKinds*.

To initialize these two arrays, a random integer, from 0 to 2 inclusive, is chosen as the value of each element of the array *shapeKinds*. The 0 indicates a rectangle, the 1 an oval, and the 2 a triangle. Depending on the value of the *shapeKinds* element the corresponding element in the *shapes* array is initialized to the appropriate shape object. For example, if *shapeKinds* [3] has been initialized to the value 1 then *shapes* [3] will be initialized to be an *Oval* object. As each shape object is initialized, random numbers are chosen to control its size and position in the applet display area. The applet methods

> *getSize ().width*

and

> *getSize().height.*

obtain the width *surfaceWidth* and height *surfaceHeight* of the display area. When it comes time to draw the shapes in the *paint* method of the applet, the two related arrays, *shapeKinds* and *shapes*, are examined. For each shape, the *shapeKinds* element indicates the type of shape and the *shapes* element is the shape itself.

Here is the *ShapeTest* applet.

```
// The "ShapeTest" class.
// This applet randomly places 10 shapes on the drawing surface.

import java.applet.*;
import java.awt.*;

public class ShapeTest extends Applet
{
    protected final static int NUM_SHAPES = 10;

    // The array containing the shapes.
    Object [] shapes = new Object [NUM_SHAPES];

    // The array containing the kind of shapes (0=Rectangle, 1=Oval,
    // 2=Triangle).
    int [] shapeKinds = new int [NUM_SHAPES];

    // This method is called when the Applet object is created.
    public void init ()
    {
```

```java
// Get the width and height of the drawing surface.
int surfaceWidth = getSize ().width;
int surfaceHeight = getSize ().height;

// Create the shapes and place them randomly on the drawing
// surface.
for (int count = 0 ; count < NUM_SHAPES ; count++)
{
    int shapeKind = (int) (Math.random () * 3);
    int x = (int) (Math.random () * surfaceWidth);
    int y = (int) (Math.random () * surfaceHeight);

    if (shapeKind == 0)
    {
        int rectWidth = (int) (Math.random () * 20) + 10;
        int rectHeight = (int) (Math.random () * 20) + 10;
        shapes [count] = new Rectangle (this, x, y, rectWidth,
            rectHeight);
    }
    else if (shapeKind == 1)
    {
        int xRadius = (int) (Math.random () * 10) + 10;
        int yRadius = (int) (Math.random () * 10) + 10;
        shapes [count] = new Oval (this, x, y, xRadius, yRadius);
    }
    else if (shapeKind == 2)
    {
        int sideLength = (int) (Math.random () * 20) + 10;
        shapes [count] = new Triangle (this, x, y, sideLength);
    }
    shapeKinds [count] = shapeKind;
}
} // init method

// This method is called whenever the applet's drawing surface is
// obscured and then revealed. We call the paint method for each
// shape to redraw that shape (if the shape is currently visible).
public void paint (Graphics g)
{
    for (int count = 0 ; count < NUM_SHAPES ; count++)
    {
```

```
        // Determine the kind of shape, cast it to an object of the
        // appropriate class, and call its paint method.
        if (shapeKinds [count] == 0)
        {
            Rectangle r = (Rectangle) shapes [count];
            r.paint ();
        }
        else if (shapeKinds [count] == 1)
        {
            Oval o = (Oval) shapes [count];
            o.paint ();
        }
        else if (shapeKinds [count] == 2)
        {
            Triangle t = (Triangle) shapes [count];
            t.paint ();
        }
    }
} // paint method
} /* ShapeTest class */
```

This is the HTML file for the *ShapeTest* applet.

```
<HTML>
<BODY>
<APPLET CODE="ShapeTest.class"  WIDTH=300 HEIGHT=300>
</APPLET>
</BODY>
</HTML>
```

The *Rectangle, Oval,* and *Triangle* classes share a great deal of common code. In fact, the *show, hide, paint, move* methods, and part of their constructors are identical. While this makes them easy to create (by cutting and pasting code), it also weakens the maintainability of the code. If a bug is discovered in one of the common methods in one of the shapes (for example, the *move* method of the *Oval* class) there is no guarantee that a programmer will remember to fix the same bug in the other two classes. In a project of any size, it is almost guaranteed that the close relationship of the classes will be forgotten. Similarly, adding extra functionality is more difficult when dealing with three separate classes. Any method that must be added to one classes, must be added to all three.

As the *ShapeTest* class shows, despite much common behavior, all three classes must be treated completely separately. There is no way to take advantage of the fact that they have many of the same methods. There is also no way of ensuring that this will continue to be the case, since any one of them can be altered at any time so that the method names will no longer be identical with the other classes. The next section will deal with all of these issues.

# 14.2  An Abstract *Shape* Class as a Base Class

Using inheritance to capture the elements common to the three shapes classes produces as vastly superior implementation of the previous program. In earlier chapters we have shown how inheritance can be used to extend existing classes.

In Java, a class that contains abstract methods is itself declared abstract and cannot be instantiated. It is expected that classes that inherit from an abstract class will provide implementations of any abstract methods.

Abstract methods can be called within the abstract class prior to implementation. When a subclass inherits from the base class and provides an implementation of the method, that implementation will be executed when the method is called.

We will now create a base class that encapsulates the common behavior of the rectangle, oval, and triangle shapes but does not specify how the shapes are actually drawn. Each shape has its own *draw* and *erase* method that differs from class to class.

Here is the abstract class *Shape*. It contains all of the common elements from the three shape classes in the previous section. It declares the abstract methods *draw* and *erase*. Notice that the *Shape* class uses *draw* and *erase* even if their implementations are not yet available.

```
// The "Shape" class.
// This is an abstract class from which all shapes descend. It contains
// all the methods and data that are common to all shapes. For example,
// you can call the show and hide methods of any Shape object, even
// if you do not know the exact type of the object (Rectangle, Oval,
// or Triangle).

import java.awt.*;

public abstract class Shape
{
    protected Component surface; // The surface to draw on.
    protected int x, y; // The x, y location of the shape.
    protected boolean visible = false; // Is the shape currently visible.
    protected Color color; // The color of the shape.

    protected abstract void draw (); // The method to draw the shape.
    protected abstract void erase (); // The method to erase the shape.

    // Create a shape that is to be drawn on the surface (which should
    // be either an Applet or a Frame).
    public Shape (Component surface, int x, int y, Color color)
    {
        this.surface = surface;
        this.x = x;
        this.y = y;
        this.color = color;
    } // Shape constructor

    // If the shape is not already visible, make it visible.
    public void show ()
    {
        if (!visible)
        {
            draw ();
            visible = true;
        }
    } // show method

    // If the shape is visible, hide it.
    public void hide ()
```

```
{
    if (visible)
    {
        erase ();
        visible = false;
    }
} // hide method

// Redraw the shape if it is visible.
public void paint ()
{
    if (visible)
    {
        draw ();
    }
} // paint method

// Move the shape to a new location.
public void move (int x, int y)
{
    if (visible)
    {
        erase ();
        this.x = x;
        this.y = y;
        draw ();
    }
    else
    {
        this.x = x;
        this.y = y;
    }
} // move method
} /* Shape class */
```

The *Shape* class has the same public methods *show, hide, paint,* and *move* as the previous version of the three shape classes *Rectangle, Oval,* and *Triangle*. It has protected methods *draw* and *erase* labelled **abstract** that have no bodies. Its instance variables are the same as in each of three shape classes.

Having established the abstract class *Shape*, we will now show how each of the three individual shape classes extends the *Shape* class. Each individual shape has some additional instance variables, different bodies for their constructors, and bodies for the *draw* and *erase* methods that are abstract in the *Shape* class itself.

The new *Rectangle* class extends the *Shape* class. Note the call to **super** in the constructors for *Rectangle, Oval,* and *Triangle.* It calls the constructor of the base class and allows the consolidation of the parts of the constructors that are common to all three shapes.

Here is the new *Rectangle* class

```
// The "Rectangle" class.
// This class handles rectangles on a graphics surface. Once created, they
// can be moved, hidden, and shown again.

import java.awt.*;

public class Rectangle extends Shape
{
    protected int rectWidth, rectHeight; // The rectangle's width and height.

    // Create a rectangle that is to be drawn on the surface (which should
    // be either an Applet or a Frame).
    public Rectangle (Component surface, int x, int y, int rectWidth,
        int rectHeight)
    {
        super (surface, x, y, Color.red);
        this.rectWidth = rectWidth;
        this.rectHeight = rectHeight;
        show ();
    } // Rectangle constructor

    // Draw the shape.
    protected void draw ()
    {
        Graphics g = surface.getGraphics ();
        g.setColor (color);
        g.fillRect (x, y, rectWidth, rectHeight);
    } // draw method
```

```
// Erase the shape.
protected void erase ()
{
    Graphics g = surface.getGraphics ();
    g.setColor (surface.getBackground ());
    g.fillRect (x, y, rectWidth, rectHeight);
} // erase method
} /* Rectangle class */
```

Here is the new *Oval* class.

```
// The "Oval" class.
// This class handles ovals on a graphics surface. Once created, they
// can be moved, hidden, and shown again.

import java.awt.*;

public class Oval extends Shape
{
    protected int xRadius, yRadius; // The x and y radius of the oval.

    // Create an oval that is to be drawn on the surface (which should
    // be either an Applet or a Frame).
    public Oval (Component surface, int x, int y, int xRadius, int yRadius)
    {
        super (surface, x, y, Color.blue);
        this.xRadius = xRadius;
        this.yRadius = yRadius;
        show ();
    } // Oval constructor

    // Draw the shape.
    protected void draw ()
    {
        Graphics g = surface.getGraphics ();
        g.setColor (color);
        g.fillOval (x – xRadius, y – yRadius, 2 * xRadius, 2 * yRadius);
    } // draw method
```

```
        // Erase the shape.
        protected void erase ()
        {
            Graphics g = surface.getGraphics ();
            g.setColor (surface.getBackground ());
            g.fillOval (x - xRadius, y - yRadius, 2 * xRadius, 2 * yRadius);
        } // erase method
} /* Oval class */
```

Here is the new *Triangle* class.

```
// The "Triangle" class.
// This class handles equilateral triangles on a graphics surface. Once
// created, they can be moved, hidden, and shown again.

import java.awt.*;

public class Triangle extends Shape
{
        protected int sideLength; // The length of a side of the triangle.

        // Create a triangle that is to be drawn on the surface (which should
        // be either an Applet or a Frame).
        public Triangle (Component surface, int x, int y, int sideLength)
        {
            super (surface, x, y, Color.green);
            this.sideLength = sideLength;
            show ();
        } // Triangle constructor

        // Draw the shape.
        protected void draw ()
        {
            Graphics g = surface.getGraphics ();
            int [] xp = new int [3];
            int [] yp = new int [3];
            xp [0] = x;
            yp [0] = y;
            xp [1] = x + sideLength / 2;
            yp [1] = (int) (y - Math.sqrt (3.0) / 2.0 * sideLength);
```

```
        xp [2] = x + sideLength;
        yp [2] = y;
        g.setColor (color);
        g.fillPolygon (xp, yp, 3);
    } // draw method

    // Erase the shape.
    protected void erase ()
    {
        Graphics g = surface.getGraphics ();
        int [] xp = new int [3];
        int [] yp = new int [3];
        xp [0] = x;
        yp [0] = y;
        xp [1] = x + sideLength / 2;
        yp [1] = (int) (y - Math.sqrt (3.0) / 2.0 * sideLength);
        xp [2] = x + sideLength;
        yp [2] = y;
        g.setColor (surface.getBackground ());
        g.fillPolygon (xp, yp, 3);
    } // erase method
} /* Triangle class */
```

In the modified *ShapeTest* applet that uses the three new classes, the *shapes* array is now an array of objects of the *Shape* class rather than the more generic class *Object*. This means that in the *paint* method, the individual shapes do not have to be cast as one of the three classes that extend the *Shape* class, since the *paint* method is defined for any *Shape* object.

Here is the new *ShapeTest* applet.

```
// The "ShapeTest" class.
// This applet randomly places 10 shapes on the drawing surface.

import java.applet.*;
import java.awt.*;

public class ShapeTest extends Applet
{
    protected final static int NUM_SHAPES = 10;
```

```
// The array containing the Shape objects.
Shape [] shapes = new Shape [NUM_SHAPES];

// This method is called when the Applet object is created.
public void init ()
{
    // Get the width and height of the drawing surface.
    int surfaceWidth = getSize ().width;
    int surfaceHeight = getSize ().height;

    // Create the shapes and place them randomly on the drawing
    // surface.
    for (int count = 0 ; count < NUM_SHAPES ; count++)
    {
        int shapeKind = (int) (Math.random () * 3);
        int x = (int) (Math.random () * surfaceWidth);
        int y = (int) (Math.random () * surfaceHeight);

        if (shapeKind == 0)
        {
            int rectWidth = (int) (Math.random () * 20) + 10;
            int rectHeight = (int) (Math.random () * 20) + 10;
            shapes [count] = new Rectangle (this, x, y, rectWidth,
                rectHeight);
        }
        else if (shapeKind == 1)
        {
            int xRadius = (int) (Math.random () * 10) + 10;
            int yRadius = (int) (Math.random () * 10) + 10;
            shapes [count] = new Oval (this, x, y, xRadius, yRadius);
        }
        else if (shapeKind == 2)
        {
            int sideLength = (int) (Math.random () * 20) + 10;
            shapes [count] = new Triangle (this, x, y, sideLength);
        }
    }
} // init method
```

```
// This method is called whenever the applet's drawing surface is
// obscured and then revealed. We call the paint method for each
// shape to redraw that shape (if the shape is currently visible).
public void paint (Graphics g)
{
    // For each shape, call its paint method.
    for (int count = 0 ; count < NUM_SHAPES ; count++)
    {
        shapes [count].paint ();
    }
} // paint method
} /* ShapeTest class */
```

The HTML file for *ShapeTest* class is the same as for the previous *ShapeTest* applet.

The extraction of common elements from several classes to form a base class is called **factoring** and is a common tool in object-oriented design. If several classes share much of the same behavior (methods, internal variables, or even method definitions) it is often good design to create a common base class and have the original classes inherit from that base class. This also ensures that when a bug is fixed in the base class it is fixed in all of the subclasses. This is one of the powerful benefits of object-oriented design.

# 14.3    Method Overloading in the Base Class

One of the advantages of using inheritance from a base class is that the methods in the base class can be overloaded, that is, the same method name can be used to produce different results depending on the parameters that are specified when the method is called.

We will now show a variation on the *Shape* class that has two different constructors: one is the same as before and places the object instantiated at a particular location (*x, y*) on the drawing surface; the other places it at a random location within the drawing surface. The second version is used if an $x$ and $y$ are not included in the list of parameters.

In the new abstract *Shape* class, the method *move* is overloaded so that, if the $(x, y)$ position to which the shape is to be moved is not specified as a parameter, the shape is moved to a random location.

Here is the new *Shape* abstract class.

```
// The "Shape" class.
// This is an abstract class from which all shapes descend. It contains
// all the methods and data that are common to all shapes. For example,
// you can call the show and hide methods of any Shape object, even
// if you do not know the exact type of the object (Rectangle, Oval,
// or Triangle).

import java.awt.*;

public abstract class Shape
{
    protected Component surface; // The surface to draw on.
    protected int x, y; // The x, y location of the shape.
    protected boolean visible = false; // Is the shape currently visible.
    protected Color color; // The color of the shape.

    protected abstract void draw (); // The method to draw the shape.
    protected abstract void erase (); // The method to erase the shape.

    // Create a shape that is to be drawn on the surface (which should
    // be either an Applet or a Frame).
    public Shape (Component surface, int x, int y, Color color)
    {
        this.surface = surface;
        this.x = x;
        this.y = y;
        this.color = color;
    } // Shape constructor

    // Create a shape that is to be drawn on the surface (which should
    // be either an Applet or a Frame). Randomly place it on the
    // drawing surface.
    public Shape (Component surface, Color color)
```

```
{
    int surfaceWidth = surface.getSize ().width;
    int surfaceHeight = surface.getSize ().height;

    this.surface = surface;
    this.x = (int) (Math.random () * surfaceWidth);
    this.y = (int) (Math.random () * surfaceHeight);
    this.color = color;
} // Shape constructor

// If the shape is not already visible, make it visible.
public void show ()
{
    if (!visible)
    {
        draw ();
        visible = true;
    }
} // show method

// If the shape is visible, hide it.
public void hide ()
{
    if (visible)
    {
        erase ();
        visible = false;
    }
} // hide method

// Redraw the shape if it is visible.
public void paint ()
{
    if (visible)
    {
        draw ();
    }
} // paint method

// Move the shape to a new location.
public void move (int x, int y)
{
```

```
        if (visible)
        {
            erase ();
            this.x = x;
            this.y = y;
            draw ();
        }
        else
        {
            this.x = x;
            this.y = y;
        }
    } // move method

    // If the user does not specify the coordinates to move to, then
    // move the shape to a new random location.
    public void move ()
    {
        int surfaceWidth = surface.getSize ().width;
        int surfaceHeight = surface.getSize ().height;

        int newX = (int) (Math.random () * surfaceWidth);
        int newY = (int) (Math.random () * surfaceHeight);

        if (visible)
        {
            erase ();
            this.x = newX;
            this.y = newY;
            draw ();
        }
        else
        {
            this.x = newX;
            this.y = newY;
        }
    } // move method
} /* Shape class */
```

Here again are the three classes: *Oval, Rectangle,* and *Triangle.* This time they have been changed to take advantage of the overloaded constructor of the *Shape* class. Each has three different constructor methods: one as before, one that places the shape in a random location within the drawing surface, and one that places the shape randomly and determines the size of the shape randomly.

Here is the new *Rectangle* class.

```
// The "Rectangle" class.
// This class handles rectangles on a graphics surface. Once created, they
// can be moved, hidden, and shown again.

import java.awt.*;

public class Rectangle extends Shape
{
    protected int rectWidth, rectHeight; // The rectangle's width and height.

    // Create a rectangle that is to be drawn on the surface (which should
    // be either an Applet or a Frame).
    public Rectangle (Component surface, int x, int y, int rectWidth,
        int rectHeight)
    {
        super (surface, x, y, Color.red);
        this.rectWidth = rectWidth;
        this.rectHeight = rectHeight;
        show ();
    } // Rectangle constructor

    // Create a rectangle that is to be drawn on the surface (which should
    // be either an Applet or a Frame). Randomly place it on the
    // drawing surface.
    public Rectangle (Component surface, int rectWidth, int rectHeight)
    {
        super (surface, Color.red);
        this.rectWidth = rectWidth;
        this.rectHeight = rectHeight;
        show ();
    } // Rectangle constructor
```

```
// Create a rectangle that is to be drawn on the surface (which should
// be either an Applet or a Frame). Randomly place it on the
// drawing surface. Randomly determine the width and height
// of the rectangle.
public Rectangle (Component surface)
{
    super (surface, Color.red);
    this.rectWidth = (int) (Math.random () * 20) + 10;
    this.rectHeight = (int) (Math.random () * 20) + 10;
    show ();
} // Rectangle constructor

// Draw the shape.
protected void draw ()
{
    Graphics g = surface.getGraphics ();
    g.setColor (color);
    g.fillRect (x, y, rectWidth, rectHeight);
} // draw method

// Erase the shape.
protected void erase ()
{
    Graphics g = surface.getGraphics ();
    g.setColor (surface.getBackground ());
    g.fillRect (x, y, rectWidth, rectHeight);
} // erase method
} /* Rectangle class */
```

Here is the new *Oval* class.

```
// The "Oval" class.
// This class handles ovals on a graphics surface. Once created, they
// can be moved, hidden, and shown again.

import java.awt.*;

public class Oval extends Shape
{
    protected int xRadius, yRadius; // The x and y radius of the oval.
```

```
// Create an oval that is to be drawn on the surface (which should
// be either an Applet or a Frame).
public Oval (Component surface, int x, int y, int xRadius, int yRadius)
{
    super (surface, x, y, Color.blue);
    this.xRadius = xRadius;
    this.yRadius = yRadius;
    show ();
} // Oval constructor

// Create an oval that is to be drawn on the surface (which should
// be either an Applet or a Frame). Randomly place it on the
// drawing surface.
public Oval (Component surface, int xRadius, int yRadius)
{
    super (surface, Color.blue);
    this.xRadius = xRadius;
    this.yRadius = yRadius;
    show ();
} // Oval constructor

// Create an oval that is to be drawn on the surface (which should
// be either an Applet or a Frame). Randomly place it on the
// drawing surface. Randomly determine the x and y radius of
// the oval.
public Oval (Component surface)
{
    super (surface, Color.blue);
    this.xRadius = (int) (Math.random () * 10) + 10;
    this.yRadius = (int) (Math.random () * 10) + 10;
    show ();
} // Oval constructor

// Draw the shape.
protected void draw ()
{
    Graphics g = surface.getGraphics ();
    g.setColor (color);
    g.fillOval (x – xRadius, y – yRadius, 2 * xRadius, 2 * yRadius);
} // draw method
```

```
    // Erase the shape.
    protected void erase ()
    {
        Graphics g = surface.getGraphics ();
        g.setColor (surface.getBackground ());
        g.fillOval (x – xRadius, y – yRadius, 2 * xRadius, 2 * yRadius);
    } // erase method
} /* Oval class */
```

Here is the new *Triangle* class.

```
// The "Triangle" class.
// This class handles equilateral triangles on a graphics surface. Once
// created, they can be moved, hidden, and shown again.

import java.awt.*;

public class Triangle extends Shape
{
    protected int sideLength; // The length of a side of the triangle.

    // Create a triangle that is to be drawn on the surface (which should
    // be either an Applet or a Frame).
    public Triangle (Component surface, int x, int y, int sideLength)
    {
        super (surface, x, y, Color.green);
        this.sideLength = sideLength;
        show ();
    } // Triangle constructor

    // Create a triangle that is to be drawn on the surface (which should
    // be either an Applet or a Frame). Randomly place it on the
    // drawing surface.
    public Triangle (Component surface, int sideLength)
    {
        super (surface, Color.green);
        this.sideLength = sideLength;
        show ();
    } // Triangle constructor

    // Create a triangle that is to be drawn on the surface (which should
    // be either an Applet or a Frame). Randomly place it on the
```

```java
    // drawing surface. Randomly determine the length of a side of
    // the triangle.
    public Triangle (Component surface)
    {
        super (surface, Color.green);
        this.sideLength = (int) (Math.random () * 20) + 10;
        show ();
    } // Triangle constructor

    // Draw the shape.
    protected void draw ()
    {
        Graphics g = surface.getGraphics ();
        int [] xp = new int [3];
        int [] yp = new int [3];
        xp [0] = x;
        yp [0] = y;
        xp [1] = x + sideLength / 2;
        yp [1] = (int) (y – Math.sqrt (3.0) / 2.0 * sideLength);
        xp [2] = x + sideLength;
        yp [2] = y;
        g.setColor (color);
        g.fillPolygon (xp, yp, 3);
    } // draw method

    // Erase the shape.
    protected void erase ()
    {
        Graphics g = surface.getGraphics ();
        int [] xp = new int [3];
        int [] yp = new int [3];
        xp [0] = x;
        yp [0] = y;
        xp [1] = x + sideLength / 2;
        yp [1] = (int) (y – Math.sqrt (3.0) / 2.0 * sideLength);
        xp [2] = x + sideLength;
        yp [2] = y;
        g.setColor (surface.getBackground ());
        g.fillPolygon (xp, yp, 3);
    } // erase method
} /* Triangle class */
```

Here is the modified *ShapeTest* class that takes advantage of the alternate constructors that have been added to the individual shape classes. These individual shape classes in turn take advantage of the additional constructor of the *Shape* class itself. Each individual shape is drawn at a randomly-chosen location and has a randomly-chosen size. For the rectangles, the randomness of both location and size is set in the *ShapeTest* class. For the ovals, the randomness in size is set in the *ShapeTest* class. The *Oval* class, however, uses a new constructor that selects the random location. For the triangles, the new constructor in the *Triangle* class determines both the random location and size.

The random location of the rectangles upper-left corner is limited to points in the upper-left quadrant of the drawing surface. If the random location had been chosen using the new constructor of the *Rectangle* class, it would have been chosen randomly from the whole drawing surface.

Here is the new *ShapeTest* class.

```
// The "ShapeTest" class.
// This applet randomly places 10 shapes on the drawing surface.

import java.applet.*;
import java.awt.*;

public class ShapeTest extends Applet
{
    protected final static int NUM_SHAPES = 10;

    // The array containing the Shape objects.
    Shape [] shapes = new Shape [NUM_SHAPES];

    // This method is called when the Applet object is created.
    public void init ()
    {
        // Get the width and height of the drawing surface.
        int surfaceWidth = getSize ().width;
        int surfaceHeight = getSize ().height;

        // Create the shapes and place them randomly on the drawing
        // surface.
```

```java
for (int count = 0 ; count < NUM_SHAPES ; count++)
{
    int shapeKind = (int) (Math.random () * 3);

    if (shapeKind == 0)
    {
        // The following two lines place the upper-left corner
        // of the rectangle in the upper-left quadrant.
        int x = (int) (Math.random () * surfaceWidth / 2);
        int y = (int) (Math.random () * surfaceHeight / 2);
        int rectWidth = (int) (Math.random () * 20) + 10;
        int rectHeight = (int) (Math.random () * 20) + 10;
        shapes [count] = new Rectangle (this, x, y, rectWidth,
            rectHeight);
    }
    else if (shapeKind == 1)
    {
        int xRadius = (int) (Math.random () * 30) + 10;
        int yRadius = (int) (Math.random () * 10) + 10;
        shapes [count] = new Oval (this, xRadius, yRadius);
    }
    else if (shapeKind == 2)
    {
        shapes [count] = new Triangle (this);
    }
}
} // init method

// This method is called whenever the applet's drawing surface is
// obscured and then revealed. We call the paint method for each
// shape to redraw that shape (if the shape is currently visible).
public void paint (Graphics g)
{
    // For each shape, call its paint method.
    for (int count = 0 ; count < NUM_SHAPES ; count++)
    {
        shapes [count].paint ();
    }
} // paint method
} /* ShapeTest class */
```

# 14.4  Adding Methods to a Base Class

In the previous examples, many of the methods in the present *Shapes* base class were shared by the three offspring classes. It is also often possible to add a new method to the base class that all the offspring can use.

In the next example, we will add a method called *slide* that moves the location of the shape a small amount *dx* in the *x*-direction and simultaneously a small amount *dy* in the *y*-direction. In the *slide* method, if the new location has an *x* that is zero or equal to or greater than the surface width, the value of *dx* is reversed in sign. Similarly if *y* is zero or greater than or equal to the surface height, the value of *dy* is reversed in sign. This results in the shape bouncing off the boundaries of the surface. New instance variables *dx*, *dy*, *surfaceWidth*, and *surfaceHeight* are added to the *Shape* class. As well, a new constructor

   *Shape* ()

that randomly chooses initial small values for *dx* and *dy* is also provided. Each of the other two constructors are modified by the addition in their bodies of the statement

   **this** ();

which first executes the new constructor and then proceeds as before. As well, values of the variables *surfaceWidth* and *surfaceHeight* are initialized using the *getSize().width* and *getSize().height* of the *surface* object.

Here is the modified *Shape* class.

```
// The "Shape" class.
// This is an abstract class from which all shapes descend. It contains
// all the methods and data that are common to all shapes. For example,
// you can call the show and hide methods of any Shape object, even
// if you do not know the exact type of the object (Rectangle, Oval,
// or Triangle).

import java.awt.*;
```

```
public abstract class Shape
{
    protected Component surface; // The surface to draw on.
    protected int x, y; // The x, y location of the shape.
    protected boolean visible = false; // Is the shape currently visible.
    protected Color color; // The color of the shape.
    protected int surfaceWidth; // The width of the surface.
    protected int surfaceHeight; // The height of the surface.
    protected int dx, dy; // The increment of motion of the shape.

    protected abstract void draw (); // The method to draw the shape.
    protected abstract void erase (); // The method to erase the shape.

    // Set the initial direction of motion for the shape. This
    // constructor should not be called directly from a descendent
    // class, only from constructors in the Shape class.
    protected Shape ()
    {
        // Establish random values for dx and dy. Be sure that
        // dx and dy are not both zero.
        do
        {
            dx = (int) (Math.random () * 5) – 2;
            dy = (int) (Math.random () * 5) – 2;
        }
        while ((dx == 0) && (dy == 0));
    } // Shape constructor

    // Create a shape that is to be drawn on the surface (which should
    // be either an Applet or a Frame).
    public Shape (Component surface, int x, int y, Color color)
    {
        this (); // Set dx and dy.
        surfaceWidth = surface.getSize ().width;
        surfaceHeight = surface.getSize ().height;
        this.surface = surface;
        this.x = x;
        this.y = y;
        this.color = color;
    } // Shape constructor
```

```
// Create a shape that is to be drawn on the surface (which should
// be either an Applet or a Frame). Randomly place it on the
// drawing surface.
public Shape (Component surface, Color color)
{
    this (); // Set dx and dy.
    surfaceWidth = surface.getSize ().width;
    surfaceHeight = surface.getSize ().height;
    this.surface = surface;
    this.x = (int) (Math.random () * surfaceWidth);
    this.y = (int) (Math.random () * surfaceHeight);
    this.color = color;
} // Shape constructor

// If the shape is not already visible, make it visible.
public void show ()
{
    if (!visible)
    {
        draw ();
        visible = true;
    }
} // show method

// If the shape is visible, hide it.
public void hide ()
{
    if (visible)
    {
        erase ();
        visible = false;
    }
} // hide method

// Redraw the shape if it is visible.
public void paint ()
{
    if (visible)
    {
        draw ();
    }
} // paint method
```

```
// Move the shape to a new location.
public void move (int x, int y)
{
    if (visible)
    {
        erase ();
        this.x = x;
        this.y = y;
        draw ();
    }
    else
    {
        this.x = x;
        this.y = y;
    }
} // move method

// If the user does not specify the coordinates to move to, then
// move the shape to a new random location.
public void move ()
{
    int newX = (int) (Math.random () * surfaceWidth);
    int newY = (int) (Math.random () * surfaceHeight);

    if (visible)
    {
        erase ();
        this.x = newX;
        this.y = newY;
        draw ();
    }
    else
    {
        this.x = newX;
        this.y = newY;
    }
} // move method

// Slide the shape in the direction specified by dx, dy. If the shape
// has slid off the edge of the drawing surface, reverse the direction
// of that motion increment.
```

```
    public void slide ()
    {
        if ((x < 0) || (x >= surfaceWidth))
            dx = -dx;
        if ((y < 0) || (y >= surfaceHeight))
            dy = -dy;
        move (x + dx, y + dy);
    } // slide method
} /* Shape class */
```

The new *ShapeTest* class makes use of the *slide* method of *Shape* to move the ten shapes of random type (*Oval*, *Rectangle*, and *Triangle*), random location, and random size around the drawing surface.

The *start* method slides each one of the 10 shapes 10,000 times and then stops. The result is that the shapes are moved around in straight lines and bounced off the borders of the drawing surface. In the *move* method, the shape is erased in its current position then drawn in its new position. This creates the illusion that the shapes are animated in a straight line motion with bounces.

Here is the new *ShapeTest* class.

```
// The "ShapeTest" class.
// This applet randomly places 10 shapes on the drawing surface
// and then moves the shapes around the screen, bouncing them
// off the edges.

import java.applet.*;
import java.awt.*;

public class ShapeTest extends Applet
{
    protected final static int NUM_SHAPES = 10;

    // The array containing the Shape objects.
    Shape [] shapes = new Shape [NUM_SHAPES];

    // This method is called when the Applet object is created.
    public void init ()
    {
```

```
// Get the width and height of the drawing surface.
int surfaceWidth = getSize ().width;
int surfaceHeight = getSize ().height;

// Create the shapes and place them randomly on the drawing
// surface.
for (int count = 0 ; count < NUM_SHAPES ; count++)
{
    int shapeKind = (int) (Math.random () * 3);

    if (shapeKind == 0)
    {
        // The following two lines place the upper–left corner
        // of the rectangle in the upper–left quadrant.
        int x = (int) (Math.random () * surfaceWidth / 2);
        int y = (int) (Math.random () * surfaceHeight / 2);
        int rectWidth = (int) (Math.random () * 20) + 10;
        int rectHeight = (int) (Math.random () * 20) + 10;
        shapes [count] = new Rectangle (this, x, y, rectWidth,
            rectHeight);
    }
    else if (shapeKind == 1)
    {

        int xRadius = (int) (Math.random () * 30) + 10;
        int yRadius = (int) (Math.random () * 10) + 10;
        shapes [count] = new Oval (this, xRadius, yRadius);
    }
    else if (shapeKind == 2)
    {
        shapes [count] = new Triangle (this);
    }

}
} // init method

// This method is called when the Applet object is activated. Slide
// the shapes around the drawing surface for 10,000 iterations. Do
// not be surprised if there are occasional long pauses while Java
// garbage collects.
public void start ()
{
    setVisible (true); // Make the applet surface visible.
```

```
        for (int i = 0 ; i < 10000 ; i++)
            for (int count = 0 ; count < NUM_SHAPES ; count++)
                shapes [count].slide ();
} // start method

// This method is called whenever the applet's drawing surface is
// obscured and then revealed. We call the paint method for each
// shape to redraw that shape (if the shape is currently visible).
public void paint (Graphics g)
{
    // For each shape, call its paint method.
    for (int count = 0 ; count < NUM_SHAPES ; count++)
    {
        shapes [count].paint ();
    }
} // paint method
} /* ShapeTest class */
```

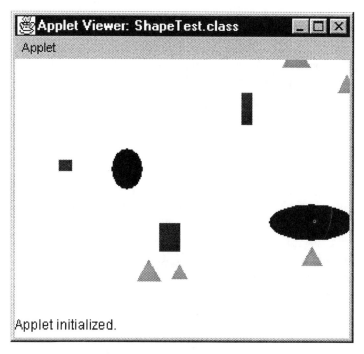

Figure 14.2 Bouncing Shapes

Using this new *ShapeTest* class changes only the base class. Although there were no changes to the *Rectangle, Oval,* and *Triangle* classes, functionality was added to all the descendant classes of *Shape*. This is another example of the advantages of the object-oriented paradigm. Figure 14.2 shows the appearance of the applet display area at a particular moment. The actual display is constantly moving.

# 14.5  Improving Efficiency of Extended Classes

After the *ShapeTest* applet has been running for some time (seconds to minutes depending upon the hardware and JVM) the shape's motion will suddenly pause for several seconds before resuming. This recurs regularly.

While there is nothing in the program to explicitly cause the pause, it occurs because of the program's structure. Java **garbage collects** unused objects. This means that most implementations of Java use new memory every time an object is instantiated until there is no memory left, whereupon it goes through all available memory looking for unused objects that it can return to the free memory list. This process can be time consuming.

Our program allocates and discards hundreds, if not thousands, of objects per second. In the *draw* and *erase* methods of *Rectangle, Oval* and *Triangle*, a *Graphics* object is allocated and then discarded when the method is finished. Since the *draw* and *erase* methods are called continuously in order to slide a shape across the screen, and because *Graphics* objects contain a great deal of data, it is possible to use all of the available free memory very quickly. This leads to frequent **garbage collection**. This section illustrates the occasional need to design programs to take into account real world constraints such as limited memory.

In the following version of the *Shape* class, we declare a **static** *Graphics* object to store the graphics context upon which all shapes will be drawn. This saves space over the alternative (each *Shape* object storing its own graphics context). This requires, however, that all

*Shapes* must be placed on the same surface and that the graphics context, surface width and height, and background color must be declared **static**. This reduces the *Shape* class' flexibility, so there is a trade-off between memory usage and flexibility.

In the constructor

>   *Shape (Component surface)*

the particular values of these four **static** class variables are assigned if this is the first *Shape* instantiated. After the variables are asssigned, the graphics context is set and will not be assigned again. Each of the other constructors first calls the constructor *Shape (Component surface)* with the statement

>   **this** (*surface*);

The *draw* and *erase* methods of the *Shape* class differ only in the color in which the shape is drawn. Changing the *Shape* class to take advantage of the similarity of the *draw* and *erase* methods also improves clarity and reliability. The new class provides bodies for *draw* and *erase* that were formerly abstract methods. These both use the newly-defined *drawShape* method.

Here is the new, more efficient *Shape* class.

```
// The "Shape" class.
// This is an abstract class from which all shapes descend. It contains
// all the methods and data that are common to all shapes. For example,
// you can call the show and hide methods of any Shape object, even
// if you do not know the exact type of the object (Rectangle, Oval,
// or Triangle).

import java.awt.*;

public abstract class Shape
{
        // The static variables common to all Shape objects. Note that all
        // Shape objects must appear on one graphics context (drawing surface).
        // We could have not made these static, and traded off using more
        // memory (a graphics context for each Shape, rather than just one)
        // for greater flexibility in the class.
```

```
protected static Graphics g; // The graphics context (drawing surface).
protected static int surfaceWidth; // The width of the surface.
protected static int surfaceHeight; // The height of the surface.
protected static Color backgroundColor; //The surface's background color.

protected int x, y; // The x, y location of the shape.
protected boolean visible = false; // Is the shape currently visible.
protected Color color; // The color of the shape.
protected int dx, dy; // The increment of motion of the shape.

// The method to draw the shape in a specified color.
protected abstract void drawShape (Color shapeColor);

// The first time a Shape object is instantiated, set the
// surface's graphics context, width, height, and background
// color. Also set the direction of motion for the shape
// whenever a Shape object is instantiated. This
// constructor should not be called directly from a descendent
// class, only from constructors in the Shape class.
public Shape (Component surface)
{
    if (g == null)
    {
        g = surface.getGraphics ();
        surfaceWidth = surface.getSize ().width;
        surfaceHeight = surface.getSize ().height;
        backgroundColor = surface.getBackground ();
    }

    // Establish random values for dx and dy. Be sure that
    // dx and dy are not both zero.
    do
    {
        dx = (int) (Math.random () * 5) – 2;
        dy = (int) (Math.random () * 5) – 2;
    }
    while ((dx == 0) && (dy == 0));
} // Shape constructor

// Create a shape that is to be drawn on the surface (which should
// be either an Applet or a Frame).
public Shape (Component surface, int x, int y, Color color)
```

```
    {
        this (surface); // Set static variables, dx, and dy.
        this.x = x;
        this.y = y;
        this.color = color;
    } // Shape constructor

    // Create a shape that is to be drawn on the surface (which should
    // be either an Applet or a Frame). Randomly place it on the
    // drawing surface.
    public Shape (Component surface, Color color)
    {
        this (surface); // Set static variables, dx, and dy.
        this.x = (int) (Math.random () * surfaceWidth);
        this.y = (int) (Math.random () * surfaceHeight);
        this.color = color;
    } // Shape constructor

    // If the shape is not already visible, make it visible.
    public void show ()
    {
        if (!visible)
        {
            draw ();
            visible = true;
        }
    } // show method

    // If the shape is visible, hide it.
    public void hide ()
    {
        if (visible)
        {
            erase ();
            visible = false;
        }
    } // hide method

    // Redraw the shape if it is visible.
    public void paint ()
    {
        if (visible)
```

```
    {
        draw ();
    }
} // paint method

// Move the shape to a new location.
public void move (int x, int y)
{
    if (visible)
    {
        erase ();
        this.x = x;
        this.y = y;
        draw ();
    }
    else
    {
        this.x = x;
        this.y = y;
    }
} // move method

// If the user does not specify the coordinates to move to, then
// move the shape to a new random location.
public void move ()
{
    int newX = (int) (Math.random () * surfaceWidth);
    int newY = (int) (Math.random () * surfaceHeight);

    if (visible)
    {
        erase ();
        this.x = newX;
        this.y = newY;
        draw ();
    }
    else
    {
        this.x = newX;
        this.y = newY;
    }
} // move method
```

```
// Slide the shape in the direction specified by dx, dy. If the shape
// has slid off the edge of the drawing surface, reverse the direction
// of that motion increment.
public void slide ()
{
    if ((x < 0) || (x >= surfaceWidth))
        dx = -dx;
    if ((y < 0) || (y >= surfaceHeight))
        dy = -dy;
    move (x + dx, y + dy);
} // slide method

// Draw the shape by drawing it in the shape's color.
protected void draw ()
{
    drawShape (color);
} // draw method

// Erase the shape by drawing it in the applet's background color.
protected void erase ()
{
    drawShape (backgroundColor);
} // erase method
} /* Shape class */
```

In the new more efficient *Rectangle* class, there are no *draw* and *erase* methods but the abstract method *drawShape* is given a body. Everything else is the same.

Here is the new *Rectangle* class.

```
// The "Rectangle" class.
// This class handles rectangles on a graphics surface. Once created, they
// can be moved, hidden, and shown again.

import java.awt.*;

public class Rectangle extends Shape
{
    protected int rectWidth, rectHeight; // The rectangle's width and height.
```

```java
// Create a rectangle that is to be drawn on the surface (which should
// be either an Applet or a Frame).
public Rectangle (Component surface, int x, int y, int rectWidth,
    int rectHeight)
{
    super (surface, x, y, Color.red);
    this.rectWidth = rectWidth;
    this.rectHeight = rectHeight;
    show ();
} // Rectangle constructor

// Create a rectangle that is to be drawn on the surface (which should
// be either an Applet or a Frame). Randomly place it on the
// drawing surface.
public Rectangle (Component surface, int rectWidth, int rectHeight)
{
    super (surface, Color.red);
    this.rectWidth = rectWidth;
    this.rectHeight = rectHeight;
    show ();
} // Rectangle constructor

// Create a rectangle that is to be drawn on the surface (which should
// be either an Applet or a Frame). Randomly place it on the
// drawing surface. Randomly determine the width and height
// of the rectangle.
public Rectangle (Component surface)
{
    super (surface, Color.red);
    rectWidth = (int) (Math.random () * 20) + 10;
    rectHeight = (int) (Math.random () * 20) + 10;
    show ();
} // Rectangle constructor

// Draw the shape in the specified color.
protected void drawShape (Color shapeColor)
{
    g.setColor (shapeColor);
    g.fillRect (x, y, rectWidth, rectHeight);
} // drawShape method
} /* Rectangle class */
```

Here is the *drawShape* method for the *Oval* class.

```
// Draw the shape in the specified color.
protected void drawShape (Color shapeColor)
{
    g.setColor (shapeColor);
    g.fillOval (x – xRadius, y – yRadius, 2 * xRadius, 2 * yRadius);
} // drawShape method
```

Here is the *drawShape* method for the *Triangle* class.

```
// Draw the shape in the specified color.
protected void drawShape (Color shapeColor)
{
    int [] xp = new int [3];
    int [] yp = new int [3];
    xp [0] = x;
    yp [0] = y;
    xp [1] = x + sideLength / 2;
    yp [1] = (int) (y – Math.sqrt (3.0) / 2.0 * sideLength);
    xp [2] = x + sideLength;
    yp [2] = y;
    g.setColor (shapeColor);
    g.fillPolygon (xp, yp, 3);
} // drawShape method
```

# 14.6  Class Hierarchies

So far in this chapter we have been describing a class hierarchy in which a parent class *Shape* has three offspring classes: *Rectangle, Oval,* and *Triangle* as shown in Figure 14.3. We will now add to this hierarchy by having a class *Square* extend the *Rectangle* class.

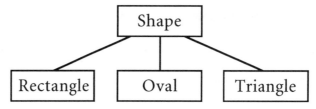

Figure 14.3 Simple Class Hierarchy

Here is the *Square* class.

```
// The "Square" class.
// This class handles squares on a graphics surface. Once created, they
// can be moved, hidden and, shown again.

import java.awt.*;

public class Square extends Rectangle
{
    // Create a square that is to be drawn on the surface (which should
    // be either an Applet or a Frame) by creating a rectangle with
    // height and width the same.
    public Square (Component surface, int x, int y, int side)
    {
        super (surface, x, y, side, side);
        color = Color.gray;
    } // Square constructor

    // Create a square that is to be drawn on the surface (which should
    // be either an Applet or a Frame) by creating a rectangle with
    // height and width the same. Randomly place it on the
    // drawing surface.
    public Square (Component surface, int side)
    {
        super (surface, side, side);
        color = Color.gray;
    } // Square constructor

    // Create a square that is to be drawn on the surface (which should
    // be either an Applet or a Frame) by creating a rectangle with
```

```
    // height and width the same. Randomly place it on the
    // drawing surface. Randomly determine the length of a side
    // of the square.
    public Square (Component surface)
    {
        super (surface);
        color = Color.gray;
        rectWidth = (int) (Math.random () * 20) + 10;
        rectHeight = rectWidth;
    } // Square constructor
} /* Square class */
```

References to **super** in *Square* refer to the constructor in the *Rectangle* class. We will now extend the *Oval* class to produce a class *Circle*.

Here is the *Circle* class.

```
// The "Circle" class.
// This class handles circles on a graphics surface. Once created, they
// can be moved, hidden, and shown again.

import java.awt.*;

public class Circle extends Oval
{
    // Create a circle that is to be drawn on the surface (which should
    // be either an Applet or a Frame) by creating an oval with
    // x and y radius the same.
    public Circle (Component surface, int x, int y, int radius)
    {
        super (surface, x, y, radius, radius);
        color = Color.yellow;
    } // Circle constructor

    // Create a circle that is to be drawn on the surface (which should
    // be either an Applet or a Frame) by creating an oval with
    // x and y radius the same. Randomly place it on the
    // drawing surface.
    public Circle (Component surface, int radius)
    {
```

```
        super (surface, radius, radius);
        color = Color.yellow;
    } // Circle constructor

    // Create a circle that is to be drawn on the surface (which should
    // be either an Applet or a Frame) by creating an oval with
    // x and y radius the same. Randomly place it on the
    // drawing surface. Randomly determine the radius of the circle.
    public Circle (Component surface)
    {
        super (surface);
        xRadius = (int) (Math.random () * 10) + 10;
        yRadius = xRadius;
        color = Color.yellow;
    } // Circle constructor
} /* Circle class */
```

Notice that the reference to **super** in *Circle* refers to the constructor of class *Oval*.

We will now extend the *Circle* class so that it adds eyes to the basic circle. The new extended class, called *Face*, has *draw* and *erase* methods that override the corresponding methods of the *Shape* class and a *drawShape* method that overrides the *drawShape* of *Circle*. The new *drawShape* also contains a call to the *drawShape* of *Circle* to color the circle before the eyes are added.

Here is the *Face* class.

```
// The "Face" class.
// This class handles Faces on a graphics surface. Once created, they
// can be moved, hidden, and shown again.

import java.awt.*;

public class Face extends Circle
{
    // The color the features (such as mouth and eyes) should be drawn in.
    protected static Color FEATURE_COLOR = Color.black;
```

```
// Create a face that is to be drawn on the surface (which should
// be either an Applet or a Frame).
public Face (Component surface, int x, int y, int radius)
{
    super (surface, x, y, radius);
    color = Color.pink;
} // Face constructor

// Create a face that is to be drawn on the surface (which should
// be either an Applet or a Frame). Randomly place it on the
// drawing surface.
public Face (Component surface, int radius)
{
    super (surface, radius);
    color = Color.pink;
} // Face constructor

// Create a face that is to be drawn on the surface (which should
// be either an Applet or a Frame). Randomly place it on the
// drawing surface. Randomly determine the radius of the face.
public Face (Component surface)
{
    super (surface);
    color = Color.pink;
} // Face constructor

// The new form of drawShape requires two parameters. The color of
// the base image and the color of the features to be placed on
// the image.
public void draw ()
{
    drawShape (color, FEATURE_COLOR);
} // draw method

// Note that in terms of drawing, we are slightly inefficient
// because we draw the features in the background color when
// they have already been erased. Doing this however, it makes
// the program easier to understand.
public void erase ()
{
    drawShape (backgroundColor, backgroundColor);
} // erase method
```

```
// Draw the face. We do this by drawing a circle using the super
// class and then drawing the eyes.
protected void drawShape (Color shapeColor, Color featureColor)
{
    super.drawShape (shapeColor); // Draw the circle.

    // Draw the eyes.
    g.setColor (featureColor);
    g.fillOval (x – xRadius / 3 – xRadius / 6, y – xRadius / 3 – xRadius / 6,
        xRadius / 3, xRadius / 3);
    g.fillOval (x + xRadius / 3 – xRadius / 6, y – xRadius / 3 – xRadius / 6,
        xRadius / 3, xRadius / 3);
} // drawShape method
} /* Face class */
```

Figure 14.4 shows the current state of the class hierarchy.

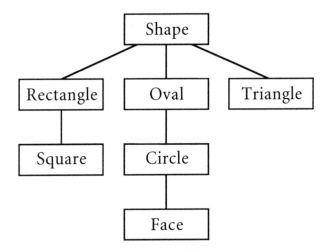

**Figure 14.4 Class Hierarchy**

Notice that all objects in the hierarchy can be considered as *Shape* objects.

We will now add two classes that extend the *Face* class: the *Sad* class and the *Happy* class. The *Sad* class is shown here. It adds a drooping mouth to *Face*. References to **super** in this class refer to *Face*.

```
// The "Sad" class.
// This class handles "sad faces" on a graphics surface. Once created, they
// can be moved, hidden, and shown again.

import java.awt.*;

public class Sad extends Face
{
    // Create a face that is to be drawn on the surface (which should
    // be either an Applet or a Frame).
    public Sad (Component surface, int x, int y, int radius)
    {
        super (surface, x, y, radius);
        color = Color.cyan;
    } // Sad constructor

    // Create a face that is to be drawn on the surface (which should
    // be either an Applet or a Frame). Randomly place it on the
    // drawing surface.
    public Sad (Component surface, int radius)
    {
        super (surface, radius);
        color = Color.cyan;
    } // Sad constructor

    // Create a face that is to be drawn on the surface (which should
    // be either an Applet or a Frame). Randomly place it on the
    // drawing surface. Randomly determine the radius of the face.
    public Sad (Component surface)
    {
        super (surface);
        color = Color.cyan;
    } // Sad constructor

    // Draw the sad face. We do this by drawing a face (without mouth)
    // using the super class and then drawing the mouth.
    protected void drawShape (Color shapeColor, Color featureColor)
    {
        super.drawShape (shapeColor, featureColor); // Draw the face.
```

```
            // Draw the frown.
            g.setColor (featureColor);
            for (int i = 0 ; i < 2 ; i++)
            {
                g.drawArc (x – 2 * xRadius / 3 – i, y + xRadius / 6 – i,
                    4 * xRadius / 3 + 2 * i, 4 * xRadius / 3 + 2 * i, 45, 90);
            }
    } // drawShape method
} /* Sad class */
```

The *Happy* class adds a smiling mouth to *Face*.

```
// The "Happy" class.
// This class handles "happy faces" on a graphics surface. Once created,
// they can be moved, hidden, and shown again.

import java.awt.*;

public class Happy extends Face
{
    // Create a face that is to be drawn on the surface (which should
    // be either an Applet or a Frame).
    public Happy (Component surface, int x, int y, int radius)
    {
        super (surface, x, y, radius);
        color = Color.magenta;
    } // Happy constructor

    // Create a face that is to be drawn on the surface (which should
    // be either an Applet or a Frame). Randomly place it on the
    // drawing surface.
    public Happy (Component surface, int radius)
    {
        super (surface, radius);
        color = Color.magenta;
    } // Happy constructor

    // Create a face that is to be drawn on the surface (which should
    // be either an Applet or a Frame). Randomly place it on the
    // drawing surface. Randomly determine the radius of the face.
```

```
public Happy (Component surface)
{
    super (surface);
    color = Color.magenta;
} // Happy constructor

// Draw the happy face. We do this by drawing a face (without mouth)
// using the super class and then drawing the mouth.
protected void drawShape (Color shapeColor, Color featureColor)
{
    super.drawShape (shapeColor, featureColor); // Draw a face.
    // Draw the smile.
    g.setColor (featureColor);
    for (int i = 0 ; i < 2 ; i++)
    {
        g.drawArc (x – 2 * xRadius / 3 – i, y – 2 * xRadius / 3 – i,
            4 * xRadius / 3 + 2 * i, 4 * xRadius / 3 + 2 * i, 180, 180);
    }
} // drawShape method
} /* Happy class */
```

We will now extend the *Happy* class to the *Rabbit* class which adds ears and whiskers to the happy face.

```
// The "Rabbit" class.
// This class handles "rabbit faces" on a graphics surface. Once created,
// they can be moved, hidden, and shown again.

import java.awt.*;

public class Rabbit extends Happy
{
    // Create a rabbit face that is to be drawn on the surface (which
    // should be either an Applet or a Frame).
    public Rabbit (Component surface, int x, int y, int radius)
    {
        super (surface, x, y, radius);
        color = Color.orange;
    } // Rabbit constructor
```

```
// Create a rabbit face that is to be drawn on the surface (which
// should be either an Applet or a Frame). Randomly place it
// on the drawing surface.
public Rabbit (Component surface, int radius)
{
    super (surface, radius);
    color = Color.orange;
} // Rabbit constructor

// Create a rabbit face that is to be drawn on the surface (which
// should be either an Applet or a Frame). Randomly place it
// on the drawing surface. Randomly determine the radius of
// the face.
public Rabbit (Component surface)
{
    super (surface);
    color = Color.orange;
} // Rabbit constructor

// Draw the rabbit face. We do this by drawing a happy face
// using the super class and then drawing the ears, nose, and
// whiskers.
protected void drawShape (Color shapeColor, Color featureColor)
{
    super.drawShape (shapeColor, featureColor); // Draw the happy face.

    // Draw the ears.
    g.setColor (shapeColor);
    g.fillOval (x – 2 * xRadius / 3, y – 2 * xRadius,
        xRadius / 3, 3 * xRadius / 2);
    g.fillOval (x + xRadius / 3, y – 2 * xRadius,
        xRadius / 3, 3 * xRadius / 2);

    // Draw the nose.
    g.setColor (featureColor);
    g.fillOval (x – xRadius / 10, y, xRadius / 5, yRadius / 5);

    // Draw the whiskers.
    g.drawLine (x – xRadius / 4, y, x – 3 * xRadius / 2, y – xRadius / 3);
    g.drawLine (x – xRadius / 4, y + xRadius / 10,
        x – 3 * xRadius / 2, y + xRadius / 10);
```

*g.drawLine* (*x* − *xRadius* / 4, *y* + *xRadius* / 5,
   *x* − 3 * *xRadius* / 2, *y* + *xRadius* / 5 + *xRadius* / 3);
*g.drawLine* (*x* + *xRadius* / 4, *y*, *x* + 3 * *xRadius* / 2, *y* − *xRadius* / 3);
*g.drawLine* (*x* + *xRadius* / 4, *y* + *xRadius* / 10,
   *x* + 3 * *xRadius* / 2, *y* + *xRadius* / 10);
*g.drawLine* (*x* + *xRadius* / 4, *y* + *xRadius* / 5,
   *x* + 3 * *xRadius* / 2, *y* + *xRadius* / 5 + *xRadius* / 3);
   } // drawShape method
} /* Rabbit class */

Figure 14.5. illustrates the class hierarchy

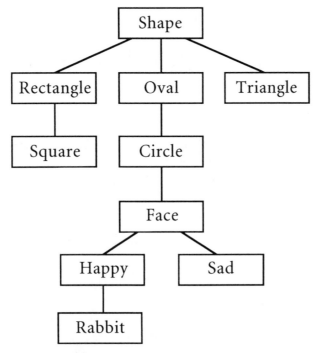

**Figure 14.5 Class Hierarchy**

Again all objects instantiated from member classes of this hierarchy are *Shape* objects.

Now that we have all these classes assembled, we can program an applet in which shapes of all these different kinds bounce around the screen.

Here is the *ShapeTest* class that uses all the classes.

```
// The "ShapeTest" class.
// This applet randomly places 20 shapes on the drawing surface
// and then moves the shapes around the screen, bouncing them
// off the edges.

import java.applet.*;
import java.awt.*;

public class ShapeTest extends Applet
{
    protected final static int NUM_SHAPES = 20;

    // The array containing the Shape objects.
    Shape [] shapes = new Shape [NUM_SHAPES];

    // This method is called when the Applet object is created.
    public void init ()
    {
        // Get the width and height of the drawing surface.
        int surfaceWidth = getSize ().width;
        int surfaceHeight = getSize ().height;

        // Create the shapes and place them randomly on the drawing
        // surface.
        for (int count = 0 ; count < NUM_SHAPES ; count++)
        {
            int shapeKind = (int) (Math.random () * 9);

            if (shapeKind == 0)
            {
                // The following two lines place the upper–left corner
                // of the rectangle in the upper–left quadrant.
                int x = (int) (Math.random () * surfaceWidth / 2);
                int y = (int) (Math.random () * surfaceHeight / 2);
                int rectWidth = (int) (Math.random () * 20) + 10;
                int rectHeight = (int) (Math.random () * 20) + 10;
                shapes [count] = new Rectangle (this, x, y, rectWidth,
                    rectHeight);
            }
```

```
            else if (shapeKind == 1)
            {
                int xRadius = (int) (Math.random () * 30) + 10;
                int yRadius = (int) (Math.random () * 10) + 10;
                shapes [count] = new Oval (this, xRadius, yRadius);
            }
            else if (shapeKind == 2)
            {
                shapes [count] = new Triangle (this);
            }
            else if (shapeKind == 3)
            {
                shapes [count] = new Circle (this);
            }
            else if (shapeKind == 4)
            {
                shapes [count] = new Square (this);
            }
            else if (shapeKind == 5)
            {
                int radius = (int) (Math.random () * 30) + 20;
                shapes [count] = new Face (this, radius);
            }
            else if (shapeKind == 6)
            {
                int radius = (int) (Math.random () * 30) + 20;
                shapes [count] = new Happy (this, radius);
            }
            else if (shapeKind == 7)
            {
                int radius = (int) (Math.random () * 30) + 20;
                shapes [count] = new Sad (this, radius);
            }
            else if (shapeKind == 8)
            {
                int radius = (int) (Math.random () * 20) + 10;
                shapes [count] = new Rabbit (this, radius);
            }
        }
    } // init method
```

```
// This method is called when the Applet object is activated. Slide the
// shapes around the drawing surface.
public void start ()
{
    setVisible (true); // Make the applet surface visible.

    // An infinite loop. In each iteration, every shape has its
    // slide method called.
    while (true)
        for (int count = 0 ; count < NUM_SHAPES ; count++)
            shapes [count].slide ();
} // start method

// This method is called whenever the applet's drawing surface is
// obscured and then revealed. We call the paint method for each
// shape to redraw that shape (if the shape is currently visible).
public void paint (Graphics g)
{
    for (int count = 0 ; count < NUM_SHAPES ; count++)
    {
        shapes [count].paint ();
    }
} // paint method
} /* ShapeTest class */
```

# 14.7 Java Interfaces

Inheritance is a very useful concept and there are times when we might wish to expand upon it. In several types of problems, the most elegant solution involves classes that would inherit behavior from more than one class. For example, having developed a class to deal with employees and a class to implement linked lists, we might want to create a class that combines both behaviors and creates a linked list of employees. This new class would inherit from both the employees and linked list classes. This is called **multiple inheritance.**

Powerful as multiple inheritance is, it is also fraught with complications. For example, how are variables and methods with the same name in both base classes handled. In response to these complications, some languages do not allow multiple inheritance at all. Others, like C++, allow full multiple inheritance.

Java takes a middle ground approach. It does not allow full multiple inheritance. Instead, it allows a class to inherit from one class and implement any number of interfaces. An interface is a set of abstract methods along with constants (variables defined **final static**). A class that implements an interface must provide bodies for all the abstract methods in the interface. The new class is both an object of the base class and an object of the interfaces it implements.

An interface has at least one abstract method which is defined in any class that implements it. As an example, here is the definition of an interface called *Colorable*. It has two abstract methods: *setColor* and *getColor*.

```
// The "Colorable" interface.
// This interface is implemented by classes that have a color that
// can be set and read. How this is implemented is up to the
// class. Any Object of a class that implements Colorable can be
// passed as parameter of type Colorable.
import java.awt.*;

public interface Colorable
{
    public abstract void setColor (Color color);
    public abstract Color getColor ();
} /* Colorable interface */
```

The new abstract class *Shape* that implements the *Colorable* interface is exactly the same as the last one we gave except for the addition of the methods *setColor* and *getColor* shown here. Note that all *Shape* objects can now also be considered *Colorable* objects.

```java
// The "Shape" class.
// This is an abstract class from which all shapes descend. It contains
// all the methods and data that are common to all shapes. For example,
// you can call the show and hide methods of any Shape object, even
// if you do not know the exact type of the object (Rectangle, Oval,
// or Triangle).

import java.awt.*;

public abstract class Shape implements Colorable
{
    ... Class and object variables as before ...
    ... Constructors as before ...
    ... Methods show, hide, paint, move, slide, draw, and erase as before ...

    // Change the color of the shape.
    public void setColor (Color color)
    {
        if (visible)
        {
            erase ();
            this.color = color;
            draw ();
        }
        else
        {
            this.color = color;
        }
    } // setColor method

    // Get the shape's current color.
    public Color getColor ()
    {
        return color;
    } // setColor method
} /* Shape class */
```

Here is a new *Text* class that places text on the screen. Once placed, the text cannot be hidden or moved. The *Text* class also implements *Colorable*. This means that any object of the *Text* class is also an object of the *Colorable* class.

```
// The "Text" class.
// This class places text on the screen. It also implements the
// "Colorable" interface, so the text's color can be changed.

import java.awt.*;

public class Text implements Colorable
{
    // The static variable common to all Text objects.
    protected static Graphics g; // The graphics context (drawing surface).

    protected String text; // The text to be displayed on the screen.
    protected int x, y; // The x, y location of the text.
    protected int size; // The point size of the text.
    protected Font font; // The font of the text.
    protected Color textColor; // The color of the text.

    // Create the text object.
    public Text (Component surface, String text, int x, int y,
        String textFace, int style, int size, Color color)
    {
        // Set the class variable g, if necessary.
        if (g == null)
        {
            g = surface.getGraphics ();
        }

        // Set the object variables.
        this.text = text;
        this.x = x;
        this.y = y;
        font = new Font (textFace, style, size);
        textColor = color;

        paint (); // Make it visible.
```

```
    } // Text constructor

    // Change the color of the text.
    public void setColor (Color color)
    {
        textColor = color;
        paint ();
    } // setColor method

    // Get the current color of the text.
    public Color getColor ()
    {
        return textColor;
    } // getColor method

    // Redraw the text.
    public void paint ()
    {
        g.setColor (textColor);
        g.setFont (font);
        g.drawString (text, x, y);
    } // paint method
} /* Text class */
```

Before giving the *ShapeTest* class we will look at another class, called *ColorCycler*, which contains a method called *cycleColors*. The *cycleColor* method cycles the color of any object that implements the *Colorable* interface through a spectrum of colors. The details of how this cycling is done may not be clear, but the result of each call to *cycleColor* is to move the color of an object from its present color to its neighboring color in the spectrum.

Here is the *ColorCycler* class.

```
// The "ColorCycler" class.
// This class is used to change the color of an object which
// implements the Colorable interface in a smooth progression
// from red to orange then yellow, green, blue, and violet.
// The class has no non-static elements, so it should never
// be instantiated.
```

```java
import java.awt.*;

public class ColorCycler
{
    // The total number of colors in the color sequence.
    static final int NUM_COLORS = 100;
    // The Color objects in the color sequence.
    static Color [] spectrum;

    // The static clause causes initialization when the class is first
    // loaded (as opposed to constructors, which cause initialization
    // when an object is first instantiated). Only static variables
    // may be assigned values in the static clause.

    // The purpose of the initialization is to create a smooth
    // sequence of colors from red through orange, yellow, green,
    // blue, and violet.
    static
    {
        spectrum = new Color [NUM_COLORS];
        int orangeBreak = NUM_COLORS / 5;
        int yellowBreak = NUM_COLORS * 2 / 5;
        int greenBreak = NUM_COLORS * 3 / 5;
        int blueBreak = NUM_COLORS * 4 / 5;
        for (int i = 0 ; i < NUM_COLORS ; i++)
        {
            // The location (from 0 - 1) from the lower bound of the color
            // range to the higher bound (0 = lower bound,
            // 1 = upper bound).
            float location;
            if (i <= orangeBreak)
            {
                location = (float) i / orangeBreak;
                spectrum [i] = new Color (1.0f, (float) (0.6 * location), 0.0f);
            }
            else if (i <= yellowBreak)
            {
                location = (float) (i - orangeBreak) /
                    (yellowBreak - orangeBreak);
                spectrum [i] =
                    new Color (1.0f, (float) (0.6 + 0.4 * location), 0.0f);
            }
```

```
        else if (i <= greenBreak)
        {
            location = (float) (i – yellowBreak) /
                (greenBreak – yellowBreak);
            spectrum [i] = new Color ((float) (1.0 – location), 1.0f, 0.0f);
        }
        else if (i <= blueBreak)
        {
            location = (float) (i – greenBreak) / (blueBreak – greenBreak);
            spectrum [i] = new Color (0.0f, (float) (1.0 – location), location);
        }
        else
        {
            location = (float) (i – blueBreak) /
                ((NUM_COLORS – 1) – blueBreak);
            spectrum [i] = new Color ((float) (0.6 * location), 0.0f, 1.0f);
        }
    }
} // static clause

// This method reads the current color of the Colorable object and
// determines which color in the color sequence is closest to that
// color. It then sets the object's color to the next color in the
// sequence. While this may take a little time the first time that
// cycleColor is called (getting the closest match of the object's
// color to a color in the color sequence is time consuming),
// subsequent calls will be fairly quick (as the object's color
// will be one of the colors in the sequence).
// Note this method is static, so a ColorCycler object does not have
// to be instantiated in order to use it.
public static void cycleColors (Colorable object)
{
    Color c = object.getColor ();

    // See if the current color matches any of the colors in the
    // color sequence.
    for (int count = 0 ; count < NUM_COLORS ; count++)
    {
        if (c == spectrum [count])
        {
            object.setColor (spectrum [(count + 1) % NUM_COLORS]);
            return;
```

```
            }
      }

      // If no color matched, see which color in the color sequence is the
      // closest match and use that. (This is likely only to occur the
      // first time this method is called for a particular Colorable
      // object.)
      int closest = 0;
      int distance = Integer.MAX_VALUE;
      for (int count = 0 ; count < NUM_COLORS ; count++)
      {

            int redDiff = spectrum [count].getRed () – c.getRed ();
            int greenDiff = spectrum [count].getGreen () – c.getGreen ();
            int blueDiff = spectrum [count].getBlue () – c.getBlue ();
            int totalDiff = (redDiff * redDiff) + (greenDiff * greenDiff) +
                  (blueDiff * blueDiff);

            if (totalDiff < distance)
            {
                  distance = totalDiff;
                  closest = count;
            }

      }

      object.setColor (spectrum [(closest + 1) % NUM_COLORS]);
   } // cycleColors method
} /* ColorCycler interface */
```

In the following version of the *ShapeTest* class, the sentences of text remain in their fixed positions on the drawing surface while the *cycleColor* method changes their colors. The shapes bounce about as before, except now they also have changing colors. This applet runs indefinitely until the user closes the window. This program provides a good example of how increasingly complex results can be achieved by inheritance and implementing interfaces.

Figure 14.6 shows the display area of the applet at a particular moment. There are 20 shapes of different sizes in different colors located randomly. The shapes are randomly-chosen from all the shapes in the hierarchy and as they bounce about the color of each is cycling over the spectrum of colors.

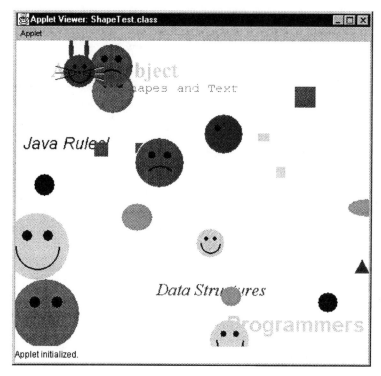

Figure 14.6 Bouncing of 20 Shapes Selected Randomly from 8 Possible Shapes with 5
Sentences at Rest, all Change Color.


Here is the new *ShapeTest* class.

```
// The "ShapeTest" class.
// This applet randomly places 20 shapes and 5 text sentences
// on the drawing surface. It moves the shapes around the screen,
// bouncing them off the edges. At the same time, the colors of
// both the shapes and the sentences are constantly changing.

import java.applet.*;
import java.awt.*;

public class ShapeTest extends Applet
{
    protected final static int NUM_SHAPES = 10;
```

```java
protected final static int NUM_SENTENCES = 5;

// The array containing the Text objects.
Text [] sentences = new Text [NUM_SENTENCES];
// The array containing the Shape objects.
Shape [] shapes = new Shape [NUM_SHAPES];

// This method is called when the Applet object is created.
public void init ()
{
    // Get the width and height of the drawing surface.
    int surfaceWidth = getSize ().width;
    int surfaceHeight = getSize ().height;

    // Create the Text objects and place them on the screen.
    sentences [0] = new Text (this, "A Text Object", 50, 50,
        "Serif", Font.BOLD, 30, Color.red);
    sentences [1] = new Text (this, "Java Rules!", 10, 150,
        "SanSerif", Font.ITALIC, 24, Color.green);
    sentences [2] = new Text (this, "Shapes and Text", 150, 70,
        "Monospaced", 0, 18, Color.blue);
    sentences [3] = new Text (this, "Data Structures", 200, 350,
        "Serif", Font.ITALIC, 24, Color.orange);
    sentences [4] = new Text (this, "Programmers Unite!", 300, 400,
        "SanSerif", Font.BOLD, 30, Color.magenta);

    // Create the shapes and place them randomly on the drawing
    // surface.
    for (int count = 0 ; count < NUM_SHAPES ; count++)
    {
        int shapeKind = (int) (Math.random () * 9);

        if (shapeKind == 0)
        {
            // The following two lines place the upper-left corner
            // of the rectangle in the upper-left quadrant.
            int x = (int) (Math.random () * surfaceWidth / 2);
            int y = (int) (Math.random () * surfaceHeight / 2);
            int rectWidth = (int) (Math.random () * 20) + 10;
            int rectHeight = (int) (Math.random () * 20) + 10;
            shapes [count] = new Rectangle (this, x, y, rectWidth,
                rectHeight);
```

```
        }
        else if (shapeKind == 1)
        {
            int xRadius = (int) (Math.random () * 30) + 10;
            int yRadius = (int) (Math.random () * 10) + 10;
            shapes [count] = new Oval (this, xRadius, yRadius);
        }
        else if (shapeKind == 2)
        {
            shapes [count] = new Triangle (this);
        }
        else if (shapeKind == 3)
        {
            shapes [count] = new Circle (this);
        }
        else if (shapeKind == 4)
        {
            shapes [count] = new Square (this);
        }
        else if (shapeKind == 5)
        {
            int radius = (int) (Math.random () * 30) + 20;
            shapes [count] = new Face (this, radius);
        }
        else if (shapeKind == 6)
        {
            int radius = (int) (Math.random () * 30) + 20;
            shapes [count] = new Happy (this, radius);
        }
        else if (shapeKind == 7)
        {
            int radius = (int) (Math.random () * 30) + 20;
            shapes [count] = new Sad (this, radius);
        }
        else if (shapeKind == 8)
        {
            int radius = (int) (Math.random () * 20) + 10;
            shapes [count] = new Rabbit (this, radius);
        }
    }
} // init method
```

```
// This method is called when the Applet object is activated. Slide the
// shapes around the drawing surface while changing their colors.
public void start ()
{
    setVisible (true); // Make the applet surface visible.

    // An infinite loop. In each iteration, every Text object
    // has its color changed and every Shape object has its
    // color changed and its slide method called.
    while (true)
    {
        // Change the colors of each Text object.
        for (int count = 0 ; count < NUM_SENTENCES ; count++)
        {
            ColorCycler.cycleColors (sentences [count]);
        }

        // Change the color and slide each Shape object.
        for (int count = 0 ; count < NUM_SHAPES ; count++)
        {
            ColorCycler.cycleColors (shapes [count]);
            shapes [count].slide ();
        }
    }
} // start method

// This method is called whenever the applet's drawing surface is
// obscured and then revealed. We call the paint method for each
// shape to redraw that shape (if the shape is currently visible).
public void paint (Graphics g)
{
    for (int count = 0 ; count < NUM_SHAPES ; count++)
    {
        shapes [count].paint ();
    }
    for (int count = 0 ; count < NUM_SENTENCES ; count++)
    {
        sentences [count].paint ();
    }
} // paint method
} /* ShapeTest class */
```

# 14.8  Chapter Summary

In this chapter we have shown how an abstract class that forms a base class can simplify the coding of a number of offspring classes that inherit from it. Examples were given of drawing different shapes where the class for each shape extended an abstract class *Shape*.

## Abstract Classes

An abstract class is one that contains some methods that have no bodies, that is, remain abstract. Any class that inherits from an abstract class must provide bodies for its abstract methods. The advantage of having abstract classes over keeping entirely separate classes for each offspring is that code that would be common to the offsprings is in the superclass and need not be repeated. This idea was illustrated by extending the abstract class *Shape* to the classes: *Rectangle, Oval,* and *Triangle.*

## Method Overloading in the Base Class

Greater variety in the offspring class could be achieved by having several different constructor methods in the base class and several versions of some methods such as the *move* method of *Shape*. To refer to a constructor method of the parent class, the word **super** is used. To refer to another constructor of the same class, the word **this** is used.

## Adding Methods to a Base Class

Greater functionality can be achieved in all offspring classes if methods are added to the base class.

## Improving the Efficiency of Operation in Classes

In our shape drawing hierarchy, it is more efficient to have a drawing surface for graphics instantiated once and stored in the base class than each time drawing is required. This requires less memory.

## Class Hierarchies

One of the great advantages in inheritance is that superclass methods need not be repeated in the subclass unless they are to be changed and overridden. Another advantage is that any object of a subclass is an object of the superclass.

This means that it is possible to have arrays of the superclass object that consist of objects of various subclasses of that superclass. For example, objects of *Rectangle*, *Oval*, and *Triangle* were all *Shape* objects. We can represent class hierarchies using diagrams to show the class relationships.

## Java Interfaces

Since a class cannot inherit from two different classes in Java, the Java interface provides a way to approximate that effect. To illustrate this idea we defined an interface *Colorable* and implemented the *Shape* class.

# 14.9  Technical Terms

ancestor class                                garbage collection

factoring                                     multiple inheritance

final static                                  super class

# 14.10    Exercises

1.  The *Shape* hierarchy could have been designed with no abstract class *Shape*. Instead, the ancestor class could have been *Oval* with *Triangle* and *Rectangle* inheriting from *Oval* and overriding the *draw* and the *erase* methods. Discuss the advantages and disadvantages of this hierarchy.

2.  Design a class hierarchy (specifying data and public methods) for a library automation system that includes books, periodicals, audio tapes, and software. Each type of item should contain information particular to the item (that is ISSN for periodicals). The system should have the means to enter items into the collection, remove items from the collection, check items in and out and inquire into the status of an item.

3.  Implement the class hierarchy in Exercise 2. Test your design by creating a new class for video tapes in the collection.

4.  Create a text-only main program to run the library automation system. Create a new set of classes for library card holders and provide some way of adding and removing card holders.

5.  Create a GUI application or applet front end to the library automation system.

6.  The *slide* method of *Shape* bounces objects whenever *x* or *y* go over an edge. This means that for objects like the *Oval*, the object bounces when the center of the oval hits an edge. Modify the necessary class or classes so that the shapes bounce whenever they touch an edge. Is there a way of doing this without having to have multiple implementations of the *slide* method?

7.  If you obscure the *ShapeTest* applet window by dragging another window over top of it, you will occasionally see part of a shape left behind. Explain how this can occur. Modify the *Shape* class to minimize this occurring. Can it be eliminated entirely?

# Chapter 15

# Records in Java

In the chapter on arrays we introduced the idea of a structured data type. An array is a sequence of items that are all of the same data type. The arrays we have shown so far are sequences of fairly primitive data types or *String* objects. The sequence of the items is determined by an index. In this chapter we will present the way that records are represented in Java.

# 15.1 Records

In Java objects consist of instance variables and methods that operate on these variables. The instance variables are the fields of the object. The object is the obvious way to represent a data type called **record** that consists of a number of fields which may be of primitive data types or may be structured data types such as other objects.

Here is a definition of a class that might be suitable for recording the name and phone number of a person.

```java
// The "PhoneRecord" class.
public class PhoneRecord
{
    protected String name, phone;

    // Constructor.
    public PhoneRecord (String name, String phone)
    {
        this.name = name;
        this.phone = phone;
    } // PhoneRecord constructor

    // Method to change name.
    public void setName (String newName)
    {
        name = newName;
    } // setName method

    // Method to change phone.
    public void setPhone (String newPhone)
```

```
    {
        phone = newPhone;
    } // setPhone method

    // Method to get name.
    public String getName ()
    {
        return name;
    } // getName method

    // Method to get phone.
    public String getPhone ()
    {
        return phone;
    } // getPhone method
} /* PhoneRecord class */
```

The fields *name* and *phone* of the record are the instance variables and are labelled **protected**. Their values can be set by the *PhoneRecord* class methods *setName* and *setPhone*, or retrieved by the methods *getName* and *getPhone*.

To instantiate an object called *person* of type *PhoneRecord* and initialize it to the name "Maria Sanchez" and phone "(407)716-2780" would require the statement

```
PhoneRecord person = new PhoneRecord ("Maria Sanchez",
                        " (407)716-2780");
```

To output the record's fields would require a statement of this sort

*c.println (person.getName () + " " + person.getPhone ());*

which would produce the result

Maria Sanchez (407)716-2780

On the surface this seems to be a rather round about way of setting and getting values of the instance variables. If they were labelled **public** in the first place then the same output result could be obtained by the statement

*c.println (person.name + " " + person.phone);*

This however is out of the spirit of object-oriented programming since one of the main points is to protect instance variables from being interfered with by other objects in any way except by the methods of the class.

Frequently the *set* and *get* methods check to see that what is being done is appropriate. In the *PhoneRecord* class there is no checking going on.

As well as *set* and *get* methods a class that is used for records can have other methods, for example, to read or write the record.

# 15.2  Arrays of Records

We can combine the *PhoneRecord* structured data type with the structured type **array** and have an array of such records. To declare an array of phone records for a list of 50 friends we would use

> *PhoneRecord friend* [] = **new** *PhoneRecord* [50];

The phone number of the 6th friend in the array could be output by the statement

> *c.println (friend* [5].*getPhone* ());

One of the most important operations on an array of records is to search for a particular record.

Searching an array of records for a particular record is very similar to searching related arrays. One of the fields of the record is designated as the **key**. The other field or fields can be retrieved once the index for the record, whose key field matches the key value for the record being sought, is found. If the key values of the array of records are not in sorted order, a sequential search must be done. If they are sorted, the much more efficient binary search may be used; so it is important to be able to sort arrays of records.

One advantage of the record object is that an entire record can be moved (copied) from one memory location to another. Many sorting methods involve swapping two records in the array.

Here is a method for swapping the record with index *i* with the record with index *j* in an array *list* whose records are objects of *PhoneRecord* class. (This method assumes that the *PhoneRecord* has already been defined.)

```
// Method to swap i and jth record in list.
public void swap (PhoneRecord list [], int i, int j)
{
    PhoneRecord temp = list [i];
    list [i] = list [j];
    list [j] = temp;
} // swap method
```

As an example of an array of records we will look at a class called *CardDeck* that has methods to generate and shuffle a deck of playing cards, as well as to print the deck.

There are 52 cards in the deck consisting of equal numbers of 4 suits: spades, hearts, diamonds, and clubs which we will represent by their first letters "S", "H", "D", and "C". In each suit there are 13 cards: namely a 2, 3, 4, 5, 6, 7, 8, 9, 10, Jack, Queen, King, and Ace. To the face cards: Jack, Queen, King, and Ace we assign the values 11, 12, 13, and 14. Each card can be represented by a record with two fields; one for the suit and one for the value. Here is the definition for the class *CardType*. We will not define any *set* methods as the deck of cards will not be changed once it is instantiated.

```
// The "CardType" class.
public class CardType
{
    protected int value;
    protected String suit;

    // Constructor.
    public CardType (int value, String suit)
    {
        this.value = value;
        this.suit = suit;
    } // CardType constructor
```

```
// Method to get value of card.
public int getValue ()
{
    return value;
} // getValue method

// Method to get suit of card.
public String suit ()
{
    return suit;
} // suitMethod
} /* CardType class */
```

The deck of cards will be represented by the class *CardDeck.*

```
// The "CardDeck" class.
import hsa.Console;

public class CardDeck
{
    final int CARDS_IN_DECK = 52;
    final int NUMBER_OF_SUITS = 4;
    final int CARDS_IN_SUIT = 13;
    final String [] suit = {"S", "H", "D", "C"};
    CardType [] deck = new CardType [CARDS_IN_DECK + 1];

    // Constructor for deck.
    public CardDeck ()
    {
        int card = 1;   //Note deck[0] not used.
        for (int whichSuit = 1; whichSuit <= NUMBER_OF_SUITS;
            whichSuit ++)
        {
            for (int whichValue = 2; whichValue <= 14; whichValue ++)
            {
                deck [card] = new CardType (whichValue, suit [whichSuit]);
                card ++;
            }
        }
```

```
    } // CardDeck constructor

    // Method to swap ith and jth card.
    protected void swap (int i, int j)
    {
        CardType temp = deck [i];
        deck [i] = deck [j];
        deck [j] = temp;
    } // swap method

    // Method to shuffle deck.
    public void shuffleDeck ()
    {
        for (int whichCard = 0; whichCard < CARDS_IN_DECK;
            whichCard ++)
        {
            // Generate random integer between 1 and CARDS_IN_DECK.
            int where = (int) (Math.random () * CARDS_IN_DECK) + 1;
            swap (whichCard, where);
        }
    } // shuffleDeck method

    // Method to print deck.
    public void printDeck (Console c)
    {
        for (int card = 1; card <= CARDS_IN_DECK; card ++)
        {
            c.println (deck [card].getSuit () + "  " + deck [card].getValue ());
        }
    } // printDeck method
} /* CardDeck class */
```

Here is a driver program to test the class *cardDeck*.

```
// The "CardDeckTest" class.
import java.awt.*;
import hsa.Console;

public class CardDeckTest
{
```

```
static public void main (String [] args)
{
    Console c = new Console ();
    CardDeck deck = new CardDeck ();
    deck.printDeck (c);
    deck.shuffleDeck ();
    deck.printDeck (c);
} // main method
} /* CardDeckTest class */
```

The deck as it is first constructed is sorted like a freshly-opened deck of cards, with the suits in order from spades to clubs and within each suit the values in order from 2, 3 ... to King, and Ace. Here is the algorithm used to shuffle the deck in the *shuffleDeck* method.

For each card in deck in turn:

• generate a random number between 1 and *CARDS_IN_DECK*, and

• swap the card with the card that the random number locates.

## 15.2.1  Two-Dimensional Arrays of Records

A two-dimensional array of records can be used to deal four hands of 13 cards each suitable for a game of bridge. The class *CardDeck* will be extended to deal hands and list the hands. The class will be called *PlayBridge*.

```
// The "PlayBridge" class.
import hsa.Console;

public class PlayBridge extends CardDeck
{
    // Additional constants and variables.
    final int NUMBER_OF_HANDS = 4;
    final int CARDS_IN_HAND = 13;
    CardType hand [] [] = new CardType [NUMBER_OF_HANDS + 1]
                                       [CARDS_IN_HAND + 1];
```

```
    // Constructor.
    public PlayBridge ()
    {
        // Calls constructor of CardDeck to generate deck.
        super ();
    } // PlayBridge constructor

    // Method for dealing hands from deck.
    public void dealHands ()
    {
        // Deal one card to each hand in turn repeatedly.
        int card = 1;
        for (int cardCount = 1; cardCount <= CARDS_IN_HAND;
            cardCount ++)
        {
            for (int handCount = 1 ; handCount <= NUMBER_OF_HANDS ;
                handCount ++)
            {
                hand [handCount] [cardCount] = deck [card];
                // Move to deal next card.
                card ++;
            }
        }
    } // dealHands method

    // Method for listing hands.
    public void listHands (Console c)
    {
        // Hands are listed one card to a line unsorted.
        for (int whichHand = 1; whichHand <= NUMBER_OF_HANDS;
            whichHand ++)
        {
            c.println ("Here are the cards for hand " + whichHand);
            for (int whichCard = 1; whichCard <= CARDS_IN_HAND;
                whichCard ++)
            {
                c.println (hand [whichHand] [whichCard].suit + hand
                                [whichHand] [whichCard].value);
            }
        }
    } // listHands method
} /* PlayBridge class */
```

Here is a test program to see the result of shuffling and dealing a deck.

```
// The "PlayBridgeTest" class.
import hsa.Console;

public class PlayBridgeTest
{
    static public void main (String [] args)
    {
        Console c = new Console ();
        PlayBridge deck = new PlayBridge ();
        deck.shuffleDeck ();
        deck.dealHands ();
        deck.listHands (c);
    } // main method
} /* PlayBridgeTest class */
```

# 15.3  Storing Records in Binary Files

Arrays of records are often stored in a file to save them from one use to another. The records must be stored or retrieved field-by-field. One way to store these is in the form of a text file. To do this each field is stored by a *println* statement and retrieved by a *readLine* statement. Storing data in text files was discussed in Chapter 6.

Records stored in text form must be read sequentially. A more common and useful form of storage of records is in binary form. This permits the user to access any one record as easily as any other; it permits **random access** to the records. In text form records take up different amounts of space, and require different numbers of bytes to store them since, for example in phone records, some names are longer than others.

In binary form all records are of equal length, that is, they require the same number of bytes. This means that the position of the beginning of the fourth record in the file will be at a point that is three times the length of a single record in bytes.

To achieve a fixed record length all *String* fields must be stored as character arrays of fixed length. For example, in a phone record the phone number requires 13 characters. This can be stored as 13 bytes. In Java each character is represented in Unicode by two bytes. Although this in fact, is out of the spirit of Java, in storing records in binary form, only the first byte of the Unicode character is stored. This byte corresponds to the ASCII representation of a character and, if only the Roman alphabet is used, is sufficient. Java uses Unicode representation so that characters from all languages can be represented.

As an example of storing records in binary form we will look at the storage of student records. For each student we will store a name, address, year, and average mark. This will illustrate how integers and real numbers are handled as well as strings. Here is the definition of the class *StudentRecord*.

```
// The "StudentRecord" class.
import java.io.*;

public class StudentRecord
{
    protected String name;          // Allow 30 characters.
    protected String address;// Allow 40 characters.
    protected int year;             // Needs 4 bytes.
    protected double average;       // Needs 8 bytes.
    protected static final int RECORD_SIZE = 82;

    // Constructor reads record from file.
    public StudentRecord (RandomAccessFile input) throws IOException
    {
        // Allow 30 bytes for name.
        byte [] nameBytes = new byte [30];
        input.readFully (nameBytes);
        name = new String (nameBytes, 0);
        // Allow 40 bytes for address.
        byte [] addressBytes = new byte [40];
        input.readFully (addressBytes);
        address = new String (addressBytes, 0);
        year = input.readInt ();
        average = input.readDouble ();
```

```
} // StudentRecord constructor

// Constructor uses data from keyboard.
public StudentRecord (String name, String address, int year,
            double average)
{
    this.name = name;
    this.address = address;
    this.year = year;
    this.average = average;
} // StudentRecord constructor

// Method to get address.
public String getAddress ()
{
    return address;
} // getAddress method

// Method to get average.
public double getAverage ()
{
    return average;
} // getAverage method

// Method to get year.
public int getYear ()
{
    return year;
} // getYear method

// Method to get record size.
public static int recordSize ()
{
    return RECORD_SIZE;
} // recordSize method

// Method to write a record to file.
public void write (RandomAccessFile output) throws IOException
{
    byte [] nameBytes = new byte [30];
    name.getBytes (0, name.length (), nameBytes, 0);
    output.write (nameBytes);
```

```
         byte [] addressBytes = new byte [40];
         address.getBytes (0, address.length (), addressBytes, 0);
         output.write (addressBytes);
         output.writeInt (year);
         output.writeDouble (average);
      } // write method
} /* StudentRecord class */
```

The *studentRecord* class has a method for constructing a record by reading from the file and a method for writing a record to the file. For the name, an array of bytes called *nameBytes* is set up of length 30. In the *readFully* of the constructor, 30 bytes are read from the file and stored in *nameBytes*. This is then converted to a *String* and stored in *name*. The constructor

   *String (nameBytes, 0)*

assigns the bytes to the string, filling the **hibyte** part of each Unicode character with 0.

In the *write* method of *StudentRecord* the *String* class method *getBytes* copies the characters of the string into a byte array starting at the character in position 0 (the first argument of *getBytes*). The second argument is the position just past the last character (given by *length* ()). The third argument gives the name of the byte array starting at 0 (the fourth argument). The hibyte of each character is not copied.

For binary files the primitive data types are written by *writeInt* (), *writeDouble* (), *writeBoolean* (), and so on. They are read by *readInt* (), *readDouble* (), *readBoolean* (), and so on.

The size of the *StudentRecord* is 82 bytes: 30 for the name, 40 for the address, 4 for the year, and 8 for the average. This is available from the *recordSize* method of the *StudentRecord* class.

A binary file called "school" is opened for reading and writing by a statement of the form

   *RandomAccessFile schoolFile = **new** RandomAccessFile ("school", "rw");*

If the file is just for reading use "r". To position the file for reading or writing the *seek* method is used. The form for reading or writing records called *student* of *StudentRecord* class is *schoolFile.seek ((***long***) recordNumber * student.recordSize ());*

The *seek* method requires a **long** argument and sets the file position. The file position is the number of bytes from the beginning of the file, the zero position. The *recordNumber* must start at record zero.

At any stage the file position can be determined by the function-type method *getFilePointer* (), which is a method of the *RandomAccessFile* class.

# 15.4 Example of Using a Binary File

We will now examine a program that reads in student records of the class *StudentRecord* and stores them in a file in binary form called "school". As each record is stored its whereabouts are recorded in an array called *directory*. This is an array of records of the class called *WhereAbouts*.

```
// The "WhereAbouts" class.
public class WhereAbouts
{
    // This is the directory record.
    protected String name;
    protected int where; // Location in file.

    // Constructor.
    public WhereAbouts (String name, int where)
    {
        this.name = name;
        this.where = where;
    } // WhereAbouts constructor

    // Method to find file location of name from directory.
    public int getLocationIfMatch (String name)
    {
        if (name.equals (this.name))
        {
            return where;
```

```
            }
        else
        {
            return –1;
        }
    } // getLocationIfMatch method
} /* WhereAbouts class */
```

Here is the *Students* class application program to read student records from the keyboard, store them in the binary file "school", and prepare a directory entry for each. The program allows the user to look up individual records randomly.

```
// The "Students" class.
import java.io.*;
import hsa.Console;

public class Students
{
    static int recordNumber = 0;
    static WhereAbouts directory [] = new WhereAbouts [100];

    // Main method to find name in directory.
    public static void main (String [] args) throws IOException
    {
        Console c = new Console ();
        String choice;
        String name, address;
        int year;
        double average;
        // Open school file to read and write.
        RandomAccessFile schoolFile =
                new RandomAccessFile ("school", "rw");
        StudentRecord student;
        while (true)
        {
            c.println ("Enter");
            c.println (" e to enter a new record");
            c.println (" f to find student information");
            c.println (" q to quit");
```

```
c.print ("Choice: ");
choice = c.readLine ();
if (choice.equals ("e"))
{
    c.print ("Enter name: ");
    name = c.readLine ();
    c.print ("Enter address: ");
    address = c.readLine ();
    c.print ("Enter year: ");
    year = c.readInt ();
    c.print ("Enter average: ");
    average = c.readDouble ();
    student = new StudentRecord (name, address, year, average);
    // Set the file position to the end of file.
    schoolFile.seek ((long) recordNumber *
                                StudentRecord.recordSize ());
    // Store record in file.
    student.write (schoolFile);
    directory [recordNumber] =
                new WhereAbouts (name, recordNumber);
    recordNumber ++;
}
else if (choice.equals ("f"))
{
    c.println ("Enter the name of the student: ");
    name = c.readLine ();
    int location = find (name);
    if (location == –1)
    {
        c.println (name + " not found");
    }
    else
    {
        schoolFile.seek ((long) location *
                                StudentRecord.recordSize ());
        student = new StudentRecord (schoolFile);
        c.println ("Name = " + name);
        c.println ("Address = " + student.getAddress ());
        c.println ("Year = " + student.getYear ());
        c.println ("Average = " + student.getAverage ());
    }
}
```

```
            else if (choice.equals ("q"))
            {
                break;
            }
        }
    } // main method

    public static int find (String name)
    {
        int count = 0;
        int location = -1;
        while (count < recordNumber && location == -1)
        {
            location = directory [count].getLocationIfMatch (name);
            count ++;
        }
        return location;
    } // find method
} /* Students class */
```

If the directory list is to be kept sorted so that a binary search is possible, as insertions occur they must be placed in their proper place in the directory. Maintaining a sorted list with insertions and deletions is described in the next chapter.

# 15.5  Records with Alternative Sets of Fields

Often it is required that a file be maintained in which records do not all have the same set of fields. For example, a file might be required to store information by the motor vehicle department for licensing purposes. Each record would have common fields, for example, license plate, name, and address, but there might be three different record types: one for passenger vehicles, one for commercial vehicles, and one for recreational vehicles.

A class would be set up called *Vehicle* with the common fields, then the three classes *Passenger, Commercial*, and *Recreational* would be defined as extending the *Vehicle* class.

Each would have its own additional fields. If a binary file is to be kept of the different vehicle types the record size must be the number of bytes required to store the longest of the three types.

If an array of such records were maintained in memory called *vehicle* it would be defined by

> *Vehicle vehicles* [] = **new** *Vehicle* [100];

Any *Vehicle* class record can be tested to see which type it belongs to using the comparison operator **instanceof**. For example, we could test the *i*th record of the *vehicles* array to see if it is for a passenger vehicle by the statement

```
if (vehicle [i] instanceOf Passenger)
{
    Passenger p = (Passenger) vehicles [i];
    p.setMake ("GM");
    p.setColor (Color.green);
        and so on
}
```

In this the methods *setMake* and *setColor* belong to the *Passenger* class. This is an example of **polymorphism**, the inclusion of a number of different forms of the base class *Vehicle*. In other programming languages this problem is solved by having **variant records**.

# 15.6 Chapter Summary

## Records as Objects

In Java objects are the natural way to represent records; the instance variables are the **fields** of the record. Since in object oriented programming direct access to the instance variables by other objects is not desired, the record object must contain *set* and *get* methods to permit the user to manipulated the variables.

The *set* and *get* methods should, in principle, provide protection against improper interference.

As well, the class that is used to instantiate records could contain other methods such as those to read and write records to files.

## Array of Records

An array of records is essentially an array of objects. If the array is to be used for the retrieval of information then one field is designated as the key field. If the array is arranged so that the key fields are in random order then a linear search is needed to locate the record with the required key.

If the array is in sorted order according to the key fields the much more efficient binary search can be used. This means that for efficiency arrays of records should be kept in sorted order. Most sorting algorithms require the movement of records from one place in the array to another, an operation that is very simple since the records are objects and are passed by reference.

## Example of Using Records

As an example of using records in both one and two dimensional arrays a program was developed to shuffle and deal a deck of cards into hands suitable for the game of bridge. A *CardType* class represented the individual cards. A class called *CardDeck* represented an array of 52 of such records. Methods were included in *CardDeck* to initialize the deck, shuffle the cards, and output the card records in the deck.

A class called *PlayBridge* extended the *CardDeck* class defining additional constants and instance variables to represent four bridge hands of 13 cards each. The hands were represented by a two-dimensional array of card records. The *PlayBridge* class had methods for dealing the hands from the deck and listing the contents of each hand.

## Storing Records in Binary Files

Records written as text files field-by-field must be accessed sequentially. Records written in binary form can be accessed randomly, as well as sequentially. In binary form all records must be the same length so individual records can be replaced in the file. Fields that are of primitive data types require a fixed number of bytes given by the data type. Strings can be of various lengths but must be stored as a fixed number of bytes. This size must be determined for each string field.

Reading of strings is by a fixed number of bytes using the *readFully* method of the *RandomAccessFile* class. Writing strings to files uses the *getBytes* method of the *RandomAccessFile* class. Primitive data types are read by *readInt* (), *readDouble* (), *readBoolean* (), and so on. They are written by the corresponding *writeInt*, *writeDouble*, *writeBoolean*, and so on.

To open a binary file of class *RandomAccessFile* called *file* for reading and writing we use

> *RandomAccessFile file* = **new** *RandomAccessFile* ("file name", "rw");

where "file name" is the external name of the file and is placed in quotes.

## Searching a Random Access File

The file position of an individual record in a random access binary file is its record index multiplied by the length of each record. The file position must be given as a **long** integer. To position the reading or writing pointer at the beginning of a record in *file* at *filePosition* the statement is

> *file.seek* ((**long**) *filePosition*);

To find the file position of the pointer at any time the *getFilePointer* () method of the *RandomAccessFile* class is used.

## Records with Alternative Sets of Fields

If a single file is kept of records that have variations in the fields that they require then a base record class is defined and variant classes created as extensions of the base class.

The common fields are instance variables in the base class and the variations are fields in the extended class or classes. Such records all belong to the base class and can be manipulated in an array or file as objects of this same class. To determine their particular or actual class the comparison operator **instanceof** is used.

# 15.7 Technical Terms

hibyte                                        random access

instanceof                                    record

# 15.8 Exercises

1.  A *StudentRecords* class is to be defined with these instance variables
    definition

    > *String name*; // Allow 40 characters.
    > **int** *mark* [] = **new int** [4];
    > **double** *average*;

    Create an array of 26 such records and initialize them with
    simulated data giving names A, B, C, D and so on to the students.
    Fill in marks for each record as random numbers between 0 and
    100. Give all the averages a temporary value of −1. Store the array
    as a file in binary form.

2.  Read the binary file created in Exercise 1, computing the average
    mark for the student and recording it in *average*. Read each record,
    process it, and return it as an updated record to the binary file.

    At the same time compute the class average for each of the four
    subjects and the overall average mark outputting them in a
    summary.

3.  Devise a program so that individual students could request
    information from the file with the proper averages. Be sure to have
    a directory created.

4.  Modify the *find* method used in the *Students* class of this chapter to
    use the binary method of search on the file created in Exercise 2.
    This is possible since the records will be sorted by name, that is, A
    first, B second, and so on.

5.  In the game of bridge the high-card point value of a hand can be calculated by assigning a 4 to an ace, 3 to a king, 2 to a queen, and 1 to a jack. Extend the *PlayBridge* class so that the number of points of each hand is displayed along with the hand itself.

6.  In a bridge game players are in pairs that cooperate with each other: player 1 is a partner of player 3, player 2 is a partner of player 4. If a team has 25 high-card points between them they can score a "game in one hand". Write a program that counts the number of times each of the two teams of players could get a game in one hand in a fixed number of deals. What is the percentage of the deals that produces a "game in one hand" situation. Try dealing 10 hands to begin, then try dealing 100 hands.

# Chapter 16

# Algorithms for Sorting Lists

In the last chapter we examined the record data type. Records are convenient data structures for keeping lists of data where several items of information are to be kept together. In many situations a list must be kept up-to-date; it must be maintained. New items are added, items are changed, and items are deleted. The purpose of keeping this list is to be able to retrieve information.

The binary search technique is vastly superior to the linear (or sequential) search for a large sized list. To obtain this efficiency, the list must be maintained in sorted order. In this chapter we will examine algorithms for sorting an unsorted list.

# 16.1  What is Sorting?

For a list such as a list of names to be sorted, the values in the list must be placed in ascending (non-decreasing) or descending (non-increasing) order. Most often lists are sorted in ascending (non-decreasing) order. For example, the names in a telephone book are sorted this way. We say non-decreasing because names could be identical. When sorting is complete the final list must be a rearrangement of the original list. It must be a **permutation** of the original values.

If a list to be sorted contains composites, like records that contain several data components, then one field is designated as the **key to the sorting**. The list is sorted in ascending or descending values of the key field.

There are a large number of different basic methods for sorting lists and these vary widely in their efficiencies. In this chapter we will examine a number of the best known sorting algorithms and compare them. For shorter lists, all methods are about equal in efficiency. For long lists the difference can be striking.

Before we begin looking at specific algorithms we will examine two fundamental manipulations called **swapping** and **shifting** which are the basis of many different kinds of sorts.

Many of the simple methods of sorting involve repeatedly exchanging two values in the list. This is called swapping.

Here is a useful method which swaps elements in a list of string values such as a list of names. We will be incorporating this method into a class that has the size of the list *listSize* and the declaration of *list* as an array of strings as instance variables.

```
// Method to swap the ith and jth elements of list of strings.
protected void swap (int i, int j)
{
    String temp = list [i];
    list [i]= list [j];
    list [j] = temp;
} // swap method
```

The *swap* action is shown in Figure 16.1.

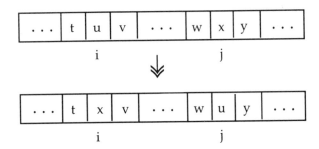

Figure 16.1 The Swap Operation

Shifting is another useful operation for sorting arrays. In a shift operation the *j*th item in the list is moved to the *i*th position (where *i* < *j*) and the *i*+*1*th to *j*th items each moved one position to the right. The list here is written horizontally with the smallest values of the array index on the left.

Figure 16.2 shows the *shift* action.

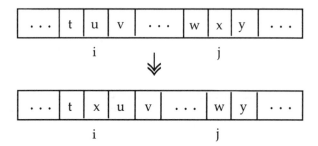

**Fig. 16.2 The Shift Operation**

Here is a method for shifting. Again it is to be part of a class that has *list* declared.

```
// Method for shifting.
protected void shift (int i, int j)
{
    String temp = list [j];
    for (int k = j; k < i; k —)
    {
        list [k] = list [k – 1];
    }
} // shift method
```

The *swap* and *shift* methods will be used in a number of algorithms.

These two methods, along with two others called *fakeData* and *printList*, are going to be incorporated into an abstract class called *Sort* which can be extended to use the various sorting algorithms. The reason the class is abstract, and therefore cannot be instantiated, is that it has a method called *sort* that has no body. When *Sort* is extended the *sort* method will be overridden by the actual sorting algorithm being implemented. We will have a different *sort* method for each algorithm. Each one of the sorting classes will be an extension of the abstract class *Sort*.

Here is the *Sort* class.

```
// The "Sort" class.
import hsa.Console;

public abstract class Sort
{
    Console c;
    int listSize;
    String list [];

    // Constructor
    public Sort (Console c, int listSize)
    {
        this.c = c;
        list = new String [listSize + 1];
        this.listSize = listSize;
        fakeData ();
    } // Sort constructor

    // Method to generate simulated data.
    protected void fakeData ()
    {
        for (int i = 1; i <= listSize; i ++)
        {
            String alphabet = "abcdefghijklmnopqrstuvwxyz";
            StringBuffer temp = new StringBuffer ();
            for (int letter = 0; letter < 4; letter ++)
            {
                // Generate a random integer between 0 and 25.
                int where = (int) (Math.random () * 26);
                temp.append (alphabet.charAt (where));
            }
            list [i] = temp.toString ();
        }
    } // fakeData method

    // Method to output list of strings.
    public void printList ()
    {
        for (int i = 1; i <= listSize; i ++)
```

```
        {
            c.print (list [i] + " ");
        }
        c.println ();
    } // printList method

    // Method to shift elements in list.
    protected void shift (int i, int j)
    {
        String temp = list [j];
        for (int k = j; k >= i + 1; k —)
        {
            list [k] = list [k – 1];
        }
        list [i] = temp;
    } // shift method

    // Abstract method to sort list.
    public abstract void sort ()

    // Method to swap the ith and jth elements of list of strings.
    public void swap (int i, int j)
    {
        String temp = list [i];
        list [i] = list [j];
        list [j] = temp;
    } // swap method
} /* Sort class */
```

Notice that the *Sort* class is labelled as **abstract**, as is the method *sort* which has no body. The instance variables *c*, *listSize*, and *list* are declared, and in the constructor the *listSize* is provided. We will not be using the array element *list* [0] so that the *list* must be stored in an array of length *listSize* + 1. The constructor calls on the **protected** method *fakeData* to compile an array of random four-letter words. The method *printList* can be used to output the elements in *list* from *list*[1] to *list* [*listSize*]. We are now ready to look at the different sorting algorithms.

# 16.2 Insertion Sort

    **Insertion sorting** is an algorithm which might be used, for example, to sort the cards of a bridge hand as they are picked up one by one. In this method there is a sorted part (the cards already picked up) and an unsorted part (the cards still on the table). As each card is picked up and inserted in its proper position in the hand, the sorted part gets longer and the unsorted part shorter.

    Figure 16.3 shows a sequence of four steps (*a, b, c,* and *d*) in this sorting method. Step *a* shows the two parts of the list at any stage: the part that is sorted and the part still unsorted. In step *b* the first value *u* of the unsorted sequence is examined. In step *c* the position where this value should be inserted is found in the sorted sequence; this is the position that contains *v*, the smallest value larger than *u* in the sorted sequence. The value *u* is inserted ahead of *v*, making the sorted sequence longer by one entry, as shown in *d*. This is accomplished by shifting all elements from *v* to the end of the list to the right thus leaving the space for *u*.

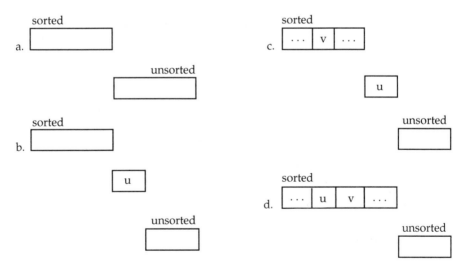

**Figure 16.3 Insertion Sorting**

If all the items are to be kept in a single array, the boundary between the sorted and the unsorted items must be identified. The sorting is done by moving the element at the boundary in the unsorted part into its proper place in the sorted part.

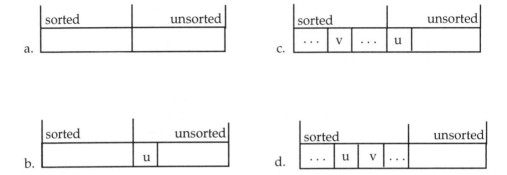

**Figure 16.4 Insertion of Next Element**

Figure 16.4 shows the moves that are made as *u* is inserted. Notice that when the insertion is made, a shift operation occurs so the *shift* method can be used.

The insertion sorting algorithm will be placed in a class called *InsertSort* which extends the *Sort* class, providing a *sort* method to override the abstract *sort* method of *Sort*. A driver program of the *InsertSortTest* class instantiates an object *sortList* of the class *InsertSort* with a *listSize* of 10 and calls the *sort* method of *InsertSort*. It prints the list before and after sorting using the *printList* method of *InsertSort*.

Here is the *InsertSortTest* class.

```
// The "InsertSortTest" class.
import java.awt.*;
import hsa.Console;

public class InsertSortTest
{
    static public void main (String [] args)
    {
```

```
        Console c = new Console ();
        InsertSort sortList = new InsertSort (c, 10);
        sortList.printList ();
        sortList.sort ();
        sortList.printList ();
    } // main method
} /* InsertSortTest */
```

In the *sort* method itself there are *print* statements that output the values of *i* and *j* and the current elements of *list* at each stage of sorting.

In the constructor of *InsertSort* the constructor of *Sort* is invoked by the keyword **super**.

Here is a listing of the *InsertSort* class.

```
// The "InsertSort" class.
import java.awt.*;
import hsa.Console;

public class InsertSort extends Sort
{
    // Constructor
    public InsertSort (Console c, int listSize)
    {
        super (c, listSize);
    } // InsertSort constructor

    //Method to sort list of strings by insertion.
    public void sort ()
    {
        for (int j = 2; j <= listSize; j ++)
        {
            // Find where to insert jth element.
            int i= 1;
            while (i != j && list [i].compareTo (list [j]) < 0)
            {
                i ++;
            }
            shift (i, j);
```

```
                    // Temporary statements to trace execution.
                    c.print (i, 3);
                    c.print (j, 3);
                    c.print (" ");
                    printList ();
                }
            } // sort method
        } /* InsertSort */
```

Here is a typical output from running the driver program.

```
ppnq rbzh bvkf bdpi zzbg jksg ekfi ykav xkfa bsbp
  2   2 ppnq rbzh bvkf bdpi zzbg jksg ekfi ykav xkfa bsbp
  3   1 bvkf ppnq rbzh bdpi zzbg jksg ekfi ykav xkfa bsbp
  4   1 bdpi bvkf ppnq rbzh zzbg jksg ekfi ykav xkfa bsbp
  5   5 bdpi bvkf ppnq rbzh zzbg jksg ekfi ykav xkfa bsbp
  6   3 bdpi bvkf jksg ppnq rbzh zzbg ekfi ykav xkfa bsbp
  7   3 bdpi bvkf ekfi jksg ppnq rbzh zzbg ykav xkfa bsbp
  8   7 bdpi bvkf ekfi jksg ppnq rbzh ykav zzbg xkfa bsbp
  9   7 bdpi bvkf ekfi jksg ppnq rbzh xkfa ykav zzbg bsbp
 10   2 bdpi bsbp bvkf ekfi jksg ppnq rbzh xkfa ykav zzbg
bdpi bsbp bvkf ekfi jksg ppnq rbzh xkfa ykav zzbg
```

One line of output is produced as each value is inserted into the sorted part of the list. The first two entries on the line give the number of values now sorted and the position to which the inserted value has been moved. The next entries show the list with this item inserted. By examining the output, it is possible to see how the process progresses. At each line the sorted part of the list becomes one element longer until, in the last line, the entire list is sorted.

# 16.3  Selection Sort

The **selection sort** is a sorting algorithm where each item in the list is examined to find the item that should be first. For a list of numbers this would be the smallest. For strings, it would be the alphabetically least. When the smallest item is found it is moved to the beginning of the list. Then the list from the 2nd entry to the last is examined to select the smallest (least) item, which is then moved to the second position. As before, the part of the list that is sorted grows and the part that is still unsorted shrinks. The smallest item just selected is swapped with the first item in the unsorted part of the list.

Figure 16.5 shows how the process proceeds.

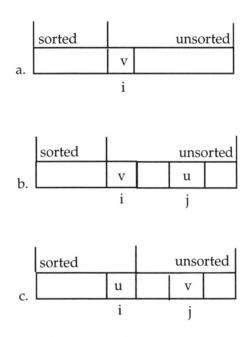

Figure 16.5 Selection Sorting

The first item $v$ in the unsorted part is in position $i$. The first $i-1$ values are sorted. The smallest value $u$ of the unsorted part is in position $locationOfSmallest$. The items in position $i$ a n d $locationOfSmallest$ are then swapped.

Here is the class *SelectSort* that extends the *Sort* class and provides the *sort* method incorporating the selection method.

A driver program for this sort algorithm is the same as *InsertSortTest* except that the *sortList* object is instantiated from the *SelectSort* class. The driver is called *SelectSortTest*.

Here is the *SelectSort* class.

```
// The "SelectSort" class.
import java.awt.*;
import hsa.Console;

public class SelectSort extends Sort
{
    // Constructor
    public SelectSort (Console c, int listSize)
    {
        super (c, listSize);
    } // SelectSort constructor

    // Method to sort list of strings by selection.
    public void sort ()
    {
        for (int i = 1; i <= listSize; i ++)
        {
            // Select smallest element.
            int whereSmall = i;
            for (int j = i + 1; j <= listSize; j ++)
            {
                if (list [j].compareTo (list [whereSmall])) < 0)
                {
                    whereSmall = j;
                }
            }
            swap (i, whereSmall);
            // Temporary statements to trace execution.
            c.print (i, 3);
            c.print (whereSmall, 3);
            c.print (" ");
            printList ();
        }
    } // sort method
} /* SelectSort class */
```

Execution of *SelectSortTest* might give these results.

```
nrbk favg jbgi jddo lezm efsl ngzl btfu xrot ejgb
  1  8 btfu favg jbgi jddo lezm efsl ngzl nrbk xrot ejgb
  2  6 btfu efsl jbgi jddo lezm favg ngzl nrbk xrot ejgb
  3 10 btfu efsl ejgb jddo lezm favg ngzl nrbk xrot jbgi
  4  6 btfu efsl ejgb favg lezm jddo ngzl nrbk xrot jbgi
  5 10 btfu efsl ejgb favg jbgi jddo ngzl nrbk xrot lezm
  6  6 btfu efsl ejgb favg jbgi jddo ngzl nrbk xrot lezm
  7 10 btfu efsl ejgb favg jbgi jddo lezm nrbk xrot ngzl
  8 10 btfu efsl ejgb favg jbgi jddo lezm ngzl xrot nrbk
  9 10 btfu efsl ejgb favg jbgi jddo lezm ngzl nrbk xrot
btfu efsl ejgb favg jbgi jddo lezm ngzl nrbk xrot
```

Here each line of the trace shows first how many values have been sorted, then the position from which the smallest was selected.

# 16.4  Bubble Sort

The next sorting algorithm we will examine is called **bubble sort**. The bubble sort algorithm works by swapping adjacent pairs in the list until all adjacent pairs are in order, at which time the entire list is sorted. It does this by making repeated **passes through the array**. The first pass compares element 1 to element 2 and swaps them if they are out of order, then compares element 2 to element 3 and swaps them if they are out of order, and so on.

In Figure 16.6, the original list to sort is $(D, B, E, C, A)$. This is shown in the top left line of the figure. Eventually this list should be rearranged to be sorted as $(A, B, C, D, E)$. This is shown in the bottom right line.

In this example the algorithm makes four passes through the array. These passes are represented by the downward pointing arrows. For a list of length $n$ (5 in this example), there are $n - 1$ passes (4 in this example). Each pass moves from left to right across the list, comparing the two elements in each pair and swapping the elements if they are out of order.

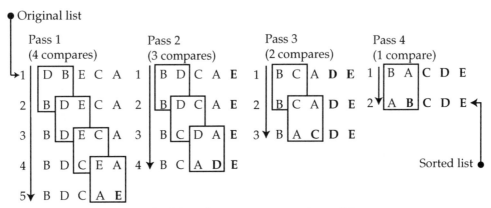

Each box does a compare, and possibly a swap.
Boldface items have reached their final positions.

**Figure 16.6 Passes of a Bubble Sort**

Pass 1 begins in line 1, comparing the first pair of items, *D* and *B*. Since *D* and *B* are out of order, they are swapped, as shown in line 2. Next, the second pair, *D* and *E*, are compared in line 2. Since they are found to be in order, they are not swapped, as shown in line 3. Pass 1 continues in this way, comparing each pair, with swapping if necessary to put them into order.

At the completion of pass 1, the swapping will have caused the largest element (*E* in this example) to be moved into the right-most position of the list (see line 5). The next pass can then stop before inspecting the right-most position. Pass 2 is just like pass 1, scanning from left to right, swapping out-of-order pairs, but it stops before reaching the right-most position. Each successive pass is similar, but each stops one position earlier, until the final pass, pass 4 in this example, handles only the left-most pair.

The term **bubble sort** comes from the idea that large elements are moved (bubbled) to the right. If we visualize the list with the first element on the bottom and the last element on the top, we can think of the bubbles (the large elements) as drifting toward the top of the list.

## 16.4.1  Top Down Design of Bubble Sort

It is also possible to develop a bubble sort method using successive refinement. In successive refinement we move step-by-step from a statement of what we hope to accomplish (the specification of the problem) to the algorithm for doing it. The specification of the problem in English is step-by-step transformed into the algorithm in Java.

In Figure 16.7 the top node gives the informal specification for sorting the list.

The first refinement, from node 1 to node 2, creates a loop whose iterations implement the passes of bubble sort. This creates the new requirement to

Swap elements in *list* [1] .. [*last*] so largest is in *list* [*last*].

This problem is solved in the next node, node 3, by an inner loop that bubbles the largest element into *list* [*last*]. The next refinement, from node 3 to node 4, introduces an **if** statement that checks to see if a pair is in order.

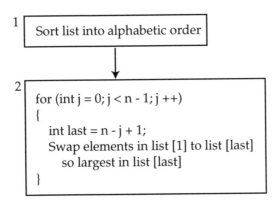

Figure 16.7 Successive Refinement for Bubble Sort

We require one final refinement, in node 4, to implement the swap of two array elements in Java, thereby completing all the refinements.

The class *BubbleSort* incorporates the *sort* which is a bubble sort. Again a driver program *BubbleSortTest* would be required.

```java
// The "BubbleSort" class.
import java.awt.*;
import hsa.Console;

public class BubbleSort extends Sort
{
    // Constructor
    public BubbleSort (Console c, int listSize)
    {
        super (c, listSize);
    } // BubbleSort constructor

    // Method to sort list of strings by bubble sort.
    public void sort ()
    {
        for (int j = 1; j < listSize; j ++)
        {
            int last = listSize - j + 1;
            // Swap elements in list 1 to last so largest is in list [last].
            for (int k = 1; k < last; k ++)
            {
                // Swap pair (k, k + 1) if out of order.
                if (list [k].compareTo (list [k + 1]) > 0)
                    swap (k, k + 1);
                // Temporary statements to trace execution.
                c.print (k, 3);
                c.print (k + 1, 3);
                c.print (" ");
                printList ();
            }
        }
    } // sort method
} /* BubbleSort class */
```

A word of caution is in order regarding top down programming. In principle, a programmer starts with a specification and refines it, step-by-step, into a program. In actual practice, the programmer more often works partly top down and partly bottom up, with various detours along the way. Even though the program has not been developed in a top down order, it should be possible to give a top down description of its structure. This is possible because the parts of the program should each correspond to specifications given at a high level in the description.

### 16.4.2  Improving Bubble Sort

In the example of bubble sort provided in Figure 16.6, each pass swaps at least one pair. If, however, a pass does no swapping, it would indicate that all of the pairs are in order, which implies that the entire list is already in order. We can therefore improve the algorithm by adding a flag (a boolean variable) that keeps track of whether a pass has done any swaps. If it has not, the algorithm should terminate without doing any further passes.

This improvement is particularly important if the list to be sorted is "almost" in order. This would be the case if we had a previously-sorted list with a few new names added.

# 16.5  Running Time for Sorting Algorithms

Because sorting is an operation that is frequently required in processing data, it is important to have it performed as efficiently as possible. One way to determine efficiency is to compare the running time of various algorithms. It is possible to analyze an algorithm to show that the running time of the bubble sort algorithm depends on the square of the number of items being sorted.

The time for many simple sorting algorithms including insertion, selection, and bubble sort depend on the square of the number of items sorted. There are also many sorting algorithms whose running time depends on the log of the number of items multiplied by the number itself; these are much faster (for large $n$) than those that depend upon the square. One of the simplest of these sorts is merge sort, which is presented next.

# 16.6 Merge Sort

**Merging** is a process whereby two (or more) sorted lists are combined to produce a single sorted list. Suppose we have an array of strings arranged so that the items from *first* to *middle* are sorted in ascending order. The other half of the array from *middle* + 1 to *last* is similarly sorted.

The merging of these two halves requires a temporary storage array called *temp* that is large enough to hold both halves. There are three index variables: *point1* that points to successive elements of the first half, *point2* that points into the second half, and *point3* that points into the merged array that is formed in *temp*.

Here is a *merge* method that will be used in the *MergeSort* class.

```
// Method to merge two sorted halves of a list.
public void merge (int first, int middle, int last)
{
    // List going from first to middle is sorted.
    // List going from middle + 1 to last is sorted.
    String temp [] = new String [last + 1];
    int point1 = first;
    int point2 = middle + 1;
    int point3 = first;
    while (point3 <= last)
    {
        // Point 3 locates item in merged list.
        if (point1 < middle + 1 && point2 > last ||
            list [point1].compareTo (list [point2]) < 0)
        {
            temp [point3] = list [point1];
            point1 ++;
        }
        else
        {
            point3 ++;
        }
    }
    // Copy merged array back to original place.
```

```
    for (int i = first; i <= last; i ++)
    {
        list [i] = temp [i]
    }
    // Temporary statements to trace execution.
    c.print (first, 3);
    c.print (last, 3);
    printList (list);
} // merge method
```

With a list of *n* strings divided into two sorted lists of *n*/2 strings each, the time to merge the two lists into a single sorted list depends on *n* the number of items, since every comparison results in one item being placed in the sorted list.

It is possible to improve the time to do a sort by dividing the list in two, sorting each half by a method such as the bubble sort, and then merging the two sorted halves. If this is such a great method, why not use it as the method for sorting each half instead of using the bubble sort? Each half of the original list could be subdivided, these quarters in turn could be subdivided, and so on until only one item is left in each part. It would not be necessary to sort the parts because they contain only one element; they are sorted already, eliminating the need for the bubble sort, or any other method for that matter. And what is more, each subdivision of a part improves the efficiency over a straight bubble sort of that part.

An analysis can show that the new sorting method has a time that depends on (*n log n*) which is a great improvement over $n^2$ dependency for the bubble sort.

Here is the method *mergeSort* that uses the *merge* method to sort the list.

```
// Recursive method that uses itself and the merge method to sort.
public void mergeSort (int first, int last)
{
    if (last > first)
    {
        int middle = (first + last) / 2;
        mergeSort (first, middle);
```

```
        mergeSort (middle + 1, last);
        merge (first, middle, last);

    }
} // mergeSort method
```

This method is a recursive method in that it calls itself. In the *sort* method, the call to *mergeSort* will give the value of *first* as 1 and *last* as *listSize*. Each time *mergeSort* is called, an activation record is set up containing the values of *first, last,* and *middle* for that particular call. If the *last* of list is the same as the *first* then the list contains only one element. No sorting is necessary and it returns from the method *mergeSort* to the method that called it, or to the *main* method when the whole list is sorted.

The stack of activation records for the recursive calls increases in size with each call to a method and shrinks when a method returns to its point of call. Following what happens as the process proceeds is not a simple matter, but Java handles all of the growing and shrinking of the stack automatically so this need not concern the user.

## 16.6.1  The Nature of Recursion

The merge sort provides an excellent example of how recursion works in sorting. It is more efficient to sort two lists of half the size of the original then merge the two halves, than to sort the list as a whole. We use the same method to sort each half of the list: divide it in half and then merge the two halves. This subdivision continues until each half contains only one item. At this point there is no need for sorting and the process ends.

The nature of recursion is that it constantly moves, on each recursive call, to a smaller problem until the problem vanishes, as it does here, or it becomes very simple. This is the **base** or **degenerate case**, for which the answer is known.

The solutions to the subproblems are then combined to produce the solution to the problem itself.

To summarize, using a recursive approach requires:

- a way to make the problem smaller,
- a way of dealing with the base (or degenerate) case, and
- a way of building up the larger result from partial results.

These requirements are satisfied for the merge sort.

- The problem is made smaller by splitting the list in two.
- The base case is a list containing a single item, which is obviously sorted.
- The large result is produced by merging two smaller results.

Here is the class *MergeSort* that uses the recursive merge sort.

```java
// The "MergeSort" class.
import hsa.Console;

public class MergeSort extends Sort
{

    // Constructor
    public MergeSort (Console c, int listSize)
    {
        super (c, listSize);
    } // MergeSort constructor

    public void merge (int first, int middle, int last)
    {
        // List going from first to middle is sorted.
        // List going from middle + 1 to last is sorted.
        String temp [] = new String [last + 1];
        int point1 = first;
        int point2 = middle + 1;
        int point3 = first;
        while (point3 <= last)
        {
            // Point 3 locates item in merged list.
            if (point1 < middle + 1 && (point2 > last ||
                list [point1].compareTo (list [point2]) < 0))
```

```
                    {
                        temp [point3] = list [point1];
                        point1 ++;
                    }
                    else
                    {
                        temp [point3] = list [point2];
                        point2 ++;
                    }
                    point3 ++;
            }
            // Copy merged array back to original place.
            for (int i= first; i <= last; i ++)
            {
                    list [i] = temp [i];
            }
            // Temporary statements to trace execution.
            c.print (first, 3);
            c.print (last, 3);
            c.print (" ");
            printList ();
    } // merge method

    // Recursive method that uses itself and the merge method to sort.
    public void mergeSort (int first, int last)
    {
            if (last > first)
            {
                    int middle = (first + last) / 2;
                    mergeSort (first, middle);
                    mergeSort (middle + 1, last);
                    merge (first, middle, last);
            }
    } // mergeSort method

    // The sort method.
    public void sort ()
    {
            mergeSort (1, listSize);
    } // sort method
} /* MergeSort class */
```

# 16.7 Quicksort

Another sorting algorithm that has a simple recursive form is the **Quicksort** algorithm. In this algorithm the list of items to be sorted is divided into two parts by choosing a **pivot item**. All entries less than the pivot are placed in the first part; those greater than the pivot are in the second part. The ideal would be to have the two parts of roughly equal length but it is hard to choose a pivot element to achieve this. For simplicity we will take as the pivot element the one in the middle of the list. First, the pivot is moved out of the way by swapping it with the first element in the list. A sweep is then made across the remainder of the list. When a value examined is larger than the pivot (that is, less than or equal to the pivot), it is swapped with the value just to the right of the boundary between the two sets of values. This makes the part containing values not larger than the pivot bigger by one element. Figure 16.8 illustrates the behavior of the algorithm.

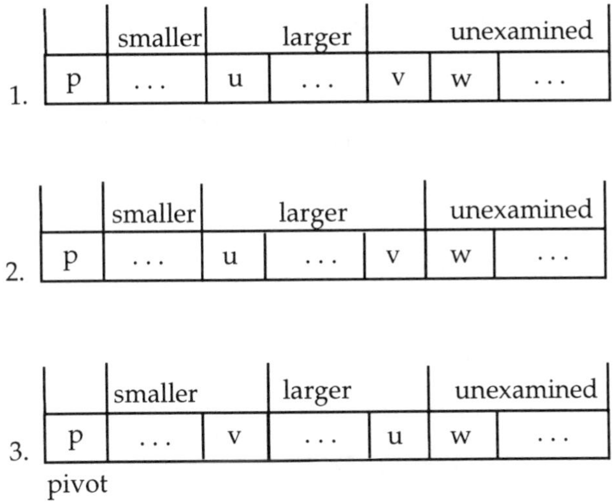

Figure 16.8 Quicksort Algorithm

In part 1 the first element *v* of the unexamined part is examined. If it is larger than the pivot value *p*, it is left where it is, as shown in part 2 of the figure. The region of smaller values stays the same, the region of larger values increases in size, and the unexamined region shrinks. If, on the other hand, *v* is not larger than the pivot *p*, it is swapped with the value *u* just to the right of the boundary between the small and large regions as in part 3 of the figure. Here the region of smaller values increases in size, the region of larger values stays the same size (although the value formerly at its left end is now at its right end), and the unexamined region has shrunk.

Once the pass across the sequence is complete, the pivot value is swapped to the boundary between the large and small regions. If the pivot choice was ideal, this should be near the middle of the list.

To implement *Quicksort* the process just described must be executed recursively. Each part is in turn split into two parts, and so on until each part contains only one element. This was also the case with the recursive merge sort. The difference here is that when the final split has taken place the list will be sorted, whereas with *mergeSort* the parts had to be merged.

Here is the recursive *quickSort* method which copes with an array between the indexes *left* and *right*.

```
// Recursive method quickSort to sort list of strings between
// index left and index right.
public void quickSort (int left, int right)
{
    int pivotPlace;
    // Place pivot at left side of list.
    swap (left, (left + right) / 2);
    int lastSmall = left;
    for (int i = left + 1; i <= right; i ++)
    {
        if (list [i].compareTo (list [left]) <= 0)
        {
            lastSmall ++;
            swap (lastSmall, i);
        }
    }
```

```
        // Place pivot at boundary.
        swap (left, lastSmall);
        pivotPlace = lastSmall;
        // Sort left part.
        if (left < pivotPlace − 1)
        {
            quickSort (left, pivotPlace − 1);
        }
        // Sort right part.
        if (pivotPlace + 1 < right)
        {
            quickSort (pivotPlace + 1, right);
        }
} // quickSort method
```

In the program that uses the recursive *quickSort* method the call to *quickSort* is:

```
        quickSort (1, size);
```

Here is the complete *QuickSort* class.

```
// The "QuickSort" class.
import hsa.Console;

public class QuickSort extends Sort
{
    // Constructor
    public class QuickSort (Console c, int listSize)
    {
        super (c, listSize);
    } // QuickSort constructor

    // Recursive method QuickSort to sort list of strings between
    // index left and index right.
    public void quickSort (int left, int right)
    {
        int pivotPlace;
        // Place pivot at left side of list.
        swap (left, (left + right) / 2);
        int lastSmall = left;
```

```
        for (int i = left + 1; i <= right; i ++)
        {
            if (list [i].compareTo (list [left]) <= 0)
            {
                lastSmall ++;
                swap (lastSmall, i);
            }
        }
        // Place pivot at boundary.
        swap (left, lastSmall);
        pivotPlace = lastSmall;
        // Sort left part.
        if (left < pivotPlace − 1)
        {
            quickSort (left, pivotPlace − 1);
        }
        // Sort right part.
        if (pivotPlace + 1 < right)
        {
            quickSort (pivotPlace + 1, right);
        }
    } // quickSort method

    // The sort method.
    public void sort ()
    {
        quickSort (1, listSize);
    } // sort method
} /* QuickSort class */
```

# 16.8 Chapter Summary

A sorting algorithm for a list must produce a permutation of the original list arranged so that the smallest (least) value comes first, the second smallest next, and so on. There are many different sorting algorithms. We examined three that involve interchanging elements in the list.

# Insertion Sort

In this algorithm the sorting proceeds from left to right. The elements on the left are sorted but the remainder is unsorted. The value at the boundary is examined and its proper position in the sorted part is determined. The values to the right are then moved to make room for it. The worst case execution depends on $n^2$.

# Selection Sort

As with the insertion sort at any stage, the elements in the left part are sorted; those in the right are not. The sorted part is extended by selecting from the unsorted part its smallest element and swapping it with the element in the unsorted part just past the boundary. This algorithm is also depends on $n^2$ in its worst case scenario.

# Bubble Sort

Here the sorted part of the list is extended by passing from the right to the left in the unsorted part, comparing adjacent elements, and exchanging them whenever they are out of order. This results in the smallest remaining value "bubbling" to the boundary. The worst case execution time depends on $n^2$.

# Recursive Sorts

In these sorts the list is split into two parts, each part is sorted, using the same method, and the parts are recombined to give a complete sorted list. The recursive splitting stops when every part contains only one element.

# Merge Sort

In this sort the list is split in the middle each time. Merging is required to recombine the parts.

## Quicksort

In this method the splitting into parts is more complex. The element in the middle is taken as a **pivot** and the rest of the elements divided into two parts; those with values less than or equal to the pivot value, and those with values greater than the pivot. Unlike the merge sort, these two parts are not necessarily the same size. When the Quicksort is applied recursively, the elements will have been moved into sequence.

# 16.9  Technical Terms

| | |
|---|---|
| bubble sort | pivot item |
| degenerate case | quick sort |
| insertion sort | selection sort |
| key to sorting | swapping |
| mergesort | switching |
| permutation | time complexity |

# 16.10    Exercises

1.  Write a method that determines the median of a list of *n* marks. The median is the mark that divides the list (if sorted) into two equal halves. If the list contains an even number of items, the halves are different by one item. Use it to find the median of a list of 100 simulated exam marks.

2.  Adapt the insertion sorting method of this chapter to work for a list of student records with fields for name, address, and year. The *swap* and *shift* methods will also have to be modified. Test the new sort method.

3  Two strings of $n$ characters are to be compared to see whether the second string could be formed by permuting the characters in the first string. Analyze the efficiency of three possible algorithms for doing this.

   a.  Scan the first string one character at a time and see if each character has a corresponding character in the second. Be sure to erase a character in the second string once it has been "used".

   b.  Sort the two strings and compare them character-by- character.

   c.  Prepare a frequency count of each character in each string and compare the counts.

4.  A variation of the selection sort is called **quadratic selection**. In this sort the list of $n$ items to be sorted is divided into 4 equal sized groups of $n/4$ each. The smallest element in each group is selected and placed in a temporary array of 4 elements. From these the smallest is selected. It is then replaced by the next smallest elements from its original group until sorting is complete. Program this algorithm. Analyze its performance. How does it compare with selection sorting?

# Chapter 17

# Self-Referential Classes and Linked Lists

In the last chapter we looked at a number of algorithms for sorting lists of strings such as the insertion, selection, bubble, and merge sorts. As well, we examined the complexity of these various algorithms in order to get an estimate of their relative efficiencies. The lists that were being sorted were stored as arrays. When sorted, the strings were stored in the array so that they were either non-decreasing or non-increasing.

Lists of records stored in an array can be sorted by the same methods. One field of the record acts as the key field in the sorting. This chapter will look at an entirely different way of storing records in memory, in which an additional field of each record indicates where the next record in the sequence is stored in memory. The field acts as a reference to the next record's location. It provides a link to the next record in the sequence.

# 17.1 Links

Links are frequently used when a number of records form a data structure. In an array of records, there is an implicit structure in the way that the records are stored in the array. The index of the array is used to find the next element in a list. When links are used, however, the individual elements have no such spatial relationship but each record contains a field that provides a **link to the next record** in the list.

For example, consider a list of names that are linked together. Each record in the list could be an object of a *LinkRecord* class defined this way.

```
// The "LinkListRecord" class.
// A class for creating self-referential records.
public class LinkListRecord
{
    protected String data;
    protected LinkListRecord next;

    // Constructor that initializes name but sets next to null.
    public LinkListRecord (String name)
```

```
    {
        data = name;
        next = null;
    } // LinkListRecord constructor

    // Constructor that initializes name and nextNode.
    public LinkListRecord (String name, LinkListRecord nextNode)
    {
        data = name;
        next = nextNode;
    } // LinkListRecord constructor

    // Method to get data in node.
    public String getData ()
    {
        return data;
    } // getData method

    // Method to get next in node.
    public LinkListRecord getNext ()
    {
        return next;
    } // getNext method

    // Method to set data in node.
    public void setData (String data)
    {
        this.data = data;
    } // setData method

    // Method to set next in node.
    public void setNext (LinkListRecord next)
    {
        this.next = next;
    } // setNext method
} /* LinkListRecord class */
```

This definition is a recursive definition, since the definition of the record type *LinkListRecord* defines the link as a reference to the record type *LinkListRecord*. It is **self-referential**.

We will now set up a simple linked list with only two records in the list. The first record of the list stores the name "alpha" and the second record stores the name "beta". To find the first record there must be a link outside the list itself to point to the first record. The first record must also have a link to the second record. Because there are only two records, the second record has a link that points to no other record. This requires a special value called **null**. Figure 17.1 shows the arrangement of this linked list.

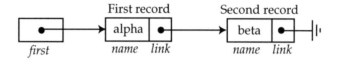

Figure 17.1 Linked List of Two Records

Here are the statements that set up this linked list.

```
first = new LinkListRecord ("alpha");
second = new LinkListRecord ("beta");
first.setNext (second);
second.setNext (null);
```

This shows how the self-referential class *LinkListRecord* is used to create a linked list

# 17.2  Singly Linked Lists

In a simple linked list each record contains a link to the next element in the list. The last element contains a **null** value link. Other lists, however, can contain more than a single link in each record. For this reason we refer to this structure as a **singly linked list**.

A more realistic example of storing names in a linked list involves inputting a list of names, and then modifying the program to output the list in reverse order. As each name is added, it is placed at the beginning of the list. The link to the list is called *last*, since it always points to the name added last. Figure 17.2 shows the growth of the list as the names *Bob, Anna*, and *Lee* are input.

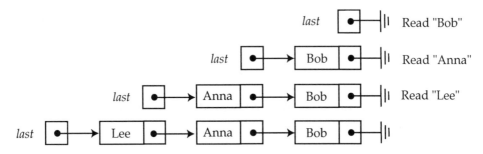

**Figure 17.2 Growth of List of Names**

Here is the *main* method that reads in the names and uses the class *LinkListRecord*.

```
// The "TestLinkListRecord" class.
// Show names inserted in linked list
// then print them in reverse order.
String name;
// Start with an empty list.
LinkListRecord last = null;
c.println ("Enter names one to a line");
while (true)
{
    String newName;
    c.println ("Enter new name, end with q");
    newName = c.readLine ();
    if (newName.equals ("q")) break;
    LinkListRecord p;
    p = new LinkListRecord (newName, last);   // Allocate new record.
    last = p;        // Set last to point to new record.
}
// Print list is reverse order.
c.println ("Here is the list in reverse order");
while (last != null)
{
    c.println (last.getData ());
    LinkListRecord p; // Declare a link.
    p = last; // Locate record to remove from list.
    last = p.getNext (); // Change last to point to next record.
}
```

In the loop, the program has a local link variable *p* which is used to allocate each new record. When the record has been allocated, its *link* field is set to *last* which currently points to the beginning of the existing list. Once the *link* field is set, the value of the link *last* is changed to point to the new record which is located by *p*.

A list that is, as this one, stored in a **last-in-first-out** basis is called a **stack**.

# 17.3  A List Class

We will now develop a list class to store items that are pairs of string information, such as names and phone numbers or names and addresses. It will permit new items to be entered and old items deleted. The items will be records where the first field of the record will act as the **key field** of the record and the second field will be the **information field**. We will be able to look up the information corresponding to any key, presuming that the key is in the list, and change the information field of any record whose key is specified. We will also be able to output the entire list.

Here is a summary of the methods that are to be provided for the list which is an abstract data type (ADT).

List: An Abstract Data Type

The list containing a set of data elements that each contain a key and information. Elements can be entered into the list. Using the key, an element can be looked up, have its information changed, or be deleted. The list can also be output.

*Methods*

**void** enter (key, info)          Add new record.

**void** delete (key)               Delete record.

**void** change (key, info)         Change information in record.

String lookUp (key)                 Find info for given key.

**void** display                    Display all records in list.

This definition of the ADT *List* is kept simple by requiring that it be used in a particular way. For example, the user must not try to delete or change an item not already in the list. If there is any doubt, the *lookUp* operation should be used before doing either of the other two operations. We will implement *List* as a class. It will use the *LinkRecord* class.

Here is the definition of the *LinkRecord* class.

```
// The "LinkRecord" class.
public class LinkRecord
{
    protected String key;
    protected String info;
    protected LinkRecord next;

    // Constructor to create a LinkRecord with key and info, link null.
    public LinkRecord (String key, String info)
    {
        this.key = key;
        this.info = info;
        next = null;
    } // LinkRecord constructor

        // Constructor to create a LinkRecord with key, info, and next.
    public LinkRecord (String key, String info, LinkRecord next)
    {
        this.key = key;
        this.info = info;
        this.next = next;
    } // LinkRecord constructor

    // Get key in LinkRecord.
    public String getKey ()
    {
        return key;
    } // getKey method

    // Get info in LinkRecord.
    public String getInfo ()
    {
```

```
        return info;
    } // getInfo method

    // Get next in LinkRecord.
    public LinkRecord getNext ()
    {
        return next;
    } // getNext method

    // Set info in this LinkRecord.
    public void setInfo (String info)
    {
        this.info = info;
    } // setInfo method

    // Set next in LinkRecord.
    public void setNext (LinkRecord next)
    {
        this.next = next;
    } // setNext method
} /* LinkRecord class */
```

Here is the driver program to test the *List* class.

```
// The "TestList" class.
// Program to test List class.
// This assumes a class LinkRecord defined.
List p;
p = new List (); // Instantiate a list.
String name, phone, info;
String command;
c.println ("Phone list program");
c.println ("You must give a command and supply requested information");
c.println ("Enter(e), Delete(d), Change(c), LookUp(l), Print(p), or Quit(q) ");
// Read and handle each command.
while (true)
{
    c.print ("Command: ");
    command = c.readLine ();
    if (command.charAt (0) == 'q') break;
```

```
switch (command.charAt (0))
{
    case 'e': // Enter.
        c.print ("Give name: ");
        name = c.readLine ();
        c.print ("Give phone number: ");
        phone = c.readLine ();
        // Look to see if already in list.
        info = p.lookUp (name);
        if (info == null)
            p.enter (name, phone);
        else
            c.println ("Item already in list");
        break;
    case 'd': // Delete.
        c.print ("Give name: ");
        name = c.readLine ();
        info = p.lookUp (name);
        if (info != null)
        {
            p.delete (name);
            c.println ("Entry is deleted");
        }
        else
            c.println ("Item is not in list");
        break;
    case 'c': // Change.
        c.print ("Give name: ");
        name = c.readLine ();
        info = p.lookUp (name);
        if (info != null)
        {
            c.print ("Give new phone number: ");
            phone = c.readLine ();
            p.change (name, phone);
        }
        else
            c.println ("Name not in book");
        break;
    case 'l':     // Lookup.
        c.print ("Give name: ");
        name = c.readLine ();
```

```
                    phone = p.lookUp (name);
                    if (phone != null)
                        c.println ("Phone number is " + phone);
                    else
                        c.println ("Name not in book");
                    break;
                case 'p': // Print.
                    p.display (c);
                    break;
                default:
                    c.println ("Command \" " + command + "\" not available");
            }
        }
        c.println ("Quitting list not saved");
```

## 17.3.1  Sample Execution of Demonstration Program

Here is the output for an execution of the program.

```
Phone list program
You must give a command and supply requested information
Enter(e), Delete(d), Change(c), LookUp(l), Print(p), or Quit(q)
Command: e
Give name: Graeme Hirst
Give phone number: (416) 555-4521
Command: e
Give name: Pam Linnemann
Give phone number: (519) 555-8372
Command: e
Give name: Inge Weber
Give phone number: (905) 555-8009
Command: l
Give name: Graeme Hirst
Phone number is: (416) 555-4521
Command: d
Give name: Pam Linnemann
Entry is deleted
Command: c
Give name: Inge Weber
Give new phone number: (905) 555-6338
```

```
Command: l
Give name: Pam Linnemann
Name not in list
Command: p
Inge Weber (905) 555-6338
Graeme Hirst    (416) 555-4521
Command: q
Quitting, list not saved.
```

The order of entries in the list will depend on the implementation. Changing an entry does not alter its position in the list.

# 17.4  Implementation of List Class

Since *List* is an abstract data type, the programmer does not need to be concerned with the details of implementation. This section, however, will illustrate how to implement the *List* class, with the list as a linked list using a self-referential class.

```
// The "List" class.
import hsa.Console;

public class List
{
    protected LinkRecord first;

    // Constructor to produce empty list.
    public List ()
    {
        first = null;
    } // List constructor

    // This method used internally not exported.
    protected LinkRecord find (String key)
    {
        LinkRecord where = first;
        while (where != null && !where.getKey ().equals (key))
        {
            where = where.getNext ();
```

```
        }
    return where;
} // find method


// Add a new item assumed not already present.
// Add to head of list.
public void enter (String key, String info)
{
    LinkRecord p = new LinkRecord (key, info, first);
    first = p;
} // enter method


// Delete item assumed already in list.
public void delete (String key)
{
    LinkRecord where;
    if (first.getKey ().equals (key))
    {
        where = first;
        first = where.getNext ();
    }
    else
    {
        LinkRecord prev = first;
        where = prev.getNext ();
        while (!where.getKey ().equals (key))
        {
            prev = where;
            where = prev.getNext ();
        }
        prev.next = where.getNext ();
    }
} // delete method


// Change info for item assumed in list.
public void change (String key, String info)
{
    LinkRecord where = find (key);
    if (where != null)
        where.setInfo (info);
} // change method
```

```
public String lookUp (String key)
{
    String info;
    LinkRecord where = find (key);
    if (where != null)
        info = where.getInfo ();
    else
        info = null;
    return info;
} // lookUp method

// Print all items in list.
public void display (Console c)
{
    LinkRecord p = first;
    if (p != null)
    {
        do
        {
            c.println (p.getKey () + "   " + p.getInfo ());
            p = p.next;
        }
        while (p != null);
    }
    else
        c.println ("There are no items in list");
} // display method
} /* List class */
```

We were able to use the *find* method in the *change* and *lookUp* methods, but not in the *delete* method. The *delete* method requires both a reference to the item preceding the item to be deleted, and the reference to the item to be deleted itself.

Although we have implemented the *List* class using a linked list it could also have been implemented using an array. The important point of using an abstract data type like *List* is that the details of implementation do not concern its user and can be changed without affecting its use.

# 17.5  Ordered Lists

Another kind of list, called the **ordered list**, is useful when the user requires printouts that are in sorted order. In this kind of list, the items are to be kept so that they are at all times sorted by key. The programmer can create a *SortedLinkedList* class from the *List* class using inheritance. The only thing that the programmer needs to do is change the *enter* method so that, instead of placing a new entry at the start of the list, it is placed in its proper sorted location.

Here is an implementation of the *SortedLinkedList* class.

```
//The "SortedLinkedList" class.
public class SortedLinkedList extends List
{
    // Override method of List to maintain sorted order.
    public void enter (String key, String info)
    {
        LinkRecord p = new LinkRecord (key, info);
        // See if item goes first in list.
        if (first == null || first.getKey ().compareTo (key) >= 0)
        {
            p.setNext (first);
            first = p;
        }
        else
        {
            // Find location to insert new entry.
            LinkRecord prev = first;
            LinkRecord follow = first.getNext ();
            while (follow != null && follow.getKey ().compareTo (key) < 0)
            {
                prev = follow;
                follow = follow.getNext ();
            }
            // Adjust links to make insertion.
            prev.setNext (p);
            p.setNext (follow);
        }
    } // enter method
} /* SortedLinkedList class */
```

The result of using this *SortedList* class with the demonstration program would be that the list output would be sorted.

## 17.5.1   Sample Execution of Demonstration Program

Here is the output for an execution of the program.

```
Phone list program
You must give a command and supply requested information
Enter(e), Delete(d), Change(c), LookUp(l), Print(p), or Quit(q)
Command: e
Give name: Pam Linnemann
Give phone number: (519) 555-8372
Command: e
Give name: Inge Weber
Give phone number: (905) 555-8009
Command: e
Give name: Graeme Hirst
Give phone number: (416) 555-4521
Command: p
Graeme Hirst    (416) 555-4521
Pam Linnemann  (519) 555-8372
Inge Weber (905) 555-8009
Command: l
Give name: Graeme Hirst
Phone number is: (416) 555-4521
Command: d
Give name: Pam Linnemann
Entry is deleted
Command: c
Give name: Inge Weber
Give new phone number: (905) 555-6338
Command: l
Give name: Pam Linnemann
Name not in list
Command: p
Graeme Hirst    (416) 555-4521
Inge Weber (905) 555-6338
Command: q
```
Quitting, list not saved.

# 17.6  Chapter Summary

This chapter has explored self-referential classes to implement linked lists.

## Links

Multiple records are usually maintained in a data structure. A list is such a structure. A list of records would have a sequence; there would be a first item in the list, a second, a third, and so on. The array index indicates the sequence in an array. The first item has an index 0, the next an index 1, and so on. In an array, the list is stored in sequential memory locations and this provides the list item sequence.

When memory is allocated using self-referential classes one of the fields of each record, called a **link**, points to the next record in the list's sequence.

A list of records containing a **key** field and one or more information fields can be kept as a **stack** according to a last-in-first-out discipline.

## List Class

A *List* class can be used to instantiate a *List* object. This object can be defined in terms of the operations *enter, delete, change, lookUp,* and *display*. A demonstration program was presented to use an instance of the *List* class to maintain a list of names and corresponding phone numbers. The name field was used as a **key** to the records for purposes of deletion, changing, and lookup.

## Linked List Implementation of List Class

The implementation of the *List* class was shown as a linked list of the data items.

## Ordered Lists

Usually an ordered list is one in which the keys of successive records are in a non-decreasing (ascending) or non-increasing (descending) order. We say the list is sorted on the key.

The *List* class can be modified to produce a *SortedList* class by inheritance. The *enter* method of *List* must be overridden with a new method to maintain the list in sorted order as each new item is entered. In this way one class can be used to create a new class, thus saving considerable effort.

# 17.7  Technical Terms

information field

keyfield

last-in-first-out

link to the next record

ordered list

self-referential

singly-linked list

stack

# 17.8  Exercises

1.  A stack is a list in which new entries go at the head (or top) of the list and are said to be pushed onto the stack. Entries are removed from the top of this list and are said to be popped from the stack. Define these operations for an ADT *Stack*.

    *push, pop, display*

    Write a demonstration program to push names onto the stack and pop them off the stack. Implement a *Stack* class using links.

2. A queue is a list in which new entries are placed at the end (or tail) of the queue and removed from the first (or head) of the queue. This is a first-in-first-out (FIFO) discipline. Write a linked implementation of a *Queue* class with operations

   *enter, leave, print*

   Write a program to test this class.

3. It is often useful to save a list in memory between one use and the next. Modify the *List* class so that the operations *load* and *save* are added. These are used to initialize the list by reading it from a file rather than initializing it as being empty. If a *save* operation is given before leaving any program that uses the list, the list can be read from the file by a *load* operation the next time the program is used.

# Chapter 18

# Advanced GUIs

In Chapter 11 we showed how a graphical interface could be built for an applet. In this chapter we will look at more advanced examples of designing and building a graphical interface for applets using the GUI components available in the Abstract Windowing Toolkit (awt) of the Java class library. As well, we will show how GUI components may be incorporated into Java application programs.

# 18.1  The MovieWicket Example Problem

The problem that we will examine is to provide an applet with a graphical user interface that implements the interface for a cashier in a movie theater wicket. There are three categories of tickets that can be purchased: adult, senior, and child.

As a customer makes a request for tickets the cashier clicks buttons on the interface (see Figure 18.1). A single click is required for each ticket requested. As this happens, a running total of the cost of the tickets is displayed. When all the tickets have been requested, the cashier clicks the button labelled "Print Ticket". When this button is pressed, a summary of the tickets requested and the total cost is displayed in the text area labelled "Total".

After the total has been displayed, clicking any one of the three ticket buttons clears the text area and the running total in order to begin the calculation for the next customer.

If at any stage the cashier wants to start over for a particular customer, for instance, if the customer changes the request, the cashier can click the button labelled "Clear" which sets everything to zero.

It is important to specify what you want to accomplish in an applet and to decide what its graphical user interface will be like before you start to create it. In the next section we will describe step-by-step the process of creating an applet named *MovieWicket* with this interface.

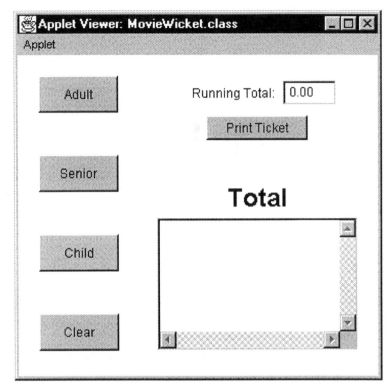

Figure 18.1 The MovieWicket Applet

## 18.2  Layout of GUIs

The GUI components of the applet must be laid out in the applet's display area. The Abstract Windowing Toolkit (awt) of the Java class library provides three basic layout managers. We have already introduced two of these: the *FlowLayout* manager and the *BorderLayout* manager.

The layout manager can be instantiated to apply to a panel or to the applet as a whole. To achieve a complicated layout, the applet is divided into panels which may themselves be divided into subpanels, and so on.

If no particular layout manager is instantiated for the panel or applet, the *FlowLayout* manager is used by default. With the *FlowLayout* manager the GUI components are laid out in rows from left to right, starting with the top row of the panel or applet. The number of GUI components that are placed in a row depends on the size of the components and the size of the container, that is, the panel or applet. When the number of components does not fill a row, a request can be made in the program to center them in the row, to left justify them, or to right justify them. The *setAlignment* method is used to specify how the components should be placed. The parameter to set alignment is

> *componentClass.alignmentType*

where *alignmentType* is LEFT, RIGHT, or CENTER. For example, the statements

> *totalLabel* = **new** *Label* ("Total");
> *totalLabel.setAlignment* (Label.CENTER);

result in the label "Total" being centered.

The *BorderLayout* manager divides the container (panel or applet) into five areas: North, South, East, West, and Center as shown in Figure 18.2.

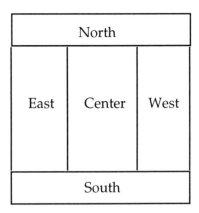

**Figure 18.2 Border Layout with all five Areas**

If the North and South areas are not used, the division is as shown in Figure 18.3.

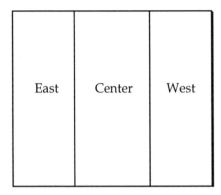

Figure 18.3 BorderLayout with only East, Center, and West

If Center is also missing then East and West fill the space.

The position of a component in a *BorderLayout* is specified by a statement of the form

*containerIdentifier.add (position, componentIdentifier);*

where the position is written as "North" for the north location. (Note that the position's first letter is capitalized and it is in quotes.)

For example, if a label called *totalLabel* is to be placed in the North position of a panel called *totalPanel* using *BorderLayout*, the statements required are:

*totalPanel.setLayout (**new** BorderLayout ());*
*totalPanel.add ("North", totalLabel);*

The third layout manager we will use is the *GridLayout* manager. The *GridLayout* manager divides the container into a certain number of rows, each with a certain number of columns. In the constructor for *GridLayout*, the arguments give respectively the number of rows and columns, as well as the horizontal spacing between rows and the vertical spacing between columns. The constructor form, including the call to make it the current layout, is

*setLayout (**new** GridLayout (rows, columns, hgap, vgap));*

As the components are added in a *GridLayout* they are placed, in sequence, from left to right in the first row, then in the second row, and so on. The components in the row take up the full space across the container.

Spacing can also be specified in the constructors for the other two layout managers. For *FlowLayout* the constructor

> setLayout (**new** *FlowLayout* (*FlowLayout.CENTER, hgap, vgap*));

specifies the alignment as well as the spacing. For *BorderLayout* the constructor

> setLayout (**new** *BorderLayout* (*hgap, vgap*));

adjusts the spacing between the five areas.

# 18.3 Layout for the MovieWicket Applet

For the *MovieWicket* example we will divide the applet into two main panels (see Figure 18.4) which we will call *westPanel* and *eastPanel*. These two panels will be placed in the applet using the *BorderLayout* manager with the *eastPanel* in the "East" position and *westPanel* in the "West" position. The other areas of the *BorderLayout* will not be present.

The *eastPanel* will be subdivided into three panels called *runningTotalPanel*, *printPanel*, and *totalPanel*. These three panels will be placed in the *eastPanel* using the *BorderLayout* manager with the three areas "North", "Center", and "South".

The *westPanel* will be laid out using the *GridLayout* manager. In this case we have specified that the four buttons are to be laid out in four rows in a single column with horizontal spacing of 30 pixels. This is the space between buttons and between the top and bottom of the panel and the buttons. The vertical spacing of 40 pixels provides a space between the sides of the panel and the buttons.

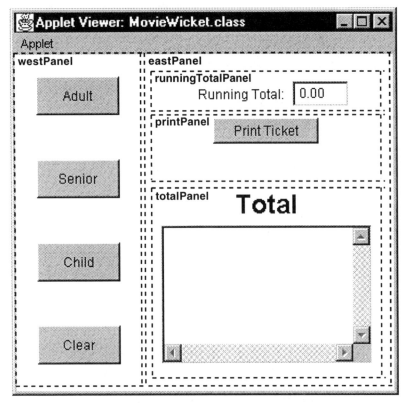

Figure 18.4 Panels in the MovieWicket Applet

Here is the part of the *MovieWicket* class that defines the GUI components and places them in the applet. The *init* method specifies their placement.

```
// The "MovieWicket" class.
import java.applet.*;
import java.awt.*;
import java.text.*;

public class MovieWicket extends Applet
{
    static final double ADULT_PRICE = 8.00;
    static final double CHILD_PRICE = 3.50;
    static final double SENIOR_PRICE = 4.50;
```

```
Button adultButton, seniorButton, childButton;
Button clearButton, printButton;

Label runningTotalLabel, totalLabel;
TextField runningTotalTextField;
TextArea totalTextArea;

int adults = 0, seniors = 0, children = 0;
double total = 0;

// Called by the system when the applet is loaded.
public void init ()
{
    // Set properties of the applet.
    setLayout (new BorderLayout ());

    // Create all the components in the applet.
    // The spaces around "Adult" are used to create a wider button.
    adultButton = new Button ("    Adult    ");
    seniorButton = new Button ("Senior");
    childButton = new Button ("Child");
    clearButton = new Button ("Clear");
    runningTotalLabel = new Label ("Running Total: ");
    runningTotalLabel.setAlignment (Label.RIGHT);
    runningTotalTextField = new TextField ("0.00");
    printButton = new Button ("   Print Ticket   ");
    totalLabel = new Label ("Total");
    totalLabel.setAlignment (Label.CENTER);
    totalLabel.setFont (new Font ("Dialog", Font.BOLD, 24));
    totalTextArea = new TextArea (7, 25); // 7 rows. 25 columns wide.

    // Layout the four buttons on the left in a panel.
    Panel westPanel = new Panel ();
    westPanel.setLayout (new GridLayout (0, 1, 30, 40));
    westPanel.add (adultButton);
    westPanel.add (seniorButton);
    westPanel.add (childButton);
    westPanel.add (clearButton);
    // Place westPanel into the applet.
    add ("West", westPanel);
```

```
        // Layout the running total label and text field.
        Panel runningTotalPanel = new Panel ();
        runningTotalPanel.add (runningTotalLabel);
        runningTotalPanel.add (runningTotalTextField);

        // Place the "Print Ticket" button in its own panel so that it
        // won't be resized to fit the entire central area.
        Panel printPanel = new Panel ();
        printPanel.add (printButton);

        // Layout the total text area and the label above it.
        Panel totalPanel = new Panel ();
        totalPanel.setLayout (new BorderLayout ());
        totalPanel.add ("North", totalLabel);
        totalPanel.add ("South", totalTextArea);

        // Place all three panels in a panel covering the right hand side.
        Panel eastPanel = new Panel ();
        eastPanel.setLayout (new BorderLayout ());
        eastPanel.add ("North", runningTotalPanel);
        eastPanel.add ("Center", printPanel);
        eastPanel.add ("South", totalPanel);

        // Place eastPanel into the applet.
        add ("East", eastPanel);
    } // init method

    // This is used to force the layout manager to give 20 pixels
    // of space around the edges.
    public Insets insets ()
    {
        return (new Insets (20, 20, 20, 20));
    } // insets method

    ... additional methods...

} /* MovieWicket class */
```

In addition to the **import statements**, the applet's declarations of the GUI components and variables, and the *init* method of the applet, there is a method *insets* which returns a component of type *Insets*. The system calls the *insets* method to determine the distance that the component should be placed from the edge of the applet. In our program, we have provided an *insets* method to create a border of width 20 pixels all around the components. This border prevents the components from running out to the edge of their containers as they would with some layouts.

# 18.4 Implementation of the Actions of the Applet

Before the applet can actually function, the buttons must be implemented so that clicking them really does something. Once the GUI interface is created, however, it is possible to run the applet as it stands to see that it produces the desired layout.

To proceed to the next step we must create the *action* method of the applet. The clicking of the *adultButton* will call the method called *addAdult*. This method will add one to the count of adults, add *ADULT_PRICE* to the running total, and clear the *totalTextArea* in case there is still something there from the previous customer.

Here is the *action* method.

```
public boolean action (Event evt, Object arg)
{
    // If the user pressed a button, call the associated method.
    if (evt.target == adultButton)
        addAdult ();
    else if (evt.target == seniorButton)
        addSenior ();
    else if (evt.target == childButton)
        addChild ();
    else if (evt.target == printButton)
        printTicket ();
    else if (evt.target == clearButton)
        clearAll ();
    else
        return false;

    return true;
} // action method
```

Here is the *addAdult* method.

```
// Called when the user pressed the "Adult" button.
protected void addAdult ()
{
    // Increment the adult counter.
    adults++;

    // Add to the total.
    total += ADULT_PRICE;

    // Display the new total.
    NumberFormat form = new DecimalFormat ("0.00");
    runningTotalTextField.setText (form.format (total));

    // Clear the previously printed ticket.
    totalTextArea.setText ("");
} // addAdult method
```

The statements

```
    NumberFormat form = new DecimalFormat ("0.00");
    runningTotalTextField.setText (form.format (total));
```

display the running total to two decimal places. These have been used before in this book. The *total* is set to zero by the *clearAll* method or when *printTicket* is called.

Here are the methods for *addChild*, and *addSenior*.

```
// Called when the user pressed the "Child" button.
protected void addChild ()
{
    // Increment the adult counter.
    children++;

    // Add to the total.
    total += CHILD_PRICE;

    // Display the new total.
    NumberFormat form = new DecimalFormat ("0.00");
```

```
    runningTotalTextField.setText (form.format (total));

    // Clear the previously printed ticket.
    totalTextArea.setText ("");
} // addChild method

// Called when the user pressed the "Senior" button.
protected void addSenior ()
{
    // Increment the adult counter.
    seniors++;

    // Add to the total.
    total += SENIOR_PRICE;

    // Display the new total.
    NumberFormat form = new DecimalFormat ("0.00");
    runningTotalTextField.setText (form.format (total));

    // Clear the previously printed ticket.
    totalTextArea.setText ("");
} // addSenior method
```

The *clearAll* method sets the counters to zero, the display running total
to zero, and *TotalTextArea* to blank.

```
// Called when the user pressed the "Clear" button.
protected void clearAll ()
{
    // Reset the counters and the total.
    adults = 0;
    seniors = 0;
    children = 0;
    total = 0;

    // Display the new running total.
    runningTotalTextField.setText ("0.00");

    // Clear the printed ticket.
    totalTextArea.setText ("");
} // clearAll method
```

The *PrintTicket* method summarizes the customer's request. The string *result* has a number of \n character combinations to indicate a new line when *result* is output in the *totalTextArea* by the *setText* method of the *TextArea* class. The variables *adults, seniors, children*, and *total* are set to zero so that they are ready for the next customer's order.

```
// Called when the user pressed the "Print Ticket" button.
protected void printTicket ()
{
    // Display the values of the counters and the total in the
    // total text area.
    String result;
    NumberFormat form = new DecimalFormat ("0.00");
    result = "Adults: " + adults + "\nSeniors: " + seniors +
        "\nChildren: " + children + "\nTotal: " + form.format (total);
    totalTextArea.setText (result);

    // Reset the counters and the total now that the ticket is printed.
    adults = 0;
    seniors = 0;
    children = 0;
    total = 0;
} // printTicket method
```

This applet was run with an HTML file that specified the applet's display area to be 350 pixels wide by 300 pixels high.

# 18.5 Drawing Using the Mouse

In the example of the movie wicket we interact with the graphical user interface by clicking buttons using the mouse. A click consists of pressing the mouse button down then releasing it, that is, letting it up. The *action* method determines which of the buttons is clicked, that is, the target of the mouse event.

We can use the mouse in another way by dragging it, that is, by pressing it down then moving it without releasing it. The event of dragging the mouse is detected by the *Component* method *mouseDrag* which has the header

**public boolean** *mouseDrag* (*Event e*, **int** *x*, *int y*)

where (*x*, *y*) are the coordinates of the mouse as it is dragged.

Here is an applet called *BallPoint* that can be used to draw in the applet's display area. As the mouse is dragged, filled circles of color are drawn. When the mouse button is released, drawing ceases until the mouse button is again depressed. This creates a ballpoint pen effect.

```
// The "BallPoint" class.
import java.applet.Applet;
import java.awt.*;

public class BallPoint extends Applet
{
    final int RADIUS = 5;

    protected void drawBall (Graphics g, int x, int y, int radius, Color clr)
    {
        g.setColor (clr);
        g.fillOval (x – radius, y – radius, 2 * radius, 2 * radius);
    } // drawBall method

    public boolean mouseDown (Event e, int x, int y)
    {
        Graphics g = getGraphics ();
        drawBall (g, x, y, RADIUS, Color.red);
        return true;
    } // mouseDown method

    public boolean mouseDrag (Event e, int x, int y)
    {
        Graphics g = getGraphics ();
        drawBall (g, x, y, RADIUS, Color.red);
        return true;
    } // mouseDrag method
} /* BallPoint class */
```

When the user presses the mouse button, the system calls the applet's *mouseDown* method. In turn *mouseDown* calls the *getGraphics* method of the *Applet* class which returns the applet's graphics context (the drawing surface). Then *mouseDown* calls *drawBall* to draw a red ball at the mouse position.

The *mouseDrag* method works exactly the same way. It calls *getGraphics* and then *drawBall*.

There is no *paint* or *update* method for this applet. This means when the applet is hidden by another window and then revealed, any part of the drawing on the applet covered by the window will have been erased and will not be redrawn.

Figure 18.5 shows a result of drawing with the *BallPoint* applet.

Figure 18.5 Drawing with the *BallPoint* applet

# 18.6 GUIs with Java Applications

We have been talking of GUIs as if they were only usable with applets. In this section we will see how a Java application program can have a graphical user interface.

To create a Java application program with a GUI, we must first create a window into which the GUI components can be placed. This is done by instantiating a window from the *Frame* class. A *Frame* is a window with a title bar and a border. The *Frame* class has methods for hiding and showing the window, and disposing of it.

The default layout manager for a *Frame* is *BorderLayout* (unlike *Applets* and *Panels* which use the *FlowLayout* default layout manager).

When the programmer creates the *Frame* he or she specifies the window title as a parameter in the constructor. For example, the Java to create a window with a title of "My Window" would be

*Frame newWindow* = **new** *Frame* ("My Window");

The size of the frame can be set by the *resize* method or it can be made just large enough to hold the GUI components that are wanted using the *pack* method. We will look at an example where the principal component in the frame is a canvas. The size of a canvas is set using the *resize* method.

To demonstrate the process of creating GUIs in an application, we will now create an application in which a user can draw two different shapes: rectangles and ovals. To draw the shapes, the user presses the mouse down at a point in the canvas to establish the top-left corner of the rectangle that encloses the shape. He or she then drags the mouse to the point that is to be the lower-right corner of the enclosing rectangle and releases it.

As the mouse moves, the program draws a black outline of the shape being created. This outline is constantly erased and updated as the mouse moves. When the mouse is released, the shape's outline is filled with the color that has been previously selected from a choice of three colors.

This is similar to the *ControlDraw* applet example in Chapter 11 where there were two buttons to select the shape to be drawn and three radio buttons to select the color. In this case, however, we will use menus to allow for the selection of the shape and color.

# 18.7 Menus

Menus make interfaces simpler but can only be used with a *Frame*.

There are three classes needed to implement menus: the *MenuBar* class, the *Menu* class, and the *MenuItem* class. Figure 18.7 shows a *Frame* with a *MenuBar* containing three *Menus* (File, Shape and Color). The Shape Menu has been selected and contains two *MenuItems* (Oval and Rectangle).

To create a menu for a *Frame*, the programmer must first create a *MenuBar*. Here is an example.

> *MenuBar myMenus* = **new** *MenuBar* ();

The *Menus* to appear in the *MenuBar* must also be created. Once the *Menus* have been created, they can be placed in the *MenuBar* using the *add* method in this way.

> *Menu fileMenu* = **new** *Menu* ("File");
> *myMenus.add (fileMenu)*;

The programmer must also create the *MenuItems* that will appear in the *Menus*. To place a *MenuItem* in a *Menu*, the programmer uses the *add* method of the *Menu* class as follows.

> *MenuItem quitItem* = **new** *MenuItem* ("Quit");
> *fileMenu.add (quitItem)*;

An item in a menu can be either an object of the *MenuItem* class or of the *CheckboxMenuItem* class. (Note the *b* of box is lower case.) A *CheckboxMenuItem* is a *MenuItem* that can have a check placed in front of its name. This is done using the *setState* method with a parameter **true**. If the parameter is set to **false** no check mark appears.

# 18.8  A Case Study Involving GUIs in a Java Application

We will now look at the development of a Java application program with a Graphical User Interface.

## 18.8.1  Problem

Write a Java application that allows the user to draw multiple ovals and rectangles.  The user should be able to select the type of shape (rectangle or oval), its dimensions, and the color. The user must also be able to clear the screen.

## 18.8.2  User Interface – Windows

Here we must write a Java application program that uses both GUIs and graphics. Our first problem is to decide how many windows the program will require. A single window (a *Frame* object in Java) would be able to contain all the necessary GUI components.

We will produce a class *PaintShape* that extends the Java *Frame* class. The *main* method will be in a class called *PaintShapeMain* and will instantiate an object of the *PaintShape* class. Once the *Frame* object of *PaintShape* is instantiated, the *main* method is finished and the program waits for input from the user.

## 18.8.3  User Interface – Component Selection

There are a few decisions about the user interface that must be made.

- How does the user control the location and size of the shape to be drawn?
- How does the user specify whether the shape should be a rectangle or oval?

- How does the user control the color of the shape to be drawn?
- How does the user clear the screen?

The answer to the first question is to use the mouse to control the location and size of the shape to be drawn. The initial mouse button press would specify the location of a corner of the rectangle (or the corner of the containing rectangle for an oval). Dragging the mouse to the diametrically opposite corner would then specify the size. Some form of visual feedback helps the user determine the size of the shape. The click-drag of the mouse is used in most GUI-based operating systems.

The shape specification (question 2) could be done in a variety of ways. We could use radio buttons to specify which shape to use when the mouse is pressed and dragged. Menus provide another possible choice but they can only be used in a window and cannot be used on an applet drawing surface. Menus are used to allow the user to select from among a large number of possible commands or to specify mutually exclusive options. Often, checkmarks are used to mark currently-selected options. We will use two menus: one to allow the user to specify the shape and another to allow the user to specify the color.

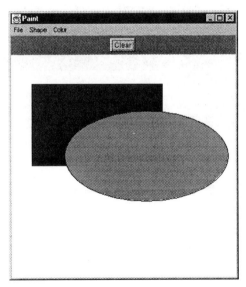

Figure 18.6 The PaintShape Application

The GUI component used to issue the command to clear the drawing area could be either a button or a command in another menu. Because we anticipate that the clear command will be called often, we choose to make it easily accessible by making it a button in the top center of the screen. Lastly, we create a separate menu for quitting the program. Figure 18.6 shows the interface we have designed for the shape-drawing Java application.

Figure 18.7 and 18.8 show the selection of the shape and the color from the program menus.

Figure 18.7 Selecting from the Shape Menu

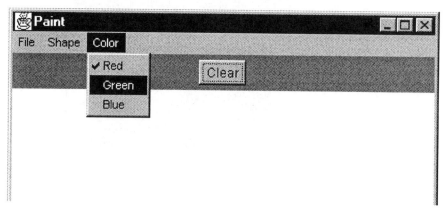

Figure 18.8 Selecting from the Color Menu

## 18.8.4   User Interface – Placement

Because we are using menus, the component placement is relatively simple. We decide to place the *Button* component for clearing the screen at the top of the screen and the *Canvas*, which contains our drawing surface, beneath it. We decide to us a *BorderLayout* to place the two components, one above the other. However, if we merely place the *Clear* button directly into the *BorderLayout*, the button will expand to fit the area allotted (across the top of the entire window). To have a normal sized button, we must place it in its own panel using *FlowLayout*. When a panel is instantiated it is, by default, defined as *FlowLayout*. The panel can then be placed in the *Frame* using *BorderLayout*.

Note that the default layout manager for an *Applet* and a *Panel* is a *FlowLayout*, and for a *Frame* is a *BorderLayout*. In this example we are using the default layout managers for the *Frame* and the *Panel* so we do not use the *setLayout* method.

We will create three menus, the *File* menu which only contains the *Quit* menu item, the *Shape* menu, which allows the user to specify the shape drawn, and the *Color* menu, which allows the user to specify the shape's color.

## 18.8.5   User Interface – Other Issues

In any GUI-based application, it is considered good form to allow the user to close the window by clicking the window's close button. Our application should also terminate execution. In Java, however, clicking the close button is not handled automatically. We must therefore override the *handleEvent* method to detect when the user clicks the close button and handle it appropriately.

## 18.8.6   The Program

Our program consists of three classes: a *PaintShapeMain* class, a *PaintShape* class, and a *PaintCanvas* class. The *PaintShape* class extends the *Frame* class. It provides the window and handles the button and menu interaction.

The *PaintCanvas* class is the drawing area for the shape and extends the *Canvas* class. We need to create a new class (as opposed to just using a *Canvas* object) because it must handle mouse button presses. Whenever *Canvas* must handle mouse or keyboard input, a new class must be created that inherits from *Canvas* and that overrides its mouse or keyboard handling methods (in this case the *mouseDown*, *mouseUp*, and *mouseDrag* methods).

The instance variables of the *PaintShape* class are:

- a *Button* (the *clearButton*),
- a *MenuItem* (the *quitItem*),
- five *CheckboxMenuItems* (*redItem*, *greenItem*, *blueItem*, *ovalItem*, *rectItem*), and
- a *PaintCanvas* (the *drawingSurface*).

*PaintShape* inherits from *Frame*. To call the constructor of *Frame* from within the constructor of *PaintShape*, we use the keyword **super**. The call to **super** sets the title bar to "Paint".

The *PaintShape* constructor also creates the menu for the *Frame*. *MenuItems* are instantiated with their labels, then the *Menus* with their labels. The *MenuItems* are then added to the *Menus*. After the *MenuBar* is instantiated, the *Menus* are added to it.

The *clearButton* is placed in a *FlowLayout* panel the panel is added in the "North" position using the default *BorderLayout* of *Frame*.

The *drawingSurface* is instantiated from the *PaintCanvas* class and added in the "South" position. The default values of *currentShape* and *currentColor* of the *drawingSurface* are set to a rectangle and red. The state of the *rectItem* and *redItem* menu items are set to **true**. This causes checkmarks to appear beside the "Rectangle" and "Red" menu items. (See Figure 18.7 and 18.8.)

To finish the construction of the *PaintShape* object, the *pack ()* method adjusts the frame size to fit the components and the *Frame* (which is initialized invisible) is made visible using the *show ()* method. Note that the size of the *drawingSurface* object is set when the *PaintCanvas* constructor is executed.

In the *PaintShape* class, the method *action* detects whether a menu item has been selected and whether the *clearButton* has been clicked.

When the user selects a color or shape menu item, the *action* method changes the current shape or color of the drawing surface then checkmarks the menu item selected by calling *setState* (**true**) for the menu item. The program then calls *setState* (**false**) for each remaining menu item to uncheck them.

If the user presses the Clear button, the *clear ()* method of the *drawingSurface* is called to clear the canvas.

If the user selects the quit menu item, the *action* method hides the *Frame* by calling the *hide ()* method. The *action* method then halts the application by calling *System.exit.*

The *handleEvent* method overrides the *Frame* class' *handleEvent.* If the user clicks the close box (the X at the top-right of the frame), *handleEvent* is called with the event WINDOW_DESTROY as the parameter. The window is then hidden by *hide ()* and the system exited using *System.exit* (0).

Here is the program for the *PaintShape* class.

```
// The "PaintShape" class.
import java.awt.*;

public class PaintShape extends Frame
{
    Button clearButton;
    MenuItem quitItem;
    CheckboxMenuItem ovalItem, rectItem, redItem, greenItem, blueItem;
    PaintCanvas drawingSurface;

    // Constructor
    public PaintShape ()
    {
        super ("Paint");

        // Create the menu items.
        quitItem = new MenuItem ("Quit Paint");
        ovalItem = new CheckboxMenuItem ("Oval");
        rectItem = new CheckboxMenuItem ("Rectangle");
        redItem = new CheckboxMenuItem ("Red");
        greenItem = new CheckboxMenuItem ("Green");
        blueItem = new CheckboxMenuItem ("Blue");
```

```
// Create the menus.
Menu fileMenu = new Menu ("File");
Menu shapeMenu = new Menu ("Shape");
Menu colorMenu = new Menu ("Color");

// Place the menu items in the menus.
fileMenu.add (quitItem);
shapeMenu.add (ovalItem);
shapeMenu.add (rectItem);
colorMenu.add (redItem);
colorMenu.add (greenItem);
colorMenu.add (blueItem);

// Place the menus into the menu bar.
MenuBar myMenus = new MenuBar ();
myMenus.add (fileMenu);
myMenus.add (shapeMenu);
myMenus.add (colorMenu);
setMenuBar (menuBar);

setBackground (Color.gray);

// We put the clear button in a panel to make it a small size.
clearButton = new Button ("Clear");
Panel p = new Panel ();
p.add (clearButton);
add ("North", p);

drawingSurface = new PaintCanvas ();
add ("South", drawingSurface);

// Set the default values for shape and color.
drawingSurface.currentShape = drawingSurface.RECTANGLE;
drawingSurface.currentColor = Color.red;
rectItem.setState (true);
redItem.setState (true);

pack ();

show ();
} // PaintShape constructor
```

```
// Handles button presses and menu item selection.
public boolean action (Event e, Object arg)
{
    if (e.target == clearButton)
    {
        drawingSurface.clear ();
    }
    if (e.target == quitItem)
    {
        hide ();
        System.exit (0);
    }
    else if (e.target == ovalItem)
    {
        drawingSurface.currentShape = drawingSurface.OVAL;
        ovalItem.setState (true);
        rectItem.setState (false);
    }
    else if (e.target == rectItem)
    {
        drawingSurface.currentShape = drawingSurface.RECTANGLE;
        ovalItem.setState (false);
        rectItem.setState (true);
    }
    else if (e.target == redItem)
    {
        drawingSurface.currentColor = Color.red;
        redItem.setState (true);
        greenItem.setState (false);
        blueItem.setState (false);
    }
    else if (e.target == greenItem)
    {
        drawingSurface.currentColor = Color.green;
        redItem.setState (false);
        greenItem.setState (true);
        blueItem.setState (false);
    }
```

```
            else if (e.target == blueItem)
            {
                drawingSurface.currentColor = Color.blue;
                redItem.setState (false);
                greenItem.setState (false);
                blueItem.setState (true);
            }
            else
            {
                return false;
            }
            return true;
    } // action method

    // Overrides the handleEvent method. It handles window
    // being closed by the user.
    public boolean handleEvent (Event evt)
    {
        switch (evt.id)
        {
            case Event.WINDOW_DESTROY:
                hide ();
                System.exit (0);
                return true;
        }
        return super.handleEvent (evt);
    } // handleEvent method
} // PaintShape class
```

The *PaintShape* window must be created by the program. This is
done in the *PaintShapeMain* application class. The *main* method
instantiates a single copy of the *PaintShape* window and exits. The
*PaintShape* window remains after the main program exits, accepting
input from the user until the user closes the window.

Here is the *PaintShapeMain* class.

```
// The "PaintShapeMain" class.
import java.awt.*;

public class PaintShapeMain
{
    public static void main (String [] args)
    {
        new PaintShape ();
    } // main method
} // PaintShapeMain class
```

The *PaintCanvas* class used by *PaintShape* is much simpler. The canvas is sized and its background set to white in the constructor. The *drawShape* method creates the outline of the shape. If *drawShape* is called a second time, with the same parameters, the shape is erased. This is done by setting the graphics context's drawing mode to *XORMode*. For example, if the program draws a black line on top of a black line in *XORMode*, the line is reset to the background color, effectively erasing it.

Care must be taken to use positive values for the *shapeWidth* and *shapeHeight*. This is done in *drawShape* and *mouseUp* by using the *Math* methods *abs* and *max*.

Aside from *currentColor* and *currentShape*, *PaintCanvas* has several other fields: *startX* and *startY* specify the initial corner of the shape (the "anchor" point); *currentX* and *currentY* specify the opposite corner of the shape the last time it was drawn.

When the user presses the mouse button while the mouse is in the *PaintCanvas*, the *mouseDown ()* method of *PaintCanvas* is called. This method sets *startX* and *startY* to the current mouse position and draws the initial shape.

As the user drags the mouse across the canvas, the system calls the *mouseDrag ()* method. Then *mouseDrag* calls *drawShape* which erases the shape outline. Next, *mouseDrag* sets *currentX* and *currentY* to the current mouse position and calls *drawShape* again to draw the shape outline from the anchor point to the current mouse location.

When the user releases the mouse button, the system calls the *mouseUp ()* method of *PaintCanvas* which erases the shape outline at the previous position and then draws the filled shape at the position of the mouse when the button was released, which is at (*finalX, finalY*). This time it does not use the *XORMode* to draw the filled shape in the current color.

Here is the program for the *PaintCanvas* class.

```
// The "PaintCanvas" class.
import java.awt.*;

class PaintCanvas extends Canvas
{
    static final int OVAL = 1;
    static final int RECTANGLE = 2;

    int currentShape;
    Color currentColor;
    protected int startX, startY, currentX, currentY;

    public PaintCanvas ()
    {
        resize (400, 400);
        setBackground (Color.white);
    } // PaintCanvas constructor

    // Clears the canvas.
    protected void clear ()
    {
        Graphics g = getGraphics ();
        g.clearRect (0, 0, size ().width, size ().height);
    } // clear method


    protected void drawShape (int cornerX, int cornerY)
    {
        Graphics g = getGraphics ();
        int x, y, shapeWidth, shapeHeight;
```

```
// Be sure shapeWidth and shapeHeight are always positive.
x = Math.min (startX, cornerX);
shapeWidth = Math.abs (cornerX - startX);
y = Math.min (startY, cornerY);
shapeHeight = Math.abs (cornerY - startY);

// Now draw the shape outline.  Use XOR mode so if the shape
// outline is already drawn there, then this will erase it.
g.setXORMode (Color.white);

if (currentShape == RECTANGLE)
{
    g.drawRect (x, y, shapeWidth, shapeHeight);
}
else
{
    g.drawOval (x, y, shapeWidth, shapeHeight);
}
} // drawShape method


public boolean mouseDown (Event e, int x, int y)
{
    startX = x;
    startY = y;
    currentX = x;
    currentY = y;
    drawShape (currentX, currentY);
    return true;
} // mouseDown method


public boolean mouseDrag (Event e, int x, int y)
{
    // Erase the shape outline in the old position.
    drawShape (currentX, currentY);

    currentX = x;
    currentY = y;

    // Draw the shape outline in the new position.
    drawShape (currentX, currentY);
```

```
        return true;
    } // mouseDrag method

    public boolean mouseUp (Event e, int finalX, int finalY)
    {
        int x, y, shapeWidth, shapeHeight;

        // Erase the shape outline in the current position.
        drawShape (currentX, currentY);

        Graphics g = getGraphics ();

        // Set the color according to the current color.
        g.setColor (currentColor);

        // Be sure shapeWidth and shapeHeight are always positive.
        x = Math.min (startX, finalX);
        shapeWidth = Math.abs (finalX – startX);
        y = Math.min (startY, finalY);
        shapeHeight = Math.abs (finalY – startY);

        // Draw the filled in color shape with a black border.
        if (currentShape == RECTANGLE)
        {
            g.fillRect (x, y, shapeWidth, shapeHeight);
            g.setColor (Color.black);
            g.drawRect (x, y, shapeWidth, shapeHeight);
        }
        else
        {
            g.fillOval (x, y, shapeWidth, shapeHeight);
            g.setColor (Color.black);
            g.drawOval (x, y, shapeWidth, shapeHeight);
        }

        return true;
    } // mouseUp method
} /* PaintCanvas class */
```

# 18.9  Chapter Summary

## Design of a Graphical User Interface

Whenever an applet is to be created with a graphical user interface, the first steps are to specify how the applet is to be used and to design a layout of the graphical components in the interface. The details of what is to happen when the user interacts with the interface must be precise.

## Layout of Interface

If a user interface is to contain a number of components: buttons, text fields, text areas, and so on, these must be laid out in the applet. There are three basic layout managers: FlowLayout, BorderLayout, and GridLayout. These can be instantiated for the whole applet or Frame or for any panel that is part of the applet or Frame.

The overall layout is planned by subdividing the applet or Frame into panels which are rectangular parts of the whole window. Panels can be in turn subdivided into panels. The GUI components are first laid out in their containing panels, then the panels laid out in their containing applet, Frame, or panel.

## FlowLayout Manager

If no layout manager is instantiated for a container (panel, applet, or *Frame*), *FlowLayout* is used by default. With this layout manager, components are placed, as they are added, from left to right in rows across the container. When one row cannot hold more components, a new row is started. The components in a row can be left justified, right justified, or centered using the key constants LEFT, RIGHT, and CENTER in the statement that sets the alignment.

## BorderLayout Manager

A *BorderLayout* manager lays out the GUI components in five areas of the container: North, South, East, West, and Center. When all of the areas are used, the North and South areas go from the left to the right side of the container. The North area is at the top of the container and the South area is at the bottom. The other three areas (West, Center, and East) are laid out between the North and South areas from the left to the right side of the container. The area in which a given component is to be placed is specified in quotation marks as the first argument in the *add* method.

If fewer than the five areas are occupied, the other areas spread out to take up the whole container.

## GridLayout Manager

The *GridLayout* manager arranges GUI components (usually all of the same type) in a number of rows and columns as specified in the *GridLayout* constructor. The components are placed, as they are added, from left to right in the rows starting with the top row.

## Implementation of the Actions of the Applet

When a button is clicked in the *MovieWicket* applet, the *action* method is called. The *Event* parameter specifies which button was clicked. For each possible button, the action method calls the appropriate method.

## Interacting with the Mouse

The behavior of the mouse can be responded to directly rather than through the *action* method. For example, the method with the header

```
public boolean mouseDrag (Event e, int x, int y)
```

yields the current coordinates ($x, y$) of the mouse when it is being held down and moved. The coordinates are constantly updated as the mouse moves.

Similarly the *mouseDown* and *mouseUp* methods give the coordinates where the mouse is pressed down and where it is released. In an example program *mouseDrag* was used to draw a ball in positions controlled by the mouse.

## Graphical User Interfaces in Applications

Java application programs that require GUIs must have a *Frame* instantiated to create a window in which the GUI components can be placed. A *Frame* is a window with a title bar and border. Its default layout manager is *BorderLayout*.

We showed an example program that has menus, a button, and a canvas to allow the user to select a shape and a color for drawing rectangles or ovals in one of three colors using the mouse. The containing rectangle of the shape was defined by pressing the mouse button down at its top-left corner and dragging the mouse to its lower-right corner and releasing it.

The way in which the *MenuBar*, *Menu*, and *MenuItem* classes were used was described. The layout of the clear button and canvas was also described.

We described how the shape outline was drawn and erased repeatedly. This was done by drawing the shape outline in the *XORMode*.

# 18.10    Exercises

1.  Write an applet that will act like the keypad of a touch-tone telephone. Display the phone number of the person being called at the top of the applet as the number is being entered. The applet should look like Figure 18.9.

| Number Called | | |
|:---:|:---:|:---:|
| 1 | 2 | 3 |
| 4 | 5 | 6 |
| 7 | 8 | 9 |
| * | 0 | # |

Figure 18.9 Touch-tone Telephone Keypad

2.  Modify the applet of Exercise 1 so that the phone number displayed will have a dash between digits that represent the area code, the exchange, and the 4-digit number. For example, numbers might be entered as 416-555-4141 or only 555-4141. The dashes are to be inserted by the programs as required.

3.  Create an applet that has the user:
    *   enter two real numbers in two text fields,
    *   select a radio button to indicate the required operation: add, subtract, multiply, or divide,
    *   press a button to execute the calculation,
    *   display the result in a third text field, and
    *   press a button to clear the calculator.

4.  Create an applet that has three radio buttons used to select the color (red, green, or blue) for drawing with a ballpoint pen effect on a canvas in the applet.

5.  Write an applet to draw rectangles in the applet. The upper-left corner of the rectangle is to be established by pressing the mouse button down. The mouse is then dragged to the lower-right corner of the wanted rectangle and released. Arrange that several rectangles can be drawn, one after the other, and remain on the screen.

6.  Modify the applet of Exercise 5 so that a rectangle is drawn as soon as the mouse starts to be dragged but is constantly updated so that it is replaced by a new rectangle as the mouse is dragged to a new point. Hint: to erase the old rectangle it must be drawn in the background color before the new rectangle is drawn.

7.  Modify the *PaintShape* and *PaintCanvas* classes to allow a fourth color for drawing the shapes.

8.  Create an application program with menus that allows the user to choose a text font, a point size, and a color for displaying the text "Happy Birthday" in the window beginning at a point at which the mouse is clicked.

# Appendices

# Appendix A

# Library Automation System Case Study

In this chapter we will present a case study that requires the use of advanced object-oriented concepts. In Chapters 11 and 18 we looked at case studies that emphasized the use of a graphical interface but had a relatively simple object-oriented design. In this new case study we will omit the design of a graphical user interface. Instead, we will use a simple text interface and concentrate on the classes necessary to the operation of a library information system.

# A.1   The Problem Specification

The problem to be solved requires us to design and create a program that will aid the librarian in supervising the library in a new school. The failure to have a clear, well-researched, and validated problem specification is the most common cause of software project catastrophes, and so we begin this process by imagining how an automated system would be used. Would there be one computer or many? Do the staff and students have direct access to the computer? Do we create one automation program or several?

To answer these questions we should explore other existing systems, examine the actual proposed library, and talk to potential users. We also need to determine the project's budget, since desirable features may have to be balanced against implementation costs.

The present library includes a collection of books and periodicals. Maintaining flexibility for the future is an important consideration. The design we create should be flexible enough to allow later changes such as the addition of audio tapes, CDs, and computer software in the library collection without rewriting major portions of the program.

The system should be able to handle two types of library cards: the student library card and the staff library card. Once again the design should allow additional types of library cards, such as for visitors, without requiring a redesign of the library automation system.

The best way to decide on the system's capabilities is through discussions with the supervisor and potential users of the library. The proposed list of capabilities should also be submitted to these people for their approval since tradeoffs made to lower costs must have the support of the user community or the system may fail. This feedback process may, in turn, result in design modifications which must be tested.

Our problem specification can now be divided into a series of lists which highlight key design decisions.

General Operations
- There will be one computer controlling the entire library.
- The librarian will be the sole operator of the computer.
- There will be a single program to perform all necessary operations.

Transactions
- Check out a library book/periodical.
- Check in a library book/periodical.
- Get information about who checked out a book/periodical.
- Get information about what books/periodicals are currently borrowed on a card,
- Get list of books/periodicals checked out or overdue.
- Get lists sorted by library item or card holder.

Maintaining the collection
- Add a book/periodical to the collection.
- Remove a book/periodical from the collection.
- List all books/periodicals in collection.

Maintaining the list of library cards
- Add a library card.
- Remove a library card.
- List all library cards..

Saving the system's information
- Save all information to disk.
- Load all information from disk.

Other desirable operations

- Print out overdue notices.
- Look up books/periodicals by title or author.
- List books/periodicals by location in the library.

We will omit all these last operations in order to keep the program relatively straight forward.

All the command options will be available in a menu to the librarian who will select a command to produce the result.

# A.2 Specifications for the Library Information System

A library consisting of books and periodicals is to be used by both staff and students. Library items may be borrowed for a period of two weeks. Each user is issued a library card. For each card a list is kept in the system of the library items that are currently on loan to that card holder including the dates on which the item is due back. As well, a list must be kept of all library items.

Libraries also need a record of the identification of the borrower (if it is currently on loan) and the date it is due to be returned. The librarian supervises borrowing and returning so that, when a transaction occurs, the two lists of library items and library cards are appropriately updated.

It should be possible to save and reload the current status of the two lists in a secondary storage file. As new library items are added to the library or items removed, the library item list is updated. Similarly, the library card list is updated as new library cards are issued or cards cancelled.

The library supervisor should also be able to output all the entries in each list, output only those library items checked out or overdue, or output the information on any individual item in either list.

# A.3 The User Interface

We will not concentrate on a fancy graphical user interface for this problem. We will use a simple text menu of the various commands available to the library supervisor and requests for information when changes are being made to either the library item list or the library card list.

# A.4 Choosing Objects and Classes

The first step in designing a larger object-oriented program is to look at the specification to find all the classes that the program might involve. It is common for a design to go through several iterations before a final decision is made on what classes are to be incorporated into the program.

In general, there are three different types of classes that we look for:

- classes that are to be instantiated multiple times
- classes that will only be instantiated once, and
- classes that are not instantiated but are essentially groups of related methods (like the *Math* class).

This last type of class often consists of a group of **static** methods. It should be noted that classes which we are only going to use a single object (the second type) could also be implemented as a set of **static** fields and **static** methods. However, this reduces the flexibility of the program. While we may only need one object of the class right now, by avoiding **static** fields and methods, we allow for the creation of multiple objects of the class at a later date.

When we look at the specification for the program, four classes are immediately obvious:

- books,
- periodicals,

- student library cards, and
- staff library cards.

In each of these classes, an object is instantiated for each physical object. For example, ten books will be stored as ten separate objects of the *Book* class.

Having decided on the four classes, we should define a preliminary set of fields and methods for the classes. The *Book* class would contain fields for title, author, ISBN, and location in the library. The *Periodical* class would contain fields for title, ISSN, issue number, and location in the library. The *StudentCard* class would contain the card holder's name and student number. The *StaffCard* class would contain the card holder's name and office number.

Methods for the *Book* class would include:

- methods to read and write the book to a file,
- methods to list all the information about the book, and
- methods to check the book out and in.

Not too surprisingly, the *Periodical* class would require a similar set of methods, although the implementation of the methods would certainly differ. For example, the information displayed about a book differs from the information displayed about a periodical.

Methods for the *StudentCard* and *StaffCard* classes are again similar. We will need methods to read and write the cards to a file and to indicate which books have been checked out on a given card.

Now that we have a list of classes, we need to create reasonable class hierarchies. As Chapter 14 illustrates, there are numerous advantages to creating class hierarchies such as:

- easier bug fixing,
- easier addition of features,
- greater program clarity,
- more compact program size, and
- greater flexibility.

To find classes that can be placed in a hierarchy, we look at classes that share a number of fields and methods in common.

The first choice is fairly obvious. The *Book* and *Periodical* classes contain a number of common fields and methods. In some cases, the implementation of the methods might differ. Often, however, many of the methods are the same with only slight differences between the objects. We must then decide whether *Book* should inherit from *Periodical*, *Periodical* inherit from *Book*, or both *Book* and *Periodical* should inherit from a new super class. Because books are not a kind of periodical and periodicals are not a kind of book, we go with the third option and make them descend from a common ancestor.

Another way of coming to the same decision is to examine the fields. If the fields and methods of one object are a superset of another, then the first object should inherit from the second. That is not the case here, so we create a separate super class containing the common fields and methods.

This common class we call *LibraryItem*. The *Book* and *Periodical* class as inherit from it. The fields of the *LibraryItem* include the title and location of the item in the library. The *Book* class contains the ISBN field and the *Periodical* class contains the ISSN and author fields and issue number fields. The *LibraryItem* item is declared **abstract** because it is not meant to be instantiated directly.

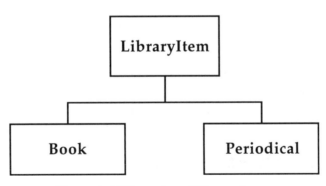

Figure A.1 Hierarchy of Library Items

The *StudentCard* and *StaffCard* classes share common fields such as the card holder name and common methods (all their methods are in common). We will create a *LibraryCard* class from which *StudentCard* and *StaffCard* inherit. The *LibraryCard* class is also declared **abstract** as it is never instantiated directly.

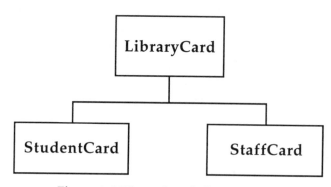

Figure A.2 Hierarchy of Library Cards

Having decided on two class hierarchies, we return to searching the specification for possible classes. Examining the specification further, we find two other objects. The library collection is an object in itself. One of its fields is a list of all the books and periodicals in the collection. Likewise, the list of library cards is an object. In this case, we are unlikely to instantiate more than a single instance of either the library collection or list of library cards. It is a good idea, however, to make these proper classes since someday our program may be required to control several library collections. Implementing the library collection as a proper class preserves the possibility of instantiating multiple objects without forcing a major rewrite of the class.

Because the library collection object will be managing the list of items that the library carries, we call the class the *LibraryItemManager*. The list of library cards becomes the *LibraryCardManager*. The data for the *LibraryItemManager* will be the collection of books and periodicals in the library that is a list of *LibraryItems*. The methods of the *LibraryItemManager* will include methods to add a book/periodical to the collection, list books/periodicals in the collection, and so on. In general, anytime the system refers to a particular book, it will use the *LibraryItemManager* to find the specific *Book* object and then use the

*Book* object's methods. Both the *LibraryItemManager* and the *LibraryCardManager* will have methods to add or remove elements from the list and to display the items on the list.

Making the *LibraryItemManager* and *LibraryCardManager* subclasses of a super class should be considered. In each case we are dealing with a list which must be managed. However, closer examination reveals that almost everything else would differ between the classes. The save and load functions would be completely different as would major aspects of creating an item to be added to the list. It is important to realize that it is possible to produce a bad class hierarchy where the subclasses have too little in common with the super class. In such a case, you can actually increase the size of the program and reduce the clarity. We decide to leave the two classes separate.

The final object is the library itself. It contains both a *LibraryItemManager* object (a book/periodical collection) and a *LibraryCardManager* object (a list of library cards). It provides the main menu to take commands from the user and call the appropriate methods in the *LibraryItemManager* and *LibraryCardManager* objects to perform the command.

This is another case where only one object of the class will be instantiated. Again, we will make this into a proper class by avoiding static fields and methods since we can imagine the day that a single program might control several smaller libraries sharing a building. Each library would have its own collection and list of library card holders. We call this class the *LibrarySupervisor*.

We will also need an application class to start the entire program. The *LibraryMain* class has a *main* method which creates a *LibrarySupervisor* object and then calls a method in *LibrarySupervisor* to make the supervisor read and execute commands.

Finally, we are likely to use a number of "helper" methods to output a string to a specified field size, read a string from a file, and so on. These are methods that are not directly related to any one class, but are used in a variety of places in the same way that methods from the *Math* class are used. Like *Math*, the *Misc* class does not need to be instantiated; all its methods are labelled as **public** and **static**.

# A.5  Choosing Fields and Methods for Each Class

Now that we have decided on the classes that we will be using we must choose appropriate fields and methods for each class.

At this point, we have only a vague idea of the fields and methods for each class. We must now produce an exact specification for the interface of each class, that is, the specification of all the public methods of each class. It is not absolutely necessary to produce a list of the fields of the class since the programmer who implements the class decides which fields to use internally. Having a list of fields, however, is helpful when determining the interface of a class.

To determine what methods and fields are required for each class, we produce a rough implementation for all the classes. This helps determine what methods are needed in the interface of each of the other classes. When this is done for all the classes in the program, we will have specified the interface for each of the classes in the design.

Once we have specified the interface for each of the classes, we can review the individual interfaces. We should consider adding methods to the interface that would make the class easier for other programs to use. Software reusability is one of the most important aspects of the object-oriented paradigm, and designing a class with an eye to its reusability is an important step in that direction.

In the rest of this section, we will examine each class in the program. After each class, we will show the class' interface "so far" in a double box. As we examine each method in the class, we will add fields and methods to the interface. The new fields and methods are shown in a single box. The box is followed by the explanation of the method's implementation. We will begin with the main program, *LibraryMain*, and work "downward".

Here is the list of classes along with fields and methods defined for them. The exact field and method names are not yet specified. As we refine the definitions, we will list fields and methods with their actual data type and names with the names in italics.

```
LibraryItem
      fields:        title, location
      methods:       load, save, list info, check out, check in
Book inherits from LibraryItem
      fields:        author, ISBN
Periodical inherits from LibraryItem
      fields:        ISSN, issue number
LibraryCard
      fields:        name
      methods:       load, save, list info, check out, check in
StudentCard
      fields:        student number
StaffCard
      fields:        office number
LibraryItemManager
      fields:        list of LibraryItems
      methods:       add an item, remove an item, list all items
LibraryCardManager
      fields:        list of LibraryCards
      methods:       add a card, remove a card, list all cards
LibrarySupervisor
      fields:        library collection, list of library cards
LibraryMain
      methods:       static void main (String[] args)
```

# A.5.1 LibraryMain – main Method

```
LibrarySupervisor
      methods:       constructor LibrarySupervisor (String fileName)
                     void handleCommands ()
```

The *LibraryMain* file contains a single method, *main*. The *main* method creates a *LibrarySupervisor* object and then calls the *handleCommand* method to make the *LibrarySupervisor* object receive and execute orders. The *LibraryMain* class contains a single static field representing the name of the file in which all the library's data is stored. This means that a separate application program is required for each library as it would be disastrous for different libraries to be saved in the same file.

## A.5.2   LibrarySupervisor class

*LibrarySupervisor*
    fields:    *LibraryItemManager libraryItemManager*
                   *LibraryCardManager libraryCardManager*
                   *String libraryDataBaseFile*

The *LibrarySupervisor* class contains a field for the library collection called *libraryItemManager*. *libraryItemManager* is an object of the *LibraryItemManager* class. The *LibrarySupervisor* class also contains a field for the list of library cards called *libraryCardManager* which is an object of the *LibraryCardManager* class. Commonly in Java programs, when only a single instance of a class is used in a class or method, the instance's name is the same as the class' except that it starts with a lower case letter rather than an upper case letter. The *LibrarySupervisor* class also has a field *libraryDataBaseFile* that contains the name of the file from which all the library data is loaded and to which it is saved.

We now examine the *LibrarySupervisor* class in detail to determine what methods and fields in other classes it will require. Here are the commands provided by *LibrarySupervisor*'s *handleCommands* method.

- Check out an item.
- Check in an item.
- List checked out items.
- List overdue books.
- Get information about a library item.
- Get information about a library card.
- Add an item to the collection.
- Remove an item from the collection.
- List the items in the collection.
- Add a library card .
- Remove a library card.
- List all the library cards.
- Exit, saving all the library's data to a file.

Because of the breadth of the *handleCommands* method, we will discuss each operation command it executes in a separate subsection.

| | |
|---|---|
| *LibraryItem* | |
| fields: | **int** *libraryItemID* |
| *LibraryCard* | |
| fields: | **int** *libraryCardID* |

This list of commands makes it obvious that we need some way of referring to a book or periodical. Rather than referring to the title, which can easily be spelled incorrectly and does not distinguish between multiple copies of the same book or periodical, each item in the library must have an ID number. The same also applies to library cards. We create two new fields for the ID numbers: *libraryItemID* in *LibraryItem* and *libraryCardID* in *LibraryCard*.

# LibrarySupervisor Constructor

| | |
|---|---|
| *LibraryItemManager* | |
| methods: | constructor *LibraryItemManager* (*DataInputStream in*) |
| | constructor *LibraryItemManager* () |
| *LibraryCardManager* | |
| methods: | constructor *LibraryCardManager* (*DataInputStream in*) |
| | constructor LibraryCardManager () |

When the *LibrarySupervisor* object is first instantiated, it attempts to read all the library data, that is, all the books, periodicals, and library cards from the file name passed as a parameter. It does this by attempting to open the library data file. If it successfully opens the library data file, it instantiates a *LibraryItemManager* object and passes in the open file as a parameter. The *LibraryItemManager* constructor must read all the data about the library items from the file.

After reading all the library items from the file, the *LibrarySupervisor* constructor instantiates a *LibraryCardManager* and passes the open file as a parameter. The *LibraryCardManager* constructor must read all the data about the library cards from the file.

If the *LibrarySupervisor* constructor is unable to open the file passed as a parameter, it creates an empty list of library cards. It creates this list by instantiating the *LibraryItemManager* and the *LibraryCardManager* objects using constructors with no parameters.

## handleCommands – Check out an item

```
LibraryItem
    fields:      int checkedOutByCardID
    methods:     void checkOutLibraryItem (int libraryCardID)
LibraryCard
    fields:      list of ints checkedOutLibraryItem
    methods:     void addLibraryItemToCheckOut (int libraryItemID)
LibraryItemManager
    methods:     LibraryItem findLibraryItemFromID (int libraryItemID)
LibraryCardManager
    methods:     LibraryCard findLibraryCardFromID (int libraryCardID)
```

The program goes through the following steps to check out a library item.

- Get the ID number of the library item to be checked out.
- Look up the *LibraryItem* object with the item ID using the *findLibraryItemFromID* method of the *LibraryItemManager* class.
- Get the ID number of the library card checking out the item.
- Look up the *LibraryCard* object with the card ID using the *findLibraryCardFromID* method of the *LibraryCardManager* class.
- Call the *checkOutLibraryItem* method of the *LibraryItem* object using the library card ID as a parameter.
- Call the *addLibraryItemToCheckOut* method of the *LibraryCard* object using the library item ID as a parameter.

New fields are needed to perform these tasks. The *LibraryItem* class needs a *checkedOutByCardID* field which contains the ID of the card used to check the item out. If it is set to zero, then the item is not checked out. The *LibraryCard* class needs a *checkedOutLibraryItem* field which is a list of the library item IDs which have been checked out with this card. The exact implementation of the list need not be decided at this time.

The *LibraryItemManager* class has a *findLibraryItemFromID* method. The method takes a library item ID as a parameter and returns the *LibraryItem* that matches the item ID. The *LibraryCardManager* class has a *findLibraryCardFromID* method. The method takes a library card ID as a parameter and returns the *LibraryItem* that matches the card ID.

The *LibraryItem* class needs a *checkOutLibraryItem* method. This method takes a library card ID as a parameter and sets the *checkedOutByCardID* field to check the item out. The *LibraryCard* class needs an *addLibraryItemToCheckOut* method. This method takes a library item ID as a parameter and adds the ID of the item to the *checkedOutLibraryItem* list.

## handleCommands – Check in an item

```
LibraryItem
    methods:        void checkInLibraryItem ()
                    int getCheckedOutByCardID ()
LibraryCard
    methods:        void removeLibraryItemFromCheckOut (int libraryItemID)
```

The program goes through the following steps To check out a library item.

- Get the ID number of the library item to be checked in.
- Look up the *LibraryItem* object with the item ID using the *findLibraryItemFromID* method of the *LibraryItemManager* class.
- Get the ID number of the library card used to check the item out using the *getCheckedOutByCardID* method of the *LibraryItem* class.
- Look up the *LibraryCard* object with the card ID using the *findLibraryCardFromID* method of the *LibraryCardManager* class.
- Call the *checkInLibraryItem* method of the *LibraryItem* object.
- Call the *removeLibraryItemFromCheckOut* method of the *LibraryCard* object using the library item ID as a parameter.

The *LibraryItem* class needs a *getCheckedOutByCardID* method. This method returns the *checkedOutByCardID* field. *LibraryItem* also needs a *checkInLibraryItem* method which sets the *checkedOutByCardID* field to zero.

*LibraryCard* needs a *removeLibraryItemFromCheckOut* method. This method takes a library item ID as a parameter and removes it from the *checkedOutLibraryItem* list.

## handleCommands – List checked out and overdue items

```
LibraryItem
    fields:        Calendar dueDate
LibraryItemManager
    methods:    void listCheckedOutLibraryItems
                        (LibraryCardManager libraryCardManager)
                void listOverdueLibraryItems
                        (LibraryCardManager libraryCardManager)
LibraryCardManager
    methods:    void listCheckedOutLibraryItems
                        (LibraryItemManager libraryItemManager)
```

Our program will allow checked out library items can be listed in either of two ways. The list of checked out library items can be sorted by library item ID or by the library card ID that checked them out. In the first case, we need a *listCheckedOutLibraryItems* method in the *LibraryItemManager* class, and in the second we need a *listCheckedOutLibraryItems* method in the *LibraryCardManager* class.

Because we will want to list the name of the card holder that checked out the book, we will need to pass the *libraryCardManager* as a parameter to the *listCheckedOutLibraryItems* method. Otherwise we would only see the library card ID and have no way of looking up the name. Likewise, to list the titles of the checked out books and periodicals, we need to pass the *libraryItemManager* as a parameter to allow the program to look up the title from the library item ID.

Listing the overdue library items is simply a call to a method in the *LibraryItemManager* class which we call *listOverdueLibraryItems*. This implies that *LibraryItem* must contain a due date that can be compared with the current date to determine if a library item is overdue. The *listOverdueLibraryItems* method takes a *libraryCardManager* as a parameter for the same reason as the *listCheckedOutLibraryItems* method does.

The *LibraryItem* class needs a *dueDate* field. We decide that the *dueDate* field should be a *Calendar* object from *java.util* package of the Java class library since *Calendar* allows calculations on dates. We will discuss the *Calendar* class in more detail later on.

Here are the three new methods in more detail. T h e *listCheckedOutLibraryItems* method of the *LibraryItemManager* class takes a *LibraryCardManager* object as a parameter and lists the checked out items in order of library item ID. It displays the card holder who checked the book out by name.

The *listOverdueLibraryItems* method displays overdue library books and the card holder who checked them out by name. This method also takes a *LibraryCardManager* object as a parameter.

*LibraryCardManager* class' *listCheckedOutLibraryItems* method lists the card ID and card holder name of each card which has checked out books. It also displays the checked out library items with their titles.

# handleCommands – Get information about a library item or card

```
LibraryItem
     methods:    abstract String longListing
                          (LibraryCardManager libraryCardManager)
Book inherits from LibraryItem
     methods:    String longListing
                          (LibraryCardManager libraryCardManager)
Periodical inherits from LibraryItem
     methods:    String longListing
                          (LibraryCardManager libraryCardManager)
LibraryCard
     methods:    abstract String longListing
                          (LibraryItemManager libraryItemManager)
StudentCard inherits from LibraryCard
     methods:    String longListing
                          (LibraryItemManager libraryItemManager)
StaffCard inherits from LibraryCard
     methods:    String longListing
                          (LibraryItemManager libraryItemManager)
```

The program goes through the following steps to list the information about individual items in the collection.

- Get the ID number of the library item to be listed.
- Look up the *LibraryItem* object with the item ID using the *findLibraryItemFromID* method of the *LibraryItemManager* class.
- Get a *String* containing all the information on the item by calling the *longListing* method of the *LibraryItem* object.
- Display the *String*.

By not passing back information about the individual fields in an item, we allow each kind of *LibraryItem* to determine what information is to be displayed, rather than forcing the *LibrarySupervisor* to know details about each kind of *LibraryItem*. In fact, *LibrarySupervisor* does not make reference to the *Book* or *Periodical* classes. It is possible to add a new kind of *LibraryItem* without modifying *LibrarySupervisor* at all! Once again, in order to allow the *LibraryItem* to translate the library card ID in the *checkedOutByCardID* field to a name, we pass a *LibraryCardManager* object as a parameter.

Because each kind of library item will have its own data that must be displayed, each subclass of *LibraryItem* must implement the *longListing* method as well. At this point in the design, the *longListing* method in *LibraryItem* could be abstract, that is, have no body at all.

Listing individual library cards occurs in much the same way. We obtain a *LibraryCard* object and then call the *longListing* method of the object to obtain a *String*. We pass a *LibraryItemManager* as a parameter to translate the library item IDs of the checked out items into titles.

The *longListing* method of the *Book* class returns a *String* detailing all the information about the calling library item, including the name of any card holder who checked it out. It takes a *LibraryCardManager* object as a parameter. The *LibrarySupervisor* currently writes out the information returned by *longListing* to standard output. This behaviour could be changed in a future version of the program (for example, to display the information in a window) without changing the *longListing* implementations.

## handleCommands – Add, Remove and List Items in Collection

> *LibraryItemManager*
> methods     **void** *addItem* ()
>                  **void** *removeItem (LibraryItem libraryItem)*
>                  **void** *listAllItems* ()

The *addItem, removeItem,* and *listAllItems* methods in the *LibraryItemManager* class add, remove, and list items in the collection. The *addItem* method has no parameters. It is responsible for getting the information about the item from the user and adding the new item to the collection. To remove an item from the collection, we get an item ID from the user, convert it to the *LibraryItem* object, and pass it as a parameter to the *removeItem* method which removes the item from library collection. The *listAllItems* method lists all the items in the library collection. The technique for displaying the data (window, console or standard output) will be decided in the *LibraryItemManager* class.

## handleCommands – Add, Remove and List Cards in the Library Card List

> *LibraryCardManager*
> methods:     **void** *addCard* ()
>                   **void** *removeCard (LibraryCard libraryCard)*
>                   **void** *listAllCards* ()

The *addCard, removeCard* and *listAllCards* methods of the *LibraryCardManager* class add, remove, and list cards in the list of library cards. The *addCard* method has no parameters. The *LibraryCardManager* is responsible for getting the information about the library card from the user and adding the new card to the list of library cards. To remove a card from the collection, we get the card's ID from the user, convert it to the *LibraryCard* object, and pass it as a parameter to the *removeCard* method which removes the card from library card list. The *listAllCards* method lists all the cards in the list. The technique for displaying the data (window, console or standard output) will be decided in the *LibraryCardManager* class.

## handleCommands – Exiting and Saving Library Data

> *LibraryItemManager*
>     methods:    **void** *save (DataOutputStream out)*
> *LibraryCardManager*
>     methods:    **void** *save (DataOutputStream out)*

When the librarian chooses to exit the program, the *LibrarySupervisor* object attempts to save all the library's data to a file. It does this by opening a file with the same name as was originally passed in to the constructor. It calls the *save* method of the *libraryItemManager* field with the open file as a parameter, which saves the content of the library collection to the file. It then calls the *save* method of the *libraryCardManager* field with the open file as a parameter, which saves the list of library cards to the file.

The *save* method of the *LibraryItemManager* class takes a *DataOutputStream* method as a parameter to the method and saves all the library items in the collection to the *DataOutputStream*. The *save* method of the *LibraryCardManager* takes a *DataOutputStream* method as a parameter to the method and saves all the list of library cards to the *DataOutputStream*.

## Class Interfaces After LibrarySupervisor

Now that we have finished analyzing *LibrarySupervisor* we can look at the list of fields and methods for our classes. We will also give actual names and data types to most of the fields in the classes. Remember, these are only guidelines for the fields and the implementer of the class is free to use different fields names as long as all the methods are correctly implemented.

> *LibraryItem*
>     fields:      *String title*
>                  *String location*
>                  **int** *libraryItemID*
>                  **int** *checkedOutByCardID*
>                  *java.util.Calendar dueDate*
>     methods:    load, save, list info
>                  **void** *checkOutLibraryItem (**int** libraryCardID)*
>                  **int** *getCheckedOutByCardID ()*

**void** *checkInLibraryItem* ()

**abstract** *String longListing*
        *(LibraryCardManager libraryCardManager)*

*Book* inherits from *LibraryItem*
    fields:    *String author*
                *String isbn*
    methods:  *String longListing*
                *(LibraryCardManager libraryCardManager)*

*Periodical* inherits from *LibraryItem*
    fields:    *String issn*
                *String issueNumber*
    methods:  *String longListing*
                *(LibraryCardManager libraryCardManager)*

*LibraryCard*
    fields:    *String name*
                **int** *libraryCardID*
                list of **ints** *checkedOutLibraryItem*
    methods:  load, save, list info
                **void** *addLibraryItemToCheckOut* (**int** *libraryItemID*)
                **void** *removeLibraryItemFromCheckOut* (**int** *libraryItemID*)
                **abstract** *String longListing*
                *(LibraryItemManager libraryItemManager)*

*StudentCard*
    fields:    *String studentNumber*
    methods:  *String longListing*
                *(LibraryItemManager libraryItemManager)*

*StaffCard*
    fields:    *String officeNumber*
    methods:  *String longListing*
                *(LibraryItemManager libraryItemManager)*

*LibraryItemManager*
    fields:    list of *LibraryItems*
    methods:  constructor *LibraryItemManager (DataInputStream in)*
                constructor *LibraryItemManager* ()
                **void** *save (DataOutputStream out)*
                *LibraryItem findLibraryItemFromID* (**int** *libraryItemID*)
                **void** *listCheckedOutLibraryItems*
                *(LibraryCardManager libraryCardManager)*
                **void** *listOverdueLibraryItems*
                *(LibraryCardManager libraryCardManager)*
                **void** *addItem* ()

```
        void removeItem (LibraryItem libraryItem)
        void listAllItems ()
LibraryCardManager
    fields:      list of LibraryCards
    methods:     constructor LibraryCardManager (DataInputStream in)
                 constructor LibraryCardManager ()
                 void save (DataOutputStream out)
                 LibraryCard findLibraryCardFromID (int libraryCardID)
                 void listCheckedOutLibraryItems
                         (LibraryItemManager libraryItemManager)
                 void addCard ()
                 void removeCard (LibraryCard libraryCard)
                 void listAllCards ()
LibrarySupervisor
    fields:      LibraryItemManager libraryItemManager
                 LibraryCardManager libraryCardManager
                 String libraryDataBaseFile
    methods:     constructor LibrarySupervisor (String fileName)
                 void handleCommands ()
LibraryMain
    methods:     static void main (String[] args)
```

## A.5.3   LibraryItemManager

We now produce a rough design of the *LibraryItemManager* class in order to determine what methods will be required in other classes. We do this by creating a design for each method in the class' interface including the constructors. We are not going to examine how the list of library items will be stored. That decision will be left up to the implementer of the *LibraryItemManager* class.

## LibraryItemManager Constructors

```
Book
    methods:     constructor Book (DataInputStream in)
Periodical
    methods:     constructor Periodical (DataInputStream in)
```

The first constructor, *LibraryItemManager (DataInputStream in)*, should read the collection from the file passed as a parameter. The file will consist of a list of data from each of the items in the collection, one after another.

We will create the appropriate object for each item (*Book* or *Periodical*) reading the object's data from the file. The best means of doing this is to have a constructor in *Book* and *Periodical* that has the *DataInputStream* as a parameter. The *LibraryItemManager* constructor reads in the number of items in the collection. For each item, it reads in the kind of item (book or periodical) and then instantiates an object of the appropriate class passing the file as a parameter to the constructor. The constructor reads the data file to get the information for the item. The item is then added to the list of items in the collection.

Note that this means that *LibraryItemManager* must be aware of the kinds of *LibraryItems* available. If we add a new kind of *LibraryItem*, we will have to modify this part of *LibraryItemManager*.

Two constructors are necessary, one for the *Book* class and one for the *Periodical* class, each taking a *DataInputStream* as a parameter.

The constructor for an empty list needs no external methods as it does not instantiate any items.

## LibraryItemManager – save Method

---

*LibraryItem*
    methods:    **abstract void** *save* (*DataOutputStream out*)
*Book* inherits from *LibraryItem*
    methods:    **void** *save* (*DataOutputStream out*)
*Periodical* inherits from *LibraryItem*
    methods:    **void** *save* (*DataOutputStream out*)

---

The *save* method uses the same technique as the constructor to make the library item objects do all the work. The *save* writes the number of items in the library collection to the data file passed in as a parameter. It then calls the *save* method of the item for each item in the collection. This means that the *LibraryItem* class will need a *save* method. The *save* method of *LibraryItem* will obviously not be the same for all kinds of *LibraryItem*, so *Book* and *Periodical* will need their own *save* methods. All the *save* methods will have the *DataOutputStream* as a parameter.

## LibraryItemManager – findLibraryItemFromID Method

| *LibraryItem* |
| methods:    **int** *getLibraryItemID* () |

The *findLibraryItemFromID* method must traverse the list of *LibraryItems* searching for the item that matches the library item ID that was passed in. It then returns the *LibraryItem* that matched. This means that we need a *getLibraryItemID* method in the *LibraryItem* class that returns the item's *libraryItemID* field.

## LibraryItemManager – listCheckedOutLibraryItems and listOverdueLibraryItems Methods

| *LibraryItem* | |
| methods: | *String getTitle* () |
| | *String getDueDate* () |
| | **boolean** *isOverdue* () |
| *LibraryCard* | |
| methods: | *String getName* () |
| *Misc* | |
| methods: | *String sizeString* (*String s*, **int** *fieldSize*) |

The *listCheckedOutLibraryItems* method goes through all the library items in the collection, checking if the ID returned by the *getCheckedOutByCardID* method of each *LibraryItem* is not zero. If it is not zero, then we list the library item on a line. We must decide what sort of information we want to list. The *listOverdueLibraryItems* method is similar, but lists items for which the item's *isOverdue* method returns **true.**

In this program, we list the ID number and title of the item, the ID and name of the library card that checked it out, and the due date. To get the title, the *LibraryItem* class needs a *getTitle* method. To obtain the item's due date in readable format, the *LibraryItem* class needs a *getDueDate* method. To obtain the name of the cardholder who checked the book out, we need to obtain the *LibraryCard* object corresponding to the library card ID. This is done using the *findLibraryCardFromID* method of the *LibraryCardManager* class to produce a *LibraryCard* and then calling the *LibraryCard*'s *getName* method. (This is the reason we passed in a *LibraryCardManager* object to this method. )

Finally, because we want a list of many items, we need to format the list. To help format the list we create a *sizeString* method in the *Misc* class that returns a *String* formatted to a certain field width. We add this method as a **public static** method to *Misc* because we anticipate it being used by many other classes and there is nothing in it that depends on a particular class.

## LibraryItemManager – addItem Method

> *Book* inherits from *LibraryItem*
>     methods:     constructor *Book* (**int** *libraryItemID*)
> *Periodical* inherits from *LibraryItem*
>     methods:     constructor *Periodical* (**int** *libraryItemID*)
> *LibraryItemManager*
>     fields:         **int** *currentLibraryItemID*

The *addItem* method is used to create new items in the collection. It requires us to instantiate a new *Book* or *Periodical* object. *LibraryItems* are never instantiated directly because everything in the collection is a book or a periodical. We ask the user for the kind of library item to be added. This requires that this section of the *LibraryItemManager* must also refer to all the different kinds of library items. If we add new kinds of library items, we will need to update the *addItem* method.

To minimize the rewriting necessary when changes are made to the *Book* or *Periodical* classes, we do not get all the information about the item in the *LibraryItemManager* class. Instead, we allow the *Book* and *Periodical* constructor to ask the user for all the information. In this way, the *LibraryItemManager* contains as little information as possible about the different kinds of *LibraryItems*.

The one field of the library item that must be assigned by the *LibraryItemManager* is the *libraryItemID*. It is important that this be unique for each item in the library. This means that the ID is passed to the *Book* or *Periodical* constructor and that *LibraryItemManager* keeps track of the IDs. The current library ID will be kept in a *currentLibraryItemID* field. The *LibraryItemManager* class guarantees that each library item gets a unique ID. It does this by issuing the IDs and incrementing the current ID by one each time a library item is created. It also means that this field must be saved in the data file along with the number of library items in the collection.

## LibraryItemManager – removeItem Method

The *removeItem* method gets passed a *LibraryItem* from the user and removes it from the library collection. This is done by searching the list of items for the specified *LibraryItem* and removing it from the list. No new methods are required.

## LibraryItemManager – listAllItems Method

```
LibraryItem
    methods:    abstract String shortListing ()
Book inherits from LibraryItem
    methods:    String shortListing ()
Periodical inherits from LibraryItem
    methods:    String shortListing ()
```

The *listAllItems* method goes through each element in the list of *LibraryItems* and calls a new method called *list* of the *LibraryItem* class. Given that we would likely wish to have a different set of data output from books and periodicals, we need to have a *shortListing* method for the *Book* and *Periodical* class. This method should return a *String* with all the information to be printed. By returning a *String* rather than outputting the data itself to the screen, we can change the display later without rewriting all the subclasses of *LibraryItem*. For example, we might wish to have the listing displayed in a window with a scrolling text box rather than being sent to standard output. This can be done by changing the *listAllCards* method rather than changing the *list* method of the *Book* and *Periodical* classes.

## Class Interfaces After LibraryItemManager

Here is the listing of the changed classes now that we have analyzed *LibraryItemManager*.

*LibraryItem*
    fields:        *String title*
                      *String location*
                      **int** *libraryItemID*
                      **int** *checkedOutByCardID*
                      *java.util.Calendar dueDate*
    methods:    **void** *checkOutLibraryItem* (**int** *libraryCardID*)
                      **int** *getCheckedOutByCardID* ()
                      **void** *checkInLibraryItem* ()
                      **abstract void** *save* (*DataOutputStream out*)
                      **abstract** *String longListing*
                                    (*LibraryCardManager libraryCardManager*)
                      **abstract** *String shortListing* ()
                      **int** *getLibraryItemID* ()
                      *String getTitle* ()
                      *Calendar getDueDate* ()

*Book* inherits from *LibraryItem*
    fields:        *String author*
                      *String isbn*
    methods:    constructor *Book* (*DataInputStream in*)
                      constructor *Book* (**int** *libraryItemID*)
                      **void** *save* (*DataOutputStream out*)
                      *String longListing*
                                    (*LibraryCardManager libraryCardManager*)
                      *String shortListing* ()

*Periodical* inherits from *LibraryItem*
    fields:        *String issn*
                      *String issueNumber*
    methods:    constructor *Periodical* (*DataInputStream in*)
                      constructor *Periodical* (**int** *libraryItemID*)
                      **void** *save* (*DataOutputStream out*)
                      *String longListing*
                                    (*LibraryCardManager libraryCardManager*)
                      *String shortListing* ()

*LibraryCard*
    fields:        *String name*
                      **int** *libraryCardID*
                      list of **ints** *checkedOutLibraryItem*
    methods:    load, save, list info
                      **void** *addLibraryItemToCheckOut* (**int** *libraryItemID*)

```
                    abstract String longListing (
                              LibraryItemManager libraryItemManager)
                    String getName ()
StudentCard
    fields:         String studentNumber
    methods:        String longListing
                              (LibraryItemManager libraryItemManager)
StaffCard
    fields:         String officeNumber
    methods:        String longListing
                              (LibraryItemManager libraryItemManager)
LibraryItemManager
    fields:         list of LibraryItems
                    int currentLibraryItemID
    methods:        constructor LibraryItemManager (DataInputStream in)
                    constructor LibraryItemManager ()
                    void save (DataOutputStream out)
                    LibraryItem findLibraryItemFromID (int libraryItemID)
                    void listCheckedOutLibraryItems
                              (LibraryCardManager libraryCardManager)
                    void listOverdueLibraryItems
                              (LibraryCardManager libraryCardManager)
                    void addItem ()
                    void removeItem ()
                    void listAllItems ()
Misc
    methods:        String sizeString (String s, int fieldSize)
```

## A.5.4   LibraryItem

The *LibraryItem* class is not meant to be instantiated directly. Several of its methods are abstract, that is, they are methods but do not necessarily contain code. They must be implemented by all subclasses of *LibraryItem*.

The *checkOutLibraryItem* and *checkInLibraryItem* methods set the *checkedOutByCardID* and *dueDate* fields. The *getCheckedOutByCardID* method returns the *checkedOutByCardID* field. The *getLibraryItemID* method returns the *libraryItemID* field. The *getTitle* method returns the *title* field. The *getDueDate* method returns the *dueDate* field. The *save*, *shortListing* and *longListing* methods are different for each kind of library item These methods may be abstract. It is only necessary that each kind of *LibraryItem* implement them.

The implementation of *LibraryItem* does not require any new methods or fields.

## A.5.5   Book

The *Book* class represents a book. In our design of this class, we will be attempting to place any code that is common to all *LibraryItems* in the *LibraryItem* class, rather than having a separate version for each kind of library item.

| *Misc* |
|---|
| methods:     *String readString (DataInputStream in)* |

The constructor will need to read all the fields from the file that is passed in as a parameter. Because there is no single method in *DataInputStream* to read as *String* from a file, we will create our own. Since our method will be used in a number of classes, we will place it in the *Misc* class. This method does not depend on any internal data, so it will be a **static** method. The method reads from a *DataInputStream* that is passed as a parameter.

| *LibraryItem* |
|---|
| methods:     constructor *LibraryItem (DataInputStream in)* |

Rather than reading in the common fields of *LibraryItem* in the constructor of each subclass of *LibraryItem*, we will use the *LibraryItem* constructor to read in the common data and then have each subclass read in the data that is specific to that subclass. This means the *LibraryItem* needs a constructor with a *DataInputStream* as a parameter.

| *LibraryItem* |
|---|
| methods:     constructor *LibraryItem* (**int** *libraryItemID*) |

The second constructor is required when the user inputs all the relevant information about the book. Once again, the best design is to have a constructor in *LibraryItem* that initializes the common fields with information from the user and then initializes the fields specific to the book.

This design can also be used for the *save, shortListing,* and *longListing* methods. The *LibraryItem* class can handle the common data, whether is it to format it for display or save it to file, and then have the methods handle the *Book* specific information. This means that the *save, shortListing,* and *longListing* methods of *LibraryItem* will not be abstract. They are not, however, to be called directly by any other class that subclasses of *LibraryItem*.

| Misc | |
|---|---|
| methods: | *String writeString (DataOutputStream out, String s)* |

The *save* method writes a number of *String* objects to the file. Just as is no single method to read a *String* from a binary file, there is no single method to write one. We create the *writeString* method of the *Misc* class to avoid duplicating the same section of program multiple times throughout the program. The method is declared **static**.

We have changed the *LibraryItem* and *Misc* classes slightly.

| LibraryItem | |
|---|---|
| fields: | *String title* |
| | *String location* |
| | **int** *libraryItemID* |
| | **int** *checkedOutByCardID* |
| | *Calendar dueDate* |
| methods: | constructor *LibraryItem (DataInputStream in)* |
| | constructor *LibraryItem* (**int** *libraryItemID*) |
| | **void** *save (DataOutputStream out)* |
| | *String shortListing ()* |
| | **void** *longListing* |
| | *(LibraryCardManager libraryCardManager)* |
| | **void** *checkOutLibraryItem* (**int** libraryCardID) |
| | **int** *getCheckedOutByCardID ()* |
| | **void** *checkInLibraryItem ()* |
| | **int** *getLibraryItemID ()* |
| | *String getTitle ()* |
| | *String getDueDate ()* |
| Misc | |
| methods: | *String sizeString (String s,* **int** *fieldSize)* |

> *String readString (DataInputStream in)*
> *String writeString (DataOutputStream out, String s)*

## A.5.6   Periodical

The *Periodical* class will not result in any further changes to the *LibraryItem* class interface. It is similar to a book except for handling different class specific fields.

## A.5.7   LibraryCardManager, LibraryCard, StudentCard, and StaffCard

We will not illustrate the development of the *LibraryCardManager*, *LibraryCard*, *StudentCard*, and *StaffCard* classes. Their development is similar to the *LibraryItemManager*, *LibraryItem*, *Book*, and *Periodical* classes. We recommend that you go through the development process with these four classes and compare the resulting set of interface with the interfaces in the next subsection.

## A.5.8   Class and Fields of the Library System

> *LibraryItem*
>     fields:      *String title*
>                   *String location*
>                   **int** *libraryItemID*
>                   **int** *checkedOutByCardID*
>                   *Calendar dueDate*
>     methods:   constructor *LibraryItem (DataInputStream in)*
>                   constructor *LibraryItem* (**int** *libraryItemID*)
>                   **void** *save (DataOutputStream out)*
>                   *String shortListing ()*
>                   **void** *longListing*
>                               (*LibraryCardManager libraryCardManager*)
>                   **void** *checkOutLibraryItem* (**int** libraryCardID)
>                   **void** *checkInLibraryItem ()*
>                   **int** *getLibraryItemID ()*

```
                         void checkInLibraryItem ()
                         int getLibraryItemID ()
                         int getCheckedOutByCardID ()
                         String getTitle ()
                         String getDueDate ()
Book inherits from LibraryItem
    fields:          String author
                     String isbn
    methods:         constructor Book (DataInputStream in)
                     constructor Book (int libraryItemID)
                     void save (DataOutputStream out)
                     String shortListing ()
                     String longListing
                             (LibraryCardManager libraryCardManager)
Periodical inherits from LibraryItem
    fields:          String issn
                     String issueNumber
    methods:         constructor Periodical (DataInputStream in)
                     constructor Periodical (int libraryItemID)
                     void save (DataOutputStream out)
                     String shortListing ()
                     String longListing
                             (LibraryCardManager libraryCardManager)
LibraryCard
    fields:          String name
                     int libraryCardID
                     list of ints checkedOutLibraryItem
    methods:         constructor LibraryCard (DataInputStream in)
                     constructor LibraryCard (int libraryCardID)
                     void save (DataOutputStream out)
                     abstract String longListing
                             (LibraryItemManager libraryItemManager)
                     void addLibraryItemToCheckOut (int libraryItemID)
                     void removeLibraryItemFromCheckOut (int libraryItemID)
                     int getLibraryCardID ()
                     String getName ()
                     String shortListing ()
StudentCard
    fields:          String studentNumber
    methods:         constructor StudentCard (DataInputStream in)
                     constructor StudentCard (int libraryCardID)
```

```
                    void save (DataOutputStream out)
                    String shortListing ()
                    String longListing
                            (LibraryItemManager libraryItemManager)
StaffCard
    fields:         String officeNumber
    methods:        constructor StaffCard (DataInputStream in)
                    constructor StaffCard (int libraryCardID)
                    void save (DataOutputStream out)
                    String shortListing ()
                    String longListing
                            (LibraryItemManager libraryItemManager)
LibraryItemManager
    fields:         list of LibraryItems
                    int currentLibraryItemID
    methods:        constructor LibraryItemManager (DataInputStream in)
                    constructor LibraryItemManager ()
                    void save (DataOutputStream out)
                    LibraryItem findLibraryItemFromID (int libraryItemID)
                    void listCheckedOutLibraryItems
                            (LibraryCardManager libraryCardManager)
                    void listOverdueLibraryItems
                            (LibraryCardManager libraryCardManager)
                    void addItem ()
                    void removeItem ()
                    void listAllItems ()
Misc
    methods:        String sizeString (String s, int fieldSize)
                    String readString (DataInputStream in)
```

## A.5.9 General Notes

The design of the library automation program has been guided by three principles.

- Design the classes so that they require as little knowledge of each other as possible. This is done so that when we modify one class' interface, it affects as few other classes as possible. A good design can be added to or changed without requiring massive rewrites.

- Design the program with clarity in mind. Make the underlying algorithms as obvious as possible. Not only does this make it easier for others to understand what has been done, it also greatly reduces the number of logic bugs that will occur in the program.

- Design the classes so that they are as flexible as possible. For example, rather than having the individual *Book* and *Periodical* classes display information about themselves, we return a *String* containing the information. The final method of display (in a window, in an hsa *Console*, or to standard output) can be changed in one location.

Unfortunately, these principles often conflict. Here are a few examples of design decision conflicts requiring judgment.

## Class Independence versus Flexibility

The code for the user interface (UI) can be unified in one or more classes, or each piece can be placed with the section of the program for which it is the interface. The advantage to the unified UI code is that it makes it simpler to change the UI to the program. Changing from a text interface to a graphical interface might not require modifying every class in the program. Also, consistency of the UI is easier to achieve by having all the code in one place.

The disadvantage to such an approach is that virtually every aspect of the program is dependent on the UI code. For example, a separate UI class would have to get data from the user for the fields in all of our classes. This would mean that a change to the otherwise internal fields of a class would necessitate a modification of the UI class. The "black box" nature of the classes could easily be lost.

Our design takes a middle route. The UI code is blended into the classes to eliminate all the classes depending on a single UI class. However, steps have been taken to unify the UI sections of many methods. For example, the *shortListing* and *longListing* methods return *Strings*. This allows the programmer to change to the UI for displaying information by modifying a single method rather than changing *LibraryItem*, *LibraryCard*, and all of their subclasses.

## Class Independence versus Clarity

Another design choice we made was to pass a *LibraryCardManager* object as a parameter to methods of the *LibraryItemManager*, *LibraryItem*, and *LibraryItem* subclasses. This was done to allow these classes to look up a card holder name from the card holder's ID. Doing this established the dependency of the *LibraryItemManager*, *LibraryItem*, and *LibraryItem* subclasses on *LibraryCardManager*. This means that if changes are made to the *LibraryCardManager* interface, we will need to examine all the dependent classes to make certain we are not changing needed methods. While this is not a problem for programs of the scale of the Library System, it is of great concern when projects contain hundreds of thousands of lines of code and involve thousands of classes. There is a great deal of difference between changing a class on which ten classes depend and changing a class on which two hundred classes depend.

If we had felt it necessary to eliminate this dependency, we could have created a method in *LibrarySupervisor* that was passed a library card ID and called the appropriate methods in the *LibraryCardManager* class. Then, instead of passing the *LibraryCardManager*, we would have passed the *LibrarySupervisor* object itself (using the keyword **this** as the parameter). The advantage to this design would be that a rewrite of *LibraryCardManager* would require only the change of the *LibrarySupervisor* class (which already depends on *LibraryCardManager* anyway). The disadvantage is that execution would be slower because there is an extra method call every time we look up a card holder's name and also we lose clarity of program design by adding a level of indirection. In our case, we chose greater clarity over increased class independence.

It is often helpful to look at the class dependencies using a diagram. Figure A.3 graphically displays the program's dependencies. A dashed line with an arrow means that a class depends on (calls methods from) another class. If there are arrows on both ends, the classes call methods from each other. In general, the fewer arrows between classes there are, the easier it is to modify the interfaces in a program's classes. Note that changes that do not modify the interface need not involve dependent classes. This is why it is preferable to properly design the interface of a class to start with rather than change the interface at a later point in time.

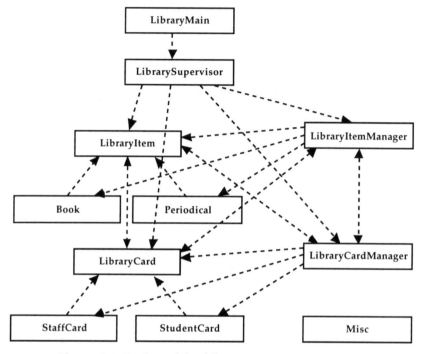

Figure A.3  Design of the Library Automation System

## Conclusion

As should be clear by now, the design of a larger system is not a clear cut set of decisions. There are many trade-offs involved. Experience allows the designer to be aware of the costs for each choice and to weigh the costs against each other.

# A.6   The Program Design

We have looked at the various classes of the library automation system program. We have also decided on the fields and methods that will be part of each class.

Having established the classes and their interfaces, we now look at implementation. We will not go into great detail as much of the implementation has been covered in the previous sections and the reasoning behind the implementation should be obvious from the class listing.

## A.6.1   LibrarySupervisor

## LibrarySupervisor – Constructor

The constructor attempts to open the library data file and then instantiate the library item collection object and the library cards object. It does this in a **try-catch** block. In this case, there are two **catch** blocks, one if a *FileNotFoundException* was generated, in which case the file was not found, and one if a *IOException* occurred, in which case an I/O error occurred when opening or reading the file.

If the open attempt succeeds, the *LibrarySupervisor* constructor instantiates the two objects using the contructors that read the list of library items and library cards from the file.

If the open fails, the program outputs a message that depends on which exception occurred. The *LibrarySupervisor* constructor then instantiates the two objects with no parameters. This creates empty copies of the library item collection and the list of library cards.

We place the statements that instantiate the two objects in the **try** block, so that if either constructor throws an *IOException* the program will print out the appropriate error message and instantiate empty copies of the library item collection and the list of library cards. This illustrates one of the advantages of exception handling. One block of error handling code handles all the possible I/O errors that can occur when reading the file. Note that we must allow the *LibraryItemManager* and *LibraryCardManager* constructors to throw *IOExceptions*.

# LibrarySupervisor – handleCommands Method

For clarity's sake we break *handleCommands* down by creating methods for use by the *LibrarySupervisor* class. These methods are called *getCommandFromKeyboard*, *executeCommand*, and *saveLibraryDatabase*. We define these methods to be **protected**.

The *getCommandFromKeyboard* method outputs the list of options and gets a legal command from the user. It returns an integer indicating the command the user selected. The *getCommandFromKeyboard* method does all the error checking.

The *getCommandFromKeyboard* method uses two nested **try-catch** blocks. The outer block handles the possibility of an *IOException* when reading from *System.in*. The inner **try-catch** block catches *NumberFormatExceptions* that might occur when attempting to convert from the *String* to an **int** using *Integer.parseInt*. The **try-catch** blocks are placed in a loop that exits only when a legal command is given.

The *executeCommand* method executes the command the user selected. This method is further broken down so that any command that takes more than two lines to execute becomes a method on its own. The *executeCommands* method is a large case statement based on the command the user entered. Here is the breakdown of the individual commands.

- Check out an item - Call the *checkOutLibraryItem* method.
- Check in an item - Call the *checkInLibraryItem* method.
- List checked out items by library item ID - Call the *listCheckedOutLibraryItems* method of the *LibraryItemManager* class.
- List checked out items by library card ID - Call the *listCheckedOutLibraryItems* method of the *LibraryCardManager* class.
- List overdue items by library item ID - Call the *listOverdueLibraryItems* method of the *LibraryItemManager* class.
- Get information about a library item - Call the *getLibraryItemInfo* method.

- Get information about a library card - Call the *getLibraryCardInfo* method.

- Add an item to the library collection - Call the *addItem* method of the *LibraryItemManager* class.

- Remove an item to the library collection - Get the library item and call the *removeItem* method of the *LibraryItemManager* class.

- List all items in the library collection - Call the *listAllItems* method of the *LibraryItemManager* class.

- Add a card to the list of library cards - Call the *addCard* method of the *LibraryCardManager* class.

- Remove a card from the list of library cards - Get the library card and call the *removeCard* method of the *LibraryCardManager* class.

- List all cards in the list of library cards - Call the *listAllCards* method of the *LibraryCardManager* class.

Once the user issues the quit command, the *handleCommands* method calls the *saveLibraryDatabase* method to save the collection of library items and the library card list. The *saveLibraryDatabase* method opens up the file as a *DataOutputStream* and passes the opened file to the *save* method of the library item collection. It then does the same for the list of library cards. The calls to the file opening and saving are placed in a **try-catch** block. This allows one block of error handling code to handle all possible I/O errors when opening, writing, and closing the file.

The design of the *checkOutLibraryItem*, *checkInLibraryItem*, *getLibraryItemInfo*, and *getLibraryCardInfo* methods is straightforward. We find, however, that we repeatedly need to get a library item or library card from the user. To avoid repeating the same section of code multiple times, we create a *getLibraryItem* method which queries the user for a library item. It looks up the *LibraryItem* object using the *findLibraryItemfromID* method of the *LibraryItemManager* class. We also create a *getLibraryCard* method which does the equivalent for library cards.

## A.6.2   LibraryItemManager

Because we have carefully hidden the implementation of the list of library items from the rest of the program, we can implement the collection of library items in a number of ways. The easiest technique is to use an array (as we have done here). To use an array, we need both the array and the number of active elements in the array. The disadvantage of a design using an array is that there is a maximum number of elements in the array. Other alternatives are to use a linked list such as the *List* class of Chapter 17 or the *Vector* class found in the *java.util* package of the Java class library.

## LibraryItemManager - Constructors

There are two constructors for *LibraryItemManager*. The first constructor has no parameters. It creates and initialized an empty array for the library items. The second constructor has an open file as a parameter. It calls the first constructor to create the array and then reads the *currentLibraryItemID* field, the number of library items in the file, and the list of library items from the file. If an *IOException* occurs while reading the file, the program throws the exception to the method that called the constructor (in this case, the *LibrarySupervisor* constructor).

To read the list of library items, the constructor reads the kind of item from the file. Once it has done that, it creates the appropriate library item and passes the file to the constructor so the constructor can read the item's data from the file.

## LibraryItemManager - save Method

The *save* method writes the *currentLibraryItemID* field, the number of library items in the collection, and the list of library items to the file. To write the list of library items, the *save* method calls the *save* method of each of the *LibraryItems* in the collection. Again, if an *IOException* occurs while reading the file, the program throws the exception to the method that called the constructor, the *saveLibraryDatabase* method of the *LibrarySupervisor* class.

## LibraryItemManager – listCheckedOutLibraryItems and listOverdueLibraryItems Methods

The two methods are implemented by going through the list of library items and printing a one-line summary of all the items that are either checked out or overdue. The one-line summary these methods produce differs from the summary produced by the *listAllItems* method in that it includes the name of the card holder who checked out the item. Thus we create a *outputShortListing* method that outputs the relevant information, converting the ID number of the library card into the card holder's name.

## LibraryItemManager – addItem Method

The *addItem* method is broken down into three parts:

- get the kind of item from the user,
- create the item and asking the user for additional information, and
- add the item to the list.

To make the program easier to understand, we create the *getItemKind* method to get the kind of item from the user, and the *createItem* method to instantiate the item. The item is added to the list of library items is inside the *addItem* method.

## LibraryItemManager – Other Methods

The *removeItem* method goes through the list of library items until a match occurs with the *LibraryItem* object passed in as a parameter. It then removes the item from the list by eliminating its place in the array.

The *listAllItems* method cycles through all the elements of the list, printing the result of the item's *shortListing* method.

The *getItemKind* method uses a **try-catch** block to catch *IOExceptions* because *addItem* does not handle them. It loops until the user gives legal input, although it allows users to cancel their request to add an item.

The *createItem* method creates the appropriate item, calling the item's constructor to get additional information about the item. The method places the constructors in a **try-catch** block so that the constructors do not have to handle *IOExceptions* themselves.

The *findLibraryItemFromID* iterates through the list of items until it finds the *LibraryItem* with an ID matching the ID passed in as a parameter. When it finds a match, it returns the matching *LibraryItem*.

# A.6.3   LibraryItem

## The Calendar Class

The *LibraryItem* class contains the fields common to the different library items. Among these fields is the *dueDate* field. which represents the date the item is due back in the library. We use the *Calendar* class of the *java.util* package to implement the *dueDate* field. This class is useful for doing date calculations. To create the initial due date, we call *Calendar.getInstance* () which returns an instance of the *Calendar* class set to the current date and time.

```
// The dueDate is instantiated to the current date and time
dueDate = Calendar.getInstance ();
```

To get a date two weeks in the future, we call the *add* method of the *Calendar* object with two parameters. We specify that we are adding days to the current date using *Calendar.DATE* for the first parameter. We specify the number of days by setting the second parameter to CHECK_OUT_TIME which has the value 14.

```
// Add two weeks to the number of days in the date
dueDate.add (Calendar.DATE, CHECK_OUT_TIME);
```

A complication occurs because we want to allow the user to return the book any time on the due date without penalty. At the moment, the *Calendar* date is set to two weeks from the minute (actually millisecond) that the book was checked out. To avoid this problem, we set the hours, minutes, and seconds of the *dueDate* object to be 11:59:59 PM. This is done using the *set* method with two parameters: the field of the *Calendar* to be set, and the value it is to be set to. We set the *Calendar.HOUR* field to 23 and the *Calendar.MINUTE* and *Calendar.SECOND* fields to 59.

```
// The library item is actually due any time during the last day, so
// set the time to 23:59:59 so that it's not overdue until the next day.
dueDate.set (Calendar.HOUR, 23);
dueDate.set (Calendar.MINUTE, 59);
dueDate.set (Calendar.SECOND, 59);
```

To determine if the due date has passed, we create a second *Calendar* object which represents the current date. We then call the *after* method with the *dueDate* field as a parameter. The *after* method returns true if the current date is after the *dueDate*, in which case the item is overdue.

```
Calendar currentDate;
currentDate = Calendar.getInstance ();
return currentDate.after (dueDate);
```

To save the *Calendar* object, we convert it into milliseconds since Jan 1, 1970. This is done by converting the *Calendar* object into a *Date* object using the *getTime* method of the *Calendar* class. The *Date* class is found in the Java class library's *java.util* package. The *Date* object can be converted into a **long** integer using the *getTime* method of the *Date* class. Note that despite having the same name, the two methods do completely different things. The **long** integer is saved to the file with the *writeLong* method of the *DataOutputStream* class.

```
out.writeLong (dueDate.getTime ().getTime ());
```

To read the *Calendar* object, the program reads in the **long** integer from the file. It creates a new *Calendar* object using *Calendar.getInstance ()*. It then creates a new *Date* object using the **long** as a parameter to the constructor. Finally, it calls the *setTime* method of the *dueDate* object using the *Date* as a parameter. This sets the *Calendar* object to represent the same date/time as the *Date* object.

```
dueDate = Calendar.getInstance ();
dueDate.setTime (new Date (dateInMillis));
```

There are a number of steps required to output the *dueDate* field as a readable *String*. First, we create a *DateFormat* object. The *DateFormat* class is in the Java class library's *java.text* package. We create a *DateFormat* object by calling the *DateFormat.getDateInstance* method with *DateFormat.MEDIUM* as a parameter. Different date formats are achieved by specifying different parameters. To get a *String*, we call the *format* method of the *DateFormat* object. This requires a *Date* object representing the date to be converted. We obtain the *Date* object using the *getTime* method of the *Calendar* class.

```
DateFormat dateFormat;
dateFormat = DateFormat.getDateInstance (DateFormat.MEDIUM);
return dateFormat.format (dueDate.getTime ());
```

## LibraryItems

The rest of *LibraryItem* is completely straightforward. We use the *readString* and *writeString* methods of *Misc* to read and write *Strings* to the *DataOutputStream* because no methods exist in the *DataOutputStream* class for writing of *Strings*. As well as saving space by avoiding duplication of code, using these methods insures that we read and write *Strings* in a compatible fashion.

## A.6.4   Book and Periodical

These two classes are also straightforward. They are designed to have the methods in *LibraryItem* handle all common data. We do this so that adding fields to *LibraryItem* does not require modifying the *Book* and *Periodical* class.

## A.6.5   LibraryCardManager

This class' design is similar to the *LibraryItemManager* class'. We do not need a separate *outputShortListing* method because there is only one method for listing of checked out items.

## A.6.6   LibraryCard, StaffCard, and StudentCard

The designs of these classes are similar to the *LibraryItem*, *Book*, and *Periodical* classes. We do not need to worry about the Calendar class because the *LibraryItem* class handles everything to do with dates.

# A.7   The Program

## A.7.1   LibraryMain

```
// The "LibraryMain" class.
// The main program for the Library Automation System.
public class LibraryMain
{
    protected static final String LIBRARY_DATA_FILE_NAME =
                                    "library.dat";

    // This method creates the LibrarySupervisor object and
    // calls the method to accept and execute orders.
    public static void main (String [] args)
    {
        LibrarySupervisor supervisor;

        // Creates the LibrarySupervisor object, passing in the name of
        // the file from which the library will be read and to which it
    // will be written.
        supervisor = new LibrarySupervisor (LIBRARY_DATA_FILE_NAME);

        // Gets commands from the user and executes them until the user
        // selects quit.
        supervisor.handleCommands ();
    } // main method
} // LibraryMain class
```

## A.7.2   LibrarySupervisor

```
// The "LibrarySupervisor" class.
// This class supervises the entire library including the
// library collection and the list of library cards.

import java.io.*;
```

```
public class LibrarySupervisor
{
    // Fields
    protected LibraryItemManager libraryItemManager;
    protected LibraryCardManager libraryCardManager;

    protected String libraryDataBaseFile;

    // The keyboard
    protected BufferedReader stdin =
        new BufferedReader (new InputStreamReader (System.in));

    // Constants
    protected static final int COMMAND_QUIT = -1;

    // The list of commands that can be entered by the librarian.
    protected static final int COMMAND_CHECK_OUT = 1;
    protected static final int COMMAND_CHECK_IN = 2;
    protected static final int COMMAND_LIST_CHECKED_OUT = 3;
    protected static final int
                COMMAND_LIST_CHECKED_OUT_BY_CARD = 4;
    protected static final int COMMAND_LIST_OVERDUE = 5;
    protected static final int COMMAND_GET_ITEM_INFO = 6;
    protected static final int COMMAND_GET_CARD_INFO = 7;
    protected static final int COMMAND_ADD_ITEM = 8;
    protected static final int COMMAND_REMOVE_ITEM = 9;
    protected static final int COMMAND_LIST_ALL_ITEMS = 10;
    protected static final int COMMAND_ADD_CARD = 11;
    protected static final int COMMAND_REMOVE_CARD = 12;
    protected static final int COMMAND_LIST_ALL_CARDS = 13;

    // These should be updated when more commands are added.
    protected static final int
                FIRST_COMMAND = COMMAND_CHECK_OUT;
    protected static final int
                LAST_COMMAND = COMMAND_LIST_ALL_CARDS;
```

```
// Create the library supervisor, reading the library's data from
// the file name in 'libraryDataFileName'.
public LibrarySupervisor (String libraryDataFileName)
{
    libraryDataBaseFile = libraryDataFileName;

    try
    {
        // Try to open the file for reading.  If it opens, instantiate
        // the collection and the list of cards, reading the data from the
        // file.
        FileInputStream fileInputStream;
        DataInputStream in;

        fileInputStream = new FileInputStream (libraryDataFileName);
        in = new DataInputStream (fileInputStream);
        libraryItemManager = new LibraryItemManager (in);
        libraryCardManager = new LibraryCardManager (in);
    }
    catch (FileNotFoundException e)
    {
        // Library data file was not found.  Instantiate an empty
        // collection and list of cards.
        System.out.println ("Library data file not found. " +
            "Starting with empty database");
        libraryItemManager = new LibraryItemManager ();
        libraryCardManager = new LibraryCardManager ();
    }
    catch (IOException e)
    {
        // An error occurred while attempting to open or read the
        // file.  Instantiate an empty collection and list of cards.
        System.out.println ("I/O Exception: " + e);
        System.out.println ("An I/O Exception occurred when " +
            " attempting to read the library data base.  Starting with " +
            " empty database");
        libraryItemManager = new LibraryItemManager ();
        libraryCardManager = new LibraryCardManager ();
    }
} // LibrarySupervisor constructor
```

```
// Get commands from the user and execute them.  Continue until
// the user selects quit.
public void handleCommands ()
{
    int command;

    do
    {
        command = getCommandFromKeyboard ();
        executeCommand (command);
    }
    while (command != COMMAND_QUIT);

    saveLibraryDatabase ();
} // handleCommands method

// Get a command from the user.
protected int getCommandFromKeyboard ()
{
    String line;
    int command;

    System.out.println ();
    System.out.println ("Commands");
    System.out.println ("—————————");
    System.out.println ("1 .. Check out an item");
    System.out.println ("2 .. Check in an item");
    System.out.println ("3 .. List checked out items by library item ID");
    System.out.println ("4 .. List checked out items by library card ID");
    System.out.println ("5 .. List overdue books");
    System.out.println ("6 .. Get information about a library item");
    System.out.println ("7 .. Get information about a library card");
    System.out.println ("8 .. Add an item to the library collection");
    System.out.println ("9 .. Remove an item from the library collection");
    System.out.println ("10 .. List all items in the library collection");
    System.out.println ("11 .. Add a library card");
    System.out.println ("12 .. Remove a library card");
    System.out.println ("13 .. List all library cards");
    System.out.println ("Q .. Quit (Saves data base)");
```

```
                // Loop until we get a legal command.
                while (true)
                {
                    System.out.println ();
                    System.out.print ("Command: ");

                    try
                    {
                        line = stdin.readLine ();
                        if (line.equalsIgnoreCase ("q"))
                        {
                            return COMMAND_QUIT;
                        }
                        try
                        {
                            command = Integer.parseInt (line);
                            if ((FIRST_COMMAND <= command) &&
                                (command <= LAST_COMMAND))
                            {
                                return command;
                            }

                            System.out.println ("Commands must be from " +
                                FIRST_COMMAND + " to " + LAST_COMMAND +
                                " or 'Q' ");
                        }
                        catch (NumberFormatException e)
                        {
                            System.out.println ("Commands must be a number " +
                                "or the letter 'q' ");
                        }
                    }
                    catch (IOException e)
                    {
                        System.out.println ("I/O Exception: " + e);
                        System.out.println ("An I/O Exception occurred when " +
                            "attempting to read a command.  Program exiting");
                        return COMMAND_QUIT;
                    }
                } // while
        } // handleCommands method
```

```java
// Get a library item ID from the user and convert it into a
// LibraryItem object.  If it fails, return null.
protected LibraryItem getLibraryItem ()
{
    int libraryItemID;
    LibraryItem libraryItem;

    while (true)
    {
        String line;

        System.out.print ("Enter the ID of the library item: ");
        try
        {
            line = stdin.readLine ();
        }
        catch (IOException e)
        {
            System.out.println ("I/O Exception: " + e);
            System.out.println ("An I/O Exception occurred when " +
                "attempting to read the library item ID. " +
                "Command cancelled");
            return null;
        }
        if (line.length () == 0)
        {
            System.out.println ("Command cancelled");
            return null;
        }
        try
        {
            libraryItemID = Integer.parseInt (line);
            break;
        }
        catch (NumberFormatException e)
        {
            System.out.println ("Library item ID must be a number");
        }
    } // while
```

```
            libraryItem = libraryItemManager.findLibraryItemFromID
                                                (libraryItemID);
        if (libraryItem == null)
        {
            System.out.println (libraryItemID +
                " is not a legal library item ID.  Command cancelled");
            return null;
        }


        return libraryItem;
    } // getLibraryItemID method

    // Get a library card ID from the user and convert it into a
    // LibraryCard object.  If it fails, return null.
    protected LibraryCard getLibraryCard ()
    {
        int libraryCardNumber;
        LibraryCard libraryCard;

        while (true)
        {
            String line;

            System.out.print ("Enter the library card number: ");
            try
            {
                line = stdin.readLine ();
            }
            catch (IOException e)
            {
                System.out.println ("I/O Exception: " + e);
                System.out.println ("An I/O Exception occurred when " +
                    "attempting to read the library card number. " +
                    "Command cancelled");
                return null;
            }
            if (line.length () == 0)
            {
                System.out.println ("Command cancelled");
                return null;
            }
```

```
        try
        {
            libraryCardNumber = Integer.parseInt (line);
            break;
        }
        catch (NumberFormatException e)
        {
            System.out.println ("Library card number must be a " +
                                              " number");

        }
    } // while

    libraryCard =
        libraryCardManager.findLibraryCardFromID (libraryCardNumber);
    if (libraryCard == null)
    {
        System.out.println (libraryCardNumber +
            " is not a legal library card number.  Command cancelled");
        return null;
    }


    return libraryCard;
} // getLibraryCardNumber method

// Check out a library item.  Get the library item to be checked out and
// the patron's library card, and then call the appropriate methods.
protected void checkOutLibraryItem ()
{
    LibraryCard libraryCard;
    LibraryItem libraryItem;

    // Get the library card number and convert it into a
    // LibraryCard object.
    libraryCard = getLibraryCard ();
    if (libraryCard == null)
        return;

    // Get the library item ID and convert it into a LibraryItem object.
    libraryItem = getLibraryItem ();
    if (libraryItem == null)
        return;
```

```
System.out.println (libraryCard.getName () + " is checking out " +
    libraryItem.getTitle ());

// Returns false if there was a problem and the command is
// cancelled.
if (libraryItem.checkOutLibraryItem (libraryCard.getLibraryCardID ()))
{
    libraryCard.addLibraryItemToCheckOut
                              (libraryItem.getLibraryItemID ());
}
} // checkOutLibraryItem method

// Check in a library item.  Get the library item to be checked in
// and call the appropriate methods.
protected void checkInLibraryItem ()
{
    int libraryCardNumber;
    LibraryCard libraryCard;
    LibraryItem libraryItem;

    // Get the library item ID and convert it into a LibraryItem object.
    libraryItem = getLibraryItem ();
    if (libraryItem == null)
        return;

    libraryCardNumber = libraryItem.getCheckedOutByCardID ();
    if (libraryCardNumber == LibraryCard.NOBODY)
    {
        System.out.println ("This book is not checked out!");
        return;
    }
    libraryCard =
        libraryCardManager.findLibraryCardFromID (libraryCardNumber);

    System.out.println (libraryItem.getTitle () + " checked out by " +
        libraryCard.getName () + " is now checked in.");

    libraryItem.checkInLibraryItem ();
    libraryCard.removeLibraryItemFromCheckOut
                              (libraryItem.getLibraryItemID ());
} // checkInLibraryItem method
```

```
// Displays all the information about a particular item in the library.
protected void getLibraryItemInfo ()
{
    LibraryItem libraryItem;

    // Get the library item ID and convert it into a LibraryItem object.
    libraryItem = getLibraryItem ();
    if (libraryItem == null)
        return;

    System.out.print (libraryItem.longListing (libraryCardManager));
} // getLibraryItemInfo method

// Displays all the information about a particular library card.
protected void getLibraryCardInfo ()
{
    LibraryCard libraryCard;

    // Get the library item ID and convert it into a LibraryItem object.
    libraryCard = getLibraryCard ();
    if (libraryCard == null)
        return;

    System.out.print (libraryCard.longListing (libraryItemManager));
} // getLibraryCardInfo method

// Executes the command that the user specified.  Asks for additional
// information as necessary.
protected void executeCommand (int command)
{
    LibraryCard libraryCard;
    LibraryItem libraryItem;

    switch (command)
    {
        case COMMAND_CHECK_OUT:
            checkOutLibraryItem ();
            break;
        case COMMAND_CHECK_IN:
            checkInLibraryItem ();
            break;
```

```
        case COMMAND_LIST_CHECKED_OUT:
            libraryItemManager.listCheckedOutLibraryItems
                                    (libraryCardManager);
            break;
        case COMMAND_LIST_CHECKED_OUT_BY_CARD:
            libraryCardManager.listCheckedOutLibraryItems
                                    (libraryItemManager);
            break;
        case COMMAND_LIST_OVERDUE:
            libraryItemManager.listOverdueLibraryItems
                                    (libraryCardManager);
            break;
        case COMMAND_GET_ITEM_INFO:
            getLibraryItemInfo ();
            break;
        case COMMAND_GET_CARD_INFO:
            getLibraryCardInfo ();
            break;
        case COMMAND_ADD_ITEM:
            libraryItemManager.addItem ();
            break;
        case COMMAND_REMOVE_ITEM:
            libraryItem = getLibraryItem ();
            libraryItemManager.removeItem (libraryItem);
            break;
        case COMMAND_LIST_ALL_ITEMS:
            libraryItemManager.listAllItems ();
            break;
        case COMMAND_ADD_CARD:
            libraryCardManager.addCard ();
            break;
        case COMMAND_REMOVE_CARD:
            libraryCard = getLibraryCard ();
            libraryCardManager.removeCard (libraryCard);
            break;
        case COMMAND_LIST_ALL_CARDS:
            libraryCardManager.listAllCards ();
            break;
    } // switch
} // executeCommand method
```

```
// Saves the library data base into the file specified in the
// constructor.
protected void saveLibraryDatabase ()
{
    FileOutputStream fileOutputStream;
    DataOutputStream out;

    try
    {
        // Opens the file and calls the save method of the
        // library items and cards.
        fileOutputStream = new FileOutputStream (libraryDataBaseFile);
        out = new DataOutputStream (fileOutputStream);
        libraryItemManager.save (out);
        libraryCardManager.save (out);
        out.close ();
    }
    catch (IOException e)
    {
        System.out.println ("I/O Exception: " + e);
        System.out.println ("An I/O Exception occurred when " +
            " attempting to write the library data base.  The library " +
            " data base was not be written successfully");
    }
} // saveLibraryDatabase method
} // LibrarySupervisor class
```

## A.7.3   LibraryItemManager

```
// The "LibraryItemManager" class.
// This class manages a list of library items (the library collection)

import java.io.*;
```

```java
public class LibraryItemManager
{
    // Fields

    // The list of LibraryItems in the collection.
    protected LibraryItem [] libraryItems;
    protected int numLibraryItems;

    // The current ID given to a new library item.
    protected int currentLibraryItemID;

    // The keyboard
    protected BufferedReader stdin =
        new BufferedReader (new InputStreamReader (System.in));

    // Constants
    protected static final int MAX_LIBRARY_ITEMS = 1000;

    protected static final int KIND_CANCEL = -1;
    protected static final int KIND_BOOK = 1;
    protected static final int KIND_PERIODICAL = 2;
    protected static final int CANCEL_CODE = -1;

    protected final static int INITIAL_LIBRARY_ITEM_ID_VALUE = 1000;

    // Constructor to initialize an empty collection.
    public LibraryItemManager ()
    {
        libraryItems = new LibraryItem [MAX_LIBRARY_ITEMS];
        numLibraryItems = 0;
        currentLibraryItemID = INITIAL_LIBRARY_ITEM_ID_VALUE;
    } // LibraryItemManager constructor

    // Constructor that reads in a list of library items
    // from the binary file 'out'.
    public LibraryItemManager (DataInputStream in) throws IOException
    {
        // Calls the constructor to initialize the empty collection.
        this ();

        int numberOfLibraryItemsInFile, libraryItemKind;
        LibraryItem libraryItem = null;
```

```
// The library items part of the data file has the following format:
//        The next library item ID to use
//        The number of library items stored
//        The library items
//
//        Each library item is stored as:
//            The library item kind
//            The library item data

// Reads the next library item ID to use.
currentLibraryItemID = in.readInt ();

// Reads the number of library items stored.
numberOfLibraryItemsInFile = in.readInt ();

// Loops for each item read in from the file.
for (int i = 0 ; i < numberOfLibraryItemsInFile ; i++)
{
    // Gets the kind of item (book or periodical).
    libraryItemKind = in.readInt ();

    // Creates the appropriate kind of LibraryItem.
    if (libraryItemKind == KIND_BOOK)
        libraryItem = new Book (in);
    else if (libraryItemKind == KIND_PERIODICAL)
        libraryItem = new Periodical (in);
    else
    {
        System.out.println ("FAILURE! Illegal library item kind = " +
            libraryItemKind);
        System.out.println ("Only " + numLibraryItems + " of " +
            numberOfLibraryItemsInFile + " loaded");
        break;
    }

    // Adds the newly created item to the list of library items.
    libraryItems [numLibraryItems] = libraryItem;
    numLibraryItems++;
}

System.out.println (numLibraryItems + " library items loaded");
} // LibraryItemManager constructor
```

```
// Saves all the items in the collection to the binary file 'out'.
public void save (DataOutputStream out) throws IOException
{
    // Writes the next library item ID to use.
    out.writeInt (currentLibraryItemID);

    // Reads the number of library items stored.
    out.writeInt (numLibraryItems);

    // Calls its 'save' method of each item in the collection.
    for (int i = 0 ; i < numLibraryItems ; i++)
    {
        // Writes the library item out to the file.
        libraryItems [i].save (out);
    }

    System.out.println (numLibraryItems + " library items saved");
} // save method

// Creates a new  library item by obtaining information from the user
// and adds the library item to the collection.
public void addItem ()
{
    int libraryItemKind;
    LibraryItem libraryItem;

    // Gets the kind of item to be added.
    libraryItemKind = getItemKind ();

    // Creates the item, obtaining the item's information from the user.
    libraryItem = createItem (libraryItemKind);
    if (libraryItem == null)
    {
        return;
    }

    // Adds the newly created item to the list of library items.
    libraryItems [numLibraryItems] = libraryItem;
    numLibraryItems++;
} // addItem method
```

```
// Removes a library item from the collection.
public void removeItem (LibraryItem libraryItem)
{
    for (int i = 0 ; i < numLibraryItems ; i++)
    {
        if (libraryItems [i] == libraryItem)
        {
            for (int j = i + 1 ; j < numLibraryItems ; j++)
            {
                libraryItems [j – 1] = libraryItems [j];
            }
            numLibraryItems—;
            return;
        } // if
    } // for
} // removeItem method

// Lists all the library items in the collection, one per line.
public void listAllItems ()
{
    for (int i = 0 ; i < numLibraryItems ; i++)
    {
        System.out.println (libraryItems [i].shortListing ());
    }
} // listAllItems method

// Lists all the checked out library items sorted by library item ID.
public void listCheckedOutLibraryItems (
    LibraryCardManager libraryCardManager)
{
    for (int i = 0 ; i < numLibraryItems ; i++)
    {
        // Lists the item if it is checked out.
        if (libraryItems [i].getCheckedOutByCardID () !=
                                LibraryCard.NOBODY)
        {
            outputShortListing (libraryItems [i], libraryCardManager);
        } // if
    } // for
} // listCheckedOutLibraryItems
```

```
// Lists all the overdue library items sorted by library item ID.
public void listOverdueLibraryItems (LibraryCardManager
                                                    libraryCardManager)
{
    for (int i = 0 ; i < numLibraryItems ; i++)
    {
        if (libraryItems [i].isOverdue ())
        {
            outputShortListing (libraryItems [i], libraryCardManager);
        } // if
    } // for
} // listOverdueLibraryItems

// Returns a LibraryItem object that has a specified library item ID.
public LibraryItem findLibraryItemFromID (int libraryItemID)
{
    for (int i = 0 ; i < numLibraryItems ; i++)
    {
        if (libraryItems [i].getLibraryItemID () == libraryItemID)
        {
            return libraryItems [i];
        }
    }

    return null;
} // findLibraryItemFromID method

// Reads the type of library item to be created from the keyboard.
protected int getItemKind ()
{
    String choice;

    while (true)
    {
        System.out.println ("Add item to the collection");
        System.out.println ();
        System.out.println ("1 .. Book");
        System.out.println ("2 .. Periodical");
        System.out.println ("Q .. Cancel");
        System.out.println ();
        System.out.print ("Choice: ");
```

```
        try
        {
            choice = stdin.readLine ();
        }
        catch (IOException e)
        {
            System.out.println ("I/O Exception: " + e);
            System.out.println ("An I/O Exception occurred when " +
                "attempting to create the library item.  " +
                "No item created");
            return KIND_CANCEL;
        }
        if (choice.equals ("1"))
            return KIND_BOOK;
        else if (choice.equals ("2"))
            return KIND_PERIODICAL;
        else if (choice.equalsIgnoreCase ("q"))
            return KIND_CANCEL;
        else
            System.out.println ("Enter 1, 2 or q");
    } // while (true)
} // getItemKind method

// Creates a library item of the specified kind.
protected LibraryItem createItem (int libraryItemKind)
{
    LibraryItem item = null;

    try
    {
        switch (libraryItemKind)
        {
            case KIND_BOOK:
                item = new Book (currentLibraryItemID);
                currentLibraryItemID++;
                break;
            case KIND_PERIODICAL:
                item = new Periodical (currentLibraryItemID);
                currentLibraryItemID++;
                break;
            case KIND_CANCEL:
                break;
        }
```

```
            System.out.println ("Library Item Created");
            // We can safely pass in null, because we know that the
            // library item has not been checked out yet.
            System.out.println (item.longListing (null));
        }
        catch (IOException e)
        {
            System.out.println ("I/O Exception: " + e);
            System.out.println ("An I/O Exception occurred when " +
                " attempting to create the library item.  No item created");
        }
        return item;
    } // createItem method

    // Outputs a single-line listing of a checked out library item.
    // This is different from the shortListing method because it
    // outputs the name of the person who checked out the item.
    protected void outputShortListing (LibraryItem libraryItem,
        LibraryCardManager libraryCardManager)
    {
        LibraryCard libraryCard;
        String dueDate;

        // Gets the library card object that checked out this item.
        libraryCard =
            libraryCardManager.findLibraryCardFromID (
            libraryItem.getCheckedOutByCardID ());

        // Outputs item ID, Title, Card Number, Card Name and due date.
        System.out.println (libraryItem.getLibraryItemID () + " " +
            Misc.sizeString (libraryItem.getTitle (), 20) +
            libraryItem.getCheckedOutByCardID () + " " +
            Misc.sizeString (libraryCard.getName (), 20) +
            libraryItem.getDueDate ());
    } // outputShortListing
} // LibraryItemManager class
```

## A.7.4   LibraryItem

```
// The "LibraryItem" class.
// This abstract class represents a generic item in the library.

import java.io.*;
import java.text.*;
import java.util.*;

public abstract class LibraryItem
{
    // Fields
    protected String title;
    protected String location;
    protected int libraryItemID;
    protected int checkedOutByCardID;
    protected Calendar dueDate;

    // The keyboard
    protected BufferedReader stdin =
        new BufferedReader (new InputStreamReader (System.in));

    // Constants
    protected static final int CHECK_OUT_TIME = 14;

    // Constructor used when information about the library item
    // is to be obtained from the user.
    public LibraryItem (int currentLibraryItemID) throws IOException
    {
        System.out.println ("Add item to collection");
        System.out.println ("————————————");
        System.out.println ();
        System.out.print ("Title: ");
        title = stdin.readLine ();
        System.out.print ("Location: ");
        location = stdin.readLine ();
        libraryItemID = currentLibraryItemID;
        checkedOutByCardID = LibraryCard.NOBODY;
        dueDate = null;
    } // LibraryItem constructor
```

```
// Constructor used when information about the library item
// is to be read from a file.
public LibraryItem (DataInputStream in) throws IOException
{
    // The kind will have already been read.

    // Reads the title (length, then the chars).
    title = Misc.readString (in);

    // Reads the location (length, then the bytes).
    location = Misc.readString (in);

    // Reads the library item ID.
    libraryItemID = in.readInt ();

    // Reads the library card ID of the card used to check the item out.
    checkedOutByCardID = in.readInt ();

    // Reads out an long representing the due date.
    long dateInMillis;
    dateInMillis = in.readLong ();
    if (dateInMillis == 0)
    {
        dueDate = null;
    }
    else
    {
        dueDate = Calendar.getInstance ();
        dueDate.setTime (new Date (dateInMillis));
    }
} // LibraryItem constructor

// Saves all the fields of LibraryItem to the binary file 'out'.
public void save (DataOutputStream out) throws IOException
{
    // Writes the title (length, then the chars).
    Misc.writeString (out, title);
    // Writes the location (length, then the chars).
    Misc.writeString (out, location);
    // Writes the library item ID.
    out.writeInt (libraryItemID);
```

```java
    // Writes the library card ID of the card used to check the item out.
    out.writeInt (checkedOutByCardID);
    // Writes out an long representing the due date.
    if (dueDate == null)
        out.writeLong (0);
    else
        out.writeLong (dueDate.getTime ().getTime ());
} // save method


// Returns a one-line listing of generic library item information.
public String shortListing ()
{
    return Misc.sizeString (title, 20) + libraryItemID;
} // shortListing method


// Returns a multi-line listing containing all the information
// of the generic library item.
public String longListing (LibraryCardManager libraryCardManager)
{
    LibraryCard libraryCard;
    String result;

    result = "Library Item ID: " + libraryItemID + "\n" +
        "Title: " + title + "\n" +
        "Location: " + location + "\n";

    if (checkedOutByCardID == LibraryCard.NOBODY)
    {
        result = result + "Not Checked Out\n";
    }
    else
    {
        libraryCard =
            libraryCardManager.findLibraryCardFromID (
            checkedOutByCardID);

        result = result + "Checked out by: " + libraryCard.getName () +
            " [Card #" + libraryCard.getLibraryCardID () + "]\n" +
            "Due Date: " +
            getDueDate () + "\n";
    }

    return result;
} // longListing method
```

```
// Checks the items out to the library card specified by libraryCardID.
public boolean checkOutLibraryItem (int libraryCardID)
{
    if ((checkedOutByCardID != LibraryCard.NOBODY) ||
                                              (dueDate != null))
    {
        System.out.println ("This book is already checked out!. " +
            "It must be checked in before it can be checked out again.");
        return false;
    }
    // Sets who checked it out.
    checkedOutByCardID = libraryCardID;
    // The dueDate is instantiated to the current date and time.
    dueDate = Calendar.getInstance ();
    // Now we add two weeks to the number of days in the date.
    dueDate.add (Calendar.DATE, CHECK_OUT_TIME);
    // The library item is actually due any time during the last day,
    // so set the time to 23:59:59 so that it's not overdue until the
    // next day.
    dueDate.set (Calendar.HOUR, 23);
    dueDate.set (Calendar.MINUTE, 59);
    dueDate.set (Calendar.SECOND, 59);
    return true;
} // checkOutLibraryItem method

// Sets the fields to specify that the item is no longer checked out.
public void checkInLibraryItem ()
{
    checkedOutByCardID = LibraryCard.NOBODY;
    dueDate = null;
} // checkInLibraryItem

// Returns the library item's ID number.
public int getLibraryItemID ()
{
    return libraryItemID;
} // getLibraryItemID method
```

```
// Returns the item's title.
public String getTitle ()
{
    return title;
} // getTitle method

// Returns the ID of the library card used to check the item out.
public int getCheckedOutByCardID ()
{
    return checkedOutByCardID;
} // getCheckedOutByCardID method

// Returns a Calendar object representing the date by which
// the item must returned.
public String getDueDate ()
{
    DateFormat dateFormat;
    dateFormat = DateFormat.getDateInstance (DateFormat.MEDIUM);
    return dateFormat.format (dueDate.getTime ());
} // getDueDate method

// Returns true if the current date is after the due date.
public boolean isOverdue ()
{
    Calendar currentDate;

    currentDate = Calendar.getInstance ();

    return currentDate.after (dueDate);
} // isOverdue method
} // LibraryItem class
```

## A.7.5   Book

```
// The "Book" class.
// This class represents a single book.

import java.io.*;
```

```
public class Book extends LibraryItem
{
    // Fields
    protected String author;
    protected String isbn;

    // Constructor used when information about the book
    // is to be obtained from the user.
    public Book (int currentLibraryItemID) throws IOException
    {
        // Obtains all the information common to all library
        // items from the user.
        super (currentLibraryItemID);

        // Obtains all the information specific to the book from the user.

        // Obtains the author from the user.
        System.out.print ("Author: ");
        author = stdin.readLine ();
        // Obtains the ISBN from the user.
        System.out.print ("ISBN: ");
        isbn = stdin.readLine ();
    } // Book constructor

    // Constructor used when information about the book
    // is to be read from a file.
    public Book (DataInputStream in) throws IOException
    {
        // Reads all the information common to all library items from file.
        super (in);

        // Reads all the information specific to the book from the file.

        // Reads the author from the file.
        author = Misc.readString (in);

        // Reads the ISBN from the file.
        isbn = Misc.readString (in);
    } // Book constructor
```

```
// Saves all the fields of Book to the binary file 'out'.
public void save (DataOutputStream out) throws IOException
{
    // Writes out what kind of object this is.
    out.writeInt (LibraryItemManager.KIND_BOOK);
    // Saves the information common to all library items to the file.
    super.save (out);
    // Writes all the information specific to the book to the file.
    // Writes the author to the file.
    Misc.writeString (out, author);
    // Writes the ISBN to the file.
    Misc.writeString (out, isbn);
} // save method

// Returns a one-line listing about the book.
public String shortListing ()
{
    return "Book: " + super.shortListing () + " " +
        Misc.sizeString (author, 20) + isbn;
} // shortListing method

// Returns a multi-line listing containing all the information
// about the book.
public String longListing (LibraryCardManager libraryCardManager)
{
    return "Type: Book\n" +
        super.longListing (libraryCardManager) +
        "Author: " + author + "\n" +
        "ISBN: " + isbn + "\n";
} // longListing method
} // Book class
```

## A.7.6   Periodical

```
// The "Periodical" class.
// This class represents a single periodical.

import java.io.*;
```

```
public class Periodical extends LibraryItem
{
    // Fields
    public String issn;
    public String issueNumber;

    // Constructor used when information about the periodical
    // is to be obtained from the user.
    public Periodical (int currentLibraryItemID) throws IOException
    {
        super (currentLibraryItemID);
        System.out.print ("ISSN: ");
        issn = stdin.readLine ();
        System.out.print ("Issue Number: ");
        issueNumber = stdin.readLine ();
    } // Book constructor

    // Constructor used when information about the periodical
    // is to be read from a file.
    public Periodical (DataInputStream in) throws IOException
    {
        // Reads the data common to all library items from the file.
        super (in);

        // Reads the issn (length, then the bytes).
        issn = Misc.readString (in);

        // Reads the issueNumber (length, then the bytes).
        issueNumber = Misc.readString (in);
    } // Book constructor

    // Saves all the fields of Periodical to the binary file 'out'.
    public void save (DataOutputStream out) throws IOException
    {
        // Writes out what kind of object this is.
        out.writeInt (LibraryItemManager.KIND_PERIODICAL);
        // Saves the information common to all library items to the file.
        super.save (out);
        // Writes all the information specific to the periodical to the file.
        // Writes the ISSN to the file.
        Misc.writeString (out, issn);
        // Writes the issue number to the file.
        Misc.writeString (out, issueNumber);
    } // save method
```

```
// Returns a one-line listing about the periodical.
public String shortListing ()
{
    return "Prdcl: " + super.shortListing () + " " + issn;
} // shortListing method

// Returns a multi-line listing containing all the information
// about the periodical.
public String longListing (LibraryCardManager libraryCardManager)
{
    return "Type: Periodical" +
        super.longListing (libraryCardManager) +
        "ISSN: " + issn + "\n" +
        "Issue Number: " + issueNumber + "\n";
} // longListing method
} // Periodical class
```

## A.7.7   LibraryCardManager

```
// The "LibraryCardManager" class.
// This class manages a list of library cards.

import java.io.*;

public class LibraryCardManager
{
    // Fields

    // This is the list of LibraryCards.
    protected LibraryCard [] libraryCards;
    protected int numLibraryCards;

    // The current ID given to a new library card.
    protected int currentLibraryCardID;

    protected BufferedReader stdin =
        new BufferedReader (new InputStreamReader (System.in));
```

```
// Constants
protected static final int MAX_LIBRARY_CARDS = 1000;

protected static final int KIND_CANCEL = -1;
protected static final int KIND_STUDENT = 1;
protected static final int KIND_STAFF = 2;
protected static final int CANCEL_CODE = -1;

protected final static int INITIAL_LIBRARY_CARD_ID_VALUE = 100;

// Constructor to initialize an empty list of library cards.
public LibraryCardManager ()
{
    libraryCards = new LibraryCard [MAX_LIBRARY_CARDS];
    numLibraryCards = 0;
    currentLibraryCardID = INITIAL_LIBRARY_CARD_ID_VALUE;
} // LibraryCardManager constructor

// Constructor that reads in a list of library cards
// from the binary file 'out'.
public LibraryCardManager (DataInputStream in) throws IOException
{
    // Calls the constructor to initialize the empty list.
    this ();

    int numberOfLibraryCardsInFile, libraryCardKind;
    LibraryCard libraryCard = null;

    // The library cards part of the data file has the following format:
    //        The next library card number to use
    //        The number of library cards stored
    //        The library cards
    //
    //        Each library card is stored as:
    //            The library card kind
    //            The library card data

    // Reads the next library card ID to use.
    currentLibraryCardID = in.readInt ();

    // Reads the number of library cards stored.
    numberOfLibraryCardsInFile = in.readInt ();
```

```
// Loops for each card read in from the file.
for (int i = 0 ; i < numberOfLibraryCardsInFile ; i++)
{
    // Gets the kind of card (student or staff card).
    libraryCardKind = in.readInt ();

    // Creates the appropriate kind of LibraryCard.
    if (libraryCardKind == KIND_STUDENT)
        libraryCard = new StudentCard (in);
    else if (libraryCardKind == KIND_STAFF)
        libraryCard = new StaffCard (in);
    else
    {
        System.out.println ("FAILURE! Illegal library card kind = " +
            libraryCardKind);
        System.out.println ("Only " + numLibraryCards + " of " +
            numberOfLibraryCardsInFile + " loaded");
        break;
    }

    // Adds the newly created card to the list of library cards.
    libraryCards [numLibraryCards] = libraryCard;
    numLibraryCards++;
}

System.out.println (numLibraryCards + " library cards loaded");
} // LibraryCardManager constructor

// Saves all the cards in the list to the binary file 'out'.
public void save (DataOutputStream out) throws IOException
{
    // Writes the next library card ID to use.
    out.writeInt (currentLibraryCardID);

    // Reads the number of library cards stored.
    out.writeInt (numLibraryCards);

    for (int i = 0 ; i < numLibraryCards ; i++)
    {
        // Writes the library card out.
        libraryCards [i].save (out);
    }
```

```
        System.out.println (numLibraryCards + " library cards saved");
} // save method

// Creates a new library card by obtaining information from the user
// and adds the library card to the list of library cards.
public void addCard ()
{
    int libraryCardKind;
    LibraryCard libraryCard;

    // Gets the kind of card to be added.
    libraryCardKind = getCardKind ();

    // Creates the card, obtaining the card's information from the user.
    libraryCard = createCard (libraryCardKind);
    if (libraryCard == null)
    {
        return;
    }

    // Adds the newly created card to the list of library cards.
    libraryCards [numLibraryCards] = libraryCard;
    numLibraryCards++;
} // addCard method

// Removes a library card from the collection.
public void removeCard (LibraryCard libraryCard)
{
    for (int i = 0 ; i < numLibraryCards ; i++)
    {
        if (libraryCards [i] == libraryCard)
        {
            for (int j = i + 1 ; j < numLibraryCards ; j++)
            {
                libraryCards [j - 1] = libraryCards [j];
            }
            numLibraryCards—;
            return;
        } // if
    } // for
} // removeCard method
```

```
// Lists all the library cards in the list, one per line.
public void listAllCards ()
{
    for (int i = 0 ; i < numLibraryCards ; i++)
    {
        System.out.println (libraryCards [i].shortListing ());
    }
} // listAllCards method

// Lists all the checked out library items sorted by the ID number of
// the library card that checked them out.
public void listCheckedOutLibraryItems (LibraryItemManager
                                                    libraryItemManager)
{
    LibraryCard libraryCard;
    String dueDate;

    for (int i = 0 ; i < numLibraryCards ; i++)
    {
        for (int j = 0 ; j < libraryCards [i].getNumCheckedOutItems () ; j++)
        {
            int libraryItemID;
            LibraryItem libraryItem;

            // Gets the library item object that are checked out
            // with this card.
            libraryItemID = libraryCards [i].getCheckedOutItemID (j);
            libraryItem =
                libraryItemManager.findLibraryItemFromID (libraryItemID);

            // Outputs card ID, card name, item ID, item title and
            // due date.
            System.out.println (libraryCards [i].getLibraryCardID () +
                " " + Misc.sizeString (libraryCards [i].getName (), 20) +
                libraryItem.getLibraryItemID () + " " +
                Misc.sizeString (libraryItem.getTitle (), 20) +
                libraryItem.getDueDate ());
        } // for
    } // for
} // listCheckedOutLibraryItems
```

```java
// Returns a LibraryCard object that has a specified library item ID.
public LibraryCard findLibraryCardFromID (int libraryCardID)
{
    for (int i = 0 ; i < numLibraryCards ; i++)
    {
        if (libraryCards [i].getLibraryCardID () == libraryCardID)
        {
            return libraryCards [i];
        }
    }

    return null;
} // findLibraryCardFromID method

// Reads the type of library card to be created from the keyboard.
protected int getCardKind ()
{
    String choice;

    while (true)
    {
        System.out.println ("Create a library card");
        System.out.println ();
        System.out.println ("1 .. Student");
        System.out.println ("2 .. Staff");
        System.out.println ("Q .. Cancel");
        System.out.println ();
        System.out.print ("Choice: ");
        try
        {
            choice = stdin.readLine ();
        }
        catch (IOException e)
        {
            System.out.println ("I/O Exception: " + e);
            System.out.println ("An I/O Exception occured when " +
                "attempting to create the library card.  No card " +
                "created");
            return KIND_CANCEL;
        }
```

```
        if (choice.equals ("1"))
            return KIND_STUDENT;
        else if (choice.equals ("2"))
            return KIND_STAFF;
        else if (choice.equalsIgnoreCase ("q"))
            return KIND_CANCEL;
        else
            System.out.println ("Enter 1, 2 or q");
    } // while (true)
} // getCardKind method

// Creates a library card of the specified kind.
protected LibraryCard createCard (int libraryCardKind)
{
    LibraryCard card = null;

    try
    {
        switch (libraryCardKind)
        {
            case KIND_STUDENT:
                card = new StudentCard (currentLibraryCardID);
                currentLibraryCardID++;
                break;
            case KIND_STAFF:
                card = new StaffCard (currentLibraryCardID);
                currentLibraryCardID++;
                break;
            case KIND_CANCEL:
                break;
        }

        System.out.println ("Library Card Created");
        // We can safely pass in null, because we no that the
        // library card has no books checked out on it yet.
        System.out.println (card.longListing (null));
    }
    catch (IOException e)
    {
        System.out.println ("I/O Exception: " + e);
        System.out.println ("An I/O Exception occured when " +
            "attempting to create the library card.  No card created");
```

```
        }
        return card;
    } // createCard method
} // LibraryCardManager class
```

## A.7.8  LibraryCard

```java
// The "LibraryCard" class.
// This abstract class represents a generic library card.

import java.io.*;

public abstract class LibraryCard
{
    // Fields
    protected String name;
    protected int libraryCardID;
    protected int [] checkedOutLibraryItems;
    protected int numCheckedOutLibraryItems;

    // The keyboard
    protected BufferedReader stdin =
        new BufferedReader (new InputStreamReader (System.in));

    // Constants
    protected static final int MAX_CHECKED_OUT_ITEMS = 100;
    public static final int NOBODY = -1;

    // Constructor used when information about the library card
    // is to be obtained from the user.
    public LibraryCard (int currentLibraryCardNumber) throws IOException
    {
        System.out.println ("Create library card");
        System.out.println ("————————————————");
        System.out.println ();
        System.out.print ("Name: ");
        name = stdin.readLine ();
        libraryCardID = currentLibraryCardNumber;
        checkedOutLibraryItems = new int [MAX_CHECKED_OUT_ITEMS];
        numCheckedOutLibraryItems = 0;
    } // LibraryCard constructor
```

```
// Constructor used when information about the library card
// is to be read from a file.
public LibraryCard (DataInputStream in) throws IOException
{
    // The kind will have already been read.

    // Reads the title (length, then the chars).
    name = Misc.readString (in);

    // Reads the library card number.
    libraryCardID = in.readInt ();

    // Reads the number of checked out books.
    numCheckedOutLibraryItems = in.readInt ();

    // Initializes the array of checked out library items.
    checkedOutLibraryItems = new int [MAX_CHECKED_OUT_ITEMS];

    for (int i = 0 ; i < numCheckedOutLibraryItems ; i++)
    {
        checkedOutLibraryItems [i] = in.readInt ();
    } // for
} // LibraryCard constructor

// Saves all the fields of LibraryCard to the binary file 'out'.
public void save (DataOutputStream out) throws IOException
{
    // Writes the name to the file.
    Misc.writeString (out, name);
    // Writes the library card ID to the file.
    out.writeInt (libraryCardID);
    // Writes the number of items checked out to the file.
    out.writeInt (numCheckedOutLibraryItems);
    // Writes the list of library items IDs checked out on this card.
    for (int i = 0 ; i < numCheckedOutLibraryItems ; i++)
    {
        out.writeInt (checkedOutLibraryItems [i]);
    }
} // save method
```

```
// Returns a one–line listing of generic library card information.
public String shortListing ()
{
    return Misc.sizeString (name, 20) + libraryCardID;
} // shortListing method

// Returns a multi–line listing containing all the information
// of the generic library card.
public String longListing (LibraryItemManager libraryItemManager)
{
    int libraryItemID;
    LibraryItem libraryItem;
    String result;

    result = "Library Card Number: " + libraryCardID + "\n" +
        "Name: " + name + "\n";

    if (numCheckedOutLibraryItems == 0)
    {
        result = result + "No Library Items Checked Out\n";
    }
    else
    {
        for (int i = 0 ; i < numCheckedOutLibraryItems ; i++)
        {
            libraryItemID = checkedOutLibraryItems [i];

            libraryItem =
                libraryItemManager.findLibraryItemFromID (libraryItemID);

            result = result + "Checked out: " + libraryItem.getTitle () +
                " [Item ID #" + libraryItemID + "]   Due Date: " +
                libraryItem.getDueDate () + "\n";
        } // for
    } // else

    return result;
} // longListing method
```

```java
// Adds a library item to the list of checked out library items.
public void addLibraryItemToCheckOut (int checkedOutLibraryItemID)
{
    checkedOutLibraryItems [numCheckedOutLibraryItems] =
        checkedOutLibraryItemID;
    numCheckedOutLibraryItems++;
} // addLibraryItemToCheckOut method

// Removes a library item from the list of checked out library items.
public void removeLibraryItemFromCheckOut (int
                                    checkedOutLibraryItemID)
{
    for (int i = 0 ; i < numCheckedOutLibraryItems ; i++)
    {
        if (checkedOutLibraryItems [i] == checkedOutLibraryItemID)
        {
            for (int j = i + 1 ; j < numCheckedOutLibraryItems ; j++)
            {
                checkedOutLibraryItems [j – 1] = checkedOutLibraryItems [j];
            }
            numCheckedOutLibraryItems—;
            return;
        }
    }

    System.out.println ("Problem! Library item to be removed from the " +
        "list of checked out items wasn't in the list!");
} // removeLibraryItemToCheckOut method

// Returns the card's ID number.
public int getLibraryCardID ()
{
    return libraryCardID;
} // getLibraryCardID method

// Returns the card holder's name.
public String getName ()
{
    return name;
} // getName method
```

```
    // Returns the number of items checked out by this card.
    public int getNumCheckedOutItems ()
    {
        return numCheckedOutLibraryItems;
    } // getNumCheckedOutItems

    // Returns the ID of the checked out library item
    // specified by checkedOutIndex.
    public int getCheckedOutItemID (int checkedOutIndex)
    {
        return checkedOutLibraryItems [checkedOutIndex];
    } // getCheckedOutItemID method
} // LibraryCard class
```

## A.7.9   StaffCard

```
// The "StaffCard" class.
// This class represents a library card issued to a staff member.

import java.io.*;

public class StaffCard extends LibraryCard
{
    // Fields
    protected String officeNumber;

    // Constructor used when information about the staff library card
    // is to be obtained from the user.
    public StaffCard (int currentLibraryCardID) throws IOException
    {
        // Obtains all the information common to all library
        // cards from the user.
        super (currentLibraryCardID);

        // Obtains all the information specific to the staff library
        // card from the user.

        // Obtains the office number from the user.
        System.out.print ("Office Number: ");
        officeNumber = stdin.readLine ();
    } // StaffCard constructor
```

```
// Constructor used when information about the staff library card
// is to be read from a file.
public StaffCard (DataInputStream in) throws IOException
{
    // Reads all the information common to all library cards from file.
    super (in);

    // Reads all the information specific to the staff library
    // card from the file.

    // Reads the office number from the file.
    officeNumber = Misc.readString (in);
} // StaffCard constructor

// Saves all the fields of StaffCard to the binary file 'out'.
public void save (DataOutputStream out) throws IOException
{
    // Writes out what kind of object this is.
    out.writeInt (LibraryCardManager.KIND_STAFF);
    // Saves the information common to all library cards to the file.
    super.save (out);
    // Writes all the information specific to the staff library
    // card to the file.
    // Writes the office number to the file.
    Misc.writeString (out, officeNumber);
} // save method

// Returns a one-line listing about the staff library card.
public String shortListing ()
{
    return "Staff: " + super.shortListing () + " " + officeNumber;
} // shortListing method

// Returns a multi-line listing containing all the information
// about the staff library card.
public String longListing (LibraryItemManager libraryItemManager)
{
    return "Type: Staff Card\n" +
        super.longListing (libraryItemManager) +
        "Office Number: " + officeNumber + "\n";
} // longListing method
} // StaffCard class
```

## A.7.10 StudentCard

```
// The "StudentCard" class.
// This class represents a library card issued to a student.

import java.io.*;

public class StudentCard extends LibraryCard
{
    // Fields
    protected int studentNumber;

    // Constructor used when information about the student library card
    // is to be obtained from the user.
    public StudentCard (int currentLibraryCardID) throws IOException
    {
        // Obtains all the information common to all library
        // cards from the user.
        super (currentLibraryCardID);

        // Obtains all the information specific to the student library
        // card from the user.

        // Obtains the student number from the user.
        System.out.print ("Student Number: ");
        while (true)
        {
            String line = stdin.readLine ();
            try
            {
                studentNumber = Integer.parseInt (line);
                break;
            }
            catch (NumberFormatException e)
            {
                System.out.println ("The library item ID is a number.");
            }
        }
    } // StudentCard constructor
```

```java
// Constructor used when information about the student library card
// is to be read from a file.
public StudentCard (DataInputStream in) throws IOException
{
    // Reads all the information common to all library.
    // cards from the file
    super (in);

    // Reads all the information specific to the student library
    // card from the file.

    // Reads the student number from the file.
    studentNumber = in.readInt ();
} // StudentCard constructor

// Saves all the fields of StudentCard to the binary file 'out'.
public void save (DataOutputStream out) throws IOException
{
    // Writes out what kind of object this is.
    out.writeInt (LibraryCardManager.KIND_STUDENT);
    // Saves the information common to all library cards to the file.
    super.save (out);
    // Writes all the information specific to the student library
    // card to the file.
    // Writes the student number to the file.
    out.writeInt (studentNumber);
} // save method

// Returns a one-line listing about the staff library card.
public String shortListing ()
{
    return "Student: " + super.shortListing () + " " + studentNumber;
} // shortListing method

// Returns a multi-line listing containing all the information
// about the student library card.
public String longListing (LibraryItemManager libraryItemManager)
{
    return "Type: Student Card\n" +
        super.longListing (libraryItemManager) +
        "Student Number: " + studentNumber + "\n";
} // longListing method
} // StudentCard class
```

## A.7.11  Misc

```
// The "Misc" class.
// This class contains methods to perform various miscellaneous duties.

import java.io.*;

public class Misc
{
    // Returns the string 's' formatted to fit in a field of size 'fieldSize'.
    public static String sizeString (String s, int fieldSize)
    {
        StringBuffer sp = new StringBuffer (s);

        for (int i = s.length () ; i < fieldSize ; i++)
        {
            sp.append (" ");
        }

        // Always have at least 1 space
        sp.append (" ");

        return sp.toString ();
    } // sizeString method

    // Reads String objects in the file 'in'. The String must be
    // saved as the length of the String followed by the bytes in
    // the String (see the writeString method).
    public static String readString (DataInputStream in) throws IOException
    {
        int stringSize;
        char [] chars;

        stringSize = in.readInt ();
        chars = new char [stringSize];
        for (int i = 0 ; i < stringSize ; i++)
            chars [i] = in.readChar ();
        return new String (chars);
    } // readString method
```

```
// Writes a String object to the file 'out'. The String is saved
// as the length followed by the bytes in the String.
public static void writeString (DataOutputStream out, String s)
    throws IOException
{
    out.writeInt (s.length ());
    out.writeChars (s);
} // writeString method
} // Misc class
```

# A.8   Exercises

1.  The library has decided to add audio tapes to the collection. Write
    a new class called *Audio* that inherits from *LibraryItem* and modify
    the existing program to support the *Audio* class. An audio tape has
    a title, an artist, and a music classification.

2.  The library occasionally wishes to loan an item to a guest. Create a
    *GuestCard* class that inherits from *LibraryCard*. Modify the
    program to support the *GuestCard* class. A guest library card
    should have a street address.

3.  Modify the program so that when an overdue item is checked in, a
    message appears indicating there is a fine and the amount of the
    fine. The fine is set at 25 cents per day.

4.  It has been decided that periodicals can only be checked out for a
    week at a time. Modify the program to allow different kinds of
    library items to have different check out periods.

5.  Modify the *LibraryItemManager* and *LibraryCardManager* classes
    to store the list of library items and cards in a linked list rather than
    array.

6.  Write a new program for a computer meant to be accessible to the
    public. The program should allow the user to ask for information
    about any library item given the item's title or the ID number. If
    the item is checked out, the program should display the due date
    but not the card ID or name.

7.  **Major Project** Add a GUI interface to the Library Automation
    System.

# Appendix B : Reserved Words

This is the list of reserved words in Java. They cannot be used as identifiers.

| | | | |
|---|---|---|---|
| abstract | boolean | break | byte |
| byvalue | case | cast | catch |
| char | class | const | continue |
| default | do | double | else |
| extends | final | finally | float |
| for | future | generic | goto |
| if | implements | import | inner |
| instanceof | int | interface | long |
| native | new | operator | outer |
| package | private | protected | public |
| rest | return | short | static |
| super | switch | synchronized | this |
| throw | throws | transient | try |
| var | void | volatile | while |

This is the list of reserved identifiers in Java.

| | | |
|---|---|---|
| true | false | null |

# Appendix C : Java Class Library

This is the list of the classes found in the Java class libraries that are used in this book along with their associated methods.

## Classes Sorted by Package

java.applet
    Applet

java.awt
    BorderLayout
    Button
    Canvas
    Checkbox
    CheckboxGroup
    CheckboxMenuItem
    Color
    Component
    Dialog
    Dimension
    Event
    FileDialog
    FlowLayout
    Font
    FontMetrics
    Frame
    Graphics
    GridLayout
    Image
    Label

java.awt (continued...)
    MediaTracker
    Menu
    MenuBar
    MenuItem
    Panel
    Point
    PrintJob
    Scrollbar
    TextArea
    TextField
    Toolkit

java.awt.event
    ActionEvent
    ActionListener
    AdjustmentEvent
    AdjustmentListener
    KeyEvent
    KeyListener
    MouseEvent
    MouseListener
    WindowEvent
    WindowListener

java.awt.image
    ImageObserver

java.io
    BufferedReader
    DataInputStream
    DataOutputStream
    FileInputStream
    FileOutputStream
    FileReader
    FileWriter
    IOException
    PrintWriter

java.lang
    Boolean
    Character
    Double
    Integer
    Math

java.lang (continued...)
    Object
    Runnable
    RuntimeException
    String
    StringBuffer
    System
    Thread

java.text
    DateFormat
    DecimalFormat

java.util
    Calendar
    Date
    Hashtable
    Stack
    StringTokenizer
    Vector

# Descriptions

This is the list of selected methods available for use in each class, along with a short description. In some of these cases, the methods listed will actually be methods defined in a parent class but commonly used in the listed class.

## Applet                    java.applet      Extend this class to create an applet.

void **init** ()
  Called by the system when the applet is loaded.

void **start** ()
  Called by the system when the applet is made active.

void **stop** ()
  Called by the system when the applet is made inactive.

void **destroy** ()
  Called by the system when the applet is discarded.

void **paint** (Graphics g)
  Called by the system when the applet drawing surface must be redrawn.

void **showStatus** (String message)
  Displays *message* in the status bar.

void **setLayout** (LayoutManager layout)
  Sets the Applet's layout manager to *layout*.

void **add** (Component comp)
  Adds Component *comp* to the Applet using the Applet's layout manager.

void **add** (String direction, Component comp)
  Used when the Applet's layout manager is BorderLayout. Add component *comp* to the frame in the area specified by *direction*. Possible values for *direction* are "North", "South", "East", "West", and "Center".

boolean **action** (Event evt, Object arg)
  Called by the system when a button is clicked or an ENTER in pressed in a text field in the Applet. The Button or TextField object that was clicked or had Return pressed is passed as the *target* field in *evt*. The method must return true if the event was handled and false if the event was not handled.

boolean **mouseDown** (Event evt, int x, int y)
  Called by the system when the mouse button is pressed. The location of the mouse click is passed as *x* and *y*.

boolean **keyDown** (Event evt, int key)
> Called by the system when a key is pressed. The keystroke pressed is passed as *key*.

boolean **handleEvent** (Event evt)
> Called by the system when an event occurs. Used for handling scrollbar events.

void **addKeyListener** (KeyListener listener)
> Add a listener for keystrokes.

void **addMouseListener** (MouseListener listener)
> Add a listener for mouse button presses.

boolean **setVisible** (boolean visible)
> Used in the Applet's start and init methods to make the surface visible before drawing to it.

void **setBackground** (Color c)
> Sets the background color of the applet to the color *c*.

Graphics **getGraphics** ()
> Returns the graphics context of the applet. Used for drawing in the applet when not in the paint method.

Image **getImage** (URL url)
> Returns an image object that will be loaded from *url*.

Image **createImage** (int width, int height)
> Creates an offscreen bitmap of the specified width and height.

boolean **prepareImage** (Image img, ImageObserver observer)
> Starts an image loading monitoring its status with *observer*. The observer parameter can be null. Returns true if all the image's data has already been loaded.

Dimension **getSize** ()
> Returns the size of the applet's allocated drawing surface in pixels. The size is specified by the HTML's HEIGHT and WIDTH attribute in the APPLET tag. Dimension has two fields, *height* and *width*. The applet's height is returned by getSize ().height and the applet's width by getSize ().width.

# ActionEvent            java.awt.event      Java 1.1 action event object.

Object **getSource** ()
> Returns the object that generated the ActionEvent.

# ActionListener         java.awt.event      Java 1.1 action event handler interface.

abstract void **actionPerformed** (ActionEvent e)
> Called when an action event occurs.

# AdjustmentEvent

java.awt.event     Java 1.1 scrollbar event object.

Adjustable **getAdjustable** ()
>    Returns the scrollbar that generated the AdjustmentEvent.

int **getValue** ()
>    Returns the new value of the scrollbar

int **getAdjustmentType** ()
>    Returns what the event was. One of UNIT_INCREMENT, UNIT_DECREMENT, BLOCK_INCREMENT, BLOCK_DECREMENT, and TRACK.

# AdjustmentListener

java.awt.event     Java 1.1 scrollbar event handler interface.

abstract void **adjustmentValueChanged** (AdjustmentEvent e)
>    Called when an adjustment event occurs.

# Boolean

java.lang          Wrapper class for **boolean** primitive data type.

**Boolean** (boolean b)
>    Constructor.

boolean **booleanValue** ()
>    Returns the boolean value contained by the object.

static Boolean **valueOf** (String s)
>    Returns a Boolean object holding the value represented by *s*.

# BorderLayout

java.awt           Places components along edges and in the center.

**BorderLayout** ()
>    Constructor.

**BorderLayout** (int hgap, int vgap)
>    Constructor – Specifies the horizontal gap *hgap* and the vertical gap *vgap* between components.

# BufferedReader

java.io            Reads ASCII data from file.

**BufferedReader** (FileReader reader)
>    Constructor – Opens *reader* for reading of ASCII text.

void **close** () throws IOException
>   Closes the file.

int **read** () throws IOException
>   Reads a character from the file. Returns –1 if the end-of-file was reached.

String **readLine** () throws IOException
>   Returns a line of input from the file (without the Return). Returns null if the end-of-file was reached before reading any characters.

# Button                              java.awt          A GUI button.

**Button** (String label)
>   Constructor – Creates a Button with label set to *label*.

String **getLabel** ()
>   Returns the Button's label.

void **setEnabled** (boolean enabled)
>   Sets whether the button is enabled or disabled. Disabled buttons cannot be pressed.

void **addActionListener** (ActionListener listener)
>   Attaches an ActionListener object to the Button. Causes the actionPerformed method of the listener to be called whenever the button is clicked.

# Calendar                           java.util          A date/time that can be used for calculations.

Calendar **getInstance** ()
>   Returns a Calendar object.

void **add** (int field, int amount)
>   Adds the value *amount* to the part of the date specified by *field*.

void **set** (int field, int value)
>   Sets the part of the date specified by *field* to *value*.

Date **getTime** ()
>   Returns a Date object representing the date/time stored in the Calendar object.

void **setTime** (Date d)
>   Sets the Calendar object to the date represented by the Date object *d*.

boolean **after** (Calendar cal)
>   Returns **true** if the date stored in the Calendar object if after the date stored in *cal*.

final static int YEAR, MONTH, DATE, HOUR, MINUTE, SECOND, MILLISECOND
>   Field names that can be used in the *add* and *set* methods.

# Canvas

java.awt

Extend this class to create a surface on which to draw.

**Canvas** ()
> Constructor.

void **addNotify** ()
> Called by the system when the Canvas peer is created.

void **paint** ()
> Called by the system when the Canvas must be redrawn.

void **setSize** (int width, int height)
> Changes the canvas to have width *width* and height *height*.

Dimension **getSize** ()
> Returns the size of the canvas in pixels. Dimension has two fields, *height* and *width*. The canvas' height is returned by getSize ().height and the canvas' width by getSize ().width.

# Character

java.lang

Wrapper class for **char** primitive data type.

**Character** (char ch)
> Constructor.

char **charValue** ()
> Returns the boolean value contained by the object.

static char **toUpperCase** (char ch)
> Converts *ch* to uppercase.

static char **toLowerCase** (char ch)
> Converts *ch* to lowercase.

# Checkbox

java.awt

A GUI check box.

**Checkbox** (String label)
> Constructor – Creates a checkbox with label set to *label*.

**Checkbox** (String label, CheckboxGroup group, boolean state)
> Constructor – Creates a radio button checkbox with label set to *label*. If *state* is true, the checkbox is checked, otherwise it is unchecked. This constructor is used for creating radio buttons.

String **getLabel** ()
> Returns the checkbox's label.

Boolean **getState** ()
> Returns true if the checkbox is checked.

void **setState** (Boolean state)
> Sets the checkbox to checked if *state* is true, unchecks the checkbox if *state* is false.

void **setEnabled** (boolean enabled)
> Sets whether the checkbox is enabled or disabled. Disabled checkboxes cannot have their state changed.

# CheckboxGroup      java.awt      Makes check boxes into radio buttons.

**CheckboxGroup** ()
> Constructor.

# CheckboxMenuItem      java.awt      A checkable menu item.

**CheckboxMenuItem** (String itemName)
> Constructor – Creates a menu item called *itemName* that can be marked with a checkmark.

boolean **getState** ()
> Returns true if the menu item is marked with a checkmark.

void **setEnabled** (Boolean newEnabled)
> Enables (make the menu item selectable) if *newEnabled* is true. Disables (dims the menu item and makes it unselectable) if *newEnabled* is false.

void **setState** (boolean newState)
> Marks the menu item with a checkmark if *newState* is true. Eliminates the checkmark if *newState* is false.

# Color      java.awt      A color.

**Color** (int red, int green, int blue)
> Constructor – Creates a Color with specified *red*, *green*, and *blue* components. Values must be in range $0 - 255$.

final static Color **black, blue, cyan, darkGray, gray, green, lightGray, magenta, orange, pink, red, white, yellow**
> Predefined colors.

# Component      java.awt      Base class for GUI components.

Image **createImage** (int width, int height)
> Creates an offscreen bitmap of the specified *width* and *height*.

boolean **prepareImage** (Image img, ImageObserver observer)
> Starts an image loading monitoring its status with *observer*. The *observer* parameter can be null. Returns true if all the image's data has already been loaded.

Toolkit **getToolkit** ()
Returns the Toolkit used by the component.

Graphics **getGraphics** ()
Returns the graphics context of the component.

Dimension **getSize** ()
Returns a Dimension object specifying the width and height of the component.

# DataInputStream          java.io          Reads binary data from a file.

**DataInputStream** (FileInputStream stream)
Constructor – Opens *stream* for reading of binary data.

boolean **readBoolean** () throws IOException
Returns a boolean value read from the file. Throws an EOFException if end-of-file was reached when attempting to read from the file.

char **readChar** () throws IOException
Returns a char value read from the file. Throws an EOFException if end-of-file was reached when attempting to read from the file.

double **readDouble** () throws IOException
Returns an 8-byte double value read from the file. Throws an EOFException if end-of-file was reached when attempting to read from the file.

void **readFully** (byte[] buffer) throws IOException
Reads *buffer.length* bytes into *buffer*. Throws an EOFException if end-of-file was reached when attempting to read from the file.

int **readInt** () throws IOException
Returns a 32-bit int value read from the file. Throws an EOFException if end-of-file was reached when attempting to read from the file.

String **readLine** () throws IOException
Returns a line of input from the file (without the Return). Returns null if the end-of-file was reached before reading any characters.

# DataOutputStream          java.io          Writes binary data to a file.

**DataOutputStream** (FileOutputStream stream)
Constructor – Opens *stream* for writing of binary data.

void **write** (byte[] buffer) throws IOException
Writes *buffer.length* bytes from *buffer* into the file.

void **writeBoolean** (boolean val) throws IOException
Writes the boolean value *val* into the file.

void **writeChar** (char val) throws IOException
Writes the character *val* into the file.

void **writeDouble** (double val) throws IOException
    Writes the 8-byte double *val* into the file.

void **writeInt** (int val) throws IOException
    Writes the 32-bit int *val* into the file.

# Date                                    java.util            Represents dates and times.

**Date** ()
    Constructor – Creates a Date object representing the current date and time..

**Date** (long timeInMillis)
    Constructor – Creates a Date object representing the time in milliseconds since Jan 1, 1970.

**getTime** ()
    Returns the date represented by the object as the tim e in milliseconds since Jan 1, 1970.

# DateFormat                            java.text            Used to format dates and times

DateFormat **getDateInstance** (int style)
DateFormat **getTimeInstance** (int style)
DateFormat **getDateTimeInstance** (int style)
    Returns a date, time or date and time formatter based on *style*.

String **format** (Date d)
    Returns the String of the date formatted in accordance with the style specified in the constructor.

final static int DEFAULT, FULL, LONG, MEDIUM, SHORT
    Style names that can be used in *get…* methods.

# DecimalFormat                         java.text            Used to format floating point numbers.

**DecimalFormat** (String formatString)
    Constructor – Creates a formatter based on *formatString*.
        #    Digit, zeros show as absent.
        0    Digit, zeros show as 0.
        .    Decimal place.
        –    Locale-specific negative sign.

String **format** (double number)
    Returns the String of the number formatted in accordance with the *formatString* specified in the constructor.

# Dialog                          java.awt              Extend this class to create a dialog.

**Dialog** (Frame parent, String title, boolean modal)
    Constructor.

void **setVisible** (boolean visible)
    Makes the dialog appear or disappear.

void **dispose** ()
    Hides and destroys the dialog.

void **setLayout** (LayoutManager layout)
    Sets the Dialog's layout manager to *layout*.

void **add** (Component comp)
    Adds component *comp* to the Dialog using the Dialog's layout manager.

void **add** (String direction, Component comp)
    Used when the Dialog's layout manager is BorderLayout. Adds component *comp* to
    the Dialog in the area specified by *direction*. Possible values for *direction* are "North",
    "South", "East", "West", and "Center".

void **pack** ()
    Lays out all the component placed in the Dialog using their respective
    LayoutManagers and then shrinks the Dialog to the smallest size that fits all the
    components.

void **setSize** (int width, int height)
    Changes the Dialog to have width *width* and height *height*.

void **setLocation** (int x, int y)
    Moves the Dialog to have its upper-left corner at $(x, y)$ with respect to the upper-left
    corner of the screen.

Dimension **getSize** ()
    Returns the size of the Dialog in pixels. Dimension has two fields, *height* and *width*.
    The Dialog's height is returned by getSize ().height and the Frame's width by
    getSize ().width.

boolean **action** (Event evt, Object arg)
    Called by the system when a button is clicked or ENTER is pressed in a text field in
    the Dialog. The Button or TextField object that was clicked or had ENTER pressed is
    passed as the *target* field in *evt*. The method must return true if the event was handled
    and false if the event was not handled.

boolean **handleEvent** (Event evt)
    Called by the system when any event occurs in the Dialog. The *id* field of Event *evt* is
    set to Event.WINDOW_DESTROY when the Close button (the X on the right hand
    side of the Dialog's title bar) has been pressed in the Dialog. The method must return
    true if the event was handled and false if the event was not handled.

boolean **mouseDown** (Event evt, int x, int y)
> Called by the system when the mouse button is pressed. The location of the mouse click is passed as *x* and *y*.

boolean **keyDown** (Event evt, int key)
> Called by the system when a key is pressed. The keystroke pressed is passed as *key*.

void **addKeyListener** (KeyListener listener)
> Add a listener for keystrokes.

void **addMouseListener** (MouseListener listener)
> Add a listener for mouse button presses.

void **addWindowListener** (WindowListener listener)
> Add a listener for window events such as the dialog's close box being pressed.

# Dimension                java.awt        Specifies a size (height and width).

> A Dimension object is returned by methods that return an object's size.
> > e.g.  Toolkit.getDefaultToolkit ().getScreenSize ()

int **height, width**
> The height and width of the size.

# Double                  java.lang       Wrapper class for **double** primitive data type.

**Double** (double d)
> Constructor.

boolean **doubleValue** ()
> Returns the double value contained by the object.

static Double **valueOf** (String s) throws NumberFormatException
> Returns a Double object holding the value represented by *s*.

static String **toString** (double d)
> Returns a String containing the string representation of *d*.

# Event                   java.awt        Passed to action, handleEvent, mouseDown, and keyDown methods.

Object **target**
> The object that generated the event. The Button object if a button was pressed or the TextField object if Return was pressed in a text field.

int **id**

> The type of event. This is set to the constant Event.ACTION_EVENT for a button click or a Return pressed in a text field. id is set to Event.WINDOW_DESTROY if the Close button (the X on the right side of the Frame's title bar) is clicked.

final static int **ACTION_EVENT**

> The value of the id field of the Event object when a button is clicked or Return is pressed in a text field.

final static int **WINDOW_DESTROY**

> The value of the id field of the Event object when the Close button on a Frame is clicked.

final static int **SCROLL_LINE_DOWN, SCROLL_LINE_UP, SCROLL_PAGE_DOWN, SCROLL_PAGE_UP, SCROLL_ABSOLUTE**

> The value of the id field of the Event object when a scrollbar has been changed using the scroll arrows, clicking in the scrollbar or dragging the scrollbox.

# FileDialog

java.io — Creates a file dialog box to allow the user to specify a file to be loaded or saved.

**FileDialog** (Frame parent, String title, int mode)

> Constructor – Creates a file dialog. The *mode* parameter is one of FileDialog.LOAD or FileDialog.SAVE.

void **show** ()

> Makes the dialog appear and blocks until the dialog is dismissed. The system will hide the dialog when the dialog is dismissed.

String **getFile** ()

> Once the file dialog has been shown, getFile returns the filename selected or null if the Cancel button was pressed.

String **getDirectory** ()

> Once the file dialog has been shown, getDirectory returns the directory that the selected file is located in or null if the Cancel button was pressed.

# FileInputStream

java.io — Opens a file to be used as a DataInputStream.

**FileInputStream** (String fileName) throws FileNotFoundException

> Constructor – Creates a FileInputStream object for the file of name *fileName*. The object can then be used as an argument to the DataInputStream constructor.

# FileOutputStream

java.io     Opens a file to be used as a DataOutputStream.

**FileOutputStream** (String fileName) throws IOException
Constructor – Creates a FileOutputStream object for the file of name *fileName*. The object can then be used as an argument to the DataOutputStream constructor.

# FileReader

java.io     Opens a file to be used as a BufferedReader.

**FileReader** (String fileName) throws FileNotFoundException
Constructor – Creates a FileReader object for the file of name *fileName*. The object can then be used as an argument to the BufferedReader constructor.

# FileWriter

java.io     Opens a file to be used as a PrintWriter.

**FileWriter** (String fileName) throws IOException
Constructor – Creates a FileWriter object for the file of name *fileName*. The object can then be used as an argument to the PrintWriter constructor.

# FlowLayout

java.awt     Places components left-to-right, top-to-bottom.

**FlowLayout** ()
Constructor.

**FlowLayout** (int alignment)
Constructor – Sets the alignment of the components to *alignment*.
*alignment* must be one of the constants defined in the FlowLayout class.

**FlowLayout** (int alignment, int hgap, int vgap)
Constructor – Sets the alignment of the components to *alignment* and the horizontal and vertical gaps between the components to *hgap* and *vgap*. *alignment* must be one of the constants defined in the FlowLayout class.

final static int **LEFT, CENTER, RIGHT**
Allowed values for *alignment* in the FlowLayout constructors.

## Font
java.awt          A font for drawing text.

**Font** (String name, int style, int size)
>    Constructor – Creates a font with the font name of *name*, the font style set to *style*, and point size set to *size*. *style* must be one or a combination of the constants defined in the Font class.

final static int **BOLD, ITALIC, PLAIN**
>    Allowed values for *style* in the Font constructor. To get bold italic, use the style Font.BOLD+Font.ITALIC.

## FontMetrics
java.awt          The measurements of a font.

>    A FontMetrics object is returned by the getFontMetrics () method in the Applet, Frame, Component or Toolkit class.
>        e.g.  Toolkit.getDefaultToolkit ().getFontMetrics (font)

**Figure B.1 The FontMetrics attributes**

int **charWidth** (char ch)
>    Returns the width of the character *ch* in pixels.

int **getAscent** ()
>    Returns the font's ascent in pixels.

int **getDescent** ()
>    Returns the font's descent in pixels.

int **getHeight** ()
>    Returns the font's total height in pixels.

int **stringWidth** (String text)
>    Returns the width of the String *text* in pixels.

# Frame                          java.awt          Extend this class to create a window.

**Frame** ()
> Constructor.

**Frame** (String title)
> Constructor – Creates a Frame with the window title set to *title*.

void **setVisible** (boolean visible)
> Makes the frame appear or disappear.

void **dispose** ()
> Hides and destroys the window.

void **setLayout** (LayoutManager layout)
> Sets the Frame's layout manager to *layout*.

void **add** (Component comp)
> Adds component *comp* to the Frame using the Frame's layout manager.

void **add** (String direction, Component comp)
> Used when the Frame's layout manager is BorderLayout. Adds component *comp* to the Frame in the area specified by *direction*. Possible values for *direction* are "North", "South", "East", "West", and "Center".

void **pack** ()
> Lays out all the component placed in the Frame using their respective LayoutManagers and then shrinks the Frame to the smallest size that fits all the components.

void **setSize** (int width, int height)
> Changes the Frame to have width *width* and height *height*.

void **setLocation** (int x, int y)
> Moves the Frame to have its upper-left corner at $(x, y)$ with respect to the upper-left corner of the screen.

Dimension **getSize** ()
> Returns the size of the Frame in pixels. Dimension has two fields, *height* and *width*. The Frame's height is returned by getSize ().height and the Frame's width by getSize ().width.

Image **createImage** (int width, int height)
> Creates an offscreen bitmap of the specified width and height.

boolean **prepareImage** (Image img, ImageObserver observer)
> Starts an image loading monitoring its status with *observer*. The *observer* parameter can be null. Returns true if all the image's data has already been loaded.

boolean **action** (Event evt, Object arg)
> Called by the system when a button is clicked or a Return is pressed in a text field in the Frame. The Button or TextField object that was clicked or had Return pressed is passed as the *target* field in *evt*. The method must return true if the event was handled and false if the event was not handled.

boolean **handleEvent** (Event evt)
> Called by the system when any event occurs in the Frame. The *id* field of Event *evt* is set to Event.WINDOW_DESTROY when the Close button (the X on the right hand side of the Frame's title bar) has been pressed in the Frame. The method must return true if the event was handled and false if the event was not handled.

boolean **mouseDown** (Event evt, int x, int y)
> Called by the system when the mouse button is pressed. The location of the mouse click is passed as *x* and *y*.

boolean **keyDown** (Event evt, int key)
> Called by the system when a key is pressed. The keystroke pressed is passed as *key*.

Toolkit **getToolkit** ()
> Returns the Toolkit used by the component.

void **addKeyListener** (KeyListener listener)
> Adds a listener for keystrokes.

void **addMouseListener** (MouseListener listener)
> Adds a listener for mouse button presses.

void **addWindowListener** (WindowListener listener)
> Adds a listener for window events such as the window's close box being pressed.

# Graphics                            java.awt         A graphics context that can be drawn upon.

> A Graphics object is passed as a parameter to the paint method or is returned by the getGraphics methods of various Components.
> > e.g.  canvas.getGraphics ()

void **clearRect** (int x, int y, int width, int height)
> Clears the rectangle to the background color.

void **draw3DRect** (int x, int y, int width, int height, boolean raised)
> Draws a 3-D rectangle. It appears raised if *raised* is true.

void **drawArc** (int x, int y, int width, int height, int startAngle, int arcAngle)
> Draws an arc. The arc is inscribed in the rectangle defined by the upper-left corner ($x$, $y$) with width of *width* and height of *height*. It starts at *startAngle* degrees and goes counterclockwise for *arcAngle* degrees.

void **drawImage** (Image img, int x, int y, ImageObserver observer)
> Draws an image onto the graphics context with the upper-left corner of the image located at ($x, y$).

void **drawImage** (Image img, int x, int y, int width, int height,
> > ImageObserver observer)
> Draws an image onto the graphics context with the upper-left corner of the image located at ($x, y$). The image is scaled so that it appears on the graphics context with the specified width and height.

void **drawLine** (int x1, int y1, int x2, int y2)
> Draws a line from $(x1, y1)$ to $(x2, y2)$.

void **drawOval** (int x, int y, int width, int height)
> Draws an ellipse. The ellipse is inscribed in the rectangle defined by the upper-left corner $(x, y)$ with width of *width* and height of *height*.

void **drawPolygon** (int[] xPoints, int[] yPoints, int numPoints)
> Draws a polygon. The *xPoints* and *yPoints* arrays define the coordinates of the array of vertices. *numPoints* specifies the number of vertices in the polygon.

void **drawRect** (int x, int y, int width, int height)
> Draws a rectangle with upper-left corner at $(x, y)$ with width of *width* and height of *height*.

void **drawRoundRect** (int x, int y, int width, int height, int arcWidth, int arcHeight)
> Draws a rectangle with rounded corners with upper-left corner at $(x, y)$ with width of *width* and height of *height*. The *arcWidth* and *arcHeight* parameters are the width and height of the ellipse used to draw the rounded corners.

void **drawString** (String str, int x, int y)
> Draws the string *str* at the starting point $(x, y)$. The *y* coordinate is the base line of the text.

void **fill3DRect** (int x, int y, int width, int height, boolean raised)
> Draws a filled 3-D rectangle. It appears raised if *raised* is true.

void **fillArc** (int x, int y, int width, int height, int startAngle, int arcAngle)
> Draws a filled arc. The arc is inscribed in the rectangle defined by the upper-left corner $(x, y)$ with width of *width* and height of *height*. It starts at *startAngle* degrees and goes counterclockwise for *arcAngle* degrees.

void **fillOval** (int x, int y, int width, int height)
> Draws a filled ellipse. The ellipse is inscribed in the rectangle defined by the upper-left corner $(x, y)$ with width of *width* and height of *height*.

void **fillPolygon** (int[] xPoints, int[] yPoints, int numPoints)
> Draws a filled polygon. The *xPoints* and *yPoints* arrays define the coordinates of the array of vertices. The *numPoints* parameter specifies the number of vertices in the polygon.

void **fillRect** (int x, int y, int width, int height)
> Draws a filled rectangle with upper-left corner at $(x, y)$ with width of *width* and height of *height*.

void **fillRoundRect** (int x, int y, int width, int height, int arcWidth, int arcHeight)
> Draws a filled rectangle with rounded corners with upper-left corner at $(x, y)$ with width of *width* and height of *height*. The *arcWidth* and *arcHeight* parameters are the width and height of the ellipse used to draw the rounded corners.

void **setColor** (Color c)
> Sets the color of the graphics context. The color is used for any draw methods.

void **setFont** (Font f)
> Sets the font of the graphics context. The font is used with the drawString method.

void **setPaintMode** ()
> Sets the graphics context into paint mode. All drawing in the graphics context draws over the background.

void **setXORMode** (Color c)
> Sets the graphics context into XOR mode. All drawing in the graphics context is XOR'd with the background. The color specified by c is a special color so that any drawing done on a background of color c will not be changed.

# GridLayout                    java.awt          Places components on a grid of identically-sized cells.

**GridLayout** (int rows, int columns)
> Constructor – Specifies the number of rows and columns when laying out the components.

**GridLayout** (int rows, int columns, int hgap, int vgap)
> Constructor – Specifies the number of rows and columns when laying out the components and sets the horizontal and vertical gaps between components to be *hgap* and *vgap*.

# Hashtable                     java.util         A hash table.

**Hashtable** ()
> Constructor.

Object **get** (Object key)
> Returns the element associated with *key*.

Object **put** (Object key, Object element)
> Associates an element with a key. Returns the previous element associated with *key* if there is one and null if the key was not in the table.

Object **remove** (Object key)
> Removes the key and associated element from the hash table. It returns the element associated with *key* if there was one and null if the key was not in the table.

boolean **isEmpty** ()
> Returns true if the table is empty.

void **clear** ()
> Clears all the keys and elements from the hash table.

# Image                          java.awt          A picture.

An Image object is returned by the getImage method of the Applet or Toolkit class or the createImage method of the Component class.

e.g.  Toolkit.getDefaultToolkit ().getImage ("mountain.jpg")

Graphics **getGraphics** ()
Returns the Images graphics context.

int **getWidth** (ImageObserver observer)
Returns the image's width if it is known, otherwise it returns −1. It starts the image loading if the image is not already loaded. The *observer* parameter can be null.

int **getHeight** (ImageObserver observer)
Returns the image's height if it is known, otherwise it returns −1. It starts the image loading if the image is not already loaded. The *observer* parameter can be null.

# ImageObserver                 java.awt.image    An interface for monitoring an image being loaded.

boolean **imageUpdate** (Image img, int infoflags, int x, int y, int width, int height)
Called by the system as the image is loaded.

static int **ABORT, ERROR**
Indicates an error occurred when the image was loaded.

static int **WIDTH, HEIGHT**
Indicates that *width* and *height* parameters of imageUpdate contain the image's width and height.

static int **SOMEBITS**
Indicates a row of the image was loaded. The *y* parameter of imageUpdate contains the row loaded.

static int **ALLBITS**
Indicates the image is completely loaded.

# Integer                        java.lang         Wrapper class for **int** primitive data type.

**Integer** (int i)
Constructor.

boolean **intValue** ()
Returns the double value contained by the object.

static Integer **valueOf** (String s) throws NumberFormatException
Returns an Integer object holding the value represented by *s*.

static int **parseInt** (String s) throws NumberFormatException
>    Returns the int represented by *s*.

static String **toString** (int i)
>    Returns a String containing the string representation of *i*.


# IOException              java.io          An exception involving I/O

Ancestor class of **EOFException** and **FileNotFoundException**. Read and write errors are of the class IOException.


# KeyEvent                 java.awt.event    Java 1.1 keyboard event object.

char **getKeyChar** ()
>    Returns the character entered at the keyboard.

int **getKeyCode** ()
>    Returns the key code of the key entered at the keyboard.

boolean **isActionKey** ()
>    Returns true if the key entered at the keyboard has no character equivalent.


# KeyListener              java.awt.event    Java 1.1 keyboard event handler
>                                            interface.

abstract void **keyTyped** (KeyEvent e)
>    Called when a key is typed at the keyboard.


# Label                    java.awt          A GUI label.

**Label** (String label)
>    Constructor – Creates a Label with its text set to *label*.

**Label** (String label, int alignment)
>    Constructor – Creates a Label with its text set to *label* and its alignment set to *alignment*. *alignment* must be one of the constants defined in the Label class.

final static int LEFT, CENTER, RIGHT
>    Allowed values for *alignment* in the Label or constructor.

String **getText** ()
>    Returns the Label's text.

void **setFont** (Font font)
>    Sets the font of the Label to *font*.

# Math

java.lang          Class for math methods. Note all methods are static.

static int **abs** (int a)
static double **abs** (double a)
> Returns the absolute value of *a*.

static double **sin** (double a)
static double **cos** (double a)
static double **tan** (double a)
> Returns the sine, cosine, or tangent of angle *a* in radians.

static double **sqrt** (double a)
> Returns the square root of *a*.

static long **round** (double a)
> Returns *a*, rounded to the nearest 64-bit integer (long).

static int **min** (int a, int b)
static double **min** (double a, double b)
> Returns the minimum of *a* and *b*.

static int **max** (int a, int b)
static double **max** (double a, double b)
> Returns the maximum of *a* and *b*.

static double **pow** (double x, double y)
> Returns $x^y$.

static double **random** ()
> Returns a random number from 0.0 (inclusive) to 1.0 (exclusive).

# MediaTracker

java.awt          Used to load multiple images.

**MediaTracker** (Component comp)
> Constructor.

**addImage** (Image img, int id)
> Adds an image to be loaded by the tracker.

void **waitForAll** ()
> Starts all the images loading and waits until the loading is completed or an error occurs.

boolean **isErrorAny** ()
> Returns true if there were any errors loading an image.

# Menu                          java.awt          A single menu in a menu bar.

**Menu** (String menuName)
> Constructor – Creates a menu called *menuName*.

void **add** (MenuItem menuItem)
> Adds *menuItem* to the end of the menu.

# MenuBar                       java.awt          The menu bar at the top of the window.

**MenuBar** ()
> Constructor – Creates a menu bar. It must be placed in the Frame by calling the Frame method setMenuBar.

void **add** (Menu menuName)
> Adds *menuName* to the end of the menus on the menu bar.

# MenuItem                      java.awt          A menu item in a menu.

**MenuItem** (String itemName)
> Constructor – Creates a menu item called *itemName*.

void **setEnabled** (Boolean newEnabled)
> Enables (make the menu item selectable) if *newEnabled* is true. Disables (dims the menu item and makes it unselectable) if *newEnabled* is false.

void **addActionListener** (ActionListener listener)
> Attaches an ActionListener object to the menu item. Causes the actionPerformed method of the listener to be called whenever the menu item is selected.

# MouseEvent                    java.awt.event    Java 1.1 mouse event object.

Point **getPoint** ()
> Returns the location where the mouse was pressed or released.

int **getX** ()
> Returns the x-coordinate of the location where the mouse was pressed or released.

int **getY** ()
> Returns the y-coordinate of the location where the mouse was pressed or released.

# MouseListener          java.awt.event     Java 1.1 mouse event handler interface.

abstract void **mouseClicked** (MouseEvent e)
    Called when the mouse button is clicked (pressed and released).

abstract void **mouseEntered** (MouseEvent e)
    Called when the mouse enters the component.

abstract void **mouseExited** (MouseEvent e)
    Called when the mouse exits the component.

abstract void **mousePressed** (MouseEvent e)
    Called when the mouse button is pressed.

abstract void **mouseReleased** (MouseEvent e)
    Called when the mouse button is released.


# MouseMotionListener     java.awt.event     Java 1.1 mouse motion event handler interface.

abstract void **mouseDragged** (MouseEvent e)
    Called when the mouse is dragged (moved with the mouse button pressed) over the component.

abstract void **mouseMoved** (MouseEvent e)
    Called when the mouse moves over the component.


# Object          java.lang     Base class for all Java classes.

Object **clone** ()
    Creates a copy of the object. User-written classes must implement their own version of clone.

boolean **equals** (Object obj)
    Returns true if *obj* is equivalent to the object. User-written classes must implement their own version of equals.

int **hashCode** ()
    Computes a hashcode from the object's data. User-written classes must implement their own version of hashCode.

void **notify** ()
    Releases a thread waiting on the object. Must be called in a synchronized method.

void **notifyAll** ()
    Releases all threads waiting on the object. Must be called in a synchronized method.

String **toString** ()
> Returns a String representation of the object. User-written classes must implement
> their own version of toString.

void **wait** () throws InterruptedException
> Forces the current thread of execution to wait until released by a call to notify in the
> same object. Must be called in a synchronized method.

# Panel                              java.awt        Allows nesting of a layout within
                                                     another layout.

**Panel** ()
> Constructor.

void **setLayout** (LayoutManager layout)
> Sets the Panel's layout manager to *layout*.

void **add** (Component comp)
> Adds component *comp* to the Panel using the Panel's layout manager.

void **add** (String direction, Component comp)
> Used when the Panel's layout manager is BorderLayout. Adds component *comp* to
> the Panel in the area specified by *direction*. Possible values for *direction* are "North",
> "South", "East", "West", and "Center".

# Point                              java.awt        Specifies a location (x and y).

> A Point object is returned by methods that return an object's location.
> > e.g.  frame.getLocation ()

int **x, y**
> The x and y coordinates of the location.

# PrintJob                           java.awt        Used to send output to a printer.

> A PrintJob object is returned by the getPrintJob method in the Toolkit class.
> > e.g.  Toolkit.getDefaultToolkit ().getPrintJob (frame, fileName, null)

Graphics **getGraphics** ()
> Returns the graphics context of the page to be printed. When the graphics context is
> disposed, the contents of the graphics context will be sent to the printer.

Dimension **getPageDimension** ()
> Returns the height and width of the page in pixels. These pixels are usually about
> 1/72 of an inch regardless of the actual resolution of the printer.

void **end** ()
> Completes the print job.

# PrintWriter             java.io          Writes ASCII data to a file.

**PrintWriter** (FileWriter writer)
> Constructor – Opens *writer* for writing of ASCII text.

void **close** ()
> Closes the file.

void **print** (boolean b)
> Prints out boolean *b* as "true" or "false".

void **print** (char c)
> Prints out character *c*.

void **print** (double d)
> Prints out double *d*.

void **print** (int i)
> Prints out integer *i*.

void **print** (String str)
> Prints out string *str*.

void **println** (boolean b)
> Prints out boolean *b* as "true" or "false" followed by a Return.

void **println** (char c)
> Prints out character *c* followed by a Return.

void **println** (double d)
> Prints out double *d* followed by a Return.

void **println** (int i)
> Prints out integer *i* followed by a Return.

void **println** (String str)
> Prints out string *str* followed by a Return.

# Runnable             java.lang        Java interface for making a class concurrent.

void **run** ()
> Called in a new thread of execution when the start method of the Thread instantiated from the object is called.

# RuntimeException      java.lang        Exceptions caused by the JVM.

Ancestor class of **ArithmeticException, ClassCastException, NumberFormatException, ArrrayIndexOutOfBoundsException, EmptyStackException, StringIndexOutOfBoundsException, NegativeArraySizeException,** and **NullPointerException**. RuntimeExceptions need not be indicated in the throw clause of a method's signature.

# Scrollbar                      java.awt       Java GUI Scrollbar.

**Scrollbar** (int orientation, int value, int visible, int min, int max)
> Constructor – The *orientation* parameter is one of Scrollbar.HORIZONTAL or
> Scrollbar.VERTICAL. The *value* parameter is the initial value of the scrollbar. The
> *visible* parameter is the amount of the item being scrolled that is visible in the
> viewport. The *min* and *max* parameters are the minimum and maximum values
> between which the scrollbar can range.

int **getValue** ()
> Returns the current value of the scrollbar.

void **addAdjustmentListener** (AdjustmentListener listener)
> Attaches an AdjustmentListener object to the Scrollbar. Causes the
> adjustmentValueChanged method of the listener to be called whenever the value of
> the scrollbar changes.

# Stack                          java.util      Java implementation of a stack.

**Stack** ()
> Constructor.

boolean **empty** ()
> Returns true if the stack has no elements in it.

Object **peek** ()
> Returns the top element of the stack. Causes an EmptyStackException if the stack is
> empty.

Object **pop** ()
> Returns the top element of the stack and removes it from the stack. Causes an
> EmptyStackException if the stack is empty.

Object **push** (Object obj)
> Pushes *obj* onto the stack. Returns *obj*.

# String                        java.lang      Java Strings.

**String** (String str)
> Constructor – Creates a String object with value of *str*.

boolean **equals** (String str)
> Returns true if the String object is equal to *str*.

boolean **equalsIgnoreCase** (String str)
> Returns true if the String object is equal to *str* with case ignored.

int **compareTo** (String str)
> Returns the result of the String object compared to *str*. If the String object is less than *str*, it returns a negative value, if they are equal, it returns 0, if the String object is greater than *str*, it returns a positive value.

boolean **endsWith** (String str)
> Returns true if the String ends with *str*.

boolean **startsWith** (String str)
> Returns true if the String starts with *str*.

char **charAt** (int index)
> Returns the character at position *index* of the String object.

String **subString** (int startPosition)
> Returns the string starting from position *startPosition* of the String object.

String **subString** (int startPosition, int endPosition)
> Returns the string starting from position *startPosition* and ending at position *endPosition* – 1 of the String object.

String **concat** (String str)
> Returns the result of the String object concatenated with *str*.

int **indexOf** (int ch)
> Returns the index of the first occurrence of *ch* in the String object.

int **indexOf** (int ch, int position)
> Returns the first occurrence of *ch* in the String object starting from the position *position*.

int **indexOf** (String str, int position)
> Returns the first occurrence of *str* in the String object starting from the position *position*.

int **length** ()
> Returns the length of the String object.

String **toLowerCase** ()
> Returns a String object which is the original String object converted to lower case.

String **toUpperCase** ()
> Returns a String object which is the original String object converted to upper case.

static String **valueOf** (boolean b)
static String **valueOf** (int i)
static String **valueOf** (double d)
> Static method to convert a boolean, integer, or double to a String.

char **charAt** (int position)
> Returns the character at position *position* of the String object.

# StringBuffer

java.lang

String buffer where the contents can be changed.

**StringBuffer** ()
> Constructor.

**StringBuffer** (String str)
> Constructor – Initializes buffer to value *str*.

StringBuffer **append** (boolean b)
StringBuffer **append** (int i)
StringBuffer **append** (double d)
StringBuffer **append** (String str)
> Appends the string representation of the argument to the StringBuffer and then returns a reference to the StringBuffer.

StringBuffer **insert** (int offset, boolean b)
StringBuffer **insert** (int offset, int i)
StringBuffer **insert** (int offset, double d)
StringBuffer **insert** (int offset, String str)
> Inserts the string representation of the argument at location *offset* of the StringBuffer and then returns a reference to the StringBuffer.

void **setCharAt** (int position, char ch)
> Sets the character at position *position* to character *ch* in the StringBuffer object.

StringBuffer **reverse** ()
> Reverses the characters in the StringBuffer and then returns a reference to the StringBuffer.

int **length** ()
> Returns the number of characters in the StringBuffer.

String **toString** ()
> Returns a String representing the contents of the StringBuffer.

# StringTokenizer

java.util

Breaks a String down into tokens separated by white space.

**StringTokenizer** (String str)
> Constructor – Creates a StringTokenizer object to tokenize *str*.

int **countTokens** ()
> Returns the number of tokens remaining in the StringTokenizer.

boolean **hasMoreTokens** ()
> Returns true if there are more tokens to be read from the StringTokenizer.

String **nextToken** ()
> Returns the next token from the StringTokenizer.

# System
java.lang      Class for system functions. Note all methods are static.

static void **exit** (int exitCode)
Immediately terminates the Java program.

static final InputStream **in**
Standard input. Open as a DataInputStream to read lines from the console.

static final PrintStream **out**
Standard output. PrintStream supports most of the same methods as the PrintWriter class.

# TextArea
java.awt      A GUI text area with scrollbars for displaying large quantities of text.

**TextArea** (int rows, int cols)
Constructor – Creates a TextArea *rows* rows deep and *cols* columns wide.

**TextArea** (String str, int rows, int cols)
Constructor – Creates a TextArea *rows* rows deep and *cols* columns wide with initial value set to *str*.

void **setText** (String str)
Sets the text in the TextArea to *str*.

String **getText** ()
Returns the String containing the text in the TextArea.

void **appendText** (String str)
Appends *str* to the text in the TextArea.

void **insertText** (String str, int pos)
Inserts the String *str* into the text in the TextArea before position *pos*.

void **replaceText** (String str, int startPosition, int endPosition)
Replaces the text in the TextArea from position *startPosition* to *endPosition* – 1 with String *str*.

void **select** (int selectionStart, int selectionEnd)
Selects the text in the TextArea between *selectionStart* and *selectionEnd* (inclusive). If *selectionStart* = *selectionEnd*, the selection is just a cursor position.

void **selectAll** ()
Selects all the text in the TextArea.

# TextField

java.awt          A GUI text area for displaying
                  editabled text.

**TextField** (int cols)
    Constructor – Creates a TextField *cols* columns wide.

**TextField** (String str, int cols)
    Constructor – Creates a TextField *cols* columns wide with initial value set to *str*.

void **setText** (String str)
    Sets the text in the TextField to *str*.

String **getText** ()
    Returns the String containing the text in the TextField.

void **addActionListener** (ActionListener listener)
    Attaches an ActionListener object to the TextField. Causes the actionPerformed
    method of the listener to be called whenever ENTER is pressed in the TextField.

# Thread

java.lang         Used to create multiple threads of
                  execution.

**Thread** (Runnable obj)
    Constructor – Creates a Thread object based on the Runnable object.

void **start** ()
    Creates a new thread of execution running the Thread's run method.

void **stop** ()
    Stops the thread of execution associated with the Thread.

void **suspend** ()
    Suspends execution of a thread associated with the Thread.

void **resume** ()
    Allows the resumption of execution of a thread associated with the Thread.

void **run** ()
    The main body of the thread. The method executed in a new thread when the
    Thread's start method is called.

static void **sleep** (int millis) throws InterruptedException
    Causes the current thread to sleep for *millis* milliseconds.

# Toolkit

java.awt          Implements platform specific
                  functionality.

    A Toolkit object is returned by the getDefaultToolkit method of the Toolkit class or
    the getToolkit method of the Component class.
        e.g. Toolkit.getDefaultToolkit ()

static Toolkit **getDefaultToolkit** ()
> Returns the Toolkit object used by this platform.

String [] **getFontList** ()
> Returns an array of strings containing the names of all the fonts.

FontMetrics **getFontMetrics** (Font font)
> Returns the font metrics for *font*.

Image **getImage** (String fileName)
> Creates an Image object from the picture stored in *fileName*. Does not start the image loading.

PrintJob **getPrintJob** (Frame frame, String jobTitle, Properties props)
> Displays a print dialog box and if the user does not select Cancel, returns the PrintJob object. The first parameter is the parent frame of the print dialog box. The second parameter is the job title. The third parameter is ignored and should be set to null.

Dimension **getScreenSize** ()
> Returns the dimensions of the screen.


# Vector                          java.awt          Java's implementation of a list.

**Vector** ()
> Constructor.

int **size** ()
> Returns the number of elements in the Vector.

void **addElement** (Object obj)
> Adds *obj* to the end of the list of elements.

void **insertElementAt** (Object obj, int index)
> Inserts *obj* before the index'th element. If index is 0, then obj is inserted at the beginning of the lost of elements.

void **setElementAt** (Object obj, int index)
> Changes the *index*'th element to *obj*.

Object **elementAt** (int index)
> Returns the *index*'th element of the list.

int **indexOf** (Object obj)
> Returns the index of the element containing *obj*. Returns −1 if *obj* is not found.

boolean **isEmpty** ()
> Returns true if the vector contains no elements.

void **removeElement** (Object obj)
> Removes *obj* from the list of elements.

void **removeElementAt** (int index)
> Removes the *index*'th element of the list.

# WindowEvent                    java.awt.event      Java 1.1 window event object.

Window **getWindow** ()
    Returns the Window (Applet or Frame) that generated the event.


# WindowListener                 java.awt.event      Java 1.1 window event handler
                                                                       interface.

abstract void **windowActivated** (WindowEvent e)
    Called when the window is activated (brought to the front).

abstract void **windowClosed** (WindowEvent e)
    Called after the window is closed.

abstract void **windowClosing** (WindowEvent e)
    Called when the user has clicked the window's close box.

abstract void **windowDeactivated** (WindowEvent e)
    Called when the window is deactivated.

abstract void **windowDeiconified** (WindowEvent e)
    Called after the window is deiconified (expanded after being minimized).

abstract void **windowIconified** (WindowEvent e)
    Called after the window is iconified (minimized).

abstract void **windowOpened** (WindowEvent e)
    Called when the window is shown for the first time.

# Appendix D : HSA Class Library

The *hsa* package consists of nine classes. It is included as part of the **Ready to Program with Java™ Technology** environment. The classes make it easier for users to begin writing programs that explore the basic concepts of computer science before coming to terms with the input and output methods of the Java class library.

To ensure the easiest possible transition from using the *hsa* package to using only the Java class library, wherever possible we have made the graphics methods in the *Console* class identical to those in the Java *Graphics* class. The *print* and *println* methods of the *Console*, *Stdout*, and *TextOutputFile* are also the same as those in the Java *PrintWriter* class. In a number of cases the classes in the *hsa* package contain extra methods.

See Appendix J for information on installing the **Ready** environment.

To use the *hsa* classes in a Java class, the following line must appear in the class header:

**import** *hsa*.*;

## Classes

### Console

The Console window can hold 25 lines of 80 column text. The user can input data directly in the Console window. The output of the program appears there also. Formatted text output is provided. It supports all the basic Java Graphics class methods plus two more to draw stars and maple leaves (suitable for flags).

The Console class window has three buttons. The "Save" button saves the contents of the screen as a ".bmp" (Windows Bitmap) file. The "Print" button prints out the contents of the window. The "Quit" button quits the program immediately. It gives visual notification when the program is finished execution by changing the label in the "Quit" button to "Close".

### TextConsole

The TextConsole window is a 25x80 window used for text output. As the output scrolls off the top of the window, a scroll bar is activated that allows users to view all output from the program. The TextConsole class differs from the Console class in that all text output is kept and can be saved and printed.

The user can input data directly in the Console window. The output of the program appears there also. Formatted text output is provided.

The TextConsole class window has three buttons. The "Save" button saves all the output sent to the window to a text file. The "Print" button prints out the all the output. The "Quit" button quits the program immediately. It gives visual notification when the program is finished execution by changing the label in the "Quit" button to "Close".

## Stdin

This is a non-instantiated class to allow users to read all the Java primitive data types from standard input before they have learned about exception handling and the intricacies of the Java primitive wrapper classes. It also makes it possible to read several primitives from one line of input without having to know the StringTokenizer class.

## Stdout

This is a non-instantiated class to allow users to output formatted data to standard output without having to learn the java.text.NumberFormat class. Users can write data to fixed length fields and with a fixed number of decimal places.

## TextInputFile

This class makes it easier to read from text files. It allows the user to read any Java primitive data type from a text file and does all the conversions, string tokenizing, and exception handling automatically.

## TextOutputFile

This class makes it easier to write to text files. It's major convenience is that it handles formatted output. Users can specify field length when outputting primitive data type as well as the number of decimal places when outputting real numbers.

## FatalError

This is a class to display fatal errors. When instantiated, it displays a window with a specified message and a button labelled "Quit". When the button is pressed, the program immediately exits.

Helpful for users who want to add error checking to their program but are not yet familiar with Frames and the rest of the Java class library.

## Message

This is a class to display messages. When instantiated, it displays a window with a specified message and a button labelled "OK". When the button is pressed, the program continues execution.

## Status

A quick way of displaying changing status messages without having to learn about Frames, and so on.

# Console

## Console - General Methods and Constructors

Console ()
> Constructor.

Console (int fontSize)
> Constructor – Creates a Console window with the text size set to *fontSize*.

Console (int rows, int cols)
> Constructor – Creates a Console window with width of *cols* columns and height of *rows* rows.

Console (int rows, int cols, int fontSize)
> Constructor – Creates a Console window with width of *cols* columns, height of *rows* rows, and the text size set to *fontSize*.

Console (String title)
> Constructor – Creates a Console window and sets the window title to *title*.

Console (int fontSize, String title)
> Constructor – Creates a Console window with the text size set to *fontSize* and sets the window title to *title*.

Console (int rows, int cols, String title)
> Constructor – Creates a Console window with width of *cols* columns, height of *rows* rows, and the window title set to *title*.

Console (int rows, int cols, int fontSize, String title)
> Constructor – Creates a console window with width of *cols* columns, height of *rows* rows, the text size set to *fontSize*, and the window title set to *title*.

void **close** ()
> Closes the Console window and disposes of its contents.

## Console - Graphics Methods

void **clearRect** (int x, int y, int width, int height)
> Clears the rectangle to the background color.

void **copyArea** (int x, int y, int width, int height, int deltaX, int deltaY)
> Copies the rectangle defined by the upper-left corner $(x, y)$ with width of *width* and height of *height* to a position moved by *deltaX* and *deltaY* pixels.

void **draw3DRect** (int x, int y, int width, int height, boolean raised)
> Draws a 3-D rectangle. It appears raised if *raised* is true.

void **drawArc** (int x, int y, int width, int height, int startAngle, int arcAngle)
> Draws an arc. The arc is inscribed in the rectangle defined by the upper-left corner $(x, y)$ with width of *width* and height of *height*. It starts at *startAngle* degrees and goes counterclockwise for *arcAngle* degrees.

void **drawLine** (int x1, int y1, int x2, int y2)
    Draws a line from (*x1*, *y1*) to (*x2*, *y2*).

void **drawMapleLeaf** (int x, int y, int width, int height)
    Draws a maple leaf. The maple leaf is inscribed in the rectangle defined by the upper-left corner (*x*, *y*) with width of *width* and height of *height*.

void **drawOval** (int x, int y, int width, int height)
    Draws an ellipse. The ellipse is inscribed in the rectangle defined by the upper-left corner (*x*, *y*) with width of *width* and height of *height*.

void **drawPolygon** (int[] xPoints, int[] yPoints, int numPoints)
    Draws a polygon. The *xPoints* and *yPoints* arrays define the coordinates of the array of vertices. *numPoints* specifies the number of vertices in the polygon.

void **drawRect** (int x, int y, int width, int height)
    Draws a rectangle with upper-left corner at (*x*, *y*) with width of *width* and height of *height*.

void **drawRoundRect** (int x, int y, int width, int height, int arcWidth, int arcHeight)
    Draws a rectangle with rounded corners with upper-left corner at (*x*, *y*) with width of *width* and height of *height*. *arcWidth* and *arcHeight* are the width and height of the ellipse used to draw the rounded corners.

void **drawStar** (int x, int y, int width, int height)
    Draws a star. The star is inscribed in the rectangle defined by the upper-left corner (*x*, *y*) with width of *width* and height of *height*.

void **drawString** (String str, int x, int y)
    Draws the string *str* at the starting point (*x*, *y*). The *y* coordinate is the base line of the text.

void **fill3DRect** (int x, int y, int width, int height, boolean raised)
    Draws a filled 3-D rectangle. It appears raised if *raised* is true.

void **fillArc** (int x, int y, int width, int height, int startAngle, int arcAngle)
    Draws a filled arc. The arc is inscribed in the rectangle defined by the upper-left corner (*x*, *y*) with width of *width* and height of *height*. It starts at *startAngle* degrees and goes counterclockwise for *arcAngle* degrees.

void **fillMapleLeaf** (int x, int y, int width, int height)
    Draws a filled maple leaf. The maple leaf is inscribed in the rectangle defined by the upper-left corner (*x*, *y*) with width of *width* and height of *height*.

void **fillOval** (int x, int y, int width, int height)
    Draws a filled ellipse. The ellipse is inscribed in the rectangle defined by the upper-left corner (*x*, *y*) with width of *width* and height of *height*.

void **fillPolygon** (int[] xPoints, int[] yPoints, int numPoints)
    Draws a filled polygon. The *xPoints* and *yPoints* arrays define the coordinates of the array of vertices. *numPoints* specifies the number of vertices in the polygon.

void **fillRect** (int x, int y, int width, int height)
> Draws a filled rectangle with upper-left corner at (*x*, *y*) with width of *width* and height of *height*.

void **fillRoundRect** (int x, int y, int width, int height, int arcWidth, int arcHeight)
> Draws a filled rectangle with rounded corners with upper-left corner at (*x*, *y*) with width of *width* and height of *height*. *arcWidth* and *arcHeight* are the width and height of the ellipse used to draw the rounded corners.

void **fillStar** (int x, int y, int width, int height)
> Draws a filled star. The star is inscribed in the rectangle defined by the upper-left corner (*x*, *y*) with width of *width* and height of *height*.

int **getWidth** ()
> Returns the width of the drawing surface of the Console window in pixels.

int **getHeight** ()
> Returns the height of the drawing surface of the Console window in pixels.

void **setColor** (Color c)
> Sets the color of the graphics context. The color is used for any draw methods.

void **setFont** (Font f)
> Sets the font of the graphics context. The font is used with the drawString method.

void **setPaintMode** ()
> Sets the graphics context into paint mode. All drawing in the graphics context draws over the background.

void **setXORMode** (Color c)
> Sets the graphics context into XOR mode. All drawing in the graphics context is XOR'd with the background. The color specified by *c* is a special color so that any drawing done on a background of color *c* will not be changed.

## Console - Text Input and Output Methods

void **clear** ()
> Clears the entire Console window and sets the cursor to the upper-left corner.

int **getMaxColumns** ()
> Returns the width of the Console window in columns.

int **getMaxRows** ()
> Returns the height of the Console window in rows.

int **getColumn** ()
> Returns the column number of the current cursor position.

int **getRow** ()
> Returns the row number of the current cursor position.

void **print** (byte b)
void **print** (short s)
void **print** (int i)

void **print** (long l)
void **print** (float f)
void **print** (double d)
void **print** (boolean b)
void **print** (char c)
void **print** (String s)
  Outputs the argument to the Console window beginning at the cursor position.

void **print** (byte number, int fieldSize)
void **print** (short number, int fieldSize)
void **print** (int number, int fieldSize)
void **print** (long number, int fieldSize)
  Outputs *number* to the Console window in a field of width *fieldSize* beginning at the cursor position. If the number (when converted to String) is larger than *fieldSize*, *fieldSize* is ignored. The output is right justified within the field.

void **print** (float number, int fieldSize)
void **print** (double number, int fieldSize)
  Outputs *number* to the Console window in a field of width *fieldSize* beginning at the cursor position. The method adjusts the number of decimal places displayed to fit in the field, if possible. If the argument (when converted to String) is larger than *fieldSize*, *fieldSize* is ignored. The output is right justified within the field.

void **print** (boolean b, int fieldSize)
void **print** (char c, int fieldSize)
void **print** (String s, int fieldSize)
  Outputs the argument to the Console window in a field of width *fieldSize* beginning at the cursor position. If the argument (when converted to String) is larger than *fieldSize*, *fieldSize* is ignored. The output is left justified.

void **print** (double number, int fieldSize, int decimalPlaces)
void **print** (float number, int fieldSize, int decimalPlaces)
  Outputs *number* to the Console window in a field of width *fieldSize* with *decimalPlaces* number of decimal places beginning at the cursor position. The field width is ignored if the number will not fit. The output is right justified.

void **println** ()
  Outputs a Return at the cursor position to the Console window.

void **println** (byte b)
void **println** (short s)
void **println** (int i)
void **println** (long l)
void **println** (float f)
void **println** (double d)
void **println** (boolean b)
void **println** (char c)

void **println** (String s)
void **println** (byte b, int fieldSize)
void **println** (short s, int fieldSize)
void **println** (int i, int fieldSize)
void **println** (long l, int fieldSize)
void **println** (float f, int fieldSize)
void **println** (double d, int fieldSize)
void **println** (boolean b, int fieldSize)
void **println** (char c, int fieldSize)
void **println** (String s, int fieldSize)
void **println** (float f, int fieldSize, int decimalPlaces)
void **println** (double d, int fieldSize, int decimalPlaces)
> Identical to **print** method with same arguments, except that a Return is output after the argument.

byte **readByte** ()
> Returns the byte value (–128 to 127) read from the keyboard.

short **readShort** ()
> Returns the 2-byte integer (–32,768 to 32,767) read from the keyboard.

int **readInt** ()
> Returns the 4-byte integer (–2,147,483,648 to 2,147,483,647) read from the keyboard.

long **readLong** ()
> Returns the 8-byte integer read from the keyboard.

float **readFloat** ()
> Returns the 4-byte float read from the keyboard.

double **readDouble** ()
> Returns the 8-byte double read from the keyboard.

boolean **readBoolean** ()
> Returns the boolean value (either "true" or "false", case insensitive) read from the keyboard.

char **readChar** ()
> Returns the character read from the keyboard.

String **readString** ()
> Returns the String read from the keyboard.

String **readLine** ()
> Returns the entire line of input read from the keyboard without the Return.

char **getChar** ()
> Returns the character read from the keyboard. Does not wait for **Enter** to be pressed.

void **setTextColor** (Color c)
> Sets the color for text output from print and println methods.

void **setTextBackgroundColor** (Color c)
> Sets the background color for text output from print and println methods.

void **setCursorVisible** (boolean visible)
> Shows or hides the text cursor according to the *visible* parameter.

void **setCursor** (int row, int col)
> Sets the cursor position to row *row* and column *col*.

## Console - Example

```
import java.awt.*;
import hsa.Console;

public class TestConsole
{
    public static void main (String[] args)
    {
        Console c = new Console ();
        c.print ("Enter the radius of the circle: ");
        int radius = c.readInt ();
        c.setColor (Color.green);
        c.fillOval (c.getWidth () / 2 – radius, c.getHeight () / 2 – radius,
                radius * 2, radius * 2);
    } // main method
} /* TestConsole class */
```

# TextConsole

## TextConsole - General Methods and Constructors

TextConsole ()
> Constructor.

TextConsole (int fontSize)
> Constructor – Creates a TextConsole window with the text size set to *fontSize*.

TextConsole (int rows, int cols)
> Constructor – Creates a TextConsole window with width of *cols* columns and height of *rows* rows.

TextConsole (int rows, int cols, int fontSize)
> Constructor – Creates a TextConsole window with width of *cols* columns, height of *rows* rows, and the text size set to *fontSize*.

TextConsole (String title)
>   Constructor – Creates a TextConsole window and sets the window title to *title*.

TextConsole (int fontSize, String title)
>   Constructor – Creates a TextConsole window with the text size set to *fontSize* and sets the window title to *title*.

TextConsole (int rows, int cols, String title)
>   Constructor – Creates a TextConsole window with width of *cols* columns, height of *rows* rows, and the window title set to *title*.

TextConsole (int rows, int cols, int fontSize, String title)
>   Constructor – Creates a TextConsole window with width of *cols* columns, height of *rows* rows, the text size set to *fontSize*, and the window title set to *title*.

void **close** ()
>   Closes the TextConsole window and disposes of its contents.

## TextConsole - Text Input and Output Methods

void **print** (byte b)
void **print** (short s)
void **print** (int i)
void **print** (long l)
void **print** (float f)
void **print** (double d)
void **print** (boolean b)
void **print** (char c)
void **print** (String s)
>   Outputs the argument to the TextConsole window beginning at the cursor position.

void **print** (byte number, int fieldSize)
void **print** (short number, int fieldSize)
void **print** (int number, int fieldSize)
void **print** (long number, int fieldSize)
>   Outputs *number* to the TextConsole window in a field of width *fieldSize* beginning at the cursor position. If the number (when converted to String) is larger than *fieldSize*, *fieldSize* is ignored. The output is right justified within the field.

void **print** (float number, int fieldSize)
void **print** (double number, int fieldSize)
>   Outputs *number* to the TextConsole window in a field of width *fieldSize* beginning at the cursor position. The method adjusts the number of decimal places displayed to fit in the field, if possible. If the argument (when converted to String) is larger than *fieldSize*, *fieldSize* is ignored. The output is right justified within the field.

void **print** (boolean b, int fieldSize)
void **print** (char c, int fieldSize)
void **print** (String s, int fieldSize)
> Outputs the argument to the TextConsole window in a field of width *fieldSize* beginning at the cursor position. If the argument (when converted to String) is larger than *fieldSize*, *fieldSize* is ignored. The output is left justified.

void **print** (double number, int fieldSize, int decimalPlaces)
void **print** (float number, int fieldSize, int decimalPlaces)
> Outputs *number* to the TextConsole window in a field of width *fieldSize* with *decimalPlaces* number of decimal places beginning at the cursor position. The field width is ignored if the number will not fit. The output is right justified.

void **println** ()
> Outputs a Return at the cursor position to the TextConsole window.

void **println** (byte b)
void **println** (short s)
void **println** (int i)
void **println** (long l)
void **println** (float f)
void **println** (double d)
void **println** (boolean b)
void **println** (char c)
void **println** (String s)
void **println** (byte b, int fieldSize)
void **println** (short s, int fieldSize)
void **println** (int i, int fieldSize)
void **println** (long l, int fieldSize)
void **println** (float f, int fieldSize)
void **println** (double d, int fieldSize)
void **println** (boolean b, int fieldSize)
void **println** (char c, int fieldSize)
void **println** (String s, int fieldSize)
void **println** (float f, int fieldSize, int decimalPlaces)
void **println** (double d, int fieldSize, int decimalPlaces)
> Identical to **print** method with same arguments, except that a Return is output after the argument.

byte **readByte** ()
> Returns the byte value (−128 to 127) read from the keyboard.

short **readShort** ()
> Returns the 2-byte integer (−32,768 to 32,767) read from the keyboard.

int **readInt** ()
> Returns the 4-byte integer (−2,147,483,648 to 2,147,483,647) read from the keyboard.

long **readLong** ()
>  Returns the 8-byte integer read from the keyboard.

float **readFloat** ()
>  Returns the 4-byte float read from the keyboard.

double **readDouble** ()
>  Returns the 8-byte double read from the keyboard.

boolean **readBoolean** ()
>  Returns the boolean value (either "true" or "false", case insensitive) read from the keyboard.

char **readChar** ()
>  Returns the character read from the keyboard.

String **readString** ()
>  Returns the String read from the keyboard.

String **readLine** ()
>  Returns the entire line of input read from the keyboard without the Return.

## TextConsole - Example

```
import java.awt.*;
import hsa.TextConsole;

public class TestTextConsole
{
    public static void main (String[] args)
    {
        Console c = new TextConsole ();
        c.print ("Enter the times table: ");
        int multiplier = c.readInt ();
        for (int count = 1 ; count <= 10 ; count++)
        {
            c.print (count, 3);
            c.print (count * multiplier, 4);
        }
    } // main method
} /* TestTextConsole class */
```

# Stdin

static boolean **close** ()
>  Closes standard input to prevent further reading.

static boolean **eof** ()
>    Returns true if the next thing to be read from the keyboard is the end-of-file marker.
>    (You can generate an end-of-file by pressing either Ctrl+Z or Ctrl+D.)

static byte **readByte** ()
>    Returns the byte value (−128 to 127) read from the keyboard.

static short **readShort** ()
>    Returns the 2-byte integer (−32,768 to 32,767) read from the keyboard.

static int **readInt** ()
>    Returns the 4-byte integer (−2,147,483,648 to 2,147,483,647) read from the keyboard.

static long **readLong** ()
>    Returns the 8-byte integer read from the keyboard.

static float **readFloat** ()
>    Returns the 4-byte float read from the keyboard.

static double **readDouble** ()
>    Returns the 8-byte double read from the keyboard.

static boolean **readBoolean** ()
>    Returns the boolean value (either "true" or "false", case insensitive) read from the
>    keyboard.

static char **readChar** ()
>    Returns the character read from the keyboard.

static String **readString** ()
>    Returns the String read from the keyboard.

static String **readLine** ()
>    Returns the entire line of input read from the keyboard without the Return.

## Stdin - Example

See Stdout example.


# Stdout

```
static void print (byte b)
static void print (short s)
static void print (int i)
static void print (long l)
static void print (float f)
static void print (double d)
static void print (boolean b)
static void print (char c)
```

static void **print** (String s)
> Outputs the argument to standard output.

static void **print** (byte number, int fieldSize)
static void **print** (short number, int fieldSize)
static void **print** (int number, int fieldSize)
static void **print** (long number, int fieldSize)
> Outputs *number* to standard output in a field of width *fieldSize*. If the number (when converted to String) is larger than *fieldSize*, *fieldSize* is ignored. The output is right justified within the field.

static void **print** (float number, int fieldSize)
static void **print** (double number, int fieldSize)
> Outputs *number* to standard output in a field of width *fieldSize*. The method adjusts the number of decimal places displayed to fit in the field, if possible. If the argument (when converted to String) is larger than *fieldSize*, *fieldSize* is ignored. The output is right justified within the field.

static void **print** (boolean b, int fieldSize)
static void **print** (char c, int fieldSize)
static void **print** (String s, int fieldSize)
> Outputs the argument to standard output in a field of width *fieldSize*. If the argument (when converted to String) is larger than *fieldSize*, *fieldSize* is ignored. The output is left justified.

static void **print** (double number, int fieldSize, int decimalPlaces)
static void **print** (float number, int fieldSize, int decimalPlaces)
> Outputs *number* to standard output in a field of width *fieldSize* with *decimalPlaces* number of decimal places. The field width is ignored if the number will not fit. The output is right justified.

static void **println** ()
> Output a Return to standard output.

static void **println** (byte b)
static void **println** (short s)
static void **println** (int i)
static void **println** (long l)
static void **println** (float f)
static void **println** (double d)
static void **println** (boolean b)
static void **println** (char c)
static void **println** (String s)
static void **println** (byte b, int fieldSize)
static void **println** (short s, int fieldSize)
static void **println** (int i, int fieldSize)
static void **println** (long l, int fieldSize)

static void **println** (float f, int fieldSize)
static void **println** (double d, int fieldSize)
static void **println** (boolean b, int fieldSize)
static void **println** (char c, int fieldSize)
static void **println** (String s, int fieldSize)
static void **println** (float f, int fieldSize, int decimalPlaces)
static void **println** (double d, int fieldSize, int decimalPlaces)
    Identical to **print** method with same arguments, except that a Return is output after
    the argument.

## Stdout - Example

```
import hsa.*;

// Reads and writes number to standard input and output.
public class TestStdinStdout
{
    public static void main (String[] args)
    {
        Stdout.println ("Calculate square roots");
        while (true)
        {
            Stdout.print ("Enter a number: ");
            if (Stdin.eof ()) break;
            double number = Stdin.readDouble ();
            if (number < 0)
            {
                // Instantiating a FatalError object displays an
                // error window and then quits the program.
                new FatalError ("Attempted to take the square " +
                            "root of a negative number");
                // Never reaches here.
            }
            Stdout.println ("The square root of ");
            Stdout.print (number)
            Stdout.print (" is ");
            Stdout.println (Math.sqrt (number), 8, 5);
        }
    } // main method
} /* TestStdinStdout class */
```

# TextInputFile

**TextInputFile** ()
> Constructor – Opens standard input as a TextInputFile.

**TextInputFile** (File file)
> Constructor – Opens *file* as a TextInputFile.

**TextInputFile** (String fileName)
> Constructor – Opens file with name *fileName* as a TextInputFile. If *fileName* is "Standard Input", "Keyboard" or "Stdin" (case irrelevant), standard input is opened as a TextInputFile.

void **close** ()
> Closes the TextInputFile to prevent further reading.

boolean **eof** ()
> Returns true if the next thing to be read from the file is the end-of-file marker. (When reading from standard input, you can generate an end-of-file by pressing either Ctrl+Z or Ctrl+D.)

byte **readByte** ()
> Returns the byte value (–128 to 127) read from the file.

short **readShort** ()
> Returns the 2-byte integer (–32,768 to 32,767) read from the file.

int **readInt** ()
> Returns the 4-byte integer (–2,147,483,648 to 2,147,483,647) read from the file.

long **readLong** ()
> Returns the 8-byte integer read from the file.

float **readFloat** ()
> Returns the 4-byte float read from the file.

double **readDouble** ()
> Returns the 8-byte double read from the file.

boolean **readBoolean** ()
> Returns the boolean value (either "true" or "false", case insensitive) read from the file.

char **readChar** ()
> Returns the character read from the file.

String **readString** ()
> Returns the String read from the file.

String **readLine** ()
> Returns the entire line of input read from the file without the Return.

## TextInputFile - Example

```
import hsa.*;

// Reads a file of integers and calculate their square roots
public class TestTextInputFile
{
    public static void main (String[] args)
    {
        String fileName;
        TextInputFile f;
        int lineNumber = 1;
        Stdout.print ("Enter the file to be read: ");
        fileName = Stdin.readLine ();
        f = new TextInputFile (fileName);
        while (!f.eof ())
        {
            double number = f.readDouble ();
            Stdout.print (number, 10, 4);
            Stdout.print (" ");
            Stdout.println (Math.sqrt (number), 10, 4);
        }
        f.close ();
    } // main method
} /* TestTextInputFile class */
```

# TextOutputFile

**TextOutputFile** ()
> Constructor – Opens standard output as a TextOutputFile.

**TextOutputFile** (File file)
> Constructor – Opens *file* as a TextOutputFile.

**TextOutputFile** (String fileName)
> Constructor – Opens file with name *fileName* as a TextOutputFile. If *fileName* is "Standard Output", "Screen" or "Stdout" (case irrelevant), standard output is opened as a TextOutputFile.

**TextOutputFile** (File file, boolean append)
> Constructor – Opens *file* as a TextOutputFile. If *append* is true, any output will be appended to *file*.

**TextOutputFile** (String fileName, boolean append)
> Constructor – Opens file with name *fileName* as a TextOutputFile. If *append* is true, any output will be appended to the file. If *fileName* is "Standard Output", "Screen" or "Stdout" (case irrelevant), standard output is opened as a TextOutputFile.

void **close** ()
> Closes the TextOutputFile to prevent further writing.

void **print** (byte b)
void **print** (short s)
void **print** (int i)
void **print** (long l)
void **print** (float f)
void **print** (double d)
void **print** (boolean b)
void **print** (char c)
void **print** (String s)
> Outputs the argument to the file.

void **print** (byte number, int fieldSize)
void **print** (short number, int fieldSize)
void **print** (int number, int fieldSize)
void **print** (long number, int fieldSize)
> Outputs *number* to the file in a field of width *fieldSize*. If the number (when converted to String) is larger than *fieldSize*, *fieldSize* is ignored. The output is right justified within the field.

void **print** (float number, int fieldSize)
void **print** (double number, int fieldSize)
> Outputs *number* to the file in a field of width *fieldSize*. The method adjusts the number of decimal places displayed to fit in the field, if possible. If the argument (when converted to String) is larger than *fieldSize*, *fieldSize* is ignored. The output is right justified within the field.

void **print** (boolean b, int fieldSize)
void **print** (char c, int fieldSize)
void **print** (String s, int fieldSize)
> Outputs the argument to the file in a field of width *fieldSize*. If the argument (when converted to String) is larger than *fieldSize*, *fieldSize* is ignored. The output is left justified.

void **print** (double number, int fieldSize, int decimalPlaces)
void **print** (float number, int fieldSize, int decimalPlaces)
> Outputs *number* to the file in a field of width *fieldSize* with *decimalPlaces* number of decimal places. The field width is ignored if the number will not fit. The output is right justified.

void **println** ()
>   Output a Return to the file.

void **println** (byte b)
void **println** (short s)
void **println** (int i)
void **println** (long l)
void **println** (float f)
void **println** (double d)
void **println** (boolean b)
void **println** (char c)
void **println** (String s)
void **println** (byte b, int fieldSize)
void **println** (short s, int fieldSize)
void **println** (int i, int fieldSize)
void **println** (long l, int fieldSize)
void **println** (float f, int fieldSize)
void **println** (double d, int fieldSize)
void **println** (boolean b, int fieldSize)
void **println** (char c, int fieldSize)
void **println** (String s, int fieldSize)
void **println** (float f, int fieldSize, int decimalPlaces)
void **println** (double d, int fieldSize, int decimalPlaces)
>   Identical to **print** method with same arguments, except that a Return is output after
>   the argument.

## TextOutputFile - Example

```java
import hsa.*;

// Saves a Times table to a file.
public class TestTextOutputFile
{
    public static void main (String[] args)
    {
        String fileName;
        TextOutputFile f;
        int lineNumber = 1;
        Stdout.print ("Enter the file to be written: ");
        fileName = Stdin.readLine ();
        f = new TextOutputFile (fileName);
        f.print (" ", 6);                    // Print 6 spaces
```

```
        for (int i = 1 ; i <= 12 ; i++)   // Print numbers across top
        {
            f.print (i, 4);
        }
        for (int i = 1 ; i <= 12 ; i++)
        {
            f.print (i, 4);
            f.print (" ");
            for (int j = 1 ; j <= 12 ; j++)
            {
                f.print (i * j, 4);
            }
            f.println ();
        }
        f.close ();
    } // main method
} /* TestTextOutputFile class */
```

# FatalError

**FatalError** (String message)
> Constructor – Displays *message* in a window titled "Fatal Error" centered on the screen. When the "Quit" button is pressed, the program exits immediately.

**FatalError** (String message, Frame frame)
> Constructor – Displays *message* in a window titled "Fatal Error" centered on the Frame *frame*. When the "Quit" button is pressed, the program exits immediately.

## FatalError - Example

> See Stdout example.

# Message

**Message** (String message)
> Constructor – Displays *message* in a untitled window centered on the screen. When the "OK" button is pressed, execution returns from the call to the constructor.

**Message** (String message, String title)
> Constructor – Displays *message* in a window titled *title* centered on the screen. When the "OK" button is pressed, execution returns from the call to the constructor.

**Message** (String message, Frame frame)
> Constructor – Displays *message* in a untitled window centered on Frame *frame*. When the "OK" button is pressed, execution returns from the call to the constructor.

**Message** (String message, String title, Frame frame)
> Constructor – Displays *message* in a window titled *title* centered on Frame *frame*. When the "OK" button is pressed, execution returns from the call to the constructor.

static void **beep** ()
> Causes the computer to beep. Useful for catching the user's attention.

## Message - Example

```
import hsa.*;

// Brings up four message windows, one after another.
public class TestMessage
{
    public static void main (String[] args)
    {
        new Message ("This is the first message", "First message");
        new Message ("This is the second message",
            "Second message");
        new Message ("This is the third message",
            "Third message");
        new Message ("This is the last message", "Last message");
    } // main method
} /* TestMessage class */
```

## Status

**Status** (String message)
> Constructor – Displays *message* in a untitled window centered on the screen. The window only disappears when the hide () method is called or the user clicks the window's Close button (the X on the right hand side of the window's title bar). Execution returns from the call to the constructor immediately.

**Status** (String message, String title)
> Constructor – Displays *message* in a window titled *title* centered on the screen. The window only disappears when the hide () method is called or the user clicks the window's Close button (the X on the right hand side of the window's title bar). Execution returns from the call to the constructor immediately.

**Status** (String message, Frame frame)
> Constructor – Displays *message* in a untitled window centered on Frame *frame*. The window only disappears when the hide () method is called or the user clicks the window's Close button (the X on the right hand side of the window's title bar). Execution returns from the call to the constructor immediately.

**Status** (String message, String title, Frame frame)
> Constructor – Displays *message* in a window titled *title* centered on Frame *frame*. The window only disappears when the hide () method is called or the user clicks the

window's Close button (the X on the right hand side of the window's title bar). Execution returns from the call to the constructor immediately.

void **setMessage** (String message)
> Changes the message in the window to *message*.

void **hide** ()
> Hides the window.

void **show** ()
> Shows the window.

void **dispose** ()
> Hides the window and disposes of its contents.

## Status - Example

```
import hsa.*;

// Count number of lines in a file
public class TestStatus
{
    public static void main (String[] args)
    {
        String fileName;
        TextInputFile f;
        Status status;
        int lineNumber = 1;
        Stdout.print ("Enter the file to have lines counted: ");
        fileName = Stdin.readLine ();
        f = new TextInputFile (fileName);
        status = new Status ("Reading " +
            fileName);              // Open status window.
        while (!f.eof ())
        {
            f.readLine ();
            status.setMessage ("Reading line number " +
                lineNumber);      // Change status message.
            lineNumber++;
        }
        status.dispose ();          // Close status window.
        f.close ();
        Stdout.println ("There were " + lineNumber + " lines in " +
            fileName);
    } // main method
} /* TestStatus class */
```

# Appendix E : Operators

This is a list of the operators available in Java and their precedence.

## Mathematical Operators

| Operator | Operation | Result Type |
|---|---|---|
| Prefix + | Identity | Same as Operands |
| Prefix − | Negative | Same as Operands |
| + | Addition | Same as Operands |
| − | Subtraction | Same as Operands |
| * | Multiplication | Same as Operands |
| / | Division | Same as Operands |
| % | Remainder | int |
| < | Less Than | boolean |
| > | Greater Than | boolean |
| == | Equals | boolean |
| <= | Less Than or Equal | boolean |
| >= | Greater Than or Equal | boolean |
| != | Not Equal | boolean |

## Boolean Operators

| Operator | Operation | Result Type |
|---|---|---|
| ! | Negation | boolean |
| && | And | boolean |
| \|\| | Or | boolean |

## Bit Manipulation Operators

| Operator | Operation | Result Type |
|----------|-----------|-------------|
| & | Bitwise and | Same as Operands |
| \| | Bitwise or | Same as Operands |
| ^ | Bitwise XOR | Same as Operands |
| << | Shift left | Same as Operands |
| >> | Shift right | Same as Operands |
| >>> | Shift right (fill with 0) | Same as Operands |

## Operator Precedence

Highest precedence operators first.

(1)    [], ., (*params*), *expr*++, *expr*--
(2)    ++*expr*, --*expr*, +*expr*, -*expr*
(3)    **new**, (*type*) *expr*
(4)    *, /, %
(5)    +, -
(6)    <<, >>, >>>
(7)    <=, <, >, >=, instanceof
(8)    ==, !=
(9)    &
(10)   ^
(11)   |
(12)   &&
(13)   ||
(14)   ?:
(15)   =, +=, -=, *=, /=, %=, >>=, <<=,
       >>>=, &=, ^=, |=

Some of these operators were not introduced in this text.

# Appendix F : Applet Syntax

An applet is a Java program capable of being loaded and executed over the internet using an Java-enabled web browser. To create an applet, the class must extend the Applet class found in the java.applet package. What follows is a template for a Java applet class.

```
// The "AppletPlate" class.
import java.applet.Applet;
import java.awt.*;

public class AppletPlate extends Applet
{
    // Place instance variables here.

    public void init ()
    {
        // Any code placed here is executed when the page is loaded.
    } // init method

    public void start ()
    {
        // Any code placed here is executed when the applet is started.
    } // start method

    public void stop ()
    {
        // Any code placed here is executed when the applet is stopped.
    } // stop method

    public void paint (Graphics g)
    {
        // Any code placed here is executed whenever the applet
        // window is revealed or when the applet runs the first time.
    } // paint method
    public boolean action (Event e, Object o)
    {
        // Any code placed here is executed when a button is clicked
        // or a Return is typed in a TextField.
        return true;
    } // action method
} // AppletPlate class
```

Any method in the template that is not modified can be omitted entirely.

The HTML file can have any number of other HTML elements. To load and execute the applet, it must have the following two lines:

```
<APPLET CODE = "class-name" WIDTH=width HEIGHT=height >
</APPLET>
```

The *class-name* must be in quotation marks and is the name of the Java class file, which ends in ".class", not the Java text file, which ends in ".java". The *width* and *height* fields are the size of the applet's display area on the web page. An applet can not change the size of the drawing surface it will be using.

The user must then create the HTML file to run the applet. When the HTML file is loaded in an Internet browser, the file *class-name* will be loaded and executed. If no path name is specified in *class-name*, the Java class files must be in the same directory as the HTML file.

Here is a template for the HTML file.

```
<HTML>
<BODY>
<APPLET CODE = "class-name" WIDTH=width HEIGHT=height >
</APPLET>
</BODY>
</HTML>
```

# Appendix G : Application Syntax

An application is a Java program capable of being run without the presence of an Internet browser. To create an application, the class must have a *main* method with the parameter of *String*[] *args*. When the application is executed, the system calls the *main* method with any command line arguments passed as a parameter to *main*.

A Java application does not have an built-in drawing surface. The application can either use standard input and output, open up a Console object from the *hsa* package, or create its own Frame.

What follows is a template for a Java application class instantiating a Console object for input and output.

```
// The "BoilerPlate" class.
import java.awt.*;
import hsa.*;

public class BoilerPlate
{
    static Console c;

    static public void main (String [] args)
    {
        c = new Console ();
        // Any code placed here is executed whenever
        // the application is run.
    } // main method
} /* BoilerPlate class */
```

# Appendix H : Installing the *Ready to Program* Java IDE

This book includes a CD that contains the *Ready to Program with Java™ Techmology* program. To install the software onto your computer, insert the CD into your computer. After a few seconds, the CD will be mounted. Double click on the *My Computer* icon found on the left-hand side of the desktop. A window containing icons for all the drives on your computer will appear. Double click on the icon representing the CD. A window representing the contents of the CD will open.

The window contains two files of interest (there may be more, but they are not used here). The file *Readme.txt* is a text file that contains information about the IDE that has changed since this book was published. It is a good idea to double click the icon and read the contents of the file.

The second file is the *setup.exe* file. This file is the installer for the *Ready To Program* IDE. To install the software, double click on the icon.

This starts the installer program. The installer will display a series of windows giving you the opportunity to specify where the software is to be installed and where the shortcut should appear. Using the default location for the software and shortcuts is recommended. You get the defaults if you press the *Next>* button in every window.

After the software is installed, the installer may ask a series of configuration questions about the *Ready* IDE. If you do not understand what is being asked, accept the default values by clicking the *Next>* button. Any configuration choices made here can be changed using the *Preferences* command in the *Ready* environment.

If there are any problems with the installation or with the software in general, please use your internet browser to load

http://www.holtsoft.com/ready/support

and look for answers to your questions.

# Appendix I : License Agreement for the *Ready to Program* Java IDE

Academic License Agreement for the Ready to Program with Java™ Technology IDE ("Program")

PLEASE READ THIS AGREEMENT CAREFULLY BEFORE USING THE PROGRAM. HOLT SOFTWARE WILL ONLY LICENSE THE PROGRAM TO YOU IF YOU FIRST ACCEPT THE TERMS OF THIS AGREEMENT BY USING THE PROGRAM. IF YOU DO NOT AGREE TO THE TERMS OF THIS AGREEMENT, DO NOT INSTALL THE PROGRAM.

The Program is owned by Holt Software Associates and is copyrighted and licensed, not sold.

Holt Software Associates grants you a nonexclusive, nontransferable license for the Program. The term "Program" means the original program and all whole or partial copies of it, including portions merged into other programs. A Program consists of machine-readable instructions, audio/visual content (such as images, text, recordings, or pictures), and related licensed materials.

## 1. LICENSE

### USE OF THE PROGRAM

You may use the Program on only one machine at any one time. You agree to ensure that anyone who uses the Program (accessed either locally or remotely) does so only for your authorized use and complies with the terms of this Agreement.

A Program is considered to be in use when it resides in memory or is otherwise stored on a machine. A Program stored on a network server solely for the purpose of being distributed to other machines is not considered to be in use.

For a Program managed by a license management tool, copies may be made and stored on machines under control of that tool, but your use may not exceed the total number of users or amount of resource authorized.

You may 1) copy the Program for backup and 2) merge the Program into another program. You must reproduce the copyright notice and any other legend of ownership on each copy, or partial copy, of the Program.

You may not: 1) use, copy, merge, or transfer the Program except as provided in this Agreement; 2) reverse assemble, reverse compile, or otherwise translate the Program except as specifically permitted by law without the possibility of contractual waiver; or 3) sublicense, rent or lease the Program.

### TRANSFER OF RIGHTS AND OBLIGATIONS

You may not transfer your rights and obligations under a license for a Program to another party.

## 2. LIMITED WARRANTY

Holt Software Associates warrants that when the Program is used in the specified operating environment, it will conform to its published specifications found in Holt Software Associates manuals. Holt Software Associates does not warrant uninterrupted or error-free operation of a Program. The warranty period for a Program expires when its Program services are no longer available.

Holt Software Associates provides defect support through Technical Support. A defect related problem means the Program does not conform to specifications and could be either a code or documentation error. For information on how you may access Technical Support, or other fee-based support services, please contact Holt Software Associates or its reseller from whom you acquired this Program.

## 3. LIMITATION OF LIABILITY

HOLT SOFTWARE ASSOCIATES WILL NOT BE LIABLE FOR ANY SPECIAL, INCIDENTAL, OR INDIRECT DAMAGES OR FOR ANY ECONOMIC CONSEQUENTIAL DAMAGES (INCLUDING LOST PROFITS OR SAVINGS), EVEN IF HOLT SOFTWARE ASSOCIATES, OR ITS RESELLER, HAS BEEN ADVISED OF THE

POSSIBILITY OF SUCH DAMAGES. SOME JURISDICTIONS DO NOT ALLOW THE EXCLUSION OR LIMITATION OF INCIDENTAL OR CONSEQUENTIAL DAMAGES, SO THE ABOVE LIMITATION OR EXCLUSION MAY NOT APPLY TO YOU.

Holt Software Associates will not be liable for 1) loss of, or damage to, your records or data or 2) any damages claimed by you based on any third party claim.

This limitation of liability also applies to any developer of a Program supplied to Holt Software Associates. It is the maximum for which we are collectively responsible.

## 4. GENERAL

You may terminate your license at any time. If you do so, all your license rights to the Program are terminated. You may keep a copy of the Program in your archives. Holt Software Associates may terminate your license if you fail to comply with the terms of this Agreement. If Holt Software Associates does so, all your license rights to the Program are terminated and you must destroy all your copies of it.

You agree to comply with all applicable export laws and regulations.

Neither party may bring a legal action under this Agreement more than two years after the cause of action arose.

This Agreement is governed by the laws of the country in which you acquired the Program. In Canada, this agreement is governed by the laws of the Province of Ontario. In the United States, this agreement is governed by the laws of the State of New York.

Any other documentation with respect to this licensed program, including any such documentation referenced herein, is provided for information purposes only and does not extend or modify the material contained in the License Information.

\*   Trademark of Holt Software Associates.

\*\*  Java is a trademark of Sun Microsystems, Inc.

Windows is a trademark of Microsoft Corp.

# Appendix J : Web Resources for Java

## Holt Software

This is the website for the publisher of this book.

**www.holtsoft.com**

## Java Everything Site

This website contains an extremely large collection of Java resources (classes, example code, applets, and reference material).

**www.gamelan.com**

## Java FAQ

These are files which contain the answers to frequently asked questions about Java. They can be very helpful if you are looking for answers to specific technical questions.

**sunsite.unc.edu/javafaq/javafaq.html**

**www.best.com/~pvdl/javafaq.html**

## Java from Sun Microsystems

This is the website belonging to Sun Microsystems, the company that created and maintains the Java language. It provides the latest information about changes to the Java language.

**java.sun.com**

## Java Development Kit

You can download the Java development Kit (JDK) from this website for free. JDK is a compiler and virtual machine.

**java.sun.com/products/jdk**

## IBM Academic Program for Java

This site contains a number of useful resources for educators teaching with Java (course notes, sample projects, and demos).

**www.ibm.com/java/academic**

## Borland JBuilder

This is a website for Borlands' JBuilder development environment.

**www.borland.com/jbuilder**

## IBM VisualAge for Java

This is a website for IBM's VisualAge for Java development environment.

**www.ibm.com/ad/vajava**

## Metrowerks CodeWarrior

This is a website for Metrowerks' CodeWarrior development environment.

**www.codewarrior.com/desktop/java**

## Microsoft Visual J++

This is a website for Microsoft's Visual J++ development environment.

**www.microsoft.com/visualj**

## Symantec Visual Café for Java

This is a website for Symantec's Visual Café for Java development environment.

**www.symantec.com/domain/cafe/deved**

# Java Newsgroups

These are Internet newsgroups for discussion of the Java language.

**comp.lang.java.setup**
> comp.lang.java.programmer

**comp.lang.java.api**
> comp.lang.java.tech

# Index

# I